Scotland and America
in the Age of the Enlightenment

FOR DORIS AND PAIGE

Scotland and America in the Age of the Enlightenment

edited by
RICHARD B. SHER
and
JEFFREY R. SMITTEN

EDINBURGH UNIVERSITY PRESS

22 George Square, Edinburgh

Set in Linotron Baskerville 2
by Photoprint, Torquay
and printed in Great Britain by
Redwood Press Limited,
Melksham, Wilts.

British Library Cataloguing
in Publication Data
Scotland and America in the age
of the Enlightenment.
1. Scotland. Intellectual life,
1714–1837
2. United States. Intellectual life,
1607–1798
I. Sher, Richard B. II. Smitten,
Jeffrey R., *1941–*
941.107

ISBN 0 7486 0129 5
0 7486 0178 3 pbk

Contents

Acknowledgements

The editors are grateful to the other co-founders of the Eighteenth-Century Scottish Studies Society – Robert Kent Donovan, Roger Fechner, Donald Livingston and our first president, Ian Ross – for their early support of this project. We are also grateful to the current president of ECSSS, Roger Emerson, as well as to several of the contributors to this volume (especially Ned Landsman), for additional editorial assistance and advice. The introduction benefited particularly from their collective efforts. Ian D.L. Clark and John Murrin caught some troublesome and persistent errors at the eleventh hour, and Paige Dayton Smitten assisted with the index. We also wish to express thanks for the help we received from the Office of the Dean of Science and Liberal Arts and the Humanities Department at New Jersey Institute of Technology, and the English Department at Texas Tech University.

Finally, we are grateful to our wives and families for putting up with us during the period when production of this volume was in full swing.

Contributors

RICHARD B. SHER is an associate dean and associate professor of history at New Jersey Institute of Technology and the founding executive secretary of the Eighteenth-Century Scottish Studies Society. The author of *Church and University in the Scottish Enlightenment* (1985) and other publications on related subjects, he is now engaged in studying the Enlightenment in Glasgow and in editing Boswell's correspondence with the Scots literati for the Yale Editions of the Private Papers of James Boswell.

JEFFREY R. SMITTEN is professor of English at Texas Tech University, where he is currently chair of the department. Since 1976 he has been co-editor of the journal *The Eighteenth Century: Theory and Interpretation.* His recent work has concentrated on the Scottish Enlightenment, notably a critical biography of William Robertson, which is in progress.

DEBORAH C. BRUNTON is a postgraduate student at the University of Pennsylvania specialising in the history of eighteenth-century medical knowledge and practice. Born into a medical family in Fife, she is currently in Edinburgh writing a doctoral thesis on smallpox inoculation in Britain.

DAVID DAICHES has written some forty-five books on a wide range of literary and historical subjects, including *Robert Burns* (1957), *The Paradox of Scottish Culture* (1964), *James Boswell and His World* (1976) and *A Companion to Scottish Culture* (1982). A resident of Edinburgh, he carried out much of the research for his contribution to this volume while a fellow at the National Humanities Center, North Carolina, in 1987–88.

PETER J. DIAMOND is assistant professor of political science and director of undergraduate studies in political science at the University of Utah. He has published articles on Thomas Reid and is now revising for publication a book on Reid as a social theorist.

ROBERT KENT DONOVAN is associate professor of history at Kansas State University. His publications include *No Popery and Radicalism: Opposition to Roman Catholic Relief in Scotland, 1778–1782* (1987) as well as a number of articles on the social history of religion in Great Britain.

ANDREW HOOK is Bradley Professor and head of the Department of English Literature at the University of Glasgow. Among his publications are *Scotland and*

America: A Study of Cultural Relations, 1750–1830 (1975) and a volume covering the period 1660–1800 in the new *History of Scottish Literature* published by Aberdeen University Press (1987).

ANNE MCCLENNY KRAUSS, formerly associate professor of music at Hollins College, teaches privately and lectures in universities and museums in both the United States and Great Britain. She has edited for publication much of Alexander Reinagle's keyboard music and has frequently performed compositions by both Reinagle and James Bremner.

NED C. LANDSMAN, associate professor of history at the State University of New York at Stony Brook, is the author of *Scotland and Its First American Colony, 1683–1760* (1985) and numerous articles treating eighteenth-century Scotland and America. He is currently at work on a transatlantic study of evangelicals and the Enlightenment.

BRUCE P. LENMAN of the University of St Andrews was the James Pinkney Harrison Visiting Professor of History at the College of William and Mary while this book was in preparation. Among his many publications are *An Economic History of Modern Scotland* (1977) and three monographs in Jacobite studies. Among his many works in progress is a study of the pace of integration of aristocratic élites in eighteenth-century Britain.

DONALD W. LIVINGSTON is associate professor of philosophy and director of graduate studies in philosophy at Emory University. His publications include *Hume: A Reevaluation* (1976), which he co-edited, and *Hume's Philosophy of Common Life* (1984). He is presently writing a book on Hume's philosophy and modern politics.

THOMAS P. MILLER is assistant professor in the Ph.D. programme in rhetoric, composition and the teaching of English at the University of Arizona. Having recently edited *Selected Writings of John Witherspoon* (1990), he is now putting together a volume of essays on eighteenth-century Scottish rhetoric and society.

CHARLES E. PETERSON is a noted architect, restorationist and historian of architecture with a special interest in historic Philadelphia. As head of the Robert Smith Project, he has for many years led the effort to learn more about Smith's life and contributions to American architecture.

LEIGH ERIC SCHMIDT is assistant professor of American church history at Drew University. His publications include *Holy Fairs: Scottish Communions and American Revivals in the Early Modern Period* (1989) as well as articles on American religious history in *William and Mary Quarterly* and other journals.

ANDREW S. SKINNER is Daniel Jack Professor of political economy at the University of Glasgow. The author of numerous articles on eighteenth-century subjects as well as modern economics, he has also edited volumes on Sir James Steuart and Adam Smith and co-edited the *Wealth of Nations* for the Glasgow Edition of Smith's works. His papers on Smith are collected in *A System of Social Science* (1979).

SHANNON C. STIMSON, Fulbright Professor of English and American Studies at the University of Sussex when this book was in preparation, is associate professor of government and social studies at Harvard University, where she teaches political and constitutional theory. Her book *The American Revolution in the Law* (1990) examines connexions between British and American jurisprudence during the eighteenth century.

Illustrations

Abbreviations

I. *Institutions and Special Collections*

BL	British Library
CPP	College of Physicians, Philadelphia
EMS	Edinburgh Musical Society
EMSSB	Edinburgh Musical Society Sederunt Books, 4 vols. (1728–95), Edinburgh Public Library
EUL	Edinburgh University Library
HSP	Historical Society of Pennsylvania
NLS	National Library of Scotland

II. *Published Sources*

Blair	Hugh Blair, *Lectures on Rhetoric and Belles Lettres*. Ed. Harold F. Harding. 2 vols. Carbondale and Edwardsville, Ill., 1965.
CAS	*The Correspondence of Adam Smith*. Ed. Ernest Campbell Mossner and Ian Simpson Ross. 2nd ed. Oxford, 1987.
E	David Hume, *Essays, Moral, Political, and Literary*. Ed. Eugene F. Miller. Indianapolis, 1985.
EM	David Hume. *Enquiries concerning Human Understanding and concerning the Principles of Morals*. Ed. L.A. Selby-Bigge, rev. P.H. Nidditch. 3rd ed. Oxford, 1975.
Franklin	*The Papers of Benjamin Franklin*. Ed. Leonard W. Labaree et al. 27 vols. to date. New Haven, Conn., 1959–.
Jefferson	*The Papers of Thomas Jefferson*. Ed. Julian P. Boyd et al. 22 vols. to date. Princeton, 1950–.
HL	*The Letters of David Hume*. Ed. J.Y.T. Greig. 2 vols. Oxford, 1932.
PMHB	*Pennsylvania Magazine of History and Biography*.
SEAR	*Scotland, Europe and the American Revolution*. Ed. Owen Dudley Edwards and George Shepperson. London, 1976.
Sher	Richard B. Sher. *Church and University in the Scottish Enlightenment: The Moderate Literati of Edinburgh*. Princeton and Edinburgh, 1985.
Sloan	Douglas Sloan. *The Scottish Enlightenment and the American College Ideal*. New York, 1971.
SM	*Scots Magazine*.
SVEC	*Studies on Voltaire and the Eighteenth Century*.
THN	David Hume, *A Treatise of Human Nature*. Ed. L.A. Selby-Bigge, rev. P.H. Nidditch. 2nd ed. Oxford, 1978.

WJW *The Works of the Reverend John Witherspoon.* 2nd ed. 4 vols. Philadelphia, 1802.

WJasW *The Works of James Wilson.* Ed. Robert Green McCloskey. 2 vols. Cambridge, Mass., 1967.

WMQ *William and Mary Quarterly* (where no additional information is cited, reference is to the 'Scotland and America' issue, 3rd ser., vol. 11, April 1954).

WN Adam Smith. *An Inquiry into the Nature and Causes of the Wealth of Nations.* Ed. R.H. Campbell, A.S. Skinner and W.B. Todd. 2 vols. Oxford, 1976. (References to this source cite part, section, chapter and paragraph rather than volume and page number.)

WTR Thomas Reid. *Philosophical Works.* Ed. Sir William Hamilton. 2 vols. 1895; rpt. Hildesheim, 1967.

WV *Wealth and Virtue: The Shaping of Political Economy in the Scottish Enlightenment.* Ed. Istvan Hont and Michael Ignatieff. Cambridge, 1983.

WWR *The Works of William Robertson.* 8 vols. London, 1827.

RICHARD B. SHER

Introduction:
Scottish-American Cultural Studies, Past and Present

I

In April 1954 *William and Mary Quarterly* published a special issue devoted to Scotland and America. It began with a general historiographical essay by George Shepperson, 'Writings in Scottish-American History: A Brief Survey' (163–78), which attacked the 'Burns Supper school of Scottish-American historians'. The aim of that school was to demonstrate the importance of Scots in the making of America by drawing attention to great feats of Scottish Americans and by listing various American inventions, ideas and individuals whose roots were said to be Scottish (freedom of speech and Theodore Roosevelt were cited as examples). In sounding the death-knell for that sort of 'chauvinistic enthusiasm', Shepperson was in effect celebrating the advent of serious study of Scotland and America during a critical period in their closely interconnected histories.

The time was right. At the end of the Second World War, Thomas Jefferson Wertenbaker's lecture *Early Scotch Contributions to the United States* (Glasgow, 1945) had set the tone for a scholarly approach to its subject, and a year later the same author published the best account up to that time of the early history of America's premier Scottish-Presbyterian academy, *Princeton, 1746–1896* (Princeton, 1946). Much of the correspondence of John Witherspoon and Benjamin Rush, two giants of the Scottish-American Enlightenment, had very recently been edited for publication by L.H. Butterfield: *Letters of Benjamin Rush* (Princeton, 1951) and *John Witherspoon Comes to America: A Documentary Account* (Princeton, 1953). Concern with Rush reflected a more general interest in Scottish-American scientific and especially medical connexions, a topic being rigorously studied during, and after, the 1950s by Whitfield J. Bell, Jr.[1] Concern with Rush and especially Witherspoon also reflected growing scholarly interest in the role of Scotland in the making of the American Presbyterian Church, the American university and the American Revolution, as presented, for example, in Leonard J. Trinterud, *The Forming of an American Tradition: A Re-examination of Colonial Presbyterianism* (Philadelphia, 1949) and in some useful articles in periodicals of the time.[2] Relatively little had yet been published on Scottish influences on American political and religious philosophy or social science. As early as the 1930s, however, Gladys Bryson had treated the latter subject in some pioneering articles,[3] and in the following decades authors such as Arnaud Leavelle, A.O. Aldridge, Sydney Ahlstrom and Douglass Adair began to break the ice that previously covered the former topic.[4] In addition, a fair amount of older biographical literature was available on Americans who had emigrated from Scotland like Witherspoon, William Smith, Charles Nisbet and Hugh Henry Brackenridge;[5] who had studied in Scotland like Rush, or had studied in America with a Scottish tutor like Jefferson;[6] or who had simply travelled in Scotland like Franklin.[7]

Thus, the appearance of the 'Scotland and America' number of *WMQ* was no accident. It represented the crystalisation of a general trend, already well under way, to free eighteenth-century Scottish-American studies from the constraints of a predominantly chauvinistic approach and raise it to a higher level of scholarship than had previously existed. Whitfield J. Bell, Jr., *WMQ*'s visiting editor at the time of the 'Scotland and America' issue was, as we have seen, among those responsible for that trend. So were the regular editor of *WMQ*, Douglass Adair of the College of William and Mary in Williamsburg, Virginia, and at least one member of that journal's board of editors, L.H. Butterfield. In the 'Personal Memoir' of Douglass Adair that she prefixed to his posthumously published volume of essays, Caroline Robbins recalled that although Adair was known for putting together 'issues devoted to a single theme', 'Scotland and America' was special:

> Plans were being developed for a "Scotland and America" number. I had a piece on Francis Hutcheson's theory of colonial independence that I wanted Douglass to print. With his customary flair, he was recruiting such then unknown writers as John Clive, Bernard Bailyn, Jack Price, and others. Though by no means all opinions expressed in the April 1954 *Quarterly* were entirely agreeable to the Scots, the total response everywhere was gratifying. At least two famous scholars, a philosopher and a historian, expressed appreciation and surprise. The undertaking was a tremendous success.[8]

'Jack Price' was Jacob M. Price, then a teaching fellow at Harvard University whose article, 'The Rise of Glasgow in the Chesapeake Tobacco Trade, 1707–1775', appeared immediately after the historiographical piece by Shepperson (179–99). This was the first significant study of a fascinating and complex pattern of trade that formed the primary economic link between Scotland and America until the War of American Independence.[9] Price showed how the Glasgow tobacco merchants established their dominance in this area, and he explored the social and economic significance of that dominance for Maryland and Virginia. His sophisticated comparative analysis was the forerunner not only of his own *Capital and Credit in British Overseas Trade: The View from the Chesapeake, 1700–1776* (Cambridge, Mass., 1980) but also of Thomas M. Devine's important book, *The Tobacco Lords: A Study of the Tobacco Merchants of Glasgow*(Edinburgh, 1975), which might well have been subtitled 'The View from the Clyde'.

Next came one of the most significant essays ever published in Scottish-American cultural studies, John Clive and Bernard Bailyn's 'England's Cultural Provinces: Scotland and America' (200–13). Noting similarities in Scottish and American experiences during the eighteenth century, the authors (who were both then instructors at Harvard University) argued that 'Scotland and America were provinces, cultural as well as political and economic, of the English-speaking world whose center was London' (207). 'Scotsmen and Americans alike', they observed, 'were constantly aware that they lived on the periphery of a greater world' (208). From this awareness of provinciality came the 'sense of inferiority' that 'pervaded the culture of the two regions, affecting the great no less than the common' (209). This sense of inferiority led in turn to a series of similar characteristics: 'imitation of English ways', 'a sense of guilt regarding local mannerisms' such as speech and, at the other extreme, 'a compensatory local pride, evolving into a patriotism' that was politically effective in America but mainly sentimental in Scotland after the failure of the Jacobite rebellion of 1745 (211). 'The deepest result of this complicated involvement in British society', the authors then argued, 'was that the provincial's view of the world was discontinuous' (212):

> Two forces, two magnets, affected his efforts to find adequate standards and styles: the values associated with the simplicity and purity (real or imagined) of nativism, and those to be found in cosmopolitan sophistication. Those who could take entire satisfaction in either could maintain a consistent position. But for provincials, exposed to both, an exclusive, singular conception of either kind was too narrow. It meant a rootlessness, an alienation either from the higher sources of culture or from the familiar local environment that had formed the personality. Few whose perceptions surpassed local boundaries rested content with a simple, consistent image of themselves or of the world. Provincial culture, in eighteenth-century Scotland as in colonial America, was formed in the mingling of these visions. (212–13)

Concluding on a positive note, Clive and Bailyn suggested that the feelings of provincial alienation experienced by eighteenth-century Americans and Scots 'fostered in such men the originality and creative imagination that we associate with the highest achievements of the enlightenment in Scotland and America' (213).

The primary significance of Clive and Bailyn's essay lay in its formulation of a broad British conceptual framework for understanding eighteenth-century Scottish and American culture. Scholars working within either one of those cultures were given a means of relating their scholarship to a much greater entity, that of the British empire. This British conceptual framework, moreover, could be relevant for a variety of disciplinary perspectives, including sociology (as a case study of the 'centre' and 'periphery' model being developed by Edward Shils), political economy (as a means for understanding political and economic power relationships) and cultural psychology (as a mechanism for explaining the special concerns and motivations of particular eighteenth-century Americans and Scots). As it turned out, the biggest impact of the Clive-Bailyn thesis was on the study of Scotland's ambivalent relationship with England, quite apart from the American dimension.[10] This development suggests a possible flaw, or at least a limitation, in the thesis itself, for however successful it may be in helping to elucidate the personal feelings and collective mentalities of Americans and Scots relative to England, it provides little guidance for understanding direct interaction between Scotland and America. These British provinces may each have had similar relationships with the capital, but what of their relationships with each other? On this matter of interprovincial connexions, the Clive-Bailyn thesis has nothing to say. In so far as Scotland and America are concerned, it speaks of similarities, analogies and parallels, never of direct ties.[11]

A second limitation concerns the definition of the larger entity to which both Scotland and America belonged. A London-centred core-and-periphery model like Clive and Bailyn's defines that larger entity as the British empire. But in regard to the realm of intellectual and cultural history, one may just as easily point to an entity that was not so much British as international and that was less an empire than a republic – what contemporaries called 'the republic of letters'. The geographical capital of this republic was Paris rather than London, but even with Paris at the centre a simple core-and-periphery model is not viable in this case. Instead, one must envision a complex web of interrelated centres and peripheries, within particular countries and regions as well as throughout the western world. The cities of Aberdeen, Boston and Bordeaux, for example, were the cultural capitals of northeastern Scotland, New England and the province of Bordeaux, respectively, yet each was itself a provincial town in relation to more prominent cultural centres such as Edinburgh, London and Paris.[12] To the extent that eighteenth-century

America was a cultural province, it was a province not merely of metropolitan England but of a variety of British and European cultural centres, including Scottish ones.

Ideas flowed freely across national boundaries as well as oceans, and between provincial centres as well as capitals and provinces. Latin died out as the international language of scholarship, but vernacular translations made up the loss. If the eighteenth-century republic of letters had a true core, it lay not in a geographical capital but in a body of common values and beliefs that were shared by 'enlightened' men of letters everywhere, including science, virtue, justice, reason, toleration, cosmopolitanism, polite learning, critical methods, freedom of the press and fundamental human rights. The details varied somewhat from region to region, nation to nation, shire to shire, city to city, colony to colony, and state to state, but the overall similarity of outlook and the general sense of shared purpose and camaraderie among those who called themselves by names such as 'philosophes' and 'literati' more than justify our continuing to refer to this international movement as the 'Enlightenment', despite recent objections to the use of that term.[13]

Though the Enlightenment unquestionably reached full bloom during the second half of the eighteenth century, it began to emerge as a serious movement during the 1720s, 1730s and 1740s. That is when men of letters born at the end of the seventeenth century and beginning of the eighteenth century – including Voltaire, Montesquieu, Francis Hutcheson and Benjamin Franklin – began to fire their first shots and to mobilise the forces of the republic of letters for the battles to come. Depending on their particular circumstances and objectives, their chief weapons were books, newspapers, pamphlets and the printing presses that made them possible; academic lectures; and convivial clubs, salons, cultural societies and academies. Of the giants of this generation, Hutcheson is by far the least well known. Yet his influence was extraordinarily extensive, not only as the leading proponent of the 'moral sense' school of British philosophy but also as the founding father – along with his contemporary George Turnbull of Aberdeen and his predecessor in the Glasgow University chair, Gershom Carmichael – of enlightened Scottish academic moral philosophy in general. In her article on Hutcheson in *WMQ*, ' "When It Is That Colonies May Turn Independent": An Analysis of the Environment and Politics of Francis Hutcheson (1694–1746)' (214–51), Caroline Robbins (then professor of history at Bryn Mawr College) uncovered a dimension of Hutcheson's moral philosophy that had been virtually ignored by previous scholars. This was his political philosophy, which she considered far and away 'Hutcheson's most original contribution to eighteenth-century thought'. And 'most important in his politics', she argued, 'was his wholehearted endorsement of the right of resistance' (243), which appeared in his posthumous *System of Moral Philosophy* as early as 1755.

Rather than focus on the specific ways in which Hutcheson's innovative rationale for colonial resistance influenced Americans looking for justifications for their rebellion against British authority, Robbins dwelt on the sources of Hutcheson's radical political philosophy. These she located in the works of various Scottish, Anglo-Irish and ultimately English 'classical republican' thinkers of the seventeenth and early eighteenth centuries, including Harrington, Fletcher, Molyneux and Molesworth. Taking the issue of intellectual sources to its fullest extreme, Robbins contended that Hutcheson's radical political thought was the product 'not of his single genius, but of the environment into which he was born and in which he lived and of the tradition he inherited' (251). In her view it was not at all surprising that an Irish Scotsman (for so Hutcheson was) first formulated, out of predominantly English republican ideas, a rationale for colonial independence that had its greatest significance in America; for it was English-speaking people living outside England – 'who thought themselves or their countrymen oppressed, poorer than they ought to be, and who yet had sufficient vitality to agitate for improvement of their condition' (225) – over whom seventeenth-century English republican thought exerted its greatest appeal during the following century. Originally devised by Englishmen, the classical republicanism that spawned the first theory of colonial independence was appropriated by inhabitants of Ireland, Scotland and America 'whose position was less favored than that of the Georgian English' (251).

Robbins's article was among other things a preview of the sixth chapter of her seminal book *The Eighteenth-Century Commonwealthman* (Cambridge, Mass., 1959), which dealt with the classical republican thought of Hutcheson, Robert Wallace and other eighteenth-century Scots. Robbins's work paved the way for further studies of Hutcheson's political philosophy and its reception in America,[14] as well as for later scholarship by Bernard Bailyn, Gordon Wood and J.G.A. Pocock on the importance of the British classical republican tradition in America during the era of the Revolution and Constitution. It also demonstrated the sheer complexity of this sort of intellectual history. To understand Hutcheson's two pages on colonies published in 1755, one had to know something about English, Irish and Scottish political philosophy since the publication of Harrington's *Oceana* in 1656. It is entirely possible that Robbins exaggerated the role of this intellectual heritage or 'environment', thus unfairly minimising the importance of Hutcheson's own contribution. And it is quite possible that she particularly exaggerated the role of her native England in shaping Irish and Scottish political philosophy during the Enlightenment.[15] But these were matters of degree. After Robbins's *WMQ* article, it was clear that Scottish and American ties could not properly be treated in isolation from the broader cultural world in which they flourished.

Nearly all of the early literature on Scotland and America traced the former's contributions to the latter. This was plainly a vast and important topic. Considering the small size of their country, Scots played a disproportionately large role in the making of America – a role that extended from the realm of ideas (e.g. moral philosophy, political economy, literature, historiography, natural science and medicine) to religion and higher education, and from the province of trade to the influx of large masses of immigrants who made their mark on American culture in countless other ways. What is often forgotten, however, is that during the eighteenth century America had a considerable influence on Scotland, not only as an outlet for Scottish emigration and a centre of Scottish trade but also as a source of information about the nature of social organisation and a challenge to conventional beliefs about the British constitution and empire. If (as Robbins suggested) the Scottish Enlightenment helped to lay the foundations for America's assertion of independence, and if (as others have claimed) it also contributed to the American Constitution and the emergence of the standard American philosophy curriculum in the eighteenth and nineteenth centuries, it is nevertheless true that the idea and reality of America helped in its turn to shape the social, political and economic thought and the ideological tenets of the Scottish Enlightenment.

One of the first publications to provide a sophisticated treatment of Revolutionary America's impact on eighteenth-century Scotland was Dalphy I. Fagerstrom's 'Scottish Opinion and the American Revolution', the next article in *WMQ* (252–75). This was an excellent condensation of the author's comprehensive Edinburgh University Ph.D. thesis of 1951, 'The American Revolution in Scottish Opinion, 1763–83'. Perhaps there is no better compliment to be paid to these works than to say that they have remained the standard short and full-length studies, respectively, of this extremely important topic. One reason for this was that Fagerstrom, then an assistant professor of history at little Bethel College in St Paul, Minnesota, had thrown his net so wide. In addition to obvious sources such as the writings on America of Adam Smith and other Scottish literati, he examined obscure pamphlets and sermons, contemporary newspapers and magazines, and unpublished political papers at the Public Record Office. A second reason was that Fagerstrom offered a controversial thesis: that despite the well-known opposition to the American Revolution by many of the Scottish literati, 'significant Scottish voices were raised in favor of the Americans in the debate on the Revolution, voices which at the same time supported burgh or county reform locally and which later contributed to the opposition in Parliament' (255). The first part of this thesis flew in the face of traditional stereotypes of the Scots – in America as well as in Britain – as government lackeys with no appreciation for political liberty. The second part of the thesis took this point further – not by probing the earlier English and Anglo-Irish sources of Scottish radical thought, as Robbins had attempted to do – but by connecting such thought with social and political reform movements in late eighteenth-century Scotland. In this way Fagerstrom demonstrated that the American Revolution's impact on Scotland was as significant in certain respects as the Scottish influence on the Revolution.

In the historiographical piece that opened *WMQ*, George Shepperson had lamented 'the lack of adequate writings on migration from Scotland to America' (165). The closing contribution to the issue, Whitfield J. Bell, Jr.'s 'Scottish Emigration to America: A Letter of Dr. Charles Nisbet to John Witherspoon, 1784' (276–89), helped to define the problem more clearly. In an excellent introduction to Nisbet's letter, Bell discussed the 'flood' of Scottish emigration in the years before the American War (1763–75) and the revival of Scottish emigration immediately after the war. Nisbet, a Popular party minister at Montrose who had been, in his own words, 'known and persecuted as a friend of America during the war' (284), wrote to his old friend Witherspoon (then visiting Britain to raise money for the College of New Jersey) on 16 March 1784 to describe the desperate economic plight of '*poor* Scotland'. 'I think it incumbent on you', he pleaded, 'as a friend of mankind and of America, to say nothing of G. Britain, to encourage poor emigrants and endeavour to procure reasonable terms for them' (284). Nisbet's letter provided a glimpse of the rising rents, 'greed' of merchants and general despair that drove so many Scots to America during the late eighteenth century. The following year Nisbet himself was on a ship bound for the New World, where he took a position as president of Dickinson College in Carlisle, Pennsylvania.

In the years just after the 'Scotland and America' issue of *WMQ*, the field continued to flourish. In 1956, for example, Ian C. Graham published *Colonists from Scotland: Emigration to North America, 1707–1783* (Ithaca, N.Y., 1956), which may have seriously underestimated the scale of Scottish emigration but was nevertheless one of the fullest answers to Shepperson's appeal for better scholarship on Scottish migrations to America. Shepperson's own contribution to the subject, *British Emigration to North America*, appeared in the following year. Then came Duane Meyer's more specialised study within the same general topic: *The Highland Scots of North Carolina, 1732–1776* (Chapel Hill, N.C., 1961). Meanwhile, Charles Page Smith produced the first thorough biography of one of early America's greatest Scots, *James Wilson, Founding Father, 1742–1798* (Chapel Hill, N.C., 1956). The area opened up by Jacob Price was further explored in J.H. Soltow, 'Scottish Traders in Virginia, 1750–1775', *Economic History Review*, 2nd ser., 12 (1959): 83–98. Scottish-American Presbyterian ties were studied in works such as G.D. Henderson, 'Jonathan Edwards and Scotland', in his *The Burning Bush: Studies in Scottish Church History* (Edinburgh, 1957), 151–62. Previously cited articles by Sydney Ahlstrom (1955) and Douglass Adair (1957) explored aspects of Scottish-American philosophical and religious relations; a pioneering pamphlet by George S. Pryde, *The Scottish Universities and the Colleges of Colonial America* (Glasgow, 1957), made up in quality for what it lacked in length; and Terence Martin, *The Instructed Vision: Scottish Common Sense Philosophy and the Origins of American Fiction* (Bloomington, Ind., 1961) discovered interesting connexions that crossed disciplines as well as continents. By then, however, this impressive burst of scholarship on eighteenth-century Scotland and America was just about played out. Though nearly all the contributors to *WMQ* became leading figures in the historical profession,[16] their post-1950s scholarship went off in other directions. As I have remarked elsewhere, the 1960s proved to be an important period in eighteenth-century Scottish historiography, rivalling the remarkably productive decade and a half that preceded the First World War,[17] but it was not a good time for scholarship on Scotland and America. In eighteenth-century American history, similarly, the 1960s was an exciting era but one that generally looked inward or to England, and only rarely to Scotland.

The drought in Scottish-American studies of the eighteenth century received some welcome relief in 1971, when Douglas Sloan published his landmark study, *The Scottish Enlightenment and the American College Ideal.* Thoroughly researched and well written, Sloan's book combined a general overview of institutional foundations and influences with excellent case studies of four particular Scottish-American educators: Francis Alison, John Witherspoon, Samuel Stanhope Smith and Benjamin Rush. The next year saw the publication of another excellent investigation of academic influences, Donald H. Meyer, *The Instructed Conscience: The Shaping of the American National Ethic* (Philadelphia, 1972). By the mid-1970s the field of eighteenth-century Scottish-American cultural relations was once again thriving. Among the most useful studies that appeared around that time were Donald J. D'Elia, *Benjamin Rush: Philosopher of the American Revolution* (Philadelphia, 1974), which contains a valuable chapter on 'Edinburgh and the Scottish Enlightenment'; Andrew Hook, *Scotland and America: A Study of Cultural Relations, 1750–1835* (Glasgow, 1975) and N.T. Phillipson's discussion of that important book's thesis in 'The Export of Enlightenment', *Times Literary Supplement*, 2 July 1976: 823; Tom Devine's previously mentioned volume *The Tobacco Lords*; a number of the brief essays in *Scotland, Europe and the American Revolution*, ed. Owen Dudley

Edwards and George Shepperson (London, 1976) – the proceedings of a bicentennial conference originally published in volumes 35 and 36 of the *New Edinburgh Review*; Howard Miller, *The Revolutionary College: American Presbyterian Higher Education, 1707–1837* (New York, 1976); Jane Rendall, 'The Influence of the Edinburgh Medical School on America in the Eighteenth Century', in *The Early Years of the Edinburgh Medical School*, ed. R.G.W. Anderson and A.D.C. Simpson (Edinburgh, 1976), 95–124; Boyd S. Schlenther, 'Scottish Influences, Especially Religious, in Colonial America', *Records of the Scottish Church History Society* 19 (1976): 133–54; Martha L. Stohlman, *John Witherspoon: Parson, Politician, Patriot* (Philadelphia, 1976); William C. Lehmann, *Scottish and Scotch-Irish Contributions to Early American Life and Culture* (Port Washington, N.Y., 1978); Garry Wills, *Inventing America: Jefferson's Declaration of Independence* (New York, 1978); and a host of studies on how the American crisis was viewed by particular Scottish literati such as Hume and Smith, and on how Scottish thought may have influenced American Founding Fathers such as Jefferson and especially Madison.[18]

By this time some discussion of the influence of Scottish thought on early America was becoming obligatory in all general studies of the American Enlightenment. Examples include Donald H. Meyer, *The Democratic Enlightenment* (New York, 1976); Henry F. May, *The Enlightenment in America* (New York, 1976); D.H. Meyer, 'The Uniqueness of the American Enlightenment', and David Lundberg and Henry F. May, 'The Enlightened Reader in America' – both in the special 'American Enlightenment' issue of *American Quarterly* published in summer 1976; and (particularly in regard to Francis Hutcheson's role as one of America's 'founding forefathers') Morton White, *The Philosophy of the American Revolution* (New York, 1978). Commenting on this literature in a review essay, Daniel Walker Howe observed that 'the relevance of the Scottish Enlightenment to the American has been singled out repeatedly for particular notice.'[19] More recently, James T. Kloppenberg has written: 'In the 1970s Henry F. May and Morton White led a squadron of intellectual historians who emphasized the importance of Scottish common sense philosophy in the complex of ideas that constituted America's version of the Enlightenment.'[20]

Unfortunately, the notice given to Scotland in this literature was usually little more than perfunctory. In their effort to impose order on American intellectual life, Meyer and May lumped together nearly all Scottish thinkers as members of a more or less coherent school of common sense philosophy and practically confined their influence to the last decade of the eighteenth century and opening decades of the nineteenth century.[21] The results were rarely very illuminating. Meyer incongruously treated the contributions of John Witherspoon to the American Enlightenment within the context of the American assimilation of Scottish common sense philosophy during the 1790s, as if that were the decade of Witherspoon's prime rather than of his decline and death (in 1794).[22] Lundberg and May divided the Scots into sceptical thinkers (Hume and, remarkably, Adam Ferguson) and common sense philosophers (just about everybody else, including Adam Smith and Hugh Blair), and they as well as May in *The Enlightenment in America* stressed the didactic influence and academic institutionalisation of the latter group in the period 1800–1815,[23] when Scottish thought provided moral comfort and epistemological assurance in an era of post-Enlightenment, post-Revolution stabilisation. It is certainly true that Scottish common sense philosophy became part of the standard American college curriculum in the nineteenth century,[24] but defining the Scottish influence in this way is a gross oversimplification that is particularly misleading for the study of the American Enlightenment. Lundberg and May's own data reveal that the most popular books in eighteenth- and early nineteenth-century America included many Scottish works that do not easily fit into their system of classification, such as Hume's *Essays*, Ferguson's *Essay on the History of Civil Society* and *History of the Progress and Termination of the Roman Republic*, Kames's *Elements of Criticism* and *Sketches of the History of Man*, and above all Hume's *History of England*, Smith's *Wealth of Nations*, and Blair's *Sermons* and *Lectures on Rhetoric and Belles Lettres*.[25] If there is a pattern of Scottish influence to be found here, it will not be discovered simply by uttering the magic words 'common sense philosophy'.

Another approach marks Garry Wills's previously cited study of the Declaration of Independence, *Inventing America*, and its 1981 sequel, *Explaining America: The Federalist*. Looking closely at two of the most important documents of the new republic, Wills claimed to have discovered a far earlier and a far greater Scottish influence than had formerly been recognised. In his view this influence included, but went considerably beyond, the Scottish common sense philosophy properly so-called. Wills emphasised, and sometimes over-emphasised or misunderstood, the influence on Jefferson, Madison and Hamilton of Francis Hutcheson's notion of the moral sense as well as certain other ideas of Scottish moralists such as Hume, Smith, Kames, Ferguson, Reid and even Dugald Stewart. Equally important, he continually drew attention to the critical role of Scots as educators of the Founding Fathers, not only renowned academics such as William Smith and John Witherspoon – who is hailed as 'probably the most influential teacher in the entire history of American education' (*Explaining*, 18) – but also lesser lights such as Jefferson's tutor William Small. Wills pointed out that 'the education of our revolutionary generation can be symbolized by this fact: At age sixteen Jefferson *and* Madison *and* Hamilton were all being schooled by Scots who had to come to America as adults' (*Explaining*, 63). 'America in general had gone to school to the Scots in the last colonial period', he stated (*Inventing*, 176); and this contention bears serious consideration by historians of early America in spite of the exaggerations and factual errors for which Wills has rightly been taken to task.[26] If nothing else, Wills forcefully raised the issue of Scottish intellectual influences in America in the critical decades that preceded the institutionalisation of common sense philosophy during and after the 1790s. But intellectual historians have frequently ignored that larger issue, preferring to engage in Wills-bashing rather than in carefully examining the impact of Scotland on the American Enlightenment.[27] It is one thing, however, to expose Wills's careless claims and unfounded arguments on specific points; it is quite another to grapple seriously with his general, and quite plausible, thesis about the primacy of Scottish philosophical ideas and teachers in America during the second and third quarters of the eighteenth century.

Much of the mid- and late-1970s scholarship on Scottish and American intellectual ties that I have been discussing was inspired by the 1976 bicentennials of the American Revolution, of the publication of the *Wealth of Nations* and of the death of Hume. As the hoopla surrounding those events died down, scholarly interest in Scotland and America began to move in other directions. One of these was bibliographical sources: see the valuable (though not specifically Scottish) compilation by Thomas R. Adams, *The American Controversy: A Bibliographical Study of the British Pamphlets about the American Disputes, 1764–1783*, 2 vols. (Providence, R.I., 1980) and above all William R. Brock, *Scotus Americanus: A Survey of the Sources for Links between Scotland and America in the Eighteenth Century* (Edinburgh, 1982). The study of religious connexions benefited from contributions by Marilyn J. Westerkamp, Susan O'Brien and Leigh Eric Schmidt that are cited in the notes to Schmidt's chapter in this volume, as well as the seminal work of Ned Landsman cited below; Norman Fiering, *Jonathan Edwards's Moral Thought and Its British Context* (Chapel Hill, N.C., 1981); and Lefferts A. Loetscher, *Facing the Enlightenment and Pietism: Archibald Alexander and the Founding of Princeton Theological Seminary* (Westport, Conn. and London, 1983). America's debt to Scottish political economy and the 'four-stages theory' of social development began to claim a place in studies intended for general academic audiences, such as Forrest McDonald, *Novus Ordo Seclorum: The Intellectual Origins of the Constitution* (Lawrence, Kan., 1985), chap. 3. Business history was treated in case studies such as *A Scottish Firm in Virginia, 1767–77: W. Cuninghame and Co.*, ed. T.M. Devine (Edinburgh, 1984) and Jacob M. Price, 'The Last Phase of the Virginia-London Conseignment Trade: James Buchanan & Co., 1758–68', *WMQ*, 3rd ser., 43 (1986): 64–98.

But the biggest growth area during the 1980s was migration and settlement, well covered in studies such as Brock's *Scotus Americanus*; David Dobson, *The Original Scots Colonists of Early America, 1612–1783* (1989), which lists some 7180 immigrants, as well as Dobson's six-volume *Directory of Scottish Settlers in North America, 1625–1825*, (1985–86), his *Directory of Scots in the Carolinas, 1680–1830* (1986), and his *Directory of Scots Banished to the American Plantations, 1650–1775* (1984) – all published, along with some reprints of older works in this area, by Geneological Publishing Co. of Baltimore, Maryland; Eric Richards, *A History of the Highland Clearances*, 2 vols. (London, 1982–85); J.M. Bumsted, *The People's Clearance: Highland Emigration to British North America, 1770–1815* (Edinburgh, 1982); A. Roger Ekirch, 'The Transportation of Scottish Criminals to America during the Eighteenth Century', *Journal of British Studies* 24 (1985): 366–74 and *Bound for America: The Transportation of British Convicts to the Colonies, 1718–1775* (Oxford, 1987); Ned Landsman, *Scotland and Its First American Colony, 1683–1760* (Princeton, 1985) and 'Revivalism and Nativism in the Middle Colonies: The Great Awakening and the Scots Community in East Jersey', *American Quarterly* 34 (1982): 149–64; articles and communications on American ethnic origins in the 1980 and 1984 volumes of *WMQ*; and Bernard Bailyn, *Voyagers to the West: A Passage in the Peopling of America on the Eve of the Revolution* (New York, 1986). By providing a fascinating account of Scottish migration to America in the pre-Revolution decade that Whitefield Bell had identified, in the classic 'Scotland and America' number of *WMQ*, as the 'flood' years of Scottish emigration, Bailyn's book may be seen as a particularly fitting response, by one of that number's most renowned contributors, to George Shepperson's appeal for fresh scholarship on this subject.

II

This book and the society responsible for it both had their origins at the March 1986 meeting of the American Society for Eighteenth-Century Studies in Williamsburg, Virginia. The programme of that meeting included a panel that I organised to commemorate the publication at Williamsburg of the 'Scotland and America' issue of *WMQ* more than three decades earlier. Afterwards the members of the panel established a society dedicated to promoting the advancement of eighteenth-century Scottish studies. The three fundamental principles of the new society were simple: it would be scholarly rather than ethnic, multidisciplinary and international. Those same principles gave rise to the plan for ECSSS's first publication project: a broadly interdisciplinary collection of essays that would feature new scholarship on Scottish-American cultural relations during the age of the Enlightenment. The founders of ECSSS believed that a volume of this kind was badly needed, for such a thing had not been done since 1954, and then only on a small scale and with authors from a single discipline. Though a number of valuable studies of eighteenth-century Scottish-American cultural subjects had appeared since then, the field obviously had much more to offer. Subsequent events suggested that this was indeed a topic whose time had come.[28] We also believed that such a volume would benefit from contributions by scholars in literature, history, philosophy, religion, economics, medicine, natural science, music, architecture and other disciplines, and that it would appeal to readers interested in America as well as in Scotland, Britain generally and the Enlightenment. Even if the essays were kept to a modest length, this would be a book of substantial size, and we dared to hope it would be a book of consequence as well. Yet it could not possibly cover the entire field of Scotland and America in the age of the Enlightenment. If the collection were to have coherence, the first task would be to give it a rational and manageable organisational structure.

After one or two false starts, the editors agreed upon a plan. The chronological focus of the book would be the period of the 'high' Enlightenment in Europe and America – roughly from the 1750s through the 1780s. Preference would be given to interdisciplinary essays with something new to say in the areas of cultural and intellectual history, or to essays written from the perspective of particular disciplines, such as religion, music and architecture, that have traditionally been neglected by students of the Scottish and American Enlightenments. Our goal would not be to have the last word on Scotland and America but, quite the contrary, to open up this topic to further enquiry by suggesting its richness and complexity. To achieve this goal with the greatest degree of coherence, we decided to divide the collection into three thematic parts, each representing a general area of study about which too little is known.

In part I, 'Religion and Revolution: The Two Worlds of John Witherspoon', the 'two worlds' of the title may be taken in both a geographical and a topical sense. Geographically, they refer to the tension between Scotland and America, the old world and the new. Topically, they refer to the tension between Scottish Calvinist religion and the political thought and rhetoric of the Enlightenment and the American Revolution. It seemed logical to focus this part of the collection on the man for whom these tensions were most pronounced. As a leader of the Popular or (as he called it) Orthodox party in the Church of Scotland and an opponent of the Enlightenment during his Scottish days; as president of the College of New Jersey (later Princeton University) after 1768, and a lecturer there on moral philosophy, rhetoric and other topics; as a leader of the Presbyterian Church in America; as a strong supporter of the American Revolution and the new American republic; and as a spokesman for Scots throughout America – John Witherspoon was a figure of commanding importance. Yet scholarship on Witherspoon and the thriving transatlantic, evangelical Calvinist culture with which he was associated is astonishingly thin.

Ned C. Landsman opens this part of the book with an examination of the supposed inconsistency between Witherspoon the arch-Calvinist Scot and Witherspoon the secularised American. He argues that this apparent inconsistency disappears as soon as one understands the changing nature of late eighteenth-century Scottish Calvinist orthodoxy, as embodied by the Popular party in the kirk. As America came to be seen as a bastion of true religion, uncorrupted morals and personal liberty, Witherspoon and his colleagues embraced a new form of evangelical cosmopolitanism that shifted the American provinces from the periphery to the centre of their vision. In this new vision the polite learning and manners of the Enlightenment and the economic prosperity secured by commerce and industry were not necessarily evil and not necessarily incompatible with true religion; rather, they could be instruments of improvement or even signs of divine favour, if joined with the Calvinist piety and political liberty that America offered. Thus, in America Witherspoon could freely draw upon portions of the liberal moral philosophy of Francis Hutcheson without breaking in any significant way with the orthodox Calvinist party in Scotland.

In the next chapter I attempt to show that Witherspoon's famous sermon of 1776, *The Dominion of Providence over the Passions of Men*, used a traditional Scottish preaching mode, the Calvinist jeremiad, on behalf of the American Revolution. Scottish opponents of the Revolution (and presumably also of the Popular party) were naturally offended by Witherspoon's sermon and sought to ridicule it. But their ridicule has until now been forgotten, while *Dominion of Providence* itself has continued to be regarded as a classic text of the American Revolution. The chapter complements Ned Landsman's thesis by illustrating how Witherspoon employed at least one important component of the Scots Presbyterian tradition in the service of a vision of Calvinist piety and freedom that could be realised only in the American provinces. It also suggests a general weakness in the current scholarship on American preaching during the Revolution, too much of which confines itself either to New England alone or, at most, to New England in relation to old England – without acknowledging the extent of Scottish, Irish and European influences.

The Presbyterian jeremiad was far from being the only Scottish religious tradition that was influential in America. As Leigh Eric Schmidt demonstrates in chapter 3, the great American Presbyterian revivals of the eighteenth century frequently paralleled a rich Scottish and Scots-Irish heritage of 'sacramental festivity'. Elements of this heritage can be traced all the way back to the popular religious festivals of the pre-

Reformation period, but Presbyterians gave communion days a distinctive ritualistic form and a special place as the holiest time of the spiritual year. The anticipation and excitement surrounding such days created an atmosphere particularly conducive to revivalism, in America as in Scotland and Ulster. After stating and illustrating this thesis, Schmidt presents five observations that point in the direction of further research on this fascinating subject. To these I will add another: that the Enlightenment in Scotland and America was not the thoroughly secular phenomenon it is sometimes thought to be. I make this claim not only because Scottish Moderates and American Old Siders were more devoutly Presbyterian than secular interpretations sometimes allow but also, and more to the point, because the same New Light spirit that infused the Presbyterian revivals in America gave birth to the College of New Jersey at Princeton; and behind both developments lay Scots Presbyterian religious and intellectual values and practices. What Ned Landsman has elsewhere called the Scottish-American 'Evangelical Enlightenment' may not, therefore, be the gross contradiction in terms it may initially seem.[29] On the other hand, the last part of Schmidt's chapter discusses the hostility towards the Scottish tradition of sacramental festivals among spokesmen for the Enlightenment and emphasises the growing perception among American Presbyterians that such festivals constituted 'impediments to refinement and to disciplined social and economic advancement'. The popular rusticity, vehemence and enthusiasm of the Scottish Presbyterian evangelical tradition were in this sense direct challenges to the enlightened principles of refinement, order and decency.[30]

In chapter 4 Robert Kent Donovan provides additional evidence of both the validity and the shortcomings of the notion of a Scottish-American evangelical enlightenment. Building on Dalphy Fagerstrom's pioneering research from the 1950s, Donovan shows that leading members of the Popular party in the Church of Scotland constituted a vocal opposition to British policy during the American War, and that this opposition was rooted in the party's religious ties with evangelical Calvinists in America. The limits of this evangelical enlightenment were defined by the Popular party's bigotry and intolerance towards Roman Catholics. Anti-Catholic sentiment strengthened the bonds between evangelical Calvinists in Scotland and America and encouraged the Popular party's support for the American Revolution. It would therefore be wrong, Donovan argues, for twentieth-century commentators to describe the political views of eighteenth-century Popular party clerics as enlightened or liberal. Rather, those men supported a liberal cause and employed the rhetoric of liberty for largely illiberal reasons.

The last chapters of part I treat two different topics in a somewhat similar manner, in that both employ a comparative method to examine Witherspoon's ideas on a particular topic. Thomas P. Miller's subject in chapter 5 is rhetoric, and his approach hinges on a comparison of Witherspoon with his near contemporary in Scotland, the celebrated professor and Moderate preacher Hugh Blair. His primary contention is that although these two men enjoyed the benefit of a similar educational experience at Edinburgh University, their subsequent rhetoric lectures – Blair at his alma mater and Witherspoon at the College of New Jersey – were very different. Blair's view of his subject was essentially belletristic, reflecting 'the Moderate literati's dislocation from their own public culture'. But Witherspoon's view of rhetoric reflected the fundamentally different social context in which he found himself after emigrating to America, a context that demanded a politically activist, civic rhetoric that would contribute to 'the establishment of a national political consensus'. Both men drew upon the civic humanist tradition in rhetoric, Miller argues, but they embraced different strains of civic humanism depending upon the particular kind of 'republic' each addressed: Blair the republic of letters, Witherspoon the political republic that the American Founding Fathers were about to establish.

Peter J. Diamond's subject in chapter 6 is common sense philosophy, which was so closely associated with the land of its birth that during the nineteenth century it came to be known throughout the western world simply as 'the Scottish Philosophy'. It might just as well have been called 'the Aberdonian Philosophy', not merely because its greatest exponent, Thomas Reid, hailed from Aberdeen but also because, as Diamond shows, many of its underlying principles were developed by Aberdonian followers of Francis Hutcheson and George Turnbull, such as David Fordyce. Diamond argues that 'this Hutchesonian universe of discourse, devoted to the academic pursuit of moral and civic virtue', informed the educational thought of both Witherspoon at Princeton and William Smith at Philadelphia. Though the former was a Presbyterian minister zealous for the Revolution, and the latter was an Episcopalian clergyman whose lack of enthusiasm for the American cause cost him his academic office and may also have hurt his standing with modern scholars,[31] the emphasis here is on their similarities. Both men were born in Scotland during the 1720s and educated there during the 1730s and 1740s, when the philosophical writings of Hutcheson, Turnbull and Fordyce were in print but those of Reid were still decades away. Both were not so much philosophers as educators seeking to modify Hutcheson's moral sense philosophy 'in order to emphasise the rational and hence improvable aspects of the moral faculty'. If this direction was similar to the one later taken by Reid, Diamond believes the similarity has more to do with the Scottish intellectual context from which they both emerged, and the comparable pedagogical purposes to which their philosophical ideas were put in America, than to Reid's direct influence.

Discussion of 'the Scottish Philosophy' leads us into the second part of the volume, 'Philosophers and Founding Fathers', which focuses on some of the ways in which the American Revolution affected Scottish thinkers such as Hume, Smith, Robertson and the aristocratic 'country' Whigs as well as some of the ways in which Scottish thought and rhetoric may have influenced American Founding Fathers such as Wilson and Madison. Chapters 7 through 10 present four very different ways in which Scottish thinkers viewed the American crisis of the 1760s and 1770s. In chapter 7, Donald W. Livingston explains David Hume's remarkable support for American independence – remarkable because it was voiced so early (1768) and by a man of conservative political tastes – in terms of Hume's complete rejection of 'English barbarism', meaning particularly dangerously abstract or theoretical notions of Revolution ideology, natural rights and liberty (as in the dreaded slogan 'Wilkes and Liberty'). Removing the ideological blinders that he believed such 'fictions' placed on the eyes of most of his contemporaries, Hume was able to analyse events causally and dispassionately. He did not side with the American rebels' own ideological arguments, which to him were ultimately grounded in the same faulty premises as those of their opponents. Rather, says Livingston, he simply observed, on the basis of empirical evidence drawn from history and contemporary events, that 'a new order of political societies had spontaneously evolved in America that would have to be recognised on pain of a war that could not be won or, if it could, of a reign of terror to keep the colonies in subjection, which a liberty-loving regime such as Britain could not stomach, much less afford financially'.

As Andrew S. Skinner discusses in chapter 8, Adam Smith recommended keeping America in the British empire as part of an incorporating union based on the principles of free trade and taxation with representation. Such, at least, was his recommendation until the hardening of both sides in the conflict made that solution unthinkable and drove him reluctantly to the realisation that partial military defeat was Britain's likely fate. Skinner's thesis centres on the idea that Smith's thinking was driven by his economic analysis, which scrutinised the government's Navigation Acts in order to reveal both their considerable short-term strengths and their inherent long-term 'contradictions'. The latter would eventually become apparent from either an American or a British point of view, but both perspectives could be reduced to the single proposition that, in the long run, both the colonies and the mother country would be hurt by mercantilist restrictions. Skinner suggests further that Smith's preference for free trade was ultimately rooted in his Hutchesonian 'moral' conviction that liberty, including economic liberty, is a basic right of all people.

William Robertson adopted a more conservative position on America than either Hume or Smith. Yet Robertson's was a consistently humane conservatism, Jeffrey R. Smitten tells us in chapter 9, in that it called for British supremacy without oppression. Smitten argues that this stance towards America reflects Robertson's guiding principles of balance and moderation – principles that informed his oratory as the leader of the Moderate party in the kirk as well as his prose style as a historian. Furthermore, this stance and these principles are the key to understanding why Robertson did not complete his plan to supplement the successful history of Spanish America that he published in 1777 with a history of British America. In a state of polarisation and commitment, balance and moderation seemed to have no place. And when it became clear that America would be lost to the British empire, Robertson realised he could not write the history of British America with the happy ending he originally envisioned.

The political conservatism of Robertson and his fellow Moderates in the Church of Scotland forms a stark contrast to the pro-American sentiments of the Popular party, as treated by Robert Kent Donovan in chapter 4.[32] It may also be contrasted with a second strand of pro-American sentiment, one associated with aristocratic 'country' Whiggery. As Bruce P. Lenman explains in chapter 10, this aristocratic 'country' Whig tradition can be traced back to Andrew Fletcher of Saltoun at the turn of the eighteenth century. At the time of the American Revolution its main spokesmen were the earls of Lauderdale, Selkirk and Buchan, who opposed the American War for the same reasons that they opposed the sham elections of Scottish representative peers to sit in the House of Lords. These men refused to sell out to a corrupt ministry and paid the price by sacrificing influence and by earning reputations as outsiders or eccentrics. Their 'country' Whig scruples about America were shared by lesser born members of the Scottish landed élite, such as George Dempster, John Maclaurin (Lord Dreghorn) and James Boswell. Indeed, Boswell scholars may well find that Lenman's paradigm of Scottish aristrocratic 'country' Whiggery works better for understanding Boswell's ideology than the traditional label 'Tory', especially when that label is interpreted in a Johnsonian manner.

The last two chapters of part II turn from Scottish ideas about the American crisis to Scottish influences on some of the American Founding Fathers who helped to resolve that crisis in the years following the Revolution. James Wilson, the focus of Shannon C. Stimson's attention in chapter 11, was born in Scotland in 1747 and educated at the university nearest his home, St Andrews. In 1764, one year before Wilson's emigration to America at the age of eighteen, Thomas Reid's *An Inquiry into the Human Mind, on the Principles of Common Sense* was published at Edinburgh. In America Wilson settled in Philadelphia and became a lawyer, a signer of the Declaration of Independence, a major contributor to the Constitution, an eloquent orator in courts and assemblies, and a Supreme Court justice (as well as an unscrupulous land speculator). He was also a brilliant political and legal thinker profoundly indebted to Thomas Reid's philosophy of common sense. Stimson explores that influence in light of the apparent tension in Wilson's thought between the democratic concept of popular sovereignty and the more conservative concept of judicial review by an élite or 'supreme' court, and she demonstrates how Wilson both used and extended Reid's common sense principles to develop his own theory of jurisprudence. In particular, she shows how Wilson's common sense principles formed the basis for his faith in juries composed of common men and above all in a power of judicial review vested in 'a jury of the country', or Supreme Court.

In chapter 12 we return to the subject of rhetoric and to eighteenth-century Britain's greatest teacher of that subject, Hugh Blair. Whereas Thomas Miller contrasts the belletristic Blair with the civic-minded Witherspoon, David Daiches stresses in this chapter Blair's importance for understanding the political rhetoric of the Founding Fathers. In the Constitution and other early American writings, Daiches finds evidence of the careful intermixing of short, straightforward sentences (*style coupé*) and long sentences that build to a climax in an almost musical manner (*style périodique*) – much as Blair recommended in his remarkably influential *Lectures on Rhetoric and Belles Lettres* (1783). Tracing the first appearance of Blair's lectures in America is not easy, but it is entirely possible that manuscript sets were in circulation there well before publication. Writing of his lectures in a letter of 1780, for example, Blair lamented 'the too frequent circulation of the imperfect and corrupted copies of them in manuscript proceeding from my scholars. They are pretty publickly sold, though at a considerable price, and are even come so far as to be quoted in printed books; particularly in Kippis's new Edition of the Biographia [Britannica] under the article *Addison*.'[33] In any event, whether Blair actually shaped the style of the Founding Fathers or merely recorded for later generations stylistic rules and principles that the Founding Fathers already understood, there can be no doubt that his lectures appealed to the common needs of linguistic 'provincials' on both sides of the Atlantic.

The third part of the collection represents the first attempt to examine cultural and intellectual ties between eighteenth-century Scotland and Philadelphia from a variety of disciplinary perspectives. Philadelphia was not only the largest and wealthiest city in America during the age of the Enlightenment but its cultural centre as well. As Andrew Hook makes clear in chapter 13, which constitutes an overview of the subject and an introduction to what follows, Philadelphia's cultural ties with Edinburgh and the rest of enlightened Scotland were extraordinarily rich, though little studied by scholars. Two of the reasons for this neglect, Hook suggests, are the survival of the traditional English tendency to subsume Scotch Presbyterians under the catch-all rubric 'dissenters' and the neglected Scottishness of Episcopalians like William Smith. One might add that as a rule students of early Philadelphia are trained to have no more sensitivity to international and ethnic connexions than are students of colonial New England – or those of enlightened Scotland, for that matter. Hook locates the key to the Scottish connexion in education, noting the roles of William Smith and Francis Alison in the College of Philadelphia, of John Morgan in the Philadelphia Medical School, and of John Witherspoon at the nearby College of New Jersey (which had a much stronger Philadelphian component than is usually realised). But he also stresses the importance of other factors, such as the similar social and intellectual situations of Edinburgh and Philadelphia as provincial capitals and the importance of Benjamin Franklin's Scottish ties. It is difficult to quibble with Hook's conclusion that what the Scottish Enlightenment offered to Philadelphia was 'above all an acceptable spirit of moderation and compromise by means of which traditional morality and progressive thinking, social order and civic development, religious faith and scientific enquiry, could all be reconciled.'

In chapter 14 Deborah C. Brunton looks at relations between the medical schools at Edinburgh and Philadelphia. Taking issue with the traditional view that gives all credit for the similarity of the two schools to the latter's Edinburgh-trained founder, John Morgan, Brunton points out that though Morgan's founding plan used Edinburgh as the model for the organisation and curriculum of the new school, other professors joined in copying (sometimes literally) the innovative course material and medical theories of their Edinburgh teachers – at least until American medicine began to experience nationalistic pressures and until Edinburgh began to lose its undisputed lead in medical education around the turn of the nineteenth century. By then, Brunton argues, similarities between the two schools owed more to the similar contexts in which they functioned than to any conscious design on the part of the Philadelphia faculty. Medical professors at both schools were paid by their students and were therefore anxious to teach subjects and theories that were up-to-date and popular. Students at both schools wanted not only a good education but also appropriate credentials for future success in the medical profession. Brunton demonstrates, then, how similarities between the Philadelphia and Edinburgh medical schools during the age of the Enlightenment were the result partly of Morgan's founding plan, partly of efforts at emulation by other Edinburgh-trained professors at the new school, and partly of parallel responses to similar circumstances.

The last two chapters in the volume consider Scottish contributions to aspects of eighteenth-century Philadelphia's nonverbal culture. In chapter 15 Anne McClenny Krauss focuses on two professional musicians who emigrated to Philadelphia after establishing strong connexions with the Edinburgh Musical Society. The older of the two, James Bremner, is shown to have established in colonial Philadelphia the new musical style of orchestral writing that the earl of Kelly had brought back to Edinburgh from Mannheim. In 1786, six years after Bremner's death, Alexander Reinagle brought another innovation to Philadelphia – the replacement of the harpsichord by the pianoforte, which the Edinburgh Musical Society had permitted him to play extensively in concert. Krauss shows how both Bremner and Reinagle borrowed the form and content of their Philadelphia concert programmes from the Edinburgh Musical Society. Reinagle also adapted the EMS tradition of combining folk and classical music – a tradition that suggests the inadequacy of the 'two cultures' interpretation of eighteenth-century Scottish culture.[34] On the other hand, Krauss clearly demonstrates the aristocratic nature of the EMS, which treated accomplished professional musicians as glorified servants. America, we may suppose, promised Bremner and Reinagle the chance of a better livelihood as well as an opportunity to raise their social standing.

In the final chapter, Charles E. Peterson examines the early career of colonial America's greatest builder-architect, Robert Smith. Peterson traces Smith's likely path from birth near Dalkeith, Scotland, to Philadelphia, where he began making his mark at the middle of the eighteenth century. We then follow Smith's work on four major Philadelphia projects, moving from Gilbert Tennent's Second Presbyterian Church, to James Hamilton's Bush Hill mansion, to the College of Philadelphia during the age of William Smith, to the majestic Christ Church Steeple, which shows the influence of the great Scottish architect William Adam. When New Side evangelicals from Philadelphia and elsewhere began to lay the groundwork for a Presbyterian college between Philadelphia and New York, the job of building the new college at Princeton, New Jersey, fell to Robert Smith. Though Peterson's essay covers only a small portion of Smith's career as a builder-architect, it is more than enough to demonstrate what an important contribution this little-known Scottish carpenter made to Philadelphia and the American Enlightenment. Smith himself was a member of the American Philosophical Society, and his buildings housed numerous enlightened institutions and individuals, including Benjamin Franklin, William Smith and John Witherspoon. In a manner analagous to Bremner and Reinagle, Smith advanced from a young journeyman carpenter in Scotland to a long career of designing, constructing and financing some of the most notable buildings in America. For all these men, and presumably for many others in the arts, Philadelphia represented the height of American civilisation and sophistication and, therefore, the best opportunity outside Britain for finding appreciative audiences, students and patrons.

Scholarship on Scotland and America in the age of the Enlightenment has come a long way since George Shepperson spoke out against the 'Burns Supper school of Scottish-American historians' more than thirty-five years ago. The editors are hopeful that readers of this volume will gain a deeper appreciation for the complex nature of Scottish-American cultural connexions in the eighteenth century. Such connexions, we have tried to show, were not limited to Scottish influences on America, for America's considerable impact on Scottish culture must also be taken into account. Moreover, it seems to us equally important that Scottish influences on America should not be restricted to a few thinkers who are thought to comprise a monolithic 'school' of philosophy: not only were the intellectual contributions of eighteenth-century Scottish thinkers far more diverse than such an approach would indicate but their contributions extended into spheres of culture that have hitherto received little scholarly attention – from preaching modes and sacramental celebrations to music, architecture and rhetoric. Future study of the American Enlightenment must take these developments into account and must try to make sense of them. This book calls upon scholars to reassess tired half-truths about the roles played by Scottish ideas, values and people in shaping early American culture. Much work remains to be done. If the essays within these pages inspire further efforts to enhance our understanding of this topic, this volume will have accomplished a great deal.

NOTES

1. Whitefield J. Bell, Jr., 'Philadelphia Medical Students in Europe, 1750–1800', *PMHB* 67 (1943): 1–29; 'Some American Students of "That Shining Oracle of Physic", Dr. William Cullen of Edinburgh, 1755–1766', *Proceedings of the American Philosophical Society* 94 (1950): 275–81; and articles in the *Journal of the History of Medicine* in 1964 and 1965. See also Bell, *John Morgan: Continental Doctor* (Philadelphia, 1965) and *The Colonial Physician and Other Essays* (New York, 1975).
2. E.g., Thomas C. Pears, 'Francis Alison', *Journal of the Presbyterian Historical Society* 28 (1950): 213–25; Leonard J. Kramer, 'Presbyterians Approach the American Revolution' and 'Muskets in the Pulpit, 1776–1783', ibid., 31 (1953): 71–86, 167–80, 229–44, and 32 (1954): 37–51; Michael Kraus, 'Charles Nisbet and Samuel

Stanhope Smith: Two Eighteenth-Century Educators', *Princeton University Library Chronicle* 6 (1944): 17–36.

3. Cited in Gladys Bryson, *Man and Society: The Scottish Inquiry of the Eighteenth Century* (Princeton, 1945), 274.
4. Arnaud B. Leavelle, 'James Wilson and the Relation of the Scottish Metaphysics to American Political Thought', *Political Science Quarterly* 57 (1942): 394–410; A.O. Aldridge, 'Edwards and Hutcheson', *Harvard Theological Review* 44 (1951): 35–53; Sydney E. Ahlstrom, 'The Scottish Philosophy and American Theology', *Church History* 24 (1955): 257–72. Douglass Adair's classic contribution to this field, ' "That Politics May Be Reduced to a Science": David Hume, James Madison, and the Tenth *Federalist*', was first published in the *Huntington Library Quarterly* in 1957 (20: 343–60) and reprinted in his posthumous *Fame and the Founding Fathers: Essays by Douglass Adair*, ed. Trevor Colbourn (New York, 1974), 93–106.
5. Varnum Lansing Collins, *President Witherspoon*, 2 vols. (Princeton, 1925); Albert F. Gegenheimer, *William Smith: Educator and Churchman, 1727–1803* (Philadelphia, 1943); Samuel Miller, *Memoir of the Rev. Charles Nisbet* (New York, 1840); Claude Milton Newlin, *The Life and Writings of Hugh Henry Brackenridge* (Princeton, 1932).
6. *The Autobiography of Benjamin Rush*, ed. George W. Corner (Princeton, 1948); Nathan Goodman, *Benjamin Rush: Physician and Citizen, 1746–1813* (Philadelphia, 1934); Herbert L. Ganter, 'William Small, Jefferson's Beloved Teacher', *WMQ*, 3rd ser., 4 (1947): 505–7.
7. J. Bennett Nolan, *Benjamin Franklin in Scotland and Ireland, 1759 and 1771* (Philadelphia, 1938).
8. Caroline Robbins, 'Douglass Adair: A Personal Memoir', in Adair, *Fame and the Founding Fathers*, xvii–xxiii, quoting xx.
9. A more specialised article on this subject appeared six months later: T.C. Barker, 'Smuggling in the Eighteenth Century: The Evidence of the Scottish Tobacco Trade', *Virginia Magazine of History and Biography* 62 (1954): 387–99.
10. In David Daiches's important little book, *The Paradox of Scottish Culture: The Eighteenth-Century Experience* (London, 1964), for example, the notion of 'cultural schizophrenia' was invoked to characterise the Scottish literati's love-hate feelings about England in regard to language and other matters, and other studies have followed this line.
11. For this reason among others, J.G.A. Pocock's model for understanding the British world as a 'diversity of interacting and varyingly autonomous cultures' is far more sophisticated and useful than core-and-periphery models. See Pocock, 'British History: A Plea for a New Subject', *Journal of Modern History* 47 (1975): 601–21, and the exchange that follows with his critics (622–28), including Michael Hechter, author of the core-and-periphery classic *Internal Colonialism: The Celtic Fringe in British National Development, 1536–1966* (Berkeley, Cal., and London, 1975).
12. Roger L. Emerson, 'The Enlightenment and Social Structures', in *City and Society in the Eighteenth Century*, ed. Paul Fritz and David Williams (Toronto, 1973), 99–124.
13. John Lough, 'Reflections on Enlightenment and Lumières', *British*

Journal for Eighteenth-Century Studies 8 (1985): 1–15. For a reply to Lough and other critics, see Richard B. Sher, 'Storm Over the Literati', *Cencrastus*, no. 28 (1987–88): 42–45.

14. The most important of these is David Fate Norton, 'Francis Hutcheson in America', *SVEC* 154 (1976): 1547–68.
15. Perhaps Robbins had this point in mind when she wrote, in her personal memoir of Douglass Adair cited in n. 8 above, that 'by no means all opinions expressed in the April 1954 *Quarterly* were entirely agreeable to the Scots'.
16. Shepperson recently retired as William Robertson Professor of Commonwealth and American History at the University of Edinburgh. Jacob Price has enjoyed a distinguished career as professor of history at the University of Michigan. Bernard Bailyn is Adams University Professor at Harvard University. John Clive became William R. Kenan, Jr. Professor of History and Literature at Harvard. Caroline Robbins became Marjorie Walter Goodhart Professor of History, and later Flora Mather Stone Professor, at Bryn Mawr. Whitefield Bell, Jr. distinguished himself as an editor of the Benjamin Franklin Papers, a librarian at the American Philosophical Society, and a leading scholar of Philadelphia science and medicine.
17. Sher, 343.
18. Most of these studies are cited in Sher, 373–74.
19. Daniel Walker Howe, 'European Sources of Political Ideas in Jeffersonian America', *Reviews in American History* 10 (1982): 28–44, quoting 29.
20. James T. Kloppenberg, 'The Virtues of Liberalism: Christianity, Republicanism, and Ethics in Early American Political Discourse', *Journal of American History* 74 (1987): 9–33, quoting 10.
21. The tendency to treat almost all eighteenth-century Scottish thinkers as members of a national 'school' of common sense philosophy had its roots in nineteenth-century perceptions, particularly James McCosh's influential book *The Scottish Philosophy* (New York, 1875). Later histories of American philosophy adopted McCosh's thesis in one way or another, and most recent intellectual historians of America have continued this tradition without subjecting it to critical scrutiny.
22. Meyer, *Democratic Enlightenment*, chap. 12: 'John Witherspoon and the Education of the Public Conscience'. Meyer's thesis was that 'Witherspoon was one of several academic innovators in the 1790's . . . who were responsible for the rise of Scottish common-sense philosophy in America' (189).
23. David Lundberg and Henry F. May, 'The Enlightened Reader in America', *American Quarterly* 28 (1976): 262–71 and supporting data; May, *Enlightenment in America*, 341–50, just *after* his chapter entitled 'The Decline of the Enlightenment'. May qualified his earlier work with Lundberg when he noted that 'not all of the Scots could be assimilated to the Didactic Enlightenment' (May, *Enlightenment in America*, 344), much as Meyer observed that 'Scottish philosophy is by no means a monolithic system of ideas, and, in fact, it reflects many different points of view' (*Democratic Enlightenment*, 189). Yet both May and Meyer's conceptual frameworks for understanding

the American Enlightenment had the effect of rendering these qualifications insignificant.

24. On this point see, in addition to works by Donald Meyer, Howard Miller and others already mentioned, Daniel Howe, *The Unitarian Conscience: Harvard Moral Philosophy, 1805–1861* (Cambridge, Mass., 1970) and James D. Hoeveler, Jr., *James McCosh and the Scottish Intellectual Tradition* (Princeton, 1981).
25. Lundberg and May, 'Enlightened Reader', appended data. Most of these titles were far better represented in American libraries than were the classic texts of common sense philosophy by Reid, Kames and Dugald Stewart. Moreover, Lundberg and May's data did not include the works of several extremely popular Scottish authors whose writings were not in the common sense philosophy mould, such as the histories of William Robertson and the poetry of James Macpherson's Ossian.
26. Ronald Hamowy, 'Jefferson and the Scottish Enlightenment: A Critique of Garry Wills's *Inventing America: Jefferson's Declaration of Independence*', *WMQ*, 3rd ser., 36 (1979): 503–23; Theodore Draper, 'Hume & Madison: The Secrets of Federalist Paper No. 10', *Encounter* 58 (1982): 34–47.
27. Ronald Hamowy has every right to criticise Wills's absurd claim that Adam Ferguson and Dugald Stewart (who was born in 1753) were among the leading figures in Scottish intellectual life during the 1740s and 1750s ('Jefferson and the Scottish Enlightenment', 521), but it should also be pointed out that some important Scottish moralists *not* mentioned by Wills were quite active in those decades – most notably David Fordyce, whose extensive influence in America has scarcely been noticed except briefly by Norman Fiering in *Moral Philosophy at Seventeenth-Century Harvard: A Discipline in Transition* (Chapel Hill, N.C., 1981), 51. John P. Diggins, *The Lost Soul of American Politics: Virtue, Self-Interest, and the Foundations of Liberalism* (Chicago, 1984) attempts to refute Wills by suggesting that the relationship between 'Jeffersonian individualism' and Wills's notion of Scottish moral philosophy, with its emphasis on 'man's sociability and dependency' and the Hutchesonian precedence of 'the moral consensus of society . . . over the private interests and conscience of the individual', appears to constitute 'a study in immiscibility' (33–34). Actually a good case can be made (though Wills does not make it) for regarding Scottish moral philosophy as a major *source* of Jeffersonian individualism: one has only to read Hutcheson or Ferguson on the rights of the individual, let alone Adam Smith. See, for example, the discussion of 'civil rights' in Ferguson's *Institutes of Moral Philosophy* (pt. 7, chap. 3, sect. 3) – a book whose possible significance is greatly underestimated by Hamowy ('Jefferson and the Scottish Enlightenment', 509). It is high time to replace the fruitless dichotomy between Lockean liberalism and Scottish moralism with a more nuanced approach, towards which Kloppenberg, 'Virtues of Liberalism' constitutes a welcome step.
28. Examples include three events with which I was honoured to be affiliated. In the summer of 1986 David Daiches and Peter Jones organised 'Institute Project Scottish Enlightenment' (IPSE) at the

University of Edinburgh, and the lavishly illustrated volume they produced, along with Jean Jones, to celebrate that conference – *A Hotbed of Genius: The Scottish Enlightenment, 1730–90* (Edinburgh, 1986) – included Archie Turnbull's very readable summary of previous research, 'Scotland and America, 1730–90' (137–52). The following April the Organization of American Historians held a well-attended seminar on 'Scotland and America: The Eighteenth Century' at its annual meeting in Philadelphia. And in the summer of 1987 the National Endowment for the Humanities sponsored at Princeton and St Andrews an extremely successful institute for teachers entitled 'Scotland, the Enlightenment and the American Republic'.

29. Ned C. Landsman, 'Presbyterians and Provinciality: The Evangelical Enlightenment in the West of Scotland, 1740–75', in *Sociability and Society: The Social World of the Scottish Enlightenment*, ed. John Dwyer and Richard B. Sher, forthcoming. An important study of the relationship between Scottish notions of evangelicalism and enlightenment in the context of the American Presbyterian ideal of higher education appeared as this volume was going to press: Mark A. Noll, *Princeton and the Republic, 1768–1822: The Search for a Christian Enlightenment in the Era of Samuel Stanhope Smith* (Princeton, 1989).
30. Ned Landsman's critical examination of the Cambuslang Revival, 'Evangelists and Their Hearers: Popular Interpretation of Revivalist Preaching in Eighteenth-Century Scotland', *Journal of British Studies* 28 (1989): 120–49, demonstrates that even the evangelical clergy could not control the popular impulse towards visions, voices and premonitions among the young members of the artisan community who dominated that event.
31. Robert Lawson-Peebles, 'The Problem of William Smith: An Aberdonian in Revolutionary America', in *Aberdeen and the Enlightenment*, ed. Jennifer J. Carter and Joan H. Pittock (Aberdeen, 1987), 52–60.
32. See also Sher, chap. 7.
33. Blair to Thomas Davies, 23 Dec. 1780, Beinecke Library, Yale University.
34. Alexander Murdoch and Richard Sher, 'Literary and Learned Culture', in *People and Society in Scotland: A Social History of Modern Scotland in Three Volumes*, vol. 1: 1760–1830, ed. T.M. Devine and Rosalind Mitchison (Edinburgh, 1988), 127–42.

I. Religion and Revolution: The Two Worlds of John Witherspoon

1

NED C. LANDSMAN

Witherspoon and the Problem of Provincial Identity in Scottish Evangelical Culture

Students of Adam Smith have long referred to *das Adam Smith Problem*, by which they mean the presumed difficulty of reconciling the sympathetic and benevolent ethic of Smith's *Theory of Moral Sentiments* with the selfish or self-interested ethic in the *Wealth of Nations*. Historians have had a similar problem with Smith's countryman and exact contemporary, John Witherspoon. In Scotland Witherspoon made a name for himself within the evangelical or Popular party of the Church of Scotland largely on the basis of his published satires of the affectations of manner, the laxness of doctrine and the apparent preference for moralising over evangelising among his Moderate opponents within the kirk. Yet in America Witherspoon would become famous for establishing the same concerns with rhetoric, literature and moral philosophy as the Moderates within the curriculum of the College of New Jersey, and in a larger sense within American curricula in general.

Over the years the Adam Smith problem has shifted its contours. For some recent writers, the question has been less the reconciliation of Smith's sympathetic and selfish ethics than the extent to which both derived from the distinct and seemingly incompatible traditions of civic humanism and natural law. So, too, has the Witherspoon problem altered. To the difficulty of reconciling Witherspoon's commitment to orthodoxy with his espousal of an apparently humanistic moral philosophy has been added the equally daunting task of explaining how the thoroughly Scottish and Presbyterian Witherspoon, a reluctant emigrant from Scotland to the colonies, could within just a few years turn into a staunch American patriot, the lone clerical signer of the Declaration of Independence and the most eloquent spokesman for colonial rights among a Scottish emigrant population hardly noted for its sympathy for the American cause.

That aspect of the problem is rendered all the more apparent by Richard Sher's demonstration in the following chapter of Witherspoon's use of the jeremiad form in both his Scottish and his American preaching. The principle behind the jeremiad is that of the covenanted nation, which faces divinely ordained trials to remind it of its sworn duties as a chosen people. But since a covenant is by definition a binding, perpetual and unalterable agreement between God and nation, one wonders how Witherspoon could reconcile his belief in Scotland's covenanted role with his equally fervent transfer of loyalties from Scotland to America.

Several explanations have been offered for these supposed conflicts in Witherspoon's thought. Some have described him as inconsistent and eclectic (the latter he surely was), borrowing whatever concepts suited him without regard for inherent contradictions.[1] That description would seem to resolve the first part of the Witherspoon problem, his espousal of both evangelicalism and moral philosophy, but it does little to explain his transfer of loyalties, evidenced by the very consistency with which he employed the rhetoric of the covenant in both Scotland and America. Others have argued that Witherspoon himself changed in the years following his move from Scotland to America, as orthodox Presbyterians on both continents gradually accommodated themselves to the prevailing ways of the Moderates.[2] That interpretation would seem to leave us with the still larger problem of explaining Witherspoon's theological writings, which remained as firmly 'orthodox' in his American years as they had been before.

There remains a third possibility, which I mean to explore in this chapter. Witherspoon's apparent inconsistencies may have been just that: apparent. However eclectic this Scottish-American pastor may have been in his borrowings, his fidelity to the Popular party and to Presbyterian orthodoxy remained firm and unyielding. It was orthodoxy itself that changed during the eighteenth century. While retaining their essential commitment to the basic tenets of Reformed theology, to the mantle of John Knox and his covenanting heirs, and to the concept of a uniform Presbyterian establishment, a new generation of devout Scottish Calvinists managed to accommodate themselves in important ways not so much to the Moderates, who were their contemporaries, as to the rapidly changing culture of an eighteenth-century Scotland increasingly enmeshed in evangelicalism, enlightenment and the transatlantic world. In the process they adopted many of the same concepts, values and terms as their more 'enlightened' opponents. They committed themselves to the new learning and to the values of literary culture and refinement, although they adapted them to evangelical ends. They began to speak in the language of commercial analysis, which was becoming an increasingly important discourse throughout the provinces. Above all, they changed their view of church and nation, away from a strictly national and sectarian conception to the broader perspective of provincial Britons. In essence, they became less 'provincial' as we often employ that term today, signifying a particular and narrow viewpoint, and more 'provincial' in the less parochial sense that would be appropriate to the eighteenth-century world, in which the provinces collectively came to represent some of the most expansive, enlightened and, in their parlance, moral and virtuous segments of the British empire. That greatly expanded conception of provinciality holds a key to understanding Witherspoon's extension of a covenanted status from Scotland to America.[3]

I

John Witherspoon was born in 1723 in Yester parish in the shire of East Lothian, the son of a clergyman and a clergyman's daughter. At the age of thirteen he entered Edinburgh University, where he studied under the celebrated John Stevenson and other noted teachers of the day. Witherspoon received his Master of Arts degree in 1739 but remained to study divinity for an additional four years. Several of his contemporaries would become influential Moderate clergymen, including William Robertson, the historian and leader of the Moderates, Alexander Carlyle, the famous autobiographer, and Hugh Blair, the rhetorician and preacher.[4] But whereas their university training would lead Carlyle, Blair and Robertson to the positions that would characterise Moderatism, Witherspoon consistently maintained his allegiance to his father's persuasion as a firm proponent of Presbyterian orthodoxy.

Witherspoon's years at Edinburgh coincided with a significant division and turning point in the history of Scottish orthodoxy, which until that point had been committed to the concept of a unified Presbyterian establishment. For most of the century the proponents of orthodoxy had fought what they viewed as a rearguard battle against English and Erastian encroachments upon the doctrine, practices and independence of the Scottish kirk. That struggle involved issues of polity, as when the Union Parliament, contrary to guarantees offered in the Treaty of Union, restored the rights of 'patrons' (often local landowners, whether Presbyterian or not) to present ministers to fill vacant churches. It involved doctrinal questions as well, as reflected in the heresy trials of John Simson, professor of theology at Glasgow University, and in the repeated attacks by orthodox clergy upon such theological liberals as Francis Hutcheson and William Leechman.

By the time Witherspoon entered Edinburgh University, those issues had provoked a schism within the kirk. In 1732 Ebenezer Erskine of Stirling, a leader of the orthodox faction, denounced the willingness of the general assembly to acquiesce in cases of patronage with such vehement language that he was suspended from the church. Erskine then joined with several determined colleagues in forming an 'Associate Presbytery' and, eventually, a separate Secession Church. The seceders preached with an evangelical fervour and within a few years had established more than thirty meetings with thousands of hearers.[5]

As a group the seceders were traditionalist to an extreme. From their predecessors in covenanting days they inherited a commitment to an interpretation of Scottish history that linked Scotland's mission to the preservation of an orthodox and unvarying Presbyterian establishment. In 1744 the Associate Presbytery publicly renewed Scotland's national covenants and made them a requirement for communion within seceder meetings. Soon thereafter one group of ardent seceders excommunicated another, including Ebenezer Erskine, for failing to prohibit the swearing of a burgess oath that could be construed as endorsing the religious establishment. The seceders were nationalistic and xenophobic as well, consistently blaming the Union with England and English 'infection' for all that was wrong with the church, from patronage to heresy to witchcraft.

Despite the popularity of the seceders, the majority of orthodox ministers remained within the kirk. Their motives were varied. Some were as firmly traditional as the members of the Associate Presbytery and opposed secession precisely because it undermined the ideal of a unified Presbyterian establishment. An example of such a clergyman was John Currie of Kinglassie, a longtime friend, neighbour and synodical ally of Ebenezer Erskine. Yet Currie was never comfortable with his colleague's course, because he viewed secession from even a flawed Presbyterian establishment as a violation of Scotland's historic and covenanted role. Currie defended his position in a vehement pamphlet war with his former colleagues.[6]

Another such minister was the influential John Willison of Dundee, who was just as suspicious as the seceders of English encroachments upon the kirk. However much orthodox Presbyterians railed against defections, Willison wrote, 'our commerce with England still increasing, the prophanation of the Lord's day among us is come to a great height'. Despite his agreement with almost all of the seceders' complaints, he condemned separations among Presbyterians as 'unscriptural'. Instead, he compiled a lengthy 'Testimony' against the 'Backslidings, Corruptions, Divisions, and prevailing Evils' within the church, decrying equally the secession and the policies that had provoked it.[7]

There was another side to the Popular party, however, consisting chiefly of younger ministers who came of age after most of the ecclesiastical battles provoking the secession had ended. They were educated under new instructional methods at the universities of Glasgow and Edinburgh in the second quarter of the eighteenth century, following the same courses and often attending the same classes as their Moderate counterparts.[8] They came of age in a society increasingly experiencing and contemplating the effects of commercial growth. Early in their careers they participated in the evangelical revivals that swept through much of the Lowlands during the 1730s and 1740s. Those revivals were linked to religious awakenings throughout the British world and would shape their ideas in important ways. During those years they developed connexions with evangelical leaders throughout the Anglo-American world and with important emerging groups among the Scottish laity, including the network of merchants trading with America and the rapidly growing community of spinners and weavers.

Among those young evangelicals were several of later renown who would be close allies of Witherspoon. One was John Gillies of Glasgow, Witherspoon's colleague in the Synod of Glasgow and Ayr, and publisher of vast collections of evangelical source materials. Gillies had embarked upon his ministry just as the revival commenced. So had Thomas Gillespie, whose deposition by the general assembly in 1752 would push Witherspoon into ecclesiastical politics. As a group these ministers were far less xenophobic than their older colleagues: many of the younger evangelicals established regular communications with dissenters in England and in America, and all paid close attention to colonial affairs.[9]

The existence of transatlantic connexions was not new among Scottish Presbyterians. Almost from the beginnings of American colonisation, Scottish ministers, acting individually, had corresponded with their counterparts in the New World. Yet the transatlantic awakening of the 1730s and 1740s brought about a new stage in the development of Scottish-American religious networks, affecting both the quality and quantity of contacts. In 1742, during the height of evangelical activity in western Scotland, William McCulloch of Cambuslang, a man at the centre of the revival movement, began publishing a religious newpaper, the *Glasgow Weekly History*, dedicated to printing original narratives of religious awakenings throughout the British world, but especially in Scotland and America. It was succeeded the following year by a *Christian Monthly History* edited by James Robe, another leading revivalist; the last several issues of that publication were taken up almost entirely with colonial news. Several years later John Gillies distributed a newsletter to his Glasgow parishioners, *An Exhortation to the Inhabitants of the South Parish of Glasgow*, carrying further word of the American revivals.

The interest of Scottish Presbyterians in the American awakening represented an important shift in perspective. Previously, advocates of orthodoxy had insisted with virtual unanimity that the Church of Scotland represented the most fully reformed of the Reformed kirks and stood as the principal site of the continuing work of redemption. Now, for the first time, Scottish Presbyterians began to perceive a direct link between religious developments at home and those occurring in other parts of the British world. With the deterioration of the influence of orthodoxy within the kirk and the rise of Moderatism and Anglicisation, Scottish evangelicals began to look to the colonies as the principal hope of reformed religion. As James Robe announced on the first page of the first number of the *Christian Monthly History*, '*New-England* hath been much upon the Heart of the Religious in *Scotland* . . . Many here looked upon it, as a Part of the habitual Earth, where pure and undefiled Religion did for some time appear, and prosper more than any where else'. And as the Scottish and American awakenings waned, John Maclaurin of Glasgow, Gillies's father-in-law and a close correspondent of several colonial clergymen, developed a plan for a joint 'Concert for Prayer' in Scotland and America to reinvigorate the transatlantic revival.[10]

Nowhere was the expanded perspective of Scottish Presbyterians more evident than in the writings of John Erskine, who had attended Edinburgh University with Witherspoon and for decades ranked with him as a leader of the Popular faction in the church. During the revival the newly licensed clergyman wrote a pamphlet titled *The Signs of the Times Consider'd: or, the High Probability, that the Present Appearances in New-England, and the West of Scotland, are a Prelude of the Glorious Things Promised to the Church in the Latter Ages* (1742). It broke with longstanding traditions by according the colonial churches as significant a role as that of the Scottish kirk in anticipating the millennium. Erskine remained intensely interested in American affairs throughout his long career: during the 1760s and 1770s he published a series of pamphlets on American grievances against the empire that reiterated his identification with the concerns of both provinces, especially as they related to true religion: 'I love my country', he wrote, 'and I love the posterity of those . . . who fled from the root of oppression . . . [for] what now is . . . a seat of liberty and of true religion'.[11]

In so expanding their perspective, Scottish clergymen were to a substantial degree reflecting the larger experience of their countrymen. In the half-century after the Union, the west of Scotland underwent a period of economic and commercial growth that contemporaries attributed almost entirely to the effects of the American trade. Scotsmen were on the whole quick to take note of America's importance to Britain and to Scotland in particular. No group was more important in the Scottish awakening than the rapidly growing community of spinners and weavers in Glasgow and its environs, who dominated church sessions wherever the revival spread. Few were more dependent for their livelihoods upon transatlantic commercial connexions.[12] Evangelical ministers were never far removed from such concerns; at least half of those active in the Scottish revivals had direct family ties to the Glasgow merchant community.

William McCulloch, the Cambuslang evangelist, married the daughter of a tobacco merchant; her sister would wed another revivalist. John Gillies and Alexander Webster, evangelical leaders in Glasgow and Edinburgh respectively, were also related to trading families.[13]

II

When Witherspoon completed his divinity studies at Edinburgh University in 1743, the Scottish revival was very much alive. Although we have no direct evidence of his participation in the awakening, there is every reason to suspect his general support: John Erskine, himself a recent Edinburgh graduate, was actively promoting the revival, as was Alexander Webster, another close ally, from his Edinburgh pulpit.[14] The following year Witherspoon was invited to preach in the parish of Beith in Ayrshire, in the heart of the revival country, where he accepted a call as minister in 1745. Witherspoon remained there until 1757, when he moved to the nearby burgh of Paisley, then in a state of rapid growth due to the expansion of the weaving industry that would make it famous.

For the first decade of his ministry Witherspoon was a relatively unknown clergyman. Then, in 1752, the general assembly of the Scottish kirk, under the influence of the rising Moderates, deposed the evangelical Thomas Gillespie from his ministry. Gillespie had violated the assembly's order to officiate at the installation of an unpopular candidate as minister of Inverkeithing parish, and his removal was a major victory for the Moderate party. The following year an unsigned satirical pamphlet appeared in Glasgow bearing the title *Ecclesiastical Characteristics*, which was soon recognised as the work of Witherspoon. In that pamphlet the author criticised the actions and beliefs of his old classmates for their endorsement of unpopular presentations, and for what he regarded as their excessive concern with politeness and moral philosophy at the expense of evangelising and sound doctrine. Those concerns were well summarised in his four requirements of a good preacher:

> 1. His subjects must be confined to social duties. 2. He must recommend them only from rational considerations, viz. the beauty and comely proportions of virtue, and its advantages in the present life, without any regard to a future state of more extended self-interest. 3. His authorities must be drawn from heathen writers, *none*, or as few as possible, from Scripture. 4. He must be very unacceptable to the common people. (*WJW*, 3:219)

Witherspoon's publication won him widespread applause among the Popular party within the kirk; yet lost in the excitement of the event was the fact that not all of the traditionalists in that faction approved of his tactics. Some questioned his use of satire in writing about matters as serious as church affairs, to the point that Witherspoon felt obliged to defend his method by referring to the use of satire in the Bible and in Christian tradition. But most advocates of orthodoxy endorsed the publication, and Virginia's Samuel Davies, then in Scotland, described his use of satire as 'nothing inferior to Dean Swift', whose Tory sympathies certainly rendered him a less than exemplary model to the most traditional Presbyterians.[15]

In succeeding years Witherspoon continued to identify with the Popular party within the kirk, consistently supporting its positions in ecclesiastical debates and articulating orthodox principles in his theological writings. Yet he often upheld tradition in rather unconventional ways that reflected his recent university training. One of those ways was his continuing use of satire, as in his *History of a Corporation of Servants* (1765), an attack upon a ministry whose members Witherspoon viewed as more concerned with their places within the church structure than the results of their preaching. Another was that unlike some of his evangelical predecessors Witherspoon consistently defended the importance of learning and refinement even for an orthodox people. Witherspoon's jests in *Ecclesiastical Characteristics* clearly revealed a thorough familiarity with the intellectual schemes he satirised, including those of such supposed Moderate idols as Hutcheson and Shaftesbury. Indeed, Witherspoon accused the Moderates of unreasonably restricting their learning by attending to the wisdom only of 'heathen' rather than Christian writers and preferring socialising to study. In an address to graduating students delivered in 1775, he emphasised 'the union of piety and literature', criticising not only 'unsanctified knowledge', as was common among evangelicals, but also piety without human learning, which risked 'disgracing the most glorious truths, by a meanness and indecency . . . in their manner of handling them' (*WJW*, 3:105).

In his zeal to defend orthodoxy, Witherspoon would even battle on the terrain of moral standards, citing human ends to justify divine means. In a 1759 sermon on *The Trial of Religious Truth by Its Moral Influence*, Witherspoon defended religiosity on instrumental grounds, contending that true morality derived only from piety, which was comprehensible to all men, in contrast with more elaborate theories of morality that were 'not intended for general use' (*WJW*, 2:392).

John Erskine offered a similar argument. Erskine conceded that although nonbelievers might prove to be useful and patriotic citizens, itself a striking admission for Scottish orthodoxy, it was dangerous to rely upon such men: 'Men animated by no worthier motives than interest or honour . . . are useful to society from principles which, had circumstances varied a little, would have led them to undermine it'. Only true religion, Erskine maintained, would produce a 'constant and uniform goodness'.[16]

In making such arguments, Witherspoon and his colleagues devoted considerable attention to the exceedingly popular subject of moral philosophy. Witherspoon employed it in typically eclectic fashion. As early as 1753, in an essay published in the *Scots Magazine*, he offered an argument in line with the tenets later developed by such common sense philosophers as Thomas Reid and James Beattie to counter the determinism of Lord Kames, which he viewed as subversive of morals.[17] At other times Witherspoon sounded much like Francis Hutcheson, asserting that morality was not based primarily upon rational consideration but was written on the heart of every man, although he always took care to dissociate himself from Hutcheson's tendency towards a utilitarian ethic. And Erskine, who was known as a pre-eminently practical preacher, offered a catalogue of virtues comprising human goodness that could have been supported by any Moderate and that reflected the particular concerns of the Enlightenment. They included 'compassion and humanity, courteousness and civility, truth and integrity, diligence and application'.[18]

Witherspoon's commitment to orthodoxy, as well as his stature within orthodox circles, was largely responsible for his election to the College of New Jersey's vacant presidency in 1766, but the Paisley pastor also seemed suited to heal the breach between Old Side and New Side Presbyterians on the board of trustees. Witherspoon's position within the Popular wing of the kirk appealed to Presbyterian evangelicals, while his commitment to a modern education and a learned ministry helped appease their opponents. Francis Alison, the Old Side leader, was himself a student and disciple of Francis Hutcheson. Although Witherspoon pointedly criticised those of Hutcheson's tenets he viewed as contrary to orthodoxy and ridiculed the Moderates for their excessive devotion to that philosopher's principles, he shared some of them himself, such as the belief in a moral sense written on the heart and most of Hutcheson's Whiggish political ideals. He made those principles into the basis of his own lectures on moral philosophy.[19]

It was far from evident that Witherspoon would accept the call to Princeton in 1766. It is well known that his wife was extremely wary of the transatlantic voyage and managed to delay his move until 1768, but there were other, more substantive reasons for doubting his willingness to go to America. Witherspoon had little need to accept the post; he already held one of the most important charges in western Scotland in the rapidly growing burgh of Paisley, and he was well liked by his parishioners. In previous years he had rejected overtures concerning three traditionally important Presbyterian charges – in Dublin, at the Scots kirk in Rotterdam and in John Willison's old parish at Dundee.[20]

That Witherspoon would accept the presidency of the College of New Jersey is indicative of just how much the perspective of orthodox

Presbyterians had broadened since the awakening and how important the colonies had become in the thinking of Scottish Presbyterians. Those wider perspectives have often been overlooked by historians who have emphasised the efforts of the young Benjamin Rush, then a medical student at Edinburgh University, to persuade Witherspoon. Rush did not act alone. While the future physician worked to alleviate Witherspoon's anxieties, college trustee Richard Stockton argued Princeton's case before other Presbyterian leaders, engaging, as he wrote, 'all the eminent clergymen in Edinburgh and Glasgow' to win over Witherspoon and his wife, 'and they are determined to take her by storm'. The tone of their efforts is well illustrated by a letter Witherspoon received from a colleague, Thomas Randall of Inchture:

> I have long thought it the intention of Providence (after our abuse of our great mercies, & our dreadful degeneracy from real religion) to fix the great seat of truth and righteousness in America; and that N. Jersey seemed to promise fair for being the *nursery* of the most approved instruments, for carrying on that great design, in that wide continent.[21]

Edinburgh merchant Archibald Wallace, a man with close ties to Scottish evangelicals and American merchants, expressed similar sentiments. Although he deeply regretted the prospect of Witherspoon's departure from Scotland, Wallace wrote to Witherspoon, 'yet when this honourable & Important service calls for your help, and a door opens for your very extensive usefullness, I cannot withstand the call, to do all I can to prevail on you, to leave your native land, at the Call of him whose is the Earth and fullness thereof'. Witherspoon replied that as a result of their persuasiveness about 'the State of Religion in America', he felt 'a pretty favourable Inclination in my own Mind' to accept the call – provided, of course, that he could get his wife to agree.[22]

III

From the time Witherspoon arrived in America, he worked aggressively to strengthen the links between Scotland and the colonies. As college president, Witherspoon introduced a variety of Scottish works into the curriculum, not only in theology but also in history and moral philosophy. Within the Presbyterian Church he set out to complete the reconciliation of Old Side and New, which he would accomplish under a strictly Scottish code of discipline. Most important, Witherspoon became an active proponent of Scottish emigration to America, investing in land in several provinces and advertising for settlers in Scottish newspapers. His interest in such activities was always more than strictly financial. By 1770 nearly every organised group of Scottish emigrants venturing to America travelled first to Princeton to meet with the president, who guided them to suitable sites regardless of whether or not he had a direct interest in those places.[23]

Witherspoon was roundly criticised for those activities. As the 'emigration mania' grew in western Scotland, Scottish critics charged him with undermining the prosperity of Scotland by promoting its depopulation. In a long letter intended for the *Scots Magazine*, Witherspoon contended that his actions were not unpatriotic and that emigration helped rather than harmed his homeland. Immigration had increased the prosperity and commerce of the colonies, and Scotland had been among the principal beneficiaries of American trade. 'No part of Europe', he wrote, 'has received, or does now receive, a greater accession of wealth, from the American settlements, than Great Britain, and perhaps . . . no part of Britain . . . has risen higher by the same means, than Scotland'.[24]

Witherspoon's support for emigration was shared by several other ministers in Scotland, especially his longtime colleague in the Synod of Glasgow and Ayr, William Thom of Govan. During the 1770s Thom, using a variety of pseudonyms, wrote at least five pamphlets in favour of colonisation, making him, along with Witherspoon, a leading proponent of Scottish emigration to America. Thom employed the 'civic' language of corruption and decay in analysing Scottish society, but like many of his countrymen he adapted it to Scotland's particular circumstances within the British empire. According to Thom, the poverty of Scotland's farmers and tradesmen during the 1770s was largely the result of a growing corruption among the country's upper classes, originating in England's increasing involvement in Scottish markets. That corruption had led to rapacious and impious behaviour by Scottish landlords in raising rents beyond the tenants' means and to a monopolistic control of production and trade. The best refuge, Thom argued, was America, where religion, harmony and prosperity could still be found. Scottish fathers owed it to their children to move to a land where true religion, 'so much despised in this country, may be esteemed'. In America Scotsmen could retain the 'true old British spirit before it be totally vitiated and extinguished'. Thom imposed a providential reading upon the efforts of Scottish soldiers during the Seven Years' War, contending that Scotsmen 'had made such important conquests in that quarter of the globe, in order to secure to themselves, and their countrymen, an agreeable and happy retreat, and a large and fertile field for them and their posterity to flourish in'. Thom the pamphleteer, as much as Witherspoon the emigrant, extended the reaches of the Scottish covenant to America.[25]

When the political events of 1776 forced Witherspoon to choose his loyalties, he opted decisively for the American side, preaching and writing in favour of independence and serving in the Continental Congress.

Perhaps surprisingly, Witherspoon was still able to employ the jeremiad form in his preaching, implying that providence had selected America rather than Scotland as its chosen people. Witherspoon never fully acknowledged that distinction. Instead, his preaching demonstrated how thoroughly 'provincial' (in the sense in which the word was used above) his perspective had become. The events of 1776 were important not only to America, Witherspoon wrote, but to all of Britain and, by offering an example of the full reaches of British liberty, to all of mankind. The American colonies had been settled, by providential design, 'by the power, the learning, and the wealth of Europe' and now provided British subjects with their greatest opportunity for liberty, prosperity and true religion. In a manner reminiscent of William Thom, Witherspoon argued that America was prosperous and successful precisely in proportion to the 'degree of British liberty' and the 'purity of faith' the colonists had brought with them, which they maintained more fully than anyone else in the British world.[26]

Witherspoon was somewhat unusual among Scottish emigrants in supporting American independence, but his sentiments were not far removed from those of many of his brethren in the Popular party in Scotland, who consistently linked the cause of American liberty to the preservation of religious liberty within the empire. In his several published tracts on behalf of the American cause, John Erskine cited not only the moral and political claims of the Americans but also their attempts to secure colonial religion against Anglican encroachments. William Thom, Charles Nisbet and several others also defended the American cause.[27]

The ability of Scotsmen such as Witherspoon and Thom to extend their loyalties to America was facilitated considerably by something else they shared with their Moderate opponents: the language of commerce and political economy, which had become an increasingly popular provincial discourse with powerful political connotations. In Scotland that conceptual framework had attained its popularity just as Scotsmen were wrestling with the ramifications of their increasing involvement with the English commercial network for the prosperity and the character of their nation. Istvan Hont has pointed out that within the larger discourse on eighteenth-century Scottish political economy there lingered always the underlying question of whether or not a still-poor nation such as Scotland, by increasing its commercial ties, could ever hope to approach the prosperity of its wealthier neighbour. To Scotsmen, the overriding emphasis upon impersonal demographic and economic forces over established political relationships certainly was consistent with their faith that political and economic relationships between nations were not forever fixed by power and tradition, but were susceptible to modification and even reversal over time.[28]

What was striking was the ability of Witherspoon and Thom to reconcile commercial language with their religious and moral concerns. Early in his career Thom had set out to assess the causes of the decline of religion in Scotland, locating them primarily in the advance of commerce and an excessive market consciousness among the urban population and the landowning class. The solutions Thom offered, however, were equally commercial in orientation, linking commerce and piety. Thus Thom advocated revising the Glasgow University curriculum to provide a training more suitable to the needs of a commercial people, such as 'practical Mathematics', 'the History of our own Country, and of those in the Neighbourhood or with which we carry on Commerce, natural History, Geography, the History of Commerce, and practical Morality', along with more diligent teaching of religion even to those not enrolled in the divinity course. Later, Thom would outline a programme of collective action by Scottish farmers designed to lower the demand for farms and reduce the cost of overpriced tenancies. Such a programme, in Thom's view, was a matter not only of self-interest but of religious duty as well, since the perpetual scramble for leases had diverted everyone's mind from the duty of piety.[29]

Witherspoon, writing from the more liberal environs of America, adopted a more optimistic but equally political and moral perspective on commercial prosperity. Citing Montesquieu, he attributed the growing wealth of the colonies not to their environment but to their superior religion and morals and to their liberty, which enabled Americans to preserve their religious and moral values. He and his Scottish colleagues were even able to weave commercial themes into their preaching: their jeremiads identified a decline in commerce and prosperity as perhaps the surest signs of divine disfavour and a revival of trade as one of the marks of national regeneration.[30]

By employing the language of commerce, Witherspoon was able to support American independence without rejecting his Scottish antecedents. Rather, by emphasising impersonal forces, he was able to transfer his loyalties from Scotland the state to the kirk and people. 'What is it for a man to be a friend to his country?' he asked, echoing the sentiments of his friend John Erskine a few years before. 'Is it to wish well to the stones and the earth, or to the people that inhabit it?' Witherspoon contended that he was aiding his countrymen by encouraging them to emigrate to the more prosperous and pious American provinces; he would be helping them further through the added liberty and prosperity independence would bring.[31]

That increase in liberty and prosperity would benefit not only America but also its cultural allies in Britain, even after independence, once the artificial barriers of war and mercantile restrictions were removed. What advantage had America provided Britain, Witherspoon would ask, citing one of Hume's essays on trade, other than to serve as a trading partner? Yet the continuance of the imperial relationship and the threats to American liberty endangered American commerce, which had thrived upon minimal restrictions. By contrast, if independence were established and trade restrictions removed, America would gain in population, prosperity and trade. And once the war ended that trade would again flow naturally to Britain, reinforced by ties of religion, language and habit.[32]

Witherspoon's adoption of the perspectives of political economy and moral philosophy did not signify the abandonment of his religious concerns. Rather, he employed frameworks that were becoming increasingly prevalent among educated Scotsmen of widely varying religious and political persuasions in order to defend the necessity of piety and to secure a place for it within an increasingly commercialised provincial world. In that sense, the John Witherspoon problem has something in common with the Adam Smith problem, because (if recent readings of Smith are correct) both derive from their integration of seemingly secular and even scientific perspectives into analyses of commercial society that were intensely concerned with issues of justice or morals. Witherspoon, as a spokesman for an evangelical orthodoxy that appealed increasingly to commercial and artisan groups in western Scotland, recognised the necessity of upholding religiosity in a way that would emphasise its worldly as well as its other-worldly benefits. He saw, too, the need to articulate a view of provincial society that would allow piety a vital role. His political economy, one that linked liberty, piety and growth, incorporated a wide range of economic, moral and religious concerns. It would prove adaptable to the affairs not only of Scotland but of the American provinces as well.

NOTES

1. See, for examples, Sloan, chap. 4, which remains perhaps the best attempt to date to sort out the apparent inconsistencies; *An Annotated Edition of Lectures on Moral Philosophy by John Witherspoon*, ed. Jack Scott (Newark, Del., 1982), 6–7, 27, passim; and, to a lesser extent, Donald H. Meyer, *The Democratic Enlightenment* (New York, 1976), 187, 194.
2. See, for example, Mark A. Noll, 'The Irony of the Enlightenment for Presbyterians in the Early Republic', *Journal of the Early Republic* 5 (1985):149–75; Sher, 160–61; and Henry F. May, *The Enlightenment in America* (New York, 1976), 62–64, 346–47.
3. For a suggestive discussion of Scottish provinciality, varying somewhat from my own, see John Clive and Bernard Bailyn, 'England's Cultural Provinces: Scotland and America', *WMQ*, 200–13; and several articles by Nicholas Phillipson, especially 'Culture and

Society in the Eighteenth Century Province: The Case of Edinburgh and the Scottish Enlightenment', in *The University in Society*, ed. Lawrence Stone, 2 vols. (Princeton, 1974), 2:407–48, and 'Adam Smith as Civic Moralist', in *WV*, 179–202.

4. Sher, chap. 1.
5. John McKerrow, *History of the Secession Church* (Edinburgh, 1854) remains the standard, partisan history of that movement, which badly needs a modern treatment; see also William Ferguson, *Scotland: 1689 to the Present* (Edinburgh, 1968), chap. 4; and Callum G. Brown, *The Social History of Religion in Scotland since 1730* (Edinburgh, 1987).
6. John Currie, *An Essay on Separation: Or, a Vindication of the Church of Scotland* (Edinburgh, 1738), and *A Vindication of the Real Reformation-Principles of the Church of Scotland Concerning Separation* (Edinburgh, 1740).
7. John Willison, *A Fair and Impartial Testimony, Essayed in Name of a Number of Ministers, Elders and Christian People of the Church of Scotland* (1744), in *The Whole Works of the Reverend and Learned Mr. John Willison*, 4 vols. (Edinburgh, 1816), 4:227, 313.
8. On university training at Edinburgh and Glasgow, see especially Peter Jones, 'The Scottish Professoriate and the Polite Academy, 1720–46', in *WV*, 89–116; and Roger L. Emerson, 'Scottish Universities in the Eighteenth Century, 1690–1800', *SVEC* 167 (1977): 453–74.
9. See especially the biographical entries in *Fasti Ecclesiae Scoticanae: The Succession of Ministers in the Church of Scotland*, ed. Hew Scott, 7 vols. (Edinburgh, 1915); and *Historical Collections Relating to Remarkable Periods of the Success of the Gospel*, ed. John Gillies, 2 vols. (Glasgow, 1754).
10. *Christian Monthly History, or an Account of the Revival and Progress of Religion at Home and Abroad* (Edinburgh, 1743–46), 1st ser., no. 1 (November, 1743):1; *Historical Collections*, ed. Gillies, vol. 2, chap. 6, sect. 5. In *The American Jeremiad* (Madison, Wisc., 1978), Sacvan Bercovitch has argued that the conception of America's providential role was a New England invention that was extended to incorporate all of America. It seems that both the jeremiad, as Richard Sher argues in the following chapter, and the conception of American destiny, had broader origins among British dissenting communities, including New England Congregationalists, Scottish Presbyterians and some English dissenters.
11. John Erskine, *Shall I Go to War with My American Brethren?* (London, 1769), 3; Sir Henry Moncrieff Wellwood, *Account of the Life and Writings of John Erskine* (Edinburgh, 1818).
12. I have discussed the role of spinners and weavers in the Scottish awakening in 'Evangelists and the Their Hearers: Popular Interpretation of Revivalist Preaching in Eighteenth-Century Scotland', *Journal of British Studies* 28 (1989): 120–49.
13. Information about the families of the evangelists is drawn from D[uncan] McFarlan, *The Revivals of the Eighteenth Century, Particularly at Cambuslang* (Edinburgh, 1846), and *Fasti*, ed. Scott.
14. Those who have doubted Witherspoon's evangelical sympathies have cited his alleged authorship of *A Letter from a Blacksmith, to the*

Ministers and Elders of the Church of Scotland (London, 1758), which was highly critical of revival meetings. However, there is no solid evidence to connect Witherspoon to that publication. More to the point, by the middle years of the eighteenth century Witherspoon, Erskine and Gillespie all preached against the visionary excesses of evangelical revivals. Yet in 1742 both Erskine and Gillespie publicly defended the awakening. Witherspoon, who was several years younger, was not yet out of university in 1742, but he would soon become a close associate of Erskine, Gillespie and Webster and was allied in the church courts with almost everyone who preached in the revival.

15. *The Reverend Samuel Davies Abroad: The Diary of a Journey to England and Scotland, 1753–55*, ed. George William Pilcher (Urbana, Ill., 1967), 99; and see 'A Serious Apology for the Ecclesiastical Characteristics', in *WJW*, 3:269–312.
16. John Erskine, *The Influence of Religion on National Happiness* (Edinburgh, 1756), 14–18, and *The Education of Poor Children Recommended* (Edinburgh, 1774), 6; and see Alexander Webster, *Zeal for the Civil and Religious Interests of Mankind Recommended* (Edinburgh, 1754), 23; and David Grant, *The Living Manners of the Times, and Their Consequences* (Edinburgh, 1779), 16.
17. 'Remarks on an Essay on Human Liberty', *SM* 15 (1753):165–70.
18. Erskine, *Education of Poor Children*, 6; and see *WJW*, 2:391 and Witherspoon's *Lectures*, ed. Scott, 28, 36–37.
19. On Alison, see especially Sloan, chap. 3; and see Witherspoon's *Lectures*, ed. Scott, 27–28, 36–37, 142–44.
20. Most of the documentation concerning Witherspoon's call to Princeton can be found in *John Witherspoon Comes to America: A Documentary Account*, ed. L.H. Butterfield (Princeton, 1953).
21. Ibid., 29–33. William Gray, Presbyterian publisher in Edinburgh, had expressed a similar hope for the College of New Jersey more than a decade before, writing that 'little . . . can be done for the spiritual welfare of these parts, unless a seminary of learning is placed among them' and that 'if God, in holy and just displeasure, should remove his candlestick from us, and our garden become a wilderness, who knows but that, through divine mercy, those distant parts, now an uncultivated and barrren wilderness, may become a fruitful field'. Samuel Davies, *A Sermon Preached at Henrico, 29th April, 1753. And at Canongate, 26th May, 1754* (Edinburgh, 1754), preface.
22. *Witherspoon Comes to America*, ed. Butterfield, 24–28.
23. On Witherspoon's emigration activities, see Varnum Lansing Collins, *President Witherspoon*, 2 vols. (Princeton, 1925), 1:148–55; 'Journal of General James Whitelaw, Surveyor-General of Vermont', *Proceedings of the Vermont Historical Society* (1905–6):103–57; Alexander Thomson, *News From America: Letter 1* (Glasgow, 1774); Bernard Bailyn, *Voyagers to the West: A Passage in the Peopling of America on the Eve of the Revolution* (New York, 1986), 390–93, 610–16. Witherspoon's role in securing a Scottish code of discipline within the American Presbyterian church is considered in Leonard J. Trinterud, *The Forming of an American Tradition: A Re-examination of Colonial Presbyterianism* (Philadelphia, 1949), chap. 16.
24. 'Letter Sent to Scotland for the *Scots Magazine*', in *WJW*, 4: 281–89;

and see the letters in *SM* 34 (1772):482–83, 697–700; and *Edinburgh Advertiser*, 18 Sept. 1772.

25. Thom's pamphlets were: *A Candid Enquiry Into the Causes of the Late and the Intended Migrations From Scotland* (Glasgow, n.d.); *Seasonable Advice to the Landholders and Farmers in Scotland* (Edinburgh, 1770); *Information concerning the province of North Carolina, Addressed to Emigrants from the Highlands and Western Isles of Scotland* (Glasgow, 1773); *The Present Conduct of the Chieftains and Proprietors of Lands in the Highlands of Scotland* (London, 1773); and *Information to Emigrants, Being the Copy of a Letter from a Gentleman in North-America: Containing a Full and Particular Account of the Terms on Which Settlers May Procure Lands in North-America, Particularly in the Provinces of New-York and Pensilvania* (Glasgow, 1773). The quotes are from 'The Task-Masters', in *The Works of the Reverend William Thom* (Glasgow, 1799), 207; *Information concerning the Province of North Carolina*, 10, 32; and *Present Conduct of the Chieftains and Proprietors of Lands in the Highlands of Scotland*, 1.
26. See especially *The Dominion of Providence over the Passions of Men* (1776), in *WJW*, 3:30–31, and *An Address to the Natives of Scotland Residing in America* (1776), ibid., 50–52.
27. Erskine, *Shall I Go to War?* and *Reflections on the Rise, Progress, and Probable Consequences of the Present Contentions with the Colonies* (Edinburgh, 1776), 46–47; Grant, *Living Manners of the Times*; Whitfield J. Bell, Jr., 'Scottish Emigration to America: A Letter of Dr. Charles Nisbet to John Witherspoon, 1784', *WMQ*, 276–89; and see Sher, 267–70; and Robert Kent Donovan, chap. 4 below.
28. Istvan Hont, 'The "Rich Country-Poor Country" Debate in Scottish Classical Political Economy', in *WV*, 271–316; and see Gladys Bryson, *Man and Society: The Scottish Inquiry of the Eighteenth Century* (Princeton, 1945); Ian Simpson Ross, *Lord Kames and the Scotland of His Day* (Oxford, 1972), 340ff.; and Janet Ann Reisman, 'The Origins of American Political Economy, 1690–1781' (Ph.D. diss., Brown University, 1983), chap. 2.
29. William Thom, *An Inquiry into the Causes of the Decline of Religion* (1761); *The Defects of an University Education, and Its Unsuitableness to a Commercial People, with the Expediency and Necessity of Erecting at Glasgow, an Academy for the Instruction of Youth* (1762); *Letter of Advice to the Farmers and Land-Labourers in Scotland* (1771), all in *Works*, 1–22, 263–301, 429–50.
30. Witherspoon, 'Letter Sent to Scotland for the *Scots Magazine*'; 'Reflections on the Present State of Public Affairs, and on the Duty and Interest of America in This Important Crisis', in *WJW*, 4:293–96; and 'Observations on the Improvement of America', in *WJW*, 4:385–86. For the 'commercial jeremiads', see Grant, *Living Manners of the Times*, 16–19; Thom, 'The Task-Masters' and *Information to Emigrants*, 9–10; Erskine, *Shall I Go to War?*, 19, 22–23; and Witherspoon, *Prayer for National Prosperity and for the Revival of Religion*, *WJW*, 2:453–77, and *Dominion of Providence*.
31. 'Letter Sent to Scotland for the *Scots Magazine*', 285–86; 'Reflections on the Present State of Public Affairs'; 'Observations on the Improvement of America'; and *Address to the Natives of Scotland*, 51–52.
32. *Address to the Natives of Scotland*, 54–59.

2

RICHARD B. SHER

Witherspoon's Dominion of Providence *and the Scottish Jeremiad Tradition*

John Witherspoon's fast day sermon *The Dominion of Providence over the Passions of Men* was among the most important American jeremiads of the Revolutionary era. It was preached at Princeton on 17 May 1776 and published in late July by fellow Scot Robert Aitken of Philadelphia. Within two years it passed through several British editions. Witherspoon's student and protégé Ashbel Green believed that it 'must, at the time it was preached and published, have been powerfully felt, and have contributed not a little, to promote that sense of dependence on God, and earnest looking to him for protection and aid, which distinguished the pious and patriotic fathers of American liberty and independence'; his principal modern biographer asserted that it was this 'great discourse' that first 'thrust Dr. Witherspoon into the glare of public notice'.[1] *Dominion of Providence* marked the moment at which Witherspoon publicly and irrevocably took his stand on the side of the American Revolution. Yet remarkably little has been written about this sermon or its publishing history, and still less has been said about the Scottish Presbyterian framework from which it emerged. This chapter will show that *Dominion of Providence* was shaped chiefly by the tradition of the Scottish Presbyterian jeremiad, that it was intended in large measure for an audience steeped in that tradition, and that it was an object of special concern among those Scottish Presbyterians who objected to the particular ends for which that tradition was being employed by Witherspoon. It will also suggest that the failure of most scholars of early America to grasp these points is due chiefly to the influence of Puritan New England on the historiography of eighteenth-century American political preaching.

I

Dominion of Providence takes as its biblical text Psalm 76.10: '*Surely the Wrath of Man shall praise thee: the remainder of Wrath shalt thou restrain.*' Its general point was that God's power is absolute and that man's 'disorderly passions' are ultimately in the service of divine providence, no matter how unlikely divine control may seem at any given moment in history. Witherspoon developed this general point with three particulars. First, he argued that the process of the wrath of man praising God illustrates 'the sinfulness of our nature and state' (*WJW*, 3:20), which is responsible for all disorders in society. Second, it shows how God uses man's disorderly passions as 'the instrument in his hand for bringing sinners to repentance, and for the correction and improvement of his own children' (*WJW*, 3:24). Third, it demonstrates that there is frequently a disjunction between human intentions and the actions that follow from them on the one hand and the consequences of those actions on the other. To make this point, Witherspoon used examples from sacred and profane history in which the results were very different from those intended by the historical actors, such as the persecutors of the Protestant Reformers, of the English Puritans and of Jesus himself. In this way, the first half of Witherspoon's sermon drew from the psalmist's words the three principles of the total depravity of mankind, the corrective nature of divine punishment, and the providentially ordained consequences of man's wicked intentions and actions.

The second half of *Dominion of Providence* sought to apply these general principles 'to our present situation'. Witherspoon aimed to show that, in regard to the American case specifically: 'The ambition of mistaken princes, the cunning and cruelty of oppressive and corrupt ministers, and even the inhumanity of brutal soldiers, however dreadful, shall finally promote the glory of God, and in the mean time, while the storm continues, his mercy and kindness shall appear in prescribing bounds to their rage and fury' (*WJW*, 3:19–20; italicised in 1776 and 1777 editions). Three particular applications were employed to illustrate his central thesis. First, he observed that however important temporal issues might seem, the salvation of one's soul was primary. This point provided a foundation for what was to follow, for even if the Americans were beaten into submission, their defeat would be insignificant in the grand scheme of things. Second, he argued that it was necessary to give thanks to God for 'the singular interposition of Providence hitherto, in behalf of the American colonies' (*WJW*, 3:33), which contradicted not only British intentions but British boasts of military superiority.

Witherspoon's third and most important application of this principle was that with God's help the Americans would triumph, no matter how much stronger the British *appeared* to be. 'If your cause is just', he insisted, '– you may look with confidence to the Lord and intreat him to plead it as his own' (*WJW*, 3:36). It was at this critical juncture in his discourse that Witherspoon spoke dramatically of his personal decision to break with past precedent by introducing a 'political subject into the pulpit'. He was compelled to take a political stand because he believed that the causes of civil and religious liberty were inextricably connected: to lose the first was also to lose the second. 'At this season', he announced,

> . . . I willingly embrace the opportunity of declaring my opinion without any hesitation, that the cause in which America is now in arms, is the cause of justice, of liberty, and of human nature. So far as we have hitherto proceeded, I am satisfied that the confederacy of the colonies, has not been the effect of pride, resentment, or sedition, but of a deep and general conviction, that our civil and religious liberties, and consequently in a great measure the temporal and eternal happiness of us and our posterity, depended on the issue. (*WJW*, 3:36–37)

He refused to rail at the king, parliament, particular ministers, or the people of Britain generally 'as so many barbarous savages'. The fact that the British 'should desire unlimited dominion' – the very term connoted false pretensions to divine authority – '. . . is neither new nor wonderful.' The point was not that British policies were 'corrupt or profligate', though this might well be so. The point was that

> they are men, and therefore liable to all the selfish bias inseparable from human nature. . . . they are separated from us, independent of us, and have an interest in opposing us. Would any man who could prevent it, give up his estate, person, and family, to the disposal of his neighbour, although he had liberty to chuse the wisest and the best master? Surely not. This is the true and proper hinge of the controversy between Great-Britain and America. (*WJW*, 3:37)

Witherspoon, in other words, viewed the conflict as one between competing interests, separated by great distances that made it increasingly difficult for one interest to rule effectively over the other. Independence in such a case was a natural step, justified, appropriately enough, with a naturalistic metaphor:

> There are fixed bounds to every human thing. When the branches of a tree grow very large and weighty, they fall off from the trunk. The sharpest sword will not pierce when it cannot reach. And there is a certain distance from the seat of government, where an attempt to rule will either produce tyranny and helpless subjection, or provoke resistance and effect a separation. (*WJW*, 3:38–39)

After examining the principles of the majority of his American hearers and readers, he concluded that they were grounded not in 'a seditious and turbulent spirit', or 'a blind and factious attachment to particular persons or parties' or a 'selfish rapacious disposition', but in 'a concern for the interest of your country, and the safety of yourselves and your posterity'. The cause of America was deemed 'pure' (*WJW*, 3:39).

Moreover, the American cause was also deemed 'sacred'. The last part of the sermon was devoted to 'some exhortations to duty' founded on the principles previously established. There one reads, amidst the usual pleas for prudence, moral reformation, industry and frugality, a special exhortation to those in command of American troops: 'The cause is sacred, and the champions for it ought to be holy' (*WJW*, 3:44). This 'holy war' rhetoric brings us back to Witherspoon's earlier assertions about a just cause being worthy of divine support and about an inextricable connexion existing between civil and religious liberty. The last sentence of the sermon restates the point in a slightly different way that draws together all the principal themes of the sermon: 'God grant that in America true religion and civil liberty may be inseparable, and that the unjust attempts to destroy the one, may in the issue tend to the support and establishment of both' (*WJW*, 3:46).

Witherspoon's appeal to 'holy war' rhetoric appears somewhat surprising in light of his rather mild arguments to justify the Revolution and his refusal to waste words attacking British motives or policies. The sermon's religious framework provides the crucial clues for understanding his reasoning. Since temporal events are secretly directed by Providence, there would seem to be little need to dwell on the wicked character, intentions or actions of the British. Rather, the British are reduced to the role of agents of the Lord, unknowingly doing God's work. They are supporting actors in a cosmic drama they do not fully understand, working not for their own ends but 'for the correction and improvement of [God's] own children' (*WJW*, 3:24). For 'the wrath of man in its most tempestuous rage, fulfills [God's] will, and finally promotes the good of his chosen' (*WJW*, 3:27). Once God's 'chosen' have been identified, the particulars of the controversy fade into insignificance, along with the latest perpetrators of the 'wrath of man'. Instead of the typical catalogue of British abuses, Witherspoon provides a catalogue of historical and biblical examples of wickedness turned to righteousness by the intervention of Providence. 'The scripture abounds with instances,' he writes, citing examples from both the Old and New Testaments, 'in which the designs of oppressors were either wholly disappointed, or in execution fell far short of the malice of their intention, and in some they turned out to the honor and happiness of the persons or the people, whom they were intended to destroy.'

II

Like most historical texts, *Dominion of Providence* is comprehensible to any reasonably intelligent reader but becomes considerably more interesting when understood contextually. But to which context, or contexts, should one turn? For many historians of the American Revolutionary era, the answer to this question might seem obvious. The past quarter of a century has witnessed a growing body of sophisticated literature about the importance of 'jeremiads' in the age of the Revolution. The term itself has entered the common vocabulary of eighteenth-century scholars chiefly through the work of Perry Miller, who discussed with great subtlety and penetration the character and development of this mode of preaching among New England Puritans. As Miller showed, the jeremiad was employed on special occasions such as fast days proclaimed during times of communal hardship (famine, war, pestilence) and thanksgiving days proclaimed just after such a hardship had been successfully averted or overcome. On these occasions the entire community would be held responsible for provoking God's wrath by deviating from the straight and true path, or God would be thanked for saving the community from destruction and giving it his blessing.[2]

The jeremiad builds on four fundamental premises: the absolute sovereignty of God, the sinful nature of man, the intelligibility of Providence and (implicitly, at least) the existence of a covenant between God and his 'chosen' people. The modern covenanted people bears a close resemblance to the people of Israel in the Old Testament, and it is the job of the latter-day Jeremiah to render that resemblance explicit by means of typology or analogy. In the jeremiad, history becomes explicable as the interaction through time of an all-powerful God and his covenanted but backsliding people. 'Providence' is really a shorthand way of representing the causal agent in that interaction. Affliction represents either a providential test or providential punishment for sinfulness. Natural disasters such as famines and earthquakes show the hand of God himself, while in the case of man-made hardships such as foreign and civil wars God employs non-covenanted peoples to do his work. Since they do so unwittingly, their actions are viewed as further evidence of God's absolute sovereignty. The logic of the jeremiad therefore assumes that the history of mankind is fundamentally ironic: people may intend to do one thing, but their *real* role in the providential plan is often quite different from what they intend. From the point of view of a covenanted people, on the other hand, history contains providential messages that can, if interpreted properly, permit meaningful and effective human action.

What role did the jeremiad play in the American Revolution? It is well known that on 12 June 1775 the Continental Congress recommended that all thirteen colonies set aside the twentieth of July as a day of public fasting. Other fast days followed, and these occasions provided opportunities for some of the Revolution's supporters among the clergy to preach, and sometimes publish, jeremiads on behalf of the American cause. The first congressional fast day of 1775 produced at least nine published sermons in New England alone.[3] Perry Miller believed that these patriotic jeremiads provided the real inspiration for widespread support of the Revolution; political justifications in terms of Whig principles such as 'the social compact, inalienable rights, and the right of revolution' were mere window dressing made necessary by 'circumstances and the dominant opinion in Europe'. 'What carried the ranks of the militia and citizens', Miller wrote, 'was the universal persuasion that they, by administering to themselves a spiritual purge, acquired the energies God had always, in the manner of the Old Testament, been ready to impart to His repentant children.'[4]

Virtually all later scholarship on these patriotic American jeremiads builds on the foundations that Perry Miller established. In particular, this scholarship argues or assumes, as the case may be, that American Revolutionary jeremiads grew straight out of the Puritan tradition of seventeenth-century New England. Miller himself made this point when he stated that the Continental Congress's initial recommendation for a national fast day 'virtually took over the New England thesis' of a special covenant with God: 'in effect, Congress added the other nine colonies to New England's covenant'.[5] During the late 1970s John Berens and Sacvan Bercovitch elaborated on Miller's argument in finely crafted books that traced the chronological development of the jeremiad from New England Puritanism through, and beyond, the era of the Revolution.[6] The title of Berens's first chapter, 'New England Puritanism Writ Large', states the thesis of his entire study. He first shows how the jeremiad and other elements of New England Puritanism functioned in their pure, seventeenth-century form; he then demonstrates how these same elements were adapted and modified during the following century.

Bercovitch's work is more ambitious and more closely focused on the concept of the jeremiad, but the emphasis is once again on the continuity of the American religious experience from New England Puritanism through and beyond the Revolution. Bercovitch obliterates Alan Heimert's important distinction between the political Calvinism of the federal theology and the evangelical Calvinism of the Great Awakening.[7] In his view Jonathan Edwards himself brought about a synthesis between these two strands of Calvinist thought by drawing out and spreading through the colonies 'the proto-nationalistic tendencies of the New England Way'.[8] During the eighteenth century the jeremiad became more secular in orientation and underwent other kinds of changes, but for Bercovitch these changes represent 'extension and adaptation, not . . . transformation' (94). Like Berens, Bercovitch begins with the Puritan paradigm and proceeds to consider how that paradigm was subsequently employed and modified. Both these scholars are writing about the forging of a distinctively American sense of identity out of native (New England) religious roots.

While there is undoubtedly much to be said for this approach, I believe it creates a distorted impression by failing to take into account the important role played in America by British and European jeremiads. Perry Miller observed that the rest of the colonies were ready for the Continental Congress's recommendation for a fast day in 1775 because the federal theology doctrine formed an 'integral part' of the Westminster Confession that guided Presbyterians and even turned up in the sermons of Anglicans and Baptists.[9] But Miller made this point almost in passing, while putting his main emphasis on the New England connexion, and more recent scholarship seems to have lost all sight of it. The latest commentator on the subject simply asserts that 'the Continental Congress took a cue from New England and appointed Sunday, July 20, 1775, as a national day of fasting and humiliation'.[10] Similarly, Berens writes as if the jeremiad were a New England invention, and Bercovitch occasionally takes notice of a vaguely defined entity that he calls the 'European jeremiad' solely in order to contrast it with the unique American variety made in New England. Bercovitch seems to think that outside America the jeremiad was merely 'a lament over the ways of the world' without any grounding in the notion of a special covenant between God and his people, whereas in America it took the form of 'celebration' because of the Puritans' belief in their special 'errand' or 'destiny' to establish the New Jerusalem in the wilderness. 'In their case, they believed, God's punishments were *corrective*, not destructive' (3–9), and this sense of confidence in the future remained a distinguishing feature of the American jeremiad as the Puritan faith in Providence and millennium became secularised during the eighteenth century.

Contextual analysis of Witherspoon's sermon necessitates moving beyond the familiar New England Congregationalist paradigm to a consideration of Scottish and Scots-Irish Presbyterian factors. In the first place, it is significant that until the London edition of 1778, *Dominion of Providence* was always bound with a second, shorter work, *An Address to the Natives of Scotland Residing in America*.[11] This way of presenting the sermon to the public reveals something important about the author's aims: from the outset Witherspoon seems to have intended his sermon for an audience that was predominantly Scottish and Presbyterian. As president of the premier American Presbyterian university, as one of the leaders of the American Presbyterian Church and as the single most prominent Scottish immigrant in America, Witherspoon felt obliged not only to throw himself actively into political life (distinguishing himself as the only clergyman to sign the Declaration of Independence in the weeks between preaching and publishing *Dominion of Providence*), but also to employ his oratorical and literary powers to persuade fellow Scots and fellow Presbyterians to embrace the American cause. The notion that Witherspoon, to borrow a phrase, 'took a cue from New England' when he went to the pulpit on 17 May 1776 begins to seem all the more unlikely when one considers the intellectual and religious baggage that he brought with him from Scotland. Witherspoon was forty-five years old when he emigrated to America in 1768. The son of a Scottish Presbyterian clergyman, he not only had served as a parish minister for many years himself but had gained fame as an author and ecclesiastical leader of the staunchly Calvinist 'Popular' or 'Orthodox' party in the kirk. Until 1768 his frame of reference in all important matters was the Church of Scotland, and many of his best known Scottish writings (including his famous satire of the rival ecclesiastical party, *Ecclesiastical Characteristics*) are all but incomprehensible outside it.

In Witherspoon's day the Moderate and Popular parties in the Church of Scotland disagreed about many things, but one point on which there was no disagreement was the viability and desirability of the jeremiad tradition. The roots of the Scottish jeremiad go back to the days of the Reformation and John Knox, who believed strongly in the concept of the covenant and was more willing than John Calvin to interpret historical events as unambiguous signs of God's pleasure or displeasure with his chosen people.[12] As one recent commentator has observed, Knox was in the habit of citing Old Testament judgements against collective bodies and 'saw any widespread problem in Scotland as the result of God's corporate punishment'.[13] In an important little book Arthur Williamson has traced the political context of the emergence of the covenant idea among other sixteenth-century Scots and has contrasted the Scottish notion of the covenant with the English Puritan concept of election.[14] In England, Williamson points out, the covenant (in a communal sense) represented an escape from the established social structure, whereas 'the covenant in Scotland played a centralizing role'.[15] Indeed, sixteenth-century Scottish synonyms for covenant – 'band' and 'league' – are words signifying not merely an agreement but a close-knit process of social bonding among men, chiefly for defensive purposes. Part of Knox's achievement was to build upon the ancient Scottish custom of 'banding' by giving it a new name ('covenant') and a new orientation as a pact with God rather than an agreement among men.[16] The epilogue to Williamson's book begins with a quotation from Perry Miller that includes this important statement: 'Try as they would, Puritans could never convince themselves, let alone others, that the English people were united in a single public engagement, like the Scots.'[17]

The sermon preached at St Andrews in March 1638 by Alexander

Henderson, in an effort to secure approval for the Solemn League and Covenant, illustrates the distinctively Scots Presbyterian approach to which Miller alluded.[18] Explicating the words 'Thy people' in his biblical text (Psalm 110.3), Henderson states: 'God has authority over all indeed, but in a special manner He enters into covenant with some' (59). A covenanted people is so called, he argues, because they are both God's special 'property', recognising their absolute subjection to the Lord, and a people of special 'distinction' through their faith in Christ. With such a bond comes the assurance not only of individual salvation but of providential corporate protection in the face of temporal adversaries, for 'the Lord has made all the devices and plots of the adversars, that they have devised to further their own ends, to work contrair to these ends, and to work for the good of His own work' (62). By subscribing to the national covenant, one pledged oneself to the practice and defence of 'true religion', 'that so through abundance of bands to God ye may know yourselves to be the more bound to Him' (72). Other early modern Calvinist traditions, including the Puritan one, also employed the covenanting rhetoric of federal theology, but only in Presbyterian Scotland was this rhetoric translated into a concrete act of national unity, applied specifically to 'the present ills' of the day (66), and signed in blood.

Thus, Scottish Presbyterians were well prepared for their role in helping to formulate the Westminster Confession of Faith (1647), which spoke the language of the covenant of grace (chap. 7) and the moral law (chap. 19) and explicitly endorsed the concepts of 'solemn fastings, and thanksgivings upon special occasions'. The accompanying 'Directory for the Publick Worship of God' spelled out in detail how such fast and thanksgiving days were to be conducted, beginning with these words: 'When some great and notable judgments are either inflicted upon a people, or apparently imminent, or by some extraordinary provocations notoriously deserved; as also when some special blessing is to be sought and obtained; publick solemn fasting (which is to continue the whole day) is a duty that God expecteth from that nation or people.' Then comes a lengthy discussion of how people should dress and act on such days, and how (on fast days) ministers should preach to them 'from their hearts' of the need for 'reformation', so that God will be 'pacified towards them, by answers of grace, in pardoning of sin, in removing of judgments, in averting or preventing of plagues, and in conferring of blessings, suitable to the conditions and prayers of his people, by Jesus Christ.' On thanksgiving days, similarly, the minister 'is to begin with a word of exhortation, to stir up the people to the duty for which they are met' and proceed to specific words of thanks for the particular blessings under consideration. The sermon preached on such occasions, in other words, should be what would now be called a jeremiad.

In eighteenth-century Britain fast and thanksgiving days continued to be proclaimed during and after the appearance of such 'great and notable judgments' as war with France and the Jacobite rebellions of 1715 and 1745. And on these occasions clergymen commonly employed the traditional jeremiad. Just after the suppression of the Forty-Five, for example, a volume appeared in Edinburgh under the title *Sermons on the Rebellion, 1745* that bound together seven recently published anti-Jacobite sermons preached on special occasions: four by Scottish Presbyterians (two from each ecclesiastical party) and three by English Anglicans. The first of them, George Wishart's *Times of Publick Distress Times of Trial*, was a typical Scottish jeremiad of the sort preached to motivate people to take action during a crisis. It pronounced the Forty-Five a providential test of personal and national virtue and provided consolation by pointing out that, however dismal events may seem, 'they are ordered by an infinitely wise God, for the best purposes'. Whatever their intentions, the wicked (in this case the Jacobites) really act according to God's will and demonstrate that 'the wrath of man shall praise' God. The latter biblical passage formed the text of the third sermon in the volume, Hugh Blair's *The Wrath of Man Praising God*, which developed the idea that the Jacobite rebels (who by this time had been defeated) were the instruments of Providence for punishing a people that had responded to his bountiful blessings with sinfulness. The fourth sermon in the collection, Alexander Webster's *Heathens Professing Judaism, When the Fear of the Jews Fell upon Them*, combined the substance of two sermons delivered by one of the Church of Scotland's leading evangelical preachers on the thanksgiving day proclaimed by its general assembly for 23 June 1746. Improving on Esther 8.17, it draws parallels with ancient Israel and takes aim at secret Jacobites who have become Hanoverian supporters only after the suppression of the rebellion. Significantly, it is dedicated 'to all those whose concern for the welfare of our Jerusalem and zeal for the British Israel, commenced before the Battle of Culloden'.

These and other jeremiads on the Jacobite rebellion of 1745[19] are worthy of comment because they provide some idea of an important component in Scottish Presbyterianism when John Witherspoon was a young man. It was a component that crossed party lines within the kirk and contained a distinctive rhetoric and logic for dealing with worldly crises. On a Scottish fast day during one such crisis, the Seven Years' War, young Witherspoon had preached (and soon after published) a classical Scottish jeremiad ten years before going to America. 'Affliction springeth not out of the dust', he warned in that sermon. 'National calamity is not the rigor of an arbitrary tyrant, but the wise chastisement of a gracious father, or the punishment of a righteous judge.'[20] All the fundamental elements of the famous jeremiad that Witherspoon preached at Princeton on 17 May 1776, including the biblical text itself, were well established within the Scottish Presbyterian heritage. Whether this tradition is viewed in the long term, stretching back to the age of the Reformation, the national covenants and the Westminster Confession of Faith, or in the short term, going no further back than Witherspoon's own years in Scotland, it seems clear that the roots of *Dominion of Providence* were pure Scots Presbyterian, owing little or nothing to New England Puritanism. Indeed, there is evidence to suggest that the New England clergy sometimes looked to this Scottish tradition for inspiration, for it has been noted that during the Revolution many of them spoke of joining together to form a 'Solemn League and Covenant'.[21] Nor is it difficult to see why this was so. Whereas the New England tradition of loosely connected churches held together by a regional identity had to find ways to adapt its jeremiads to a national enterprise, the Scottish Presbyterian tradition faced no such difficulty.

The tradition of the Scottish Presbyterian jeremiad was integrated into the American Presbyterian church by Witherspoon and other Scottish and Scots-Irish clergymen. Even before the Continental Congress had declared the first national fast day, Witherspoon and his Presbyterian brethren in the Synod of New York and Philadelphia had begun formulating their political position in these terms. On 19 May 1775 the synod set the last Thursday in June as a fast day unless the Congress should make this unnecessary by setting a national fast day. One day earlier the synod had appointed Witherspoon and six other ministers to a committee charged with writing a pastoral letter on the current crisis. On the twenty-second the committee produced such a letter, and after 'a few alterations' the synod voted to print and distribute five hundred copies.[22] Believed to be primarily the work of Witherspoon himself (and therefore included in his posthumous *Works*), the pastoral letter took a position slightly more moderate than the one Witherspoon would espouse publicly a year later.[23] Yet in several important respects it was a rehearsal for *Dominion of Providence*. Some sentences in the former reappeared in the latter with very slight changes.[24] Above all, the pastoral letter of 1775 employed the rhetoric of the jeremiad, as in the following passage:

> Though for the wise ends of his Providence, it may please God, for a season, to suffer his people to lie under unmerited oppression, yet in general we may expect, that those who fear and serve him in sincerity and truth, will be favoured with his countenance and strength. It is both the character and the privilege of the children of God, that they *call upon him in the day of trouble*, and he, who *keepeth covenant and truth forever*, has said, that *his ears are always open to their cry*. We need not mention to you in how many instances the event in battles, and success in war, have turned upon circumstances which

> were inconsiderable in themselves, as well as out of the power of human prudence to foresee or direct, because we suppose you firmly believe, that after all the counsels of men, and the most probable and promising means, the Lord will do *that which seemeth him good*; nor hath his promise ever failed of its full accomplishment; 'the Lord is with you while ye be with him, and if ye seek him, he will be found of you; but if ye forsake him, he will forsake you.' 2 Chron.xv.2. (*WJW*, 3:12)

This was the language of the covenant between God and his 'children', maintained by Providence so long as a covenanted people retain their faith, even when it appears they have been forsaken.

Both the pastoral letter and *Dominion of Providence* vacillated on the thorny issue of the role of sin in bringing about the present crisis. The logic of the jeremiad called for the blame to be placed squarely on the shoulders of the 'chosen', whose sins had provoked God's wrath. 'Affliction springeth not out of the dust', the pastoral letter reminded its hearers with a biblical line lifted straight out Witherspoon's fast day sermon of 1758. It was therefore necessary to

> remember and confess not only your sins in general, but those prevalent national offences which may be justly considered as the procuring causes of public judgments; particularly profaneness and contempt of God, his name, sabbaths and sanctuary; – pride, luxury, uncleanness, and neglect of family religion and government, with the deplorable ignorance and security which certainly ought to be imputed to this as their principal cause. All these are, among us, highly aggravated by the inestimable privileges, which we have hitherto enjoyed without interruption since the first settlement of this country. (*WJW*, 3:10)

As has been shown, *Dominion of Providence* also singled out man's sinful nature as the general cause of temporal disorders, and its concluding 'exhortations to duty' emphasised the need for a reformation of manners and morals. Yet both the pastoral letter and *Dominion of Providence* were unwilling to follow this logic consistently when focusing on the roots of the American crisis. In the longer passage that is quoted above from the pastoral letter, the term 'unmerited oppression' is used to describe the Americans' situation. In *Dominion of Providence*, similarly, Witherspoon declares the motives of the Americans to be 'pure' and manages to avoid any discussion of American sinfulness when treating the conflict between Britain and America. For Americans in the process of justifying a revolution, it apparently would not do to dwell too long on parallels with the ancient Jews.

Besides the matter of sin, there was a more obvious way in which *Dominion of Providence* differed from the fast day jeremiads being preached back in Scotland during the late 1770s. Unlike most of them, it took its stand on the side of the Revolution rather than against it. Henry Ippel has discovered more than 150 published British sermons that were preached on the six British fast days of the Revolution years and the thanksgiving held in July 1784.[25] The overwhelming number of them, both in Scotland and England, opposed the Revolution, including a number that drew on the Scottish jeremiad tradition.[26] This pattern serves as a reminder that though the jeremiad is always action-oriented, the values or ideology of the preacher determine just what sort of action is called for in a given situation. The logic and rhetoric of the traditional Scottish jeremiad could be used to justify either side in a war or revolution, and this flexibility contributed to its continuing popularity as a mode of political preaching.

In Britain as well as America, the activities of Witherspoon and his Presbyterian brethren provoked opponents of the American Revolution, who believed that their words and actions were stirring up the populace. In the autumn of 1776 and spring of 1777 the British civil servant Ambrose Serle reported back from the colonies to the secretary of state in London that Witherspoon, John Rodgers (a close friend of Witherspoon and fellow member of the synod of 1775's pastoral letter committee) and other clergymen were largely responsible for the present difficulties, and that 'Presbyterianism is really at the Bottom of this whole Conspiracy, has supplied it with Vigor, and will never rest, till something is decided upon it.'[27] The recently published *Dominion of Providence* was undoubtedly one of the major objects of Searle's wrath, but it is important to remember that the size and unity of the Presbyterian church gave this and other pronouncements added force. Indeed, that sermon would not even have been preached if the synod of 1776 had not specially postponed its annual meeting so that ministers could be with their congregations on the congressionally appointed fast day.[28]

Witherspoon was a conspicuous target for Anglicans and Episcopalians like Serle who viewed Presbyterianism itself with suspicion. Before the year 1776 was out, the Scottish Episcopalian Hugo Arnot ripped into Witherspoon and his ecclesiastical party for their support of the American cause in a pseudonymous publication that was 'Dedicated to Doctor Silverspoon, Preacher of Sedition in America' and was obviously inspired by *Dominion of Providence*.[29] But the political preaching of 'Doctor Silverspoon' was still more threatening to Presbyterians in Scotland who opposed the Revolution. Not only was Witherspoon fomenting rebellion; he was doing so with the authority of the Presbyterian church in America, using the godly rhetoric of the Scottish covenanting tradition and appealing directly to Scottish immigrants in America. In an effort to discredit him, unnamed 'editors' published at Glasgow early in 1777 a second edition of *Dominion of Providence*. Like the original Philadelphia edition of

1776, this Glasgow edition included the *Address to the Natives of Scotland Residing in America*. But it also included an advertisement and 'elucidating foot notes' by 'S. R.' that sought to expose Witherspoon's radicalism and make a mockery of it.

According to the advertisement prefixed to the second edition, Witherspoon's friends in Scotland had been playing down his role in agitating for the American cause. Reprinting the sermon and address, however, 'will fully justify the allegation, and silence the doctor's friends'. The sermon, moreover, would demonstrate how Witherspoon had blended 'the most rebellious sentiments with the most sacred and important truths; and hath the audacity to affirm, that not only the *temporal* but *eternal* happiness of the revolted colonists depend upon persevering in their independency, and undauntedly opposing the arms of their lawful Sovereign.' Witherspoon had cast aspersions on parliament, the king, the government's lenient policies and the British army while drawing a veil over 'the most wanton cruelties, shocking barbarities, and unheard-of instances of rapine, murder, and devastation, on the side of the provincial army'. The intention of the editors, then, was

> to shew what artful means, and fallacious arguments have been made use of by ambitious and self-designing men, to stir up the poor infatuated Americans to the present rebellious measures; what an active hand even Dr. Witherspoon has had therein; to convince his friends, in this country, of the truth of his being a chief promoter of the American revolt; and that if he falls into the hands of government, and meets with the demerit of his offence, he hath justly and deservedly procured it to himself.[30]

Lest the unsuspecting reader should find Witherspoon's arguments convincing, the editors of the second edition kept up a running attack on the author and his ideas with their footnotes. For example, when Witherspoon announced the thesis of his sermon in the long sentence quoted in the third paragraph above, the editors inserted a note that attempted to apply the logic of the jeremiad in a different manner:

> Or, with as much propriety the doctrine might have been framed thus: 'That the haughty insolence of ambitious and aspiring clergymen, however insufferable for a time; the most rebellious measures of unnatural subjects against the best of kings and the mildest government; and the most savage cruelties and unheard-of barbarities of misled and undisciplined rebels, shall, in the issue, turn out to the glory of God, and the ruin and disgrace of the promoters, by having restraints set unto them, and disappoint written upon all their designs.'

When Witherspoon remarked upon the corruption of human nature, a footnote observed that the truth of this statement had been 'remarkably verified in the doctor's late and present conduct' in stirring up and promoting rebellion. When Witherspoon called the king 'haughty', a footnote wondered 'if the epithets of *haughty* and *insolent* are not vastly more applicable to the Doctor than the Prince'. When Witherspoon asserted that God protects those with a just cause, pure principles and prudent conduct, the editors noted that the Americans' 'cause is neither just, nor their principles pure, nor has their conduct been prudent, otherwise such a train of disappointments and unsuccessful attempts, would not have so repeatedly marked their undertakings'. And when Witherspoon declared that not merely the temporal but the 'eternal happiness of us and our posterity depended on the issue' (*WJW*, 3:37), a footnote retorted: 'Tho' the doctor, and his partizans, may alledge, the Americans being taxed at all, is an incroachment upon *civil* property, how will they be able to instruct, that their *religious* liberties have in the least been invaded; or that either their temporal or *eternal* happiness depend on the issue?'

It was a sign of the times, as well as of the place, that the review of the second edition of *Dominion of Providence* that appeared in the February 1777 issue of the primary periodical of eighteenth-century Scotland paid more attention to the hostile footnotes than to the sermon itself (*SM*, 39:93–96). The following month a front-page article featured lengthy excerpts from the *Address to the Natives of Scotland* and another long, critical footnote from the second edition of *Dominion of Providence* (*SM*, 39:113–20). In the October issue a political correspondent lambasted both parts of Witherspoon's publication in a passage as notable for its vituperative tone as for its blatant distortions of the author's arguments:

> Our correspondent is astonished at this Rev. gentleman's morals. St Paul says, the damnation of those who do evil that good may come is just: Dr Witherspoon, on the contrary, says, that even if the colonists were wrong in the present context, it would be the part both of generosity and justice, in a certain class of persons, to support them effectually in it. The Apostle condemns evil even when done that good may come: the Doctor would justify evil even when done in support of what is wrong. (*SM*, 39:533)

Later in 1777 there appeared in Glasgow a third, corrected edition of *Dominion of Providence*, to which 'S. R.' added one new critical footnote and an appendix that placed most of the responsibility for the American Revolution on Witherspoon's shoulders.[31] Still later in the year a fourth edition of the work was published at Belfast.

However much the editorial comments in the Glasgow editions of *Dominion of Providence*, as well as reviews of that work in periodicals like the *Scots Magazine*, may have mocked Witherspoon's efforts to use the tradition of the Scottish Presbyterian jeremiad in the service of the

American Revolution, it was Witherspoon who had the last laugh. The edition of his sermon published in London in 1778 not only appeared without the editorial commentary of the Glasgow editions (as well as the *Address*) but also included a new advertisement that pointed out the work's 'decency and moderation'. The reviewer in the *Monthly Review* bought this line completely,[32] and the final outcome of the war seemed to lend further credence to Witherspoon's views. As if by providential decree, America *had* triumphed over an apparently mightier opponent. Witherspoon himself did not miss the chance to drive the point home. Preaching on the congressionally appointed national thanksgiving day at the end of the war (11 December 1783), he announced that 'the separation of this country from Britain, has been of God; for every step the British took to prevent, served to accelerate it, which has generally been the case when men have undertaken to go in opposition to the course of Providence, and to make war with the nature of things' (*WJW*, 3:79). Witherspoon had never lost sight of the importance of such national, political prayer days: it was said that most, if not all, of the calls for fast days during the war years were written by him.[33]

Back in Britain, meanwhile, the logic of the jeremiad was being put to some ingenious uses. In a sermon of 1785 that bore the revealing and characteristic title *National Prosperity the Consequence of National Virtue, and National Ruin the Effect of National Wickedness*, the Revd William Duff of Aberdeenshire argued that the unsuccessful resolution of the American War was really a blessing in disguise because the bad harvest of 1783 would have caused a far more devastating 'general famine' if the war had not been over by then. 'Thus', he wrote, 'while God hath in some instances been pleased to inflict chastisements upon us, on account of our national sins, he hath likewise mitigated and removed these chastisements; and in order to lead us to repentence, and allure us to our duty, hath wrought out for us unexpected and undeserved national deliverances.' From passages like this it is clear that the Scottish jeremiad assumed, just as the New England one did, that divine punishment was essentially 'corrective' rather than 'destructive'. For implicit in the Scottish jeremiad, even more than in its New England counterpart, was the belief that God has a special relationship with a covenanted nation, which he warns, tests, punishes but ultimately rewards within the confines of this world. *Dominion of Providence* was the best known of the American Presbyterian sermons and writings that sought to put this Scottish tradition to work on behalf of the Revolution. Understanding the Scottish context from which it sprang should make one wary of studies that view the eighteenth-century tradition of national fast days and jeremiads in America as little more than an extension of a Puritan paradigm from seventeenth-century New England.

NOTES

The author wishes to thank Roger Fechner, Ned Landsman, John Murrin and Jeff Smitten for comments on earlier versions of this essay.

1. Ashbel Green, *The Life of the Rev[d] John Witherspoon*, ed. Henry Lyttleton Savage (Princeton, 1973), 150; Varnum Lansing Collins, *President Witherspoon*, 2 vols. (Princeton, 1925), 1:197, 204 and bibliography.
2. Perry Miller, *The New England Mind: From Colony to Province* (Boston, 1961).
3. These are listed in W. DeLoss Love, Jr., *The Fast and Thanksgiving Days of New England* (Boston and New York, 1895), 547–48. Considering this impressive statistic, it is surprising that the only published sermon Love lists for the congressional fast day in May 1776 is Witherspoon's.
4. Perry Miller, 'From the Covenant to the Revival', in *Nature's Nation* (Cambridge, Mass., 1967), 90–120, esp. 97.
5. Ibid., 92.
6. Sacvan Bercovitch, *The American Jeremiad* (Madison, Wisc., 1978); John F. Berens, *Providence and Patriotism in Early America, 1640–1815* (Charlottesville, Va., 1978).
7. Alan Heimert, *Religion and the American Mind* (Cambridge, Mass., 1966). As Heimert put it, 'the doctrine of the covenant on which the jeremiad hinged invariably implied a less strenuous gospel . . . [and] was uncongenial to evangelical religion' (425). The jeremiad was essentially action-oriented and therefore well-suited to convincing people that worldly behaviour of a particular kind was critically important in the eyes of God, but this tendency ran counter to the evangelical emphasis on man's inability to appease God by means of deeds.
8. Bercovitch, *American Jeremiad*, 105.
9. Miller, 'Covenant to Revival', 92.
10. Harry S. Stout, *The New England Soul: Preaching and Religious Culture in Colonial New England* (Oxford, 1986), 295. In fact the day in question was a Thursday, the traditional fast day of Scottish Presbyterians and English dissenters.
11. In the first edition (Philadelphia, 1776) only, the *Address* was printed in a reduced type size.
12. Ronald J. Vander Molen, 'Providence as Mystery, Providence as Revelation: Puritan and Anglican Modifications of John Calvin's Doctrine of Providence', *Church History* 47 (1978): 27–47; Richard L. Greaves, 'John Knox and the Covenant Tradition', *Journal of Ecclesiastical History* 24 (1973): 23–32; Roger Mason, *Kingship and Commonweal: Political Thought and Ideology in Reformation Scotland*, chap. 8 (forthcoming).
13. Richard Kyle, 'John Knox's Concept of Divine Providence and Its Influence on His Thought', *Albion* 18 (1986): 408.
14. Arthur H. Williamson, *Scottish National Consciousness in the Age of James VI* (Edinburgh, 1979). See also G.D. Henderson, *The Burning Bush: Studies in Scottish Church History* (Edinburgh, 1957), chap. 4: 'The Idea of the Covenant in Scotland'.

15. Williamson, *Scottish National Consciousness*, 79.
16. Greaves, 'John Knox and the Covenant Tradition', 28–29.
17. Williamson, *Scottish National Consciousness*, 140. In a little-known lecture published as *John Witherspoon and His Times* (Philadelphia, 1890), James McCosh placed a similar emphasis upon the differences between the English Puritan and Scottish Presbyterian traditions. Both were based on the word of God, he noted, but Presbyterianism alone stood for a comprehensive and truly national system of church polity, founded on a 'Solemn League and Covenant (1638), which was subscribed in Greyfriars' churchyard, Edinburgh, in blood drawn from the veins of the signers' (6). McCosh strove to link Witherspoon with this tradition, in part by pointing out his kinship ties with John Knox and the seventeenth-century Covenanters. The contrast between the English Puritan and Scottish Presbyterian traditions was carried straight through to McCosh's own time, and he took pride in noting that the Scots-Irish in the middle and southern states were not troubled with 'fancies, conceits and Yankee notions' (9).
18. Alexander Henderson, 'Sermon at St. Andrews', in *The Covenants and the Covenanters: Covenants, Sermons, and Documents of the Covenanted Reformation*, ed. James Kerr (Edinburgh, 1895).
19. See Sher, 40–44.
20. *Prayer for National Prosperity and for the Revival of Religion Inseparably Connected* (preached 16 February 1758), in *WJW*, 2:464. In the classic style of the Scottish jeremiad Witherspoon asserted: 'It is not, indeed, to be wondered at, that not only this nation, but the protestant states of Europe in general should be brought under the rod, as they have so shamefully departed from that purity of faith and strictness of morals which was the glory of the reformation' (*WJW*, 2:472).
21. Stout, *New England Soul*, 283. In making this point Stout does not indicate the obvious Scottish Presbyterian roots of such an enterprise.
22. *Records of the Presbyterian Church in the United States of America, 1706–1788* (1904; rpt. New York, 1969), 466–69, is the source for most of the facts in this paragraph.
23. Leonard J. Trinterud, *The Forming of an American Tradition: A Re-examination of Colonial Presbyterianism* (Philadelphia, 1949), 249. I take issue with Trinterud's claim that *Dominion of Providence* adopted the moderate position of the pastoral letter.
24. For example, the pastoral letter contains this statement: 'There is no example in history, in which civil liberty was destroyed, and the rights of conscience preserved entire' (*WJW*, 3:13). In *Dominion of Providence* one reads: 'There is not a single instance in history in which civil liberty was lost, and religious liberty preserved entire' (*WJW*, 3:37).
25. Henry P. Ippel, 'Blow the Trumpet, Sanctify the Fast', *Huntington Library Quarterly* 44 (1980–81): 43–60, 'British Sermons and the American Revolution', *Journal of Religious History* 12 (1982): 191–205.
26. For a discussion of one of these Scottish jeremiads against the Revolution, Alexander Carlyle's *The Justice and Necessity of the War*

with our American Colonies Examined (Edinburgh, 1777), see Sher, 271–72.

27. Searle to Dartmouth, 8 Nov. 1776 and 25 Apr. 1777, quoted in Leonard J. Kramer, 'Muskets in the Pulpit, 1776–1783', *Journal of the Presbyterian Historical Society* 31 (1953): 229–30.
28. Leonard J. Kramer, 'Presbyterians Approach the American Revolution', *Journal of the Presbyterian Historical Society* 31 (1953): 178.
29. *The XLV. Chapter of the Prophecies of Thomas the Rhymer, in Verse: with Notes and Illustrations, Dedicated to Doctor Silverspoon, Preacher of Sedition in America* (Edinburgh, 1776). Witherspoon was alluded to in the following lines:

    When civil discord does a state embroil
    We holy harpies feed upon the spoil.
    But see, thro' silver moon-light gliding,
    Horrid hags in triumph riding,
    Bringing news of joyful tiding,
    From Discord's dreary dome.
    Lo they bring from coast Atlantic,
    Where fears ideal, yet gigantic,
    Have render'd a whole nation frantic,
    The gentle Silverspoon. (16–17)

    In the ironically pro-American dedication to this poem, Arnot wrote: 'I wish I could send you more agreeable news from this *deluded kingdom*. We are not, however, totally destitute of friends; a majority of smugglers are in favour of us, and some *high flying clergy* in a certain *city* have betrayed their affection to our cause' (7).
30. Witherspoon, of course, did not fall into the hands of the British government, but he did have the honour of being burned in effigy by British troops in America.
31. 'It is a certain fact,' said the appendix to the third edition, 'and now undeniably confirmed, by the preceding discourses, that the doctor has had a very principal hand in fomenting the present unhappy commotions in the British empire, if not the sole hand in keeping them alive. The scheme of independency, it is said, was first planned by him' (55).
32. *Monthly Review* 58 (March 1778): 246–47: 'This discourse . . . has nothing in it irrational or illiberal. It abounds more in piety than politics; though by no means destitute of the latter; but his doctrines, in both respects, breathe a spirit so candid, and so agreeable to the moderation of the Christian character, that excepting a few passages tending to encourage the Americans in their scheme of independency, this animated and pious discourse might have been delivered, with general acceptance, and possibly with good effect, before any Fast-day audience in this kingdom, – without subjecting the Preacher to the imputation of disloyalty, or disaffection to government.' Another sympathetic reader of this edition was the English dissenter James Kenrick, as noted in Colin Bonwick, *English Radicals and the American Revolution* (Chapel Hill, N.C., 1977), 44.
33. William D. Sprague, *Annals of the American Pulpit*, 9 vols. (New York, 1858–69), 3:295.

3

LEIGH ERIC SCHMIDT

Sacramental Occasions and the Scottish Context of Presbyterian Revivalism in America

'Frequently at *Sacramental Seasons* in *New-Brunswick*', Gilbert Tennent informed readers of *The Christian History* in November 1744, 'there have been signal Displays of the divine Power and Presence: . . . O the sweet Meltings that I have often seen on such Occasions among many! *New-Brunswick* did then look like a *Field the Lord had blessed*: It was like a little *Jerusalem*, to which the scattered Tribes with eager haste repaired at Sacramental Solemnities; and there they fed on the *Fatness of God's House*, and drunk of the *River of his Pleasures*.'

Tennent's experience at New Brunswick, New Jersey, had plenty of parallels. His brother William, for example, led similarly powerful sacramental occasions not far away at such places as Freehold, Maidenhead and Hopewell. From across the border in Pennsylvania, revivalist Samuel Blair offered this summary assessment: 'Our *sacramental Solemnities* for communicating in the *Lord's Supper* have generally been very blessed Seasons of Enlivening and Enlargement to the People of God.' To the north, enclaves of Presbyterian immigrants in New England participated in similar sacramental events as early as the 1720s. To the south about a generation later (in Hanover County, Virginia, for example) the administration of the Lord's Supper among Presbyterian dissenters was regularly linked with 'special outpourings of the spirit'. Presbyterian revivalism in early America, such reports suggested, was often bound up with something rather obscurely referred to as a sacramental season or sacramental solemnity.[1]

After the Revolution, narratives of Presbyterian revivals were even more insistent that these sacramental occasions were an important basis of religious renewal. In a series of revivals in western Pennsylvania between 1781 and 1788, for example, it was observed that 'there were many sweet, solemn sacramental occasions. The most remarkable of these was at Cross-Creek, in the spring of the year 1787. — It was a very refreshing season to the pious, a time of deliverance to a number of the distressed, and of awakening to many.' During the Great Revival in Kentucky, litanies of similar successes were regularly voiced. In one account, for example, revivalist James McGready noted eighteen revivals between 1797 and 1800 in and around Logan County, Kentucky, sixteen of which were directly connected to these sacramental solemnities. 'What is truly matter of praise, wonder and gratitude to every follower of Christ', McGready concluded of the intense revivals of 1800, 'is, that every sacramental occasion in all our congregations, during the whole summer and fall, was attended with the tokens of the sweet presence and power of the Almighty Jesus.' In 1803 McGready was still basking in the rays of divine light that illumined these communions. 'I have the happiness to inform you', he related, 'that the Lord is yet doing wonders in our country. . . . Our Sacramental occasions are days of the Son of Man indeed, and are usually marked with the visible footsteps of Jehovah's majesty and glory. . . . [A]t the Sacrament in the Ridge congregation, . . . [t]here were upwards of five hundred communicants; and at the tables, through the evening, and during the greater part of the night, the people of God were so filled with such extatic raptures of divine joy and comfort, that I could compare it to nothing else than the New Jerusalem coming down from heaven to earth.' Between the early eighteenth century and the turn of the nineteenth, Presbyterian revivalism in early America often intertwined with these sacramental occasions.[2]

Behind the compact attestations of the two Tennents or McGready to the power of Presbyterian sacramental occasions loomed a long history and a complex set of rituals and devotions that too often went undescribed in their cursory narratives. To understand what lay behind these evangelistic events that were invigorating Presbyterian communities in early America, one has to move across the Atlantic to Scotland, where the rituals and piety that patterned the festal communions initially took shape. Thus, the first task of this chapter is to sketch the history of these sacramental occasions in Scotland and to describe briefly the rituals and piety long connected with them. Then the discussion will turn in the second part of the chapter to suggesting the broader significance that this Scottish form of renewal holds for interpreting revivalism in American culture. Finally, in the third and concluding section of the chapter, attention will shift to how this popular Presbyterian tradition fared in the face of Enlightenment attacks from without as well as evangelical critiques from within. This section will look, in short, at how various pressures mounted for the reform of this popular evangelical tradition.

I

At least as early as the 1620s, Presbyterian renewal in Scotland was connected with sacramental occasions similar to the ones the Tennents and McGready would herald in America. Playing off a longer tradition of sacramental festivity – embodied in the Catholic celebrations of Easter and Corpus Christi, for example – the Scottish Presbyterians attacked popular Catholic forms of devotion only to rehabilitate eucharistic spectacle, mystery and solemnity in Reformed guise. If reformulating and remoulding the popular festivity of their Catholic forebears constituted one step, another was preserving Presbyterian patterns of worship in the face of High Church opposition. From the first the Presbyterians sought to distance themselves from their prelatical adversaries on the basis of distinctive sacramental practices; they thus made specific eucharistic rituals, particularly sitting around a table to share the elements, the centrepiece of their opposition to the Anglican designs of James I and Charles I. Popular, nonconforming Presbyterian preachers, especially in the southwest and in Ulster, began to attract large crowds of disaffected Scots to sacramental occasions that preserved Reformed eucharistic practice intact without such Anglican forms as kneeling, set prayers or clerical distribution. By 1630 sacramental occasions had emerged as high days of the year for the evangelical Presbyterians of the southwest and Ulster and had been used to forward a powerful Presbyterian awakening, exemplified in the widely heralded revival at Shotts.[3]

Throughout the decades of religious strife that followed, the large communions continued to develop and thrive. In the 1650s the most zealous Presbyterians, flourishing under Cromwell's Protectorate, found the fervent, lengthy and well-attended sacramental occasions ideal for furthering their cause. People flocked to these events for several days of intense, even ecstatic devotion during which they pledged themselves to Christ and to the extreme Presbyterian party known as the Protesters. Despite often bitter opposition to these perfervid, dissent-filled gatherings, such solemnities continued even after the Restoration. Illicit communions, sometimes drawing eight to ten thousand Covenanters, troubled Charles II throughout his reign, especially in the 1670s. With the Glorious Revolution and Presbyterian triumph, the popular sacramental meetings that had helped sustain the opposition to episcopacy quickly came into their own and were soon established as a prominent event in the religious life of Presbyterian Scotland. From the 1690s into the early nineteenth century, this sacramental festival was one of the most distinctive features of the religious culture of the evangelical Presbyterians. As the high days in the year, these communion seasons were regularly times of revival. In the 1740s, for example, they would cap some of the grandest revivals in the history of evangelicalism, those at Cambuslang and Kilsyth.[4]

Most of the rituals of these occasions were in evidence by the 1620s, though solidification and elaboration were gradual and ongoing. By the early eighteenth century a clear and largely fixed form, intricate in its orchestration, was in place. Though the events obviously focused on the Lord's Supper, preparation for this central rite was extensive. Preparatory activities often began weeks in advance with prayer meetings, appropriate sermons and careful catechesis. Church sessions were doubly vigilant, admonishing the sinful and reconciling the estranged. The sacramental occasion itself formally began with a day for public fasting and humiliation, usually held on the Wednesday or Thursday before the celebration of the Lord's Supper. Sometimes the fast would be on Friday, but often this day was given over to private preparation in self-examination, secret prayer, personal covenanting and meditation. On Saturday public worship resumed with sermons, prayers and psalm-singing and also with lengthy delineations of who was worthy to partake of the Lord's Supper and who was not, admonitory advices that were constantly repeated and that were formally embodied in the ritual of fencing the table on the Sabbath. Also communion tokens, small leaden emblems of the covenant, were often distributed during the services on Saturday to the worthy who would use the tokens the next day to gain admission to the table. Preparation continued into the evening and night as people retired for fervent prayer either in groups or singly.[5]

On the Sabbath the Lord's Supper was celebrated with the communicants sitting at long, linen-covered tables and passing the consecrated elements from one to another. The multitudes at these communions usually necessitated a number of table services, so many servings that the celebration often lasted all day. While ministers took turns serving the tables and exhorting at them, others usually preached elsewhere, often outdoors from a makeshift pulpit, known as the tent, that was specially constructed for these occasions. Sometimes, given the crowds, all the services were conducted in the open air in churchyards or fields. The long services of the Sabbath closed with a thanksgiving sermon that prepared the way for further praise and blessing on Monday. After several days of devotion the Monday meetings were a fitting copestone for the whole affair, a solemn sometimes exuberant day of conversion and reaffirmation. Finally the work ended and people began to make their journeys homeward, often long treks of twenty, thirty or even fifty miles. These sacramental rituals, celebrated year after year in Ulster and Scotland, were a fundamental part of popular Presbyterian culture and an important way in which regional communities were knit out of dispersed agrarian hamlets.[6] Such rituals, woven into the fabric of Presbyterian communities in the Old World, became in turn part of the tapestry of the New World. It was these rituals, maintained almost *in toto*, that would shape innumerable Presbyterian revivals in early America, even those revivals that have long been considered quintessentially American, on the frontier at such places as Gaspar River or Cane Ridge.

The Scottish and Scots-Irish Presbyterians had developed not only their own distinctive eucharistic rituals but also their own devotional literature that would help people prepare for these occasions. Pastors such as Daniel Campbell, Robert Craighead, John Spalding and John Willison provided a spate of sacramental meditations, advices, catechisms and directions, mostly published in the decades following Presbyterian establishment in 1690. Coupled with a growing number of saintly autobiographies, such as those of Elisabeth West and John Ronald, the works of these devotional writers helped codify the practice of piety that accompanied the sacramental occasions. The works of such ministers continued to provide guidance for the Presbyterian immigrants in early America. Daniel Campbell's *Sacramental Meditations*, first published in 1698, was reprinted in America in 1740 and twice more after the Revolution. Willison, one of the most prolific Presbyterian devotional writers in the eighteenth century, was likewise influential; a number of his works went through American editions. This devotional literature, though heavily indebted to Puritan and Catholic precursors, nonetheless gave the Scottish and Scots-Irish Presbyterians guidance for private preparation for the Lord's Supper, including self-examination, meditation, secret prayer and personal covenanting. Such works reflected and helped to structure the patterns of piety that the immigrants brought with them to America. The religious experience of Presbyterians in the New World would flow in channels etched in the Old. The sacramental spirituality embodied in the communion season would be a distinguishing mark of evangelical Presbyterian piety on both sides of the Atlantic.[7]

One example among many of how this piety was expressed at the lay level occurs in the spiritual narrative of 'a single *young Woman*' from Samuel Blair's congregation in southeastern Pennsylvania. Her 'Soul Exercises and Experiences' in the early 1740s serve to underscore as well the transatlantic scope of this sacramental spirituality. Her pilgrimage, as Blair related it, began slowly. Having seen 'others so much concern'd about their Souls', she wondered why she worried so little about her own. Gradually, pressed hard by her pastor's sermons, she became more uneasy about her eternal state and was 'much troubled and cast down' for 'a few Days' after each Sabbath. As her spiritual distress deepened, she joined for the first time 'a *Society* of private Christians' for prayer, Scripture reading and 'religious Conference'. Her desperation over her own sin and corruption was only intensified by her meetings with those on similarly troubled journeys; indeed, her distress grew so marked at one point that she swooned away and fell 'both Deaf and Blind' for a time. Regaining her senses, she continued to beg Christ for relief, but such relief still eluded her. Finally, after '*some Weeks*' in this 'extreme Anguish', she came to 'a Sacramental Solemnity' and there, on the Sabbath evening after the memorial of Christ's atoning death, she found reconciliation with God. As she listened to a psalm of the pilgrim ('My thirsty soul longs veh'mently, yea faints, thy courts to see: My very heart and flesh cry out, O living God, for thee'), she finally found rest after weeks of longing. Christ had 'put by the Veil' and allowed her a foretaste of the glories of heaven.[8]

The wayfaring hardly ended here. The glimmer of assurance faded, and she yearned anew to have Jesus as 'her *own Saviour in particular*'. This second round of 'grievous Dejections' continued for 'about *two Years*' with only intermittent periods of 'Sweetness and Comfort'. Sermons occasionally consoled her, but could as easily discourage. In these two years of distress the Lord's Supper as well offered her only mixed blessings. Though she regularly 'found some Refreshing and Sweetness by that Ordinance', she remained unsettled by 'much Fear and Perplexity' over her worthiness to partake. Finally, however, peace came. 'After she had been so long under an almost alternate Succession of Troubles and Supports', Blair related, 'the *Sun of Righteousness* at last broke out upon her to the clear Satisfaction and unspeakable Ravishment of her Soul, at a *Communion Table*. There her Mind was let into the glorious Mysteries of Redemption with great Enlargement.' There, 'meditat[ing] on the *Sufferings* of the Lord Jesus', she saw in an arresting moment of contemplation that Christ had 'suffered for her Sins; that she was the very Person who by her Sins had occasioned his Sufferings, and brought Agony and Pain upon him'. While at the table, she experienced simultaneously lamentation and joy; she both mourned for sin and delighted in God's presence. As a penitent, she had met with Christ at his table.[9]

Though her soul was ravished for a time, her pilgrimage necessarily continued. She pursued holiness with diligence and sought to fend off any doubts that persisted or returned. In her efforts she found '*Sacramental Seasons*' especially to be 'blessed and precious Seasons to her' and a vital source of the Lord's 'comforting Presence.' At such occasions she continued to meditate on Christ's sufferings (for example, on 'the *Blood* and *Water* that issued from the Wound made by the Spear in her Saviour's Side') and found invigoration in such prayerful contemplation. At one '*Communion Solemnity*' in particular she experienced anew 'the Glory and Delight' of God's presence. Her spiritual life, though complex, centred on these communion occasions. Enmeshed in a web of spiritual duties, such as hearing sermons, attending prayer societies, observing family devotions and retiring to secret prayer, the sacramental season was woven into the centre of this web; all strands circled around it. The Lord's Supper, one Scottish divine intoned, 'is the *Epitome* of the whole Christian Religion, both as to Doctrine and Practice.' For Blair's exemplary saint and for many others on both sides of the Atlantic, the sacrament and the devotions surrounding it were indeed very nearly the sum of Christian piety.[10]

II

Popular evangelical traditions from Scotland, particularly evident in specific sacramental rituals and devotional disciplines, informed much of Presbyterian revivalism in early America. If discussion thus far has accentuated this Scottish background and the formative influence Old World traditions had on evangelical Presbyterianism in the colonies, it has only begun to answer the larger question of what significance these communions hold for students of revivalism and American religious history. On this score a number of points stand out; the following five observations in particular seem warranted.

First, the prominence of the sacramental occasion indicates the importance of interpreting religion in early America within a transatlantic context. Much of the initial historiography on American revivalism was heavily influenced by Frederick Jackson Turner's writings about the frontier and its formative power in shaping American culture. From Catharine Cleveland and Peter Mode through William Warren Sweet and Charles Johnson, studies of American revivalism generally assumed that Old World traditions crumpled when confronted with the exigencies of life on the frontier. The Presbyterian sacramental occasion suggests precisely the opposite: Old World traditions powerfully influenced revivalism in the New World, perhaps even with particular force on the frontier. The Great Revival in the West, long the focus of the frontier school's interpretation of American revivalism, took much of its meaning and shape not from 'the very atmosphere of life in the wilderness' but from longstanding evangelical rituals. McGready's sacramental occasions or camp meetings at Gaspar River were not so much inventions of the frontier but instead evangelistic events with a nearly two-hundred-year-old history. A number of historians, including Ned Landsman, Robert Rutter and Marilyn Westerkamp, all of whom broach Scottish materials, have begun the process of the transatlantic contextualisation of American revivalism. Close study of these sacramental festivals further underlines the profound importance of transatlantic connexions in early evangelicalism.[11]

Second, understanding these communions helps us see the relationship between revivalism and sacramentalism differently. Historians as well as theologians have often assumed that revivalism had very little truck with sacramentalism, that the two were enemies, not helpmeets. Early American revivals, we are told, were characterised by 'unharnessed emotionalism' and 'the absence of all regularity.' The fervour of conversionist piety, it is suggested, was incompatible with the solemnity of sacramental ritual. In the communion season, however, this common antithesis was dissolved; sacramentalism and revivalism happily intertwined. For these evangelical Presbyterians the Lord's Supper was the basis of renewal and evoked passionate, emotional responses. Though communion itself was generally reserved for confirming the faith of those already within the fold, the sacramental occasion was aimed at those outside it as well. The confirmation of saints was paired with the conversion of sinners. The communion season represented an evangelical Protestant synthesis of revivalism and sacramentalism.[12]

Third, exploration of the sacramental occasion suggests another way of conceiving the cycle of evangelical awakenings. Historians regularly draw lines between a first Great Awakening and a second Great Awakening. This conceptualisation suggests not only that the evangelical movement was relatively quiescent between 1750 and 1800 but also that when it revived the movement had changed substantially in theology and ritual. When it comes to the revivalism of evangelical Presbyterians, however, the standard Awakening construct warrants qualification. For the Presbyterians, the sacramental occasion, usually an annual event, tended to make the cycle of renewal within their congregations a short one; year in, year out Presbyterian communities sought and regularly found revivification in the communion season. For a century in America and longer still in Scotland, these traditional events often marked out an annual rhythm of renewal that beat at a tempo distinct from that associated with a larger cycle of awakenings. Thus revivals, at least of this type, were not so much rare and extraordinary outpourings as wonted rituals of renewal, Protestant festivals that were woven into the calendar. This continuity in the process of renewal was matched by a consistent adherence to tradition. Presbyterian revivals of the 1790s were closely in line with those of the 1730s, which in turn were closely in line with those of the seventeenth century. Change came, of course, and after 1800 it came quickly, but until then the undercurrent of Old World tradition was as strong as the tide of New World innovation. Continuity in tradition and in the patterned rhythms of renewal were critical aspects of Presbyterian revivalism in early America, suggesting that the sharpness with which the awakenings are often distinguished deserves reconsideration.[13]

Fourth, study of such traditional forms of worship opens up another way of assessing the ethnic particularity of Scottish Presbyterianism. Ned Landsman has suggested that Presbyterian revivalism in early America fed ethnic nativism more than evangelical ecumenism, and his point is well worth underscoring. There were indeed critical, abiding differences between the evangelical groups in early America. They were hardly woven into one cohesive transatlantic and intercolonial movement. The points of divergence were particularly notable in forms of worship. The sacramental occasion with its distinctive configuration of rituals – the penitential fast day, the Saturday preparatory meeting, the dispensing of communion tokens, the sitting at long tables to receive the elements, the preaching from a special outdoor pulpit known as 'the tent,' the fencing of the tables, the singing of the Scottish version of the Psalms, and the Monday thanksgiving services – presented a unique pattern of activities with which only evangelical Presbyterians were wholly familiar. The persistence of an Old World Presbyterian and Scottish identity can be traced in the long commitment of many of the immigrants and their descendants to such distinctive practices, and conversely the decline of that identity can be traced in the abandonment of such rituals. Religion and ethnicity were closely interwoven in the sacramental season.[14]

Fifth and finally, these sacramental occasions remind historians of the need to look closely at the rituals of revivalism. Scholars have long been more interested in searching out the causes and consequences of awakenings than in scrutinising the revivals themselves. Explaining why revivals happened has had priority over understanding what people were doing or experiencing at revival meetings. This sorting out of a chain of causes and effects may be of less help in understanding the profound cultural significance of revivals than the full appreciation of how particular evangelistic activities were interrelated with a given culture as a whole. The intricacy of the sacramental season suggests that interpretive or ethnographic questions need to be asked. How did these rituals help the participants make sense of their world? What did they mean to those amidst them? How were these festal occasions interwoven with the culture of which they were a part? How did specific ritual performances contribute to the formation of social relationships and patterns of authority? How were various media of communication employed in these festivals; that is, how did different actions, objects, postures, gestures, settings and words contribute to 'the total process of communication' at these events? These are the sorts of ethnographic questions that recent cultural historians, such as Peter Burke, Robert Darnton, Natalie Zemon Davis and Rhys Isaac, have been pursuing in various historical contexts.[15] Though only posed here, such questions suggest anew the importance of seeing revivals as rituals that require interpretation, as richly patterned activities that provide inlets into past cultures. The Scottish sacrament with its density of ritual further encourages the exploration of ethnographic approaches to history.

III

Study of the Scottish sacrament potentially points in several directions. There are, as we have seen, important questions about the history of these communions and their various interconnexions with revivalism, about evangelical ritual and spirituality, about transatlantic ties, about worship and ethnicity. But there are also significant questions about the fate of such popular evangelical traditions. In both Scotland and America the communions attracted thousands of spectators, wayfarers and communicants and enjoyed extensive, long-lasting popularity. As evangelical festivals, the sacramental occasions were certainly on a par with later camp meetings. Indeed, in many ways the communions represented the resilience and strength of popular religious forms, here within a Reformed context. At the same time, however, the communions suggested the vulnerability of popular religious traditions, particularly festivals, to reform. Like the Catholic traditions that went before, the communion season, too, would pass from the scene. Reformers of various stripes did not stop until these 'rude festivals' were brought under control and largely quelled.[16]

The process of reform was fuelled on one side by Enlightenment attacks. Among these critiques, two in particular gained a widespread hearing and considerable notoriety: an anonymous epistle, *A Letter from a Blacksmith, to the Ministers and Elders of the Church of Scotland* (1758), and Robert Burns's satiric poem 'The Holy Fair'. The 'blacksmith', whose work proved influential on both sides of the Atlantic, based his letter on the conviction that popular evangelicalism was in desperate need of reform, that 'low superstition', ignorance and enthusiasm sullied Presbyterian worship at every turn: in family devotions, in extemporaneous prayers, in congregational psalm-singing and, most of all, in the sacramental occasions. He set out to purge Scottish worship of its many 'indecencies and follies', all of which ultimately derived from indulging 'the perverseness of the people'. To the 'blacksmith', this popular distortion of Christianity was altogether evident in the communions. 'These religious farces' too often issued in 'popular frenzy'; the preachers worked up 'the mob to the highest pitch of enthusiasm', bringing 'the weak and ignorant to the very brink of downright madness'. 'I have seen scenes', he reported in sad disbelief, 'that had much more of the fury of the bacchanalia, than the calm, serious, sincere devotion of a christian sacrament.' Brashly distinguishing 'the rational people' from 'the common people' (whom he also referred to as 'the silly, ignorant vulgar'), the 'blacksmith' made clear the sentiments of the enlightened towards popular evangelicalism.[17]

Still more important for shaping Enlightenment attitudes towards the excesses of the sacramental occasion was Burns's masterful poem 'The Holy Fair'. In various works Burns gave expression to the anti-Calvinistic, anti-evangelical dimensions of the Scottish Enlightenment, and in 'The Holy Fair' in particular he confronted the evangelicals with colourful images of popular 'superstition' and 'hypocrisy'. Writing in satiric tones, Burns took special pleasure in depicting the histrionic folly of evangelical preachers at these occasions:

> Hear how he clears the points o' Faith
> Wi' rattlin an' thumpin!
> Now meekly calm, now wild in wrath,
> He's stampan, an' he's jumpan!
> His lengthen'd chin, his turn'd up snout,
> His eldritch squeel an' gestures,
> O how they fire the heart devout,
> Like cantharidian plaisters
> On sic a day!

As did the 'blacksmith', Burns distanced himself from the fervency and spectacle of the festal communions.[18]

Together Burns and the 'blacksmith' reflect the growing gap between popular evangelicalism and the religious sensibilities of the Enlightenment. Their views suggest how the traditional communions faced growing pressures for reform from outside the evangelical camp, from that 'candid lib'ral band' of men who were the vanguard of the Enlightenment in Scotland. As one Scottish writer concluded in 1812, the festal communions were already 'much less prevalent' than they had been when Burns published his poem in 1786, since 'the most enlightened clergymen' had taken pains to discountenance them. Similarly, another opponent of the communions and the tent preaching thanked Burns for having exposed the 'enthusiasm, fanaticism, mysticism, hypocrisy and cant' that infused these evangelical gatherings.[19] The sacramental occasions, increasingly cast as enthusiastic and licentious, were in the process seriously challenged and subverted. Enlightenment figures greatly undermined such popular religious events and helped make way for nineteenth-century interpreters who, in taking the views of Burns and the 'blacksmith' as well-nigh canonical, rejoiced that these festal gatherings for the sacrament had finally succumbed to reason and refinement.

Pressure for reform of the communions was also exerted from within the evangelical tradition itself. The lengthy, crowded sacraments were especially seen as an impediment to frequent communion, a Reformed liturgical ideal from Calvin and Knox to the Westminster divines to John Erskine and John Mason. As long as the eucharist was surrounded by days of fasting, preparation and thanksgiving, and as long as people considered sacrament days as exceptional and set above ordinary Sabbaths, it was unlikely that the Lord's Supper would be regularly administered in Presbyterian churches on a monthly, quarterly or even semiannual basis. The traditional pattern was one of annual sacraments focused almost exclusively on the summer season and involving people from over a wide region. Evangelical reformers increasingly insisted, especially from the late 1740s on, that the grandness of the Scottish sacrament had to be scaled back, that the crowds and the attendant excitement had to be brought under control. More frequent and less festal communions were held up as the undoubted scriptural and Reformed ideal.

This ideal of frequent communion was trumpeted in a variety of ways on both sides of the Atlantic. Pastors wrote pamphlets and offered catechetical instruction on the biblical and apostolic imperative to receive the sacrament as a regular part of Christian worship; some would even endorse weekly communion.[20] Official channels were also pursued; indeed, the church hierarchy thrust itself into the battle for frequent communion repeatedly. In Scotland the general assembly regularly issued acts urging more frequent communion in the hope of promoting 'the glory of God, and edification of souls' as well as taming the 'disorders' of the summer communions. In 1701, 1711, 1712, 1724 and 1751 the assembly encouraged more frequent communions and particularly wanted to see the sacrament celebrated 'throughout the several months of the year'. Likewise in America similar proposals for frequent communion were made by the Synod of Philadelphia and New York in 1787 and were also affirmed by the Synod of the Carolinas in 1789. In these instances, as was generally the case in Scotland as well, the recommendation of greater frequency was joined with suggestions to do away with the extended 'public exercises' and large gatherings of the traditional mode.[21] For all their insistence, however, advocates of frequency found the road to reform long, arduous and serpentine. Popular resistance to the persistent calls for frequent, streamlined, parochial communions ran high; through the eighteenth century, evangelical reformers largely failed to reverse popular favour for sacramental festivity.

Still the reform-minded, whether judging the sacramental occasions by the standards of the Enlightenment or by those of the Reformation or by a combination thereof, were clearly gaining momentum in the second half of the eighteenth century. The popular evangelical traditions surrounding the sacrament were increasingly subject to criticism and reform on various grounds: for enthusiasm, superstition and backwardness as well as for subversion of the biblical and Reformed principle of frequent communion. The double assault of Enlightenment satirists and zealous evangelical reformers went a long way towards discrediting this traditional form of Presbyterian renewal and revival. By the early nineteenth century the communions were clearly receding in importance and declining in power. Indeed, the eighteenth-century reformers were soon celebrated as the harbingers of clear-thinking sobriety and liturgical purity by their Victorian heirs.

The persistence, especially in America, of other popular evangelical forms, such as the camp meeting and the protracted meeting, suggests that the reformers were never completely successful, that such folk traditions often remained resilient. Whatever legacies might be adduced, however, they would not disguise the historical truth that the sacramental occasion, as a distinctive early modern and Reformed festival, was gradually undermined and eventually abandoned. Most nineteenth-century Presbyterians, viewing the immense sacramental gatherings as impediments to refinement and to disciplined social and economic advancement, were happy to let them slip into the past. But although the vital sacramental celebrations were consigned to historical remembrance, that very history remained a powerful legacy: for much of the early modern period, the Scottish sacramental occasions had been critical sources of religious revival and renewal on both sides of the Atlantic.

NOTES

1. *The Christian History*, ed. Thomas Prince, Jr., 2 vols. (Boston, 1744–45) 2:252, 294, 309–10; *Historical Collections Relating to Remarkable Periods of the Success of the Gospel*, ed. John Gillies (Edinburgh, 1754; Kelso, 1845), 501–6, 520. A narrative of the sacramental occasions in New Hampshire in the 1720s can be found in Edward L. Parker, *The History of Londonderry, Comprising the Towns of Derry and Londonderry, N. H.* (Boston, 1851), 130–31, 142–46. Much of the material for this essay is drawn from Leigh Eric Schmidt, *Holy Fairs: Scottish Communions and American Revivals in the Early Modern Period* (Princeton, 1989), and those interested in further argumentation and documentation on specific points in this essay should refer to that work.
2. *Western Missionary Magazine* 1 (1803): 173, 177, 289; James McGready, *The Posthumous Works of the Reverend and Pious James M'Gready, Late Minister of the Gospel in Henderson, K[entuck]y*, ed. James Smith (Nashville, Tenn., 1837), vii–xi.
3. For works providing useful material on the history of Scottish communions and revivals, see George B. Burnet, *The Holy Communion in the Reformed Church of Scotland, 1560–1960* (Edinburgh, 1960); W.J. Couper, *Scottish Revivals* (Dundee, 1918); William D. Maxwell, *A History of Worship in the Church of Scotland* (London, 1955). Two recent works bring transatlantic perspectives to bear on this history of Scottish revivalism: Schmidt, *Holy Fairs*; Marilyn J. Westerkamp, *Triumph of the Laity: Scots–Irish Piety and the Great Awakening, 1625–1760* (New York, 1988). Westerkamp, however, pays little attention to these sacramental occasions once she turns to American materials, and she is also more concerned with Ulster than with the Scottish foundations. For my part I stress the longer view in *Holy Fairs*: namely, that popular festivity in some degree carries over in Scotland from late medieval Catholicism. I also emphasise, in contradistinction to Westerkamp, the pressures of reform that

ultimately curtailed, or at least severely impeded, these popular religious forms.

4. On the revivals at Cambuslang and Kilsyth, see Arthur Fawcett, *The Cambuslang Revival: The Scottish Evangelical Revival of the Eighteenth Century* (London, 1971). For extended analysis of the sacramental piety of many of those who attended these and other meetings, see Schmidt, *Holy Fairs*, chap. 3.
5. The rituals of these festal communions are the subject of extended ethnographic interpretation in Schmidt, *Holy Fairs*, chap. 2. Gwen Kennedy Neville in *Kinship and Pilgrimage: Rituals of Reunion in American Protestant Culture* (New York, 1987) makes some good observations about these rituals in prologue to her cultural analysis of contemporary elaborations of this folk tradition in the American South.
6. For discussion of the structure of Scottish communities and their regional quality, see Ned C. Landsman, *Scotland and Its First American Colony, 1683–1765* (Princeton, 1985).
7. Of the abundance of Scottish devotional literature relating to the Lord's Supper, see particularly Daniel Campbell, *Sacramental Meditations on the Sufferings and Death of Christ* (Philadelphia, 1792); Robert Craighead, *Advice to Communicants, for Necessary Preparation and Profitable Improvement of the Great and Comfortable Ordinance of the Lord's Supper* (Philadelphia, 1792); John Spalding, *Synaxis Sacra; Or, A Collection of Sermons Preached at Several Communions, Together with Speeches at the Tables Both Before, At, and After That Work* (Edinburgh, 1703); John Willison, *A Sacramental Catechism: Or, A Familiar Instructor for Young Communicants* (Edinburgh, 1756); John Willison, *A Sacramental Directory, Or A Treatise Concerning the Sanctification of a Communion-Sabbath* (Edinburgh, 1716). The Puritan and Catholic debts are made most explicit in Campbell's work. For more on this literature, see Schmidt, *Holy Fairs*, esp. chap. 3.
8. *Christian History*, ed. Prince, 2:253–54; *The Psalms of David in Metre: According to the Version Approved by the Church of Scotland, and Appointed to be Used in Public Worship* (Oxford, n.d.), 45.
9. *Christian History*, ed. Prince, 2:254–56.
10. Ibid., 2:255–57; Willison, *Sacramental Catechism*, iii. A major issue in the discussion of lay piety is sorting out the interactive, tensile relationship between lay experience and ministerial prescription, a question I explore in *Holy Fairs*, chap. 3.
11. For the frontier school, see, for example, Catharine Cleveland, *The Great Revival in the West, 1797–1805* (Chicago, 1916), esp. 120–21. For recent efforts to put American revivalism in transatlantic perspective, see, for example, Richard Carwardine, *Transatlantic Revivalism: Popular Evangelicalism in Britain and America, 1790–1865* (Westport, Conn., 1978); Landsman, *Scotland and Its First American Colony*; Susan O'Brien, 'A Transatlantic Community of Saints: The Great Awakening and the First Evangelical Network, 1735–1755', *American Historical Review* 91 (1986): 811–32; Robert Sherman Rutter, 'The New Birth: Evangelicalism in the Transatlantic Community during the Great Awakening, 1739–1745' (Ph.D. diss., Rutgers University, 1982); Schmidt, *Holy Fairs*; Westerkamp, *Triumph of the Laity*.

12. Cleveland, *Great Revival*, 121; Bernard A. Weisberger, *They Gathered at the River: The Story of the Great Revivalists and Their Impact upon Religion in America* (Boston, 1958), 21. Also on the opposition between revivalism and sacramentalism, see E. Brooks Holifield, *The Covenant Sealed: The Development of Puritan Sacramental Theology in Old and New England* (New Haven, Conn., 1974), 229. Recognition of the synthesis of these strands is common on the Scottish side. See, for example, John MacInnes, *The Evangelical Movement in the Highlands of Scotland, 1688 to 1800* (Aberdeen, 1951), 5–6, 154–56, 165–66, 190–91. This synthesis is also evident in Roman Catholic forms of renewal. See Jay P. Dolan, *Catholic Revivalism: The American Experience, 1830–1900* (Notre Dame, Ind., 1978).
13. For the most influential and daring formulation of the Awakening construct, see William G. McLoughlin, *Revivals, Awakenings, and Reform: An Essay on Religion and Social Change in America, 1607–1977* (Chicago, 1978). For further discussion of the thesis, see R.C. Gordon-McCutchan, ed., 'Symposium on Religious Awakenings', *Sociological Analysis* 44 (1983): 81–122.
14. On the issue of ethnicity, see especially Ned Landsman, 'Revivalism and Nativism in the Middle Colonies: The Great Awakening and the Scots Community in East New Jersey', *American Quarterly* 34 (1982): 149–64.
15. Rhys Isaac, *The Transformation of Virginia, 1740–1790* (Chapel Hill, N.C., 1982), esp. 81n., 323–57. On this cultural history, see also Peter Burke, *The Historical Anthropology of Early Modern Italy: Essays on Perception and Communication* (Cambridge, 1987); Robert Darnton, *The Great Cat Massacre and Other Episodes in French Cultural History* (New York, 1984) esp. 3–7, 257–63; Natalie Zemon Davis, *Society and Culture in Early Modern France: Eight Essays* (Stanford, 1975), and her 'From "Popular Religion" to Religious Cultures', in *Reformation Europe: A Guide to Research*, ed. Steven Ozment (St Louis, 1982), 321–41. For an interpreter of American revivalism who focuses on questions of ritual, see Dickson D. Bruce, Jr., *And They All Sang Hallelujah: Plain-Folk Camp-Meeting Religion, 1800–1845* (Knoxville, Tenn., 1974).
16. Henry Grey Graham, *The Social Life of Scotland in the Eighteenth Century* (London, 1899), 313. I assess the reform of popular religion generally and the communion season specifically in *Holy Fairs*, chap. 4. There were some pockets of traditionalism, in the Highlands and Islands, for example, that maintained the sacramental occasions well beyond the decisive period of decline. See Trefor M. Owen, 'The "Communion Season" and Presbyterianism in a Hebridean Community', *Gwerin* 1 (1956): 53–66.
17. *A Letter from a Blacksmith to the Ministers and Elders of the Church of Scotland in which the Manner of Public Worship in that Church is Considered; Its Inconveniences and Defects Pointed Out; and Methods for Removing of Them Humbly Proposed* (London, 1758; New Haven, Conn., 1814) 7, 11, 18–38, 42, 104–5, 119, 129, 137. Dissemination of the blacksmith's *Letter* was widespread. By the 1820s there had been at least seven American editions and twice as many in Britain. For the evangelical rejoinder, see *The Modes of Presbyterian Church-Worship Vindicated: In a Letter to the Blacksmith* (London, 1763).

18. *The Poems and Songs of Robert Burns,* ed. James Kinsley, 3 vols. (Oxford, 1968), 1:132–33.
19. Ibid., 1:126; George Gleig, *A Critique on the Poems of Robert Burns* (Edinburgh, 1812), 16–17; *The Poems and Songs of Robert Burns, with a Life of the Author, Containing a Variety of Particulars, Drawn From Sources Inaccessible by Former Biographers*, ed. Hamilton Paul (Ayr, 1819), xxiv–xxxix.
20. See, for example, John Erskine, *A Humble Attempt to Promote Frequent Communicating* (Glasgow, 1749); Thomas Randall, *A Letter to a Minister from his Friend, Concerning Frequent Communicating, Occasioned by the Late Overture of the Synod of Glasgow and Air upon that Subject* (Glasgow, 1749); John M. Mason, *Letters on Frequent Communion: Addressed Originally to the Members of the Associate–Reformed Church in North America*, in *The Complete Works of John M. Mason, D.D.*, ed. Ebenezer Mason, 4 vols. (New York, 1849).
21. *Acts of the General Assembly of the Church of Scotland, 1638–1842* (Edinburgh, 1843), 458, 471–72, 568, 705; *A Draught of the Form of the Government and Discipline of the Presbyterian Church in the United States of America* (New York, 1787), 79, 84–85; *A Pastoral Letter, from the Synod of the Carolinas, to the Churches under Their Care* (Fayetteville, N.C., 1790), 16–18.

4

ROBERT KENT DONOVAN

The Popular Party of the Church of Scotland and the American Revolution

Of the two parties in the Church of Scotland during the eighteenth century, the Popular party was less favoured by powerful or fashionable people and less well-known in centres of influence and opinion. Its members remain today the more obscure despite their large numbers and their ability in crises to marshall majority support over the rival Moderate party in many parishes, presbyteries and synods.[1] Although kinship, connexion and patronage united Popular party churchmen crucially, they also shared common views. These included a firm loyalty to Reformation theology and a fervent experiential spirituality that brought them the name 'evangelical'.[2] Like the Moderates, their rivals, they had an abiding allegiance to the established church. They also displayed strict adherence to church discipline, rectitude in demeanour as in doctrine being the common hallmark of all Calvinists, however different otherwise. But the Popular party departed markedly from the Moderates in its interpretation of church discipline and its efforts to enforce it. It stood not for democracy or congregationalism but for a fuller participation by the substantial members of the parish, the lay leaders, in calling the clergy to their charges.[3] The party attacked Moderate policy, which bolstered the presentation rights of the parishes' lay patrons, who were usually the crown, the nobility and lairds, or an occasional town council.[4] This attack won it the label 'Popular', although its critics ridiculed it as the enthusiastic or 'Wild' party. Still others, regarding its members' lofty attitude towards the privileges of the church over against those of the crown and aristocracy, called them the 'High' or 'high-flying' party.[5]

Because the party in its day often favoured either lost causes, like reforming the mode of presentation to clerical charges and teaching the Gaelic Bible to illiterate Highlanders, or successful causes, like revivalism and Sunday schools, that make many liberal intellectuals uncomfortable, most twentieth-century historians have neglected it. Even when Popular party clergy and laity championed American colonial rights, a cause that succeeded and that many have chosen to applaud, their contributions have attracted less study than one might expect. The seeming contradiction of support for the American patriots by a party often seen as reactionary and obscurantist baffled contemporaries like Edmund Burke and has struck many later historians as illogical and eccentric, and therefore unworthy of attention.

But support for America the Popular party gave, and it was vocal, persistent and influential. It was also bold, given the position of the party's clergy as the beneficed ministers of a state church maintained by politicians expecting support from the incumbents of ecclesiastical office in all three kingdoms. Documents that survive the crisis of 1775–83 demonstrate that some of the kirk's leading ministers openly favoured the American cause and that they were all Popular party men. These publicists enjoyed influential positions within the party, and they represented like-minded but less outspoken churchmen on many issues. We cannot identify as emphatically pro-American many of the leaders' lesser (and unpublished) clerical colleagues, but no identifiable Popular party minister spoke or wrote in an anti-American strain. Furthermore, the party's opponents, including the Moderate clergy, who themselves either supported imperial policy, temporised about it or maintained discreet silence, attacked the entire Popular party as fomenting colonial obstreperousness.[6] In addition, when calculating the importance of the party in this regard, one must bear in mind that it was numerically the larger church party, that it represented grassroots Scotland more than did the Moderates, that in crises it could count on the support of the middling and lower ranks and that it was by no means without patrons in the aristocracy and even among occasional parliamentary politicians.[7]

At this point, however, some cautions are in order. First, the pro-American views of the Popular party did not sweep Scottish public opinion. Rather, the party introduced keen dissent into political debate, creating serious, unsettling conflict within the country during the Revolution. Second, Popular party views reveal more about the party and Scotland than they do about the colonists and America. Until historians do more research on the Popular party's political ideology, and especially its apocalyptic view of politics, we cannot fully assess its contribution to the American revolutionary ethos. Third, Popular party involvement in the American Revolution, an event historians often view as liberal and liberating, does not permit us to bestow the term 'liberal' on the Popular clergy. Devoted to many traditional ideas of the day, they remain at a spiritual remove from those of us who have benefited from the support they gave the American cause, at a distance they themselves would doubtless prefer.

I

The Scottish Popular party leaders of the 1760s and 1770s had long-standing, deep-rooted ties with America. Just as Scottish Moderates or Anglican Latitudinarians associated with like-minded clergy beyond their own communions, so Popular party men, surprisingly when one considers their reputation for narrowness, counted as colleagues ministers throughout the British Isles, Europe and the American colonies. John Erskine of Greyfriars Church, Edinburgh, the most eminent Popular party divine, learned Dutch so as to correspond with clergy in the Netherlands. He was familiar with the Protestant churches of France, Switzerland and Bohemia, and his acquaintance extended to the Greek Orthodox Church. He was familiar enough with Islam to prefer its doctrines to the regrettable heresy of Socinianism.[8] But it was towards English dissenters and especially American churchmen that Erskine and his colleagues, such as William Porteous of Glasgow, Charles Nisbet of Montrose, John Gillies of Glasgow and Colin Gillies of Greenock, felt most warm. They accepted the established churches of New England as well as the Presbyterian churches of the middle colonies as sister communions and kept up the correspondence their forebears had begun with American clergy.[9] Their colonial friends were 'New Light' or 'New Side' ministers who shared Popular party spirituality and theology in many respects. During and after the mid-century evangelical revivals – the Great Awakening in America and the Cambuslang Wark in Scotland – Erskine's correspondents included Puritan Congregationalists in Massachusetts as well as Presbyterians in New Jersey. Erskine put together the manuscript of Jonathan Edward's *History of Redemption* in 1774 and published it, while his colleague John Gillies wrote and published a memoir of the transatlantic evangelist George Whitefield.

These associations were institutionalised. The Popular party raised funds for Dartmouth, Princeton and Dickinson Colleges, supplied leaders for the last two institutions and joined American colleagues in that time-honoured academic pastime, the reciprocal awarding of honorary degrees.[10] Erskine seldom sent a letter to America unaccompanied by a parcel of books, and his gifts still repose in the Yale and Harvard libraries.[11] Scottish-American ties, then, were not simply personal or ideological but had organised, material reinforcement. The Society in Scotland for Propagating Christian Knowledge reinforced this institutionalised nexus by promoting missions among American natives and colonists. The Popular party, perhaps because it could not prevail against the Moderates' successful control of the kirk's general assembly, came to predominate in the Scottish S.P.C.K., enlisting laymen of rank and wealth and increasing its income significantly. Churchmen had originally founded the society to spread Protestantism in the remote parts of Scotland and in Roman Catholic or pagan regions. In this period Popular party leaders sought to reassert the society's original aim of evangelising against the teaching of practical subjects, which in the Enlightenment threatened to replace them.[12]

Although we may view Popular party men as sponsors or patrons of the colonial churches, support between them and Americans was reciprocal. In 1761 the American Ezra Stiles had proposed an evangelical alliance to include the New England churches, the Scots Popular party and the English dissenters. Throughout Protestantism in Great Britain, Ireland and America, those who, like Stiles, had joined in the mid-century revivals saw them as having a divine vitality that transcended mundane national boundaries. They took the geographic extent of the revivals, their apparent simultaneity and their immense fervour as a summons to cooperation and unity.[13] In 1743 Scottish Popular party clergy had set up prayer meetings for the revivals' success, and the Revd John Maclaurin of Glasgow subsequently proposed a Concert for United Extraordinary Prayer, a transatlantic society that Jonathan Edwards espoused enthusiastically.[14] This work was defensive as well as promotional, urged on by dismay over criticisms from the liberal-minded and the sceptical everywhere. Also on its agenda, stated or unstated as events dictated, was opposition to plans for an Anglican episcopate for America and defence against Romanism.[15]

Contention and bloodshed in the empire during George III's reign strengthened the evangelicals' sense of identity. John Erskine, befitting his position of intellectual, professional and social eminence, took an early and strong position in 1769 with his best-known pro-American appeal, presciently entitled *Shall I Go to War with My American Brethren?* Although he paused to criticise some American statements as rash and to assert his loyalty to George III, he attacked the Stamp Act and defended the colonists' right to tax themselves. Fear that war might disrupt Christian brotherhood throughout the empire motivated him principally, but he did not limit himself to religious issues. At this time Erskine, despite his criticism of George Grenville's government, was conservatively motivated, fearing American rebellion and concerned that 'brethren', to him a term of profound significance, might enter combat.[16]

Although D.B. Swinfen asserts in a study of the Scottish press at this time that sympathy in Scotland for America became quite muted in 1776 when colonial statesmen opted for independence, Popular party clergy continued to speak out vigorously. In that year John Erskine published one pamphlet in praise of Lord Chatham and conciliation and another in which he attacked the tea duties and the Boston Port Act and argued for better colonial political representation.[17] He also republished under his own name his pro-American tract of 1769, first printed anonymously.[18] Erskine did not give up hope for compromise in 1776, but by 1779, in his last published statement on the American War, he hinted that independence was inevitable.[19]

In 1778 and thereafter the crisis in Scotland over Lord North's Roman Catholic relief program, as we shall see, roused the Popular party mightily. John Warden M'Farlane of the Canongate Church, Edinburgh, a Popular party spokesman, argued that government should heed the party on the dangers of tolerating Catholics because it had been right about the 'disasters' of a colonial war. His colleague at Elgin, William Peterkin, took the same opportunity to belabour government's American policies and its electoral corruption in a tract also aimed at Roman Catholic relief.[20] Across the border two Presbyterian clergymen with strong Popular party ties, James Murray of Newcastle-upon-Tyne and James Fordyce of London, joined their Scottish colleagues in attacking British policy.[21] Moreover, in Scotland itself John Erskine published in 1779 an account of the debate in the kirk's general assembly on the Catholic relief issue in which he openly identified the Popular party as being in fundamental agreement on the American war.[22] Although it has been alleged that 'there was no such thing as a radical press in Scotland' at this time, the Popular party gained support for its attacks on government policies from the *Glasgow Mercury* and *Edinburgh Eight-Day Magazine*, which have not earned the label 'radical' because they supported a party often dismissed as reactionary.[23]

Support for the colonists was not limited to print. The Popular party always practised fervent, outspoken preaching, and its members took to it as a matter of course in urging conciliation towards the Americans. National fast days appointed by government to promote victory stymied some but by no means all pro-American clergy. Some ignored these occasions, merely read an official proclamation without comment or employed guest preachers less hostile to government than themselves.[24] Others used the occasion to preach conciliation and peace. David Grant, politically one of the few Popular party clergy who thoroughly merited a radical, subversive reputation, published such a fast day sermon in 1779, although most of his like-minded colleagues did not print their remarks.[25] One of these was Charles Nisbet, minister at Montrose. In one unpublished sermon he compared the governments of the British empire and the Babylonian empire to the disadvantage of the former, and in another he descanted so highly on the merits of the American cause as to lift the loyalist burgh councillors out of their pew and propel them up the aisle and out of the kirk. Montrose town councillors illustrate one attitude encountered by political preachers in this era; James Boswell illustrates another. Boswell, whose family supported the Popular party, absented himself from Hugh Blair's church in Edinburgh because that Moderate preacher supported government's prosecution of the war.[26]

The hierarchy of ecclesiastical courts through which the clergy, the laity and government sought to rule the kirk provided another arena for vocal protest. In May 1776, when the general assembly met and drafted its annual address to the Crown, an invariably grateful, laudatory formulation, Popular party delegates tried to insert into it a plea for conciliation and peace. As usual, however, the Moderate party dominated the assembly, using its numbers, prestige and government connexions to foil the Popular party men. By 1778, however, the prospect of British martial success had dimmed, and Popular party delegates, whom observers agreed enjoyed more success customarily in the kirk's lower courts, busied themselves in the Synod of Dumfries with a peace overture to the general assembly.[27] When the assembly met the following May, its members debated the overture strenuously and drafted an address to the crown in awkward contradictions bespeaking Popular-Moderate compromise.[28] Again in 1779 the assembly's Popular party delegates supported America in debate, but as in 1776 they failed to command a majority or effect a compromise.[29] Their opinions vindicated at Yorktown, however, Popular party representatives in the Synod of Galloway in 1782 passed an address congratulating the King on ending the war but also urging governmental reform.[30] Although they still could not gather enough support to insert these remarks into the annual address of the general assembly, they brought about 'a warm debate' and put the Moderate majority decidedly on the defensive, bringing partisan differences into sharp outline. As the Moderates' most recent historian remarks, 'the American crisis had forced to the surface the liberal and sometimes radical undercurrents in the ideology of the Popular party as well as the deep-seated conservatism of the Moderate literati.'[31]

Popular party actions demonstrate what historians have often observed: that for many vocal Scotsmen the kirk's representative courts passed as a native parliament. They also demonstrate that American support came not merely from scattered individuals who might mount a pulpit or write a letter to a newspaper but from men who could call on extensive connexions and who merited the designation, in eighteenth-century terms at least, of 'party'. Because they lacked the Moderates' political sophistication and powerful government patrons, they could but rarely sway the decisions of the church's governing bodies on American issues and could never do so in any dramatic way at the highest level. But they gave their opponents pause. The Moderates had to reckon with them as a sustained effort, and they also had to face apprehensions about the party's influence among the public at large. As a contemporary critic remarked of them: 'Everyone who is versant in the principles of human nature, or the history of mankind, must know what notable materials the rabble are in the hands of the clergy.'[32]

Thus far the Popular party's involvement with American affairs has appeared as a straightforward political activity, somewhat at variance with historians' common view of them as narrowly religious traditionalists but logically consistent with their ecclesiastical interests. This interpretation, however, can lead to misunderstanding. For the commitment of the Popular party to long-standing interests in transatlantic affairs was total, involving every fibre of being, conscious and unconscious, rational and irrational. Although historians who are heirs to the ideas of the American Revolution will sympathise with Scotsmen who defended those ideas, their support of the American cause was not solely rational and liberal-minded. Richard Sher correctly observes that the American crisis called forth the innate liberal or radical concerns moving deep within Calvinism and often overlooked by scholars, but the crisis also conjured up concerns that darker, illogical anxieties had produced.

The grounding of the Popular party's support for the colonists in potent, irrational anxieties helps to explain the emotional hue that coloured its advocacy. Friedhelm Voges has pointed to the sense of urgency that marked eighteenth-century Scottish evangelicals, a mood arising from their apprehensions about cultural changes menacing to the party and the church.[33] With these fears ran another anxiety, deeper and sharper yet, a sense that historical time itself was running out not only for the party but also for the Church of Christ itself. John Erskine at Edinburgh and John Gillies at Glasgow felt dark, preternatural forebodings when they searched events around them for significance. These feelings made it imperative to 'exert unlanguishing vigour as they struck at error' and told 'the unwelcome truth', lending a harshness to their views.[34]

The foreboding and alarm marking so many Popular party utterances helps to explain why pro-American views moved in an odd concatenation with other concerns that appear to have little or no logical relationship with support of the colonial cause. The party's complaint that America suffered unjustly was one in a litany of grievances strung together in a sometimes curious sequence. Members of the Popular party were threatened in the Enlightenment, when the Christian church was on the defensive all over Europe and throughout the transatlantic world. Clergymen everywhere were learning they no longer enjoyed an acknowledged right to attention and respect but had to win a following instead.[35] This lesson came home especially to clergy in the Scottish Popular party, who were the watchdogs of orthodoxy and envisioned the kirk as an institution set in judgement against the secular realm or above it.[36] In Scotland, furthermore, both ecclesiastical parties belonged to a provincial church perpetually condescended to by Anglicans, whose faith was established in the empire's principal kingdom. In this predicament each of the Scottish parties reacted differently. The Popular party rejected the Moderates' course of accommodation with urbane, latitudinarian Anglicanism and prided itself instead on representing beleaguered native Calvinism. In that position, however, it found itself attacked on one side by the Moderates for uncritical adherence to ancient Presbyterian dogma and practice, and on the other side by sectarians of the Presbyterian secessions for time-serving membership in an Erastian communion whose adherence to pristine Reformation models was insufficient.[37] More galling yet was the realisation that continued adherence to the established kirk had not brought the Popular party the power to influence its policies decisively, for while they may have represented majority sentiment in the national church and in its lower courts, in the general assembly they were outmanoeuvered at almost every turn by their more astute Moderate opponents. Frustration arising in these circumstances intensified the party's concerns and wiped out distinctions that its members in more secure or hopeful situations might have had the temperateness to make. Thus John Erskine, responding to a Moderate critic, associated the views of Popular party clergymen on America with their convictions about church government generally and with their hostility to Roman Catholicism, without sensing any incompatibility among these issues.[38] Erskine and his associates viewed the American political cause not as an isolated issue but as one strand in the variegated fabric of Popular party concerns. In this connexion, of course, they bore a decided resemblance to the American revolutionaries themselves.[39]

Like the colonial leaders, the foremost members of the Popular party believed that British imperial policy reflected a government conspiracy directed at much they held dear. American protesters in the years leading up to armed conflict complained with some justification that government planned to set up an Anglican episcopate in the colonies. They concluded that this would reduce Presbyterians and Congregationalists to the unenviable status of English dissenters. Popular party spokesmen took up this grievance because of their time-honoured antipathy to Episcopalianism. They sprang to it also because they saw themselves as the Presbyterians par excellence in Scotland, suspicious as they were of their Moderate rivals who were not as resolute about Episcopalianism.[40] As regards the unenviable English dissenters, the unwillingness of government to grant them more civil rights further grieved the Popular party. They rehearsed their grievances until they came to see them as proof of government's despotic intentions in religious affairs. As the American crisis developed, they looked for the threat of tyranny throughout the empire.[41]

Another Popular party apprehension was British government connivance with Roman Catholicism. Pamphlet literature after the peace of 1763 reveals that the Scottish Popular party was persistently on the alert about Rome, as indeed it had been during the Jacobite crisis of 1745. Evangelically-minded Scots brooded about the alleged spread of Catholicism in the Highlands, an occurrence for which little or no evidence exists. The Roman Catholics made up a very small minority, probably dwindling somewhat in these decades. Rome's few adherents were in almost every case impoverished members of the lower classes. None of them, moreover, had any political power whatsoever.[42] Nonetheless, evangelical Protestants feared them deeply, searching events everywhere for signs of their influence. When Britain acquired Grenada in 1763, government's concessions to Catholics there awoke complaints that surfaced again in the American war.[43] Worse yet was the Quebec Act of 1774, under which Lord North's government confirmed some of the Canadian Catholics' civil and ecclesiastical privileges. Scottish newspapers followed the act's passage carefully, as well as efforts by the Whig opposition to repeal it in 1775. As war broke out in the colonies, Scottish friends of America brought up the Quebec Act again as an example of a deliberate ministerial policy of ruin and despotism in America. With the exaggeration that typifies prejudice, they claimed that government's dealings with Catholics in Canada amounted to 'establishing' popery there.[44]

The threat of Roman Catholicism came home to the Popular party with a vengeance in the North ministry's plan for Catholic relief in England, Scotland and Ireland. From practical considerations, tinged with a trace of Enlightenment toleration, government decided in 1778 to grant Catholic clergy and landowners in the three kingdoms some paltry civil liberties. With the support of the parliamentary opposition, they passed an English relief act in May, followed shortly afterwards by an Irish act. They also announced that a like measure would follow for Scotland. This announcement chanced to coincide with the annual May meeting of the kirk's general assembly, where Popular party delegates, as we have seen, were already restive about the plight of their American friends. They immediately denounced Roman Catholic relief. The objections were the latest venture in voicing concerns that reached back to the Quebec Act, the Peace of Paris and the Forty-Five.[45] John Erskine had objected to British policy in the colonies as early as 1763, partly on the grounds that government rejection of American demands might drive the colonists into alliance with the popish despotisms of France and Spain. He added the same anti-Catholic arguments to his pro-American publications in 1776 and 1779, and by the latter date his fears about France and Spain had become more justified. He also attacked Roman Catholic relief head-on in the general assembly and in a new pamphlet aimed at rousing opposition to that project.[46] In the general assembly of 1778 Moderate delegates succeeded in preventing any formal protest against Catholic relief, as they had on questions relating to America. Their Popular party opponents once again took to pulpit and press, and the next nine months witnessed growing protest. A stream of tracts, sermons and Protestant catechisms issued from the clergy, and a wave of petitions and resolutions against the extension of relief to Scottish Catholics arrived in London from alarmed kirk sessions, presbyteries, burgh councils, heads of families and trade incorporations.[47] The outcry took on the characteristics of a full-fledged popular protest movement, which for several years enlisted large numbers of supporters throughout society and led the more active of them to commandeer some of the lower church courts and also to establish ad hoc Protestant defence societies.[48] Although inaugurated by Popular party ministers and fostered by them, the protest spread beyond their control and led to anti-Catholic riots at Glasgow in October 1778 and again at Edinburgh and Glasgow the following February. These actions forced government to abandon Scottish relief, a capitulation that represented an unparalleled Popular party victory with far-reaching results.[49]

The Popular party clergy who stirred up the furore maintained that their objections to relief were purely political. Their claim fitted well with their criticisms of government's political policy towards America, criticisms in which they did not distinguish between civil and ecclesiastical issues, as we have seen. They saw themselves as representatives of the time-honoured old Whig tradition, setting their faces against absolutism in church or state. Both John Erskine and William Porteous of Glasgow's Wynd Church claimed that their sole concern was subversive Catholic menaces to the security of society and the constitution. Erskine said he could countenance civil rights for Arians and deists, whom he saw as posing no political threat, and Porteous for his part claimed he could put up with Hindus and Muslims who, even assuming the British Isles might harbour them, had political aims that were to him unexceptionable.[50] Although their assertions may strike us as self-serving and delusive, those who made them were demonstrating their readiness to enter the arena of political debate and their awareness that in the cultural environs of the late eighteenth century they had better present issues whenever possible as affecting secular concerns and not merely religious ones. In this respect the spokesmen for the Presbyterian seceding denominations presented a contrast to the Popular party within the kirk, for they attacked Roman Catholic doctrine and ritual head-on, insisting heresy had no rights.

Popular party spokesmen also justified their position as a political one by making public their discovery that government had sponsored relief as part of a complicated scheme to encourage Catholic priests and landowners to enlist their parishioners and tenants in the British armed forces. Government did not discuss this scheme openly when parliament debated the relief legislation, nor did it ever publicly disclose it. There is no evidence that the Opposition in parliament, who criticised war policy but supported Catholic relief, knew about its military purpose until the Scottish outcry. Scottish protesters, however, learned that toleration alone did not initially prompt Catholic relief as government claimed. The discovery added rage to horror. They knew that recruitment of Catholics for the army, though often winked at, was illegal and would remain illegal in the future, despite government's 1778 plans. They surmised that Catholic soldiers would be used in America against the Popular party's 'coreligionists'. They also concluded that North's government had tacitly admitted that its plan was nefarious by concealing its true aims. Thus fear of a conspiracy on behalf of absolutist repression took on the appearance of accurately perceived reality. The military motive behind Catholic relief, it seemed, exonerated its Protestant foes from the charge of bigotry grounded only in enmity towards a rival communion.[51] It also provided fuel for their overall campaign to defend the Protestantism they favoured at home and in the colonies. Although historians have disagreed about the full extent of Scottish sympathy for the colonists, there is no doubt that disillusionment with the war, criticism of imperial policy and sympathy for America grew in 1778 and thereafter.[52] The hardening of Popular party suspicion of government over Roman Catholic relief helps to explain this restiveness. The Quebec Act, the war in America and Catholic relief were parts of a dangerous programme 'by which the British empire is . . . visibly embarrassed in a manner perhaps without parallel in the history of Britain'.[53]

II

Antagonism towards Roman Catholics and towards government colonial policy was complex. Opposition to government efforts in America did not profit directly from the anti-relief movement. Rather, the conflict created by debate over those issues engendered suspicion of any government move. The Popular party clergy always suspected government. Their suspicions mounted during the war and erupted over Catholic relief. Some might argue that 'No Popery' hysteria deflected the Popular party from the American cause. Certainly the volume of anti-relief protest outbalanced by far the volume of anti-war criticism, but contemporaries did not separate these issues. Although many publications against popery ignored the American problem, it came up irrepressibly in others. One anonymous pamphleteer remarked that whereas government had rebuffed American petitions for redress of grievances before the war, it had welcomed wartime Catholic petitions for relief.[54] The Popular party's opponents, furthermore, saw its anti-Catholicism and pro-Americanism as elements in the same ideology. They attacked the party spokesmen, even when they limited their comments to Roman Catholic relief, for sounding like 'correspondents from Massachusetts Bay' and said they were 'fitter for a rebellious Congress than for a Scottish Synod'.[55] This reputation continued after the defeat of relief and the American victory. A critic writing in 1788 described the Popular party as 'bigoted in their religious principles; men who are ever inclined to advance the republican part of the constitution, and who are always endeavouring, by acts suitable to the end, to insinuate themselves with the rabble'.[56] The anti-relief campaigners, in fact, substantiated their critics' opinions not only by raising a 'No Popery' mob but also by setting up American-style 'committees of correspondence' to resist relief. They also referred privately to one of the Glasgow anti-Catholic societies as a 'congress'.[57]

The pro-American/anti-Catholic amalgam figured most spectacularly in the Popular party's sometime patron, the flamboyant Lord George Gordon, brother of the fourth duke of Gordon and a member of parliament. Although Lord George gained notoriety in 1780 because of the devastating anti-Catholic riots in London that bear his name, his support of the colonists antedated his protests against Catholic relief.[58] The link between army recruiting for the American War and Catholic relief initially brought the Scottish 'No Popery' campaign to his attention. His first speech in the House of Commons on Catholicism occurred in a debate on compensating Scottish Catholics injured in the anti-relief riots, a debate in which Lord Frederick Campbell accused government of attempting to raise a 'regiment of papists'. Gordon claimed that Catholic relief violated the Act of Union, which affirmed the Presbyterian establishment. He added the revolutionary assertion that government could alter the Union only with 'joint consent of the provincial synods and the people at large in their elective and corporate capacities'.[59] David Grant, the radical pro-American Popular party minister, initiated correspondence between the party and Gordon to enlist his help on both America and Catholic relief, an overture that wiser Popular party leaders later came to regret. Lord George eagerly added attacks on relief to his criticisms of government policies at home and abroad, remarking in a characteristic speech against the supine pro-government Scots M.P.s that Lord North 'wanted to make pimps and paupers of the members, convert the Speaker into an old Bawd, and perhaps, for all he knew to introduce the Whore of Babylon'.[60] Once he took up 'No Popery' his lordship made the most of it, even adopting what he fancied was the garb of a 'strict Presbyterian'. He made a grand tour of Scotland at the behest of the Popular party clergy and the anti-Catholic societies, whipped up the Scots to demand repeal of the English Catholic Relief Act and enlisted them in the London street demonstrations that led to the Gordon riots.[61] 'No

Popery' and support of America went together for Lord George, who accused the king of 'making War against the Presbyterians of America' and voiced hope that 'the 16 [sic] Provincial Synods of the North might be as happy and as prosperous, under the divine guidance, as the 13 stars of the Western World'.[62]

Anti-Catholicism and pro-Americanism also went together for Gordon's Scottish followers. The 'Eighty-five Private Societies in and about Glasgow', an ad hoc association of trade incorporations that opposed Catholic relief, published in their 'No Popery' *Transactions* some of Gordon's parliamentary speeches that dealt not with religion but with despotism and the colonial war. They did not distinguish between his opposition to relief and his pro-American, anti-monarchical positions. Speeches he made on issues not directly involving religion were also quoted in the general assembly of 1779.[63]

Lord George Gordon's private papers and public utterances reveal him as a republican. As his amanuensis observed, 'though he abhorred the detestable usurpation of Cromwell, he admired the means by which he deposed the despotic Stuarts. . . . He was well-versed in the history of the Protectorship; his language, his manners, and customs were strongly tainted with the characteristics of that age. He always talked respectfully of the Commonwealth, regretted the Restoration, and seemed to have our republican ancestors constantly in his view.'[64] When the king's officers arrested Lord George in 1780 after the London riots, they discovered that he had proposed to Scottish correspondents 'something like the establishment of a Congress; or Political Presbytery'. David Grant and Gordon had corresponded on what they called 'the important Proposition', a proposition that Grant saw as restoring 'the days of Homer'.[65] The means by which Gordon hoped to do this was armed rebellion. In a House of Commons speech on 1 December 1778 he alluded to rumours 'that the people are about to choose a Congress or proclaim a Protector', and a year later he told the Commons that he had '150,000 men ready to execute vengeance on the present ministers and bring about a reformation'.[66] Although a Scottish correspondent had urged Gordon to obtain government approval for command of a 'Protestant Reg't of Fencibles', Grant told him that most Scots would not support the plan.[67] When the authorities arrested Gordon in London after the riots, they also arrested and examined Grant at Edinburgh and Charles Nisbet at Montrose.[68]

Although Scotsmen would not bring Lord George Gordon's hopes to life, the experiences of the Popular party clergy during the American conflict did lead to further reform activity. The prospect of colonial victory and their own success against Scottish Catholic relief emboldened them. In 1780 and for some years thereafter they mounted a more vigorous campaign against lay patronage in the kirk. By 1785 this, too, had become a full-fledged movement similar to the anti-relief movement, with a committee of correspondence, tracts, sermons and petitions from kirk sessions and even from a burgh or two.[69] Just as anti-American and anti-Catholic feeling had bolstered each other, so reinvigorated antipatronage sentiment promoted criticism of civil corruption. Popular party delegates in the general assembly of 1782 sponsored an outspoken if unsuccessful overture congratulating the king on his new ministry, urging immediate peace negotiations and recommending reform of court and parliament. One of their number, the Revd William Dun of Kirkintilloch, who advocated 'returning to first principles' in government, was arrested, tried and imprisoned for three months in 1783 for his activities.[70]

The events of the years from the Peace of Paris of 1763 to the Peace of Paris of 1783 show that the history of the Popular party of the Church of Scotland cannot be separated from the history of America. The sympathies of the Popular party clergy and some of their lay followers for the colonists, and even more their fears for them, illuminate much that went on in the politics of church and state in Scotland. But the attitude these men adopted was an odd, sometimes unsettling complex of forward-looking progressivism and reactionary traditionalism. Scottish opinion at large was always divided in these years, on America and on all other major issues. This division, together with the Popular party's fundamental traditionalism, explains why the causes it adopted, with the single exception of that involving America, did not succeed. Lay patronage continued as before despite the party's vigorous, sustained protest; civil government remained unreformed; and Scottish Roman Catholics received in 1793 the privileges withheld from them in 1778. Even on the score of American rights, Popular party ideas and actions, as we have seen, were accompanied by destructive religious prejudice and encouragement of the most deplorable mob violence. Nonetheless, when scholars examine the historical circumstances behind British capitulation to American demands for independence, they must recognise the Popular party's persistent criticism of imperial policy as significant among the warnings and discouragements leading to the nation's failure of nerve in colonial affairs.

NOTES

Research for this essay was supported by financial grants from the American Philosophical Society, the John Carter Brown Library of Americana and the Kansas State University Bureau of General Research.

1. Because the party could not muster a majority in the general assembly, historians have often assumed it was the minority party.

Ian D.L. Clark, 'From Protest to Reaction: The Moderate Regime in the Church of Scotland, 1752–1805', in *Scotland in the Age of Improvement: Essays in Scottish History in the Eighteenth Century*, ed. N.T. Phillipson and Rosalind Mitchison (Edinburgh, 1970), 213–14, 222, corrected this misconception, which contemporaries did not maintain. See George Campbell, *Lectures on Ecclesiastical History,* 2 vols. (London, 1800), l:xl–xli, and Thomas Somerville, *My Own Life and Times, 1741–1814* (Edinburgh, 1861), 78–80.

2. On popular party theology see Friedhelm Voges, 'Moderate and Evangelical Thinking in the Later Eighteenth Century: Differences and Shared Attitudes', *Records of the Scottish Church History Society* 32, pt. 2 (1985): 141–57.
3. The Popular party sought to preserve or restore 'the balance of classes and interests' so much prized by radical whig theorists according to Caroline Robbins, *The Eighteenth-Century Commonwealthman* (Cambridge, Mass., 1959), 15–16. For the party's position see Henry Moncrieff Wellwood, *Account of the Life and Writings of John Erskine. D.D.* (Edinburgh, 1818), 430ff. See also Richard Sher and Alexander Murdoch, 'Patronage and Party in the Church of Scotland, 1750–1800', in *Church, Politics and Society: Scotland 1408–1929*, ed. Norman Macdougall (Edinburgh, 1983), 205–11.
4. The Popular party sought to reform lay patronage, not to abolish it. See John Erskine, 'The Qualifications Necessary for Teachers of Christianity: Preached before the Synod of Glasgow and Ayr at Glasgow, October 2, 1750', *Discourses Preached on Several Occasions* (Edinburgh, 1798), 38–39.
5. William Ferguson, *Scotland: 1689 to the Present* (Edinburgh, 1968), 228.
6. Sher, 262–76.
7. Clark, 'From Protest to Reaction', 203, 215–16, 218–21.
8. John Erskine, *Theological Dissertations* (London, 1765), 272–76, urges frequent holy communion as practised on the Continent. His *Sketches and Hints of Church History, and Theological Controversy*, 2 vols. (Edinburgh, 1790–97) is a collection of excerpts from the works of contemporary Continental Protestant theologians and Eastern Orthodox divines.
9. Wellwood, *Erskine*, 160–61, 196, 199–201, 204–5; Samuel Miller, *Memoir of the Rev. Charles Nisbet, D.D.* (New York, 1840), 25–27.
10. Henry Reay Sefton, 'Scottish and New England Churchmen in the Eighteenth Century' (S.T.M. diss., Union Theological Seminary, 1957), 22n., 27.
11. Miller, *Nisbet*, 194–95.
12. Robert Kent Donovan, *No Popery and Radicalism: Opposition to Roman Catholic Relief in Scotland, 1778–1782* (New York, 1987) 158–62, 268–69.
13. Stiles, later president of Yale, was minister at Newport, Rhode Island, at this time. For his common front see Donovan, *No Popery and Radicalism*, 271. For Scottish accounts of these traits of the revivals, see Alexander Webster, *Divine Influence the True Spring of the Extraordinary Work at Cambuslang* (Edinburgh, 1742), esp. 6, 59; John Erskine *The Signs of the Times Consider'd: or, the High Probability, that the Present Appearances in New-England, and the West of Scotland, are a Prelude of the Glorious Things Promised to the Church in the Latter Ages*

(Edinburgh, 1742), esp. 14–17; and John Maclaurin, *Sermons and Essays*, ed. John Gillies (Glasgow, 1755), iv.

14. 'Editor's Introduction', and *An Humble Attempt to Promote Explicit Agreement and Visible Union of God's People in Extraordinary Prayer*, in *The Works of Jonathan Edwards*, ed. Stephen J. Stein, 5 vols. (New Haven, Conn., 1977), 5:36–40, 308–436, passim.
15. On anti-Romanism, see 'Editor's Introduction', in *Works of Edwards*, ed. Stein, 5:46. For anti-episcopal criticisms, see Carl Bridenbaugh, *Mitre and Sceptre: Transatlantic Faiths, Ideas, Personalities, and Politics, 1689–1775* (New York, 1962), 14–15, and Bernard Bailyn, *The Ideological Origins of the American Revolution* (Cambridge, Mass., 1967), 95–98. For contemporary Scottish criticism see John Erskine, *Shall I Go to War with My American Brethren?* (London, 1769), 17, 33.
16. D.B. Swinfen, 'The American Revolution in the Scottish Press', in *SEAR*, 67–68; Erskine, *Shall I Go to War*, 1–3, 9–14, 22–23, 30–33.
17. John Erskine, *The Equity and Wisdom of Administration, in Measures That Have Unhappily Occasioned the American Revolt, Tried by the Sacred Oracles* (Edinburgh, 1776), esp. 12; John Erskine, *Reflections on the Rise, Progress, and Probable Consequences of the Present Contentions with the Colonies* (Edinburgh, 1776), esp. 13, 29–38.
18. Wellwood, *Erskine*, 272–73.
19. John Erskine, *Prayer for Those in Civil and Military Offices Recommended . . . A Sermon Preached before the Election of the Magistrates of Edinburgh, Oct. 5, 1779* (Edinburgh, 1779), 24–25.
20. *SM* 40 (1778): 679; William Peterkin, *A Dialogue on Public Worship, between Mr. Alamode, a Young Gentlemen of Fortune; and Mr. Freeman, an Aged Country Gentleman*, 2nd ed. (Aberdeen, 1780), 34n., 37–38.
21. See James Murray, *An Impartial History of the Present War in America*, 2 vols. (London, 1778), and James Fordyce, *The Delusive and Persecuting Spirit of Popery: A Sermon, Preached in Monkwell Street, on the 10th of February last, Being a Day Appointed for a General Fast* (London, 1779), viii.
22. John Erskine, *A Narrative of the Debate in the General Assembly of the Church of Scotland, May 25, 1779; Occasioned by Apprehensions of an Intended Repeal of the Penal Statutes against Papists* (Edinburgh, 1780), iii–iv.
23. Swinfen, 'American Revolution', 67. See Donovan, *No Popery and Radicalism*, 72, 73, 239. Both publications criticised North's American policies, especially after the debacle at Saratoga, and supported the Popular party assault on Roman Catholic relief.
24. Dalphy I. Fagerstrom, 'Scottish Opinion and the American Revolution', *WMQ*, 266–67.
25. David Grant, *The Manners of the Times and Their Consequences . . . A Sermon Preached in the Tolbooth* (Edinburgh, 1779); Fagerstrom, 'Scottish Opinion', 266.
26. Fagerstrom, 'Scottish Opinion', 262–63, 266; Miller, *Nisbet*, 74–77.
27. Sher, 269–70; *Caledonian Mercury*, 16 Feb., 25 Apr., 25 May 1778; *SM* 40 (1778): 110, 220, 275.
28. *SM* 40 (1778): 267. The address described the Revolution as 'unprovoked rebellion' and its perpetrators as 'deluded men' but at the same time applauded the monarch's 'lenity' in holding out

conciliation and expressed the hope that hostilities would 'speedily terminate in a peace'.

29. See the speeches of John Thompson of Sanquhar and Colin Campbell of Renfrew in Erskine, *Narrative*, 4–8, 18–21.
30. Fagerstrom, 'Scottish Opinion', 268.
31. Sher, 275–76.
32. Hugo Arnot, *The History of Edinburgh from the Earliest Accounts to the Present Time* (Edinburgh, 1788), 288.
33. Voges, 'Moderate and Evangelical Thinking', 141, 145–46.
34. Erskine, 'Qualifications Necessary for Teachers', 5–7. See also John Gillies, *An Exhortation to the Inhabitants of the South Parish of Glasgow, Wednesday, September 26th 1750* (Glasgow, 1750), esp. 42, for an impressive illustration.
35. Voges, 'Moderate and Evangelical Thinking', 141, 145–46.
36. Clark, 'From Protest to Reaction', 206–7.
37. The sects that left the eighteenth-century church did so largely because they rejected lay patronage completely. They attacked the Popular party even in the mid-century revivals, from which all evangelicals profited. See Erskine, *Signs of the Times*, 21–23.
38. Erskine, *Narrative*, iii–iv.
39. Bailyn, *Ideological Origins*, 98, 119, 206–7n.
40. Bridenbaugh, *Mitre and Sceptre*, 211, 220, 222, 231–34, 257–58, 288; Erskine, *Shall I Go to War*, 25, 33–34; Archibald Stevenson, *The Small Success of the Gospel in Purifying the Hearts and Minds of Men Accounted for . . . A Sermon, Preached before the Society in Scotland for Propagating Christian Knowledge* (Edinburgh, 1772), 42; *Protestant Packet*, 24 Nov. 1780.
41. Erskine, *Narrative*, 10, 41; Peterkin, *Dialogue*, 48; *Scotland's Opposition to the Popish Bill: A Collection of All the Declarations and Resolutions . . . against a Proposed Repeal of the Statutes . . . for Preventing the Growth of Popery* (Edinburgh, 1780), iv, 8. In 1772 and 1773 Parliament rejected bills for the relief of English dissenting clergymen.
42. Donovan, *No Popery and Radicalism*, 166–70, 176–79. See Sher, 281. Although certainly correct in his view that some intellectual and social leaders had abandoned anti-Catholicism, Sher is too sanguine about progress at large. Prejudice against Catholics was endemic in the Protestant population throughout the English-speaking world.
43. *Glasgow Mercury*, 28 Jan. 1779, supplement; Bridenbaugh, *Mitre and Sceptre*, 333.
44. *SM* 36 (1774): 299, 302, 304, 306–9; *Edinburgh Advertiser*, 27–31 May through 24–28 June 1774, and 23–26 May 1775; *Edinburgh Magazine and Review* (July 1775); 386–87. See also Erskine, *Reflections*, 38–41.
45. *Ruddiman's Weekly Mercury*, 22 Apr. 1778; *An Address to the Protestant Interest in Scotland . . . Wherein is Clearly Demonstrated, the . . . Danger of Repealing our Penal Laws against Popery* (Glasgow and Paisley, 1779), 12; *Scotland's Opposition to the Popish Bill*, iii; Erskine, *Shall I Go to War*, 5–6, 34–35.
46. Erskine, *Equity and Wisdom*, 14; Erskine, *Prayer*, 26–29. Erskine's *Narrative* concentrated on relief. Swinfen, 'American Revolution', 69, argues that American alliances with France and Spain increased Scottish hostility towards the colonists. This was emphatically not

so for Erskine, for whom the alliances amplified distrust of North's government.

47. Robert Kent Donovan, 'Voices of Distrust: The Expression of Anti-Catholic Feeling in Scotland, 1778–1781', *Innes Review* 30 (1979): 62–76. The petitions and resolves were collected and reprinted in *Scotland's Opposition to the Popish Bill.*
48. Donovan, *No Popery and Radicalism*, 52–68, 255–57, 264–65.
49. Ibid., 23–24, 302–11; Sher, 294–97.
50. Erskine, *Narrative*, v–viii; William Porteous, *The Doctrine of Toleration Applied to the Present Times: In a Sermon, Preached . . . 10th December 1778: Being a Public Fast* (Glasgow, 1778), 9–10, 15.
51. Robert Kent Donovan, 'The Military Origins of the Roman Catholic Relief Programme of 1778', *Historical Journal* 28 (1985): 79–102, and 'Sir John Dalrymple and the Origins of Roman Catholic Relief', *Recusant History* 17 (1984): 188–96.
52. Although Swinfen disagrees with Fagerstrom on this question generally, even he agrees that discouragement about the war and disenchantment with government increased after Saratoga. Swinfen, 'American Revolution', 68, 69; Fagerstrom, 'Scottish Opinion', 255.
53. *Address to the Protestant Interest*, 6.
54. Ibid., 42.
55. *Caledonian Mercury*, 26 Oct. 1778.
56. Arnot, *History of Edinburgh*, 262.
57. George Hay, *A Memorial to the Public in Behalf of the Catholics of Edinburgh and Glasgow*, 2nd ed. (London, 1779); *Scotland's Opposition to the Popish Bill*, v–vii, 235–37; *Caledonian Mercury*, 8 Feb. 1779; *Transactions of the Eighty-five Societies in and about Glasgow, United in a General Correspondence . . . to Oppose a Repeal of the Penal Statutes against Papists* (Glasgow, 1779), 4. Most Church of Scotland clergy do not appear to have joined ad hoc anti-relief societies, although David Grant was a member of the Edinburgh Committee of Correspondence and William Porteous joined the Glasgow Committee.
58. Robert Watson, *The Life of Lord George Gordon, with a Philosophical Review of His Political Conduct* (London, 1795), 3; Donovan, *No Popery and Radicalism*, 278–79.
59. *The Parliamentary History of England* 20 (1779): 622–23; Donovan, *No Popery and Radicalism*, 146.
60. *Parliamentary History* 21 (1780): 337.
61. *The History of the Right Honourable Lord George Gordon . . . His Speeches in Parliament; and His . . . Letters to the Eighty-five Societies in Glasgow* (Edinburgh, 1780), 13.
62. The remarks are from his House of Commons speech, 2 June 1779, in *Transactions of the Eighty-five Societies*, 23. There were only fifteen synods. Gordon's error marks him as a novice in Scottish religious debate.
63. Ibid., 20–23, for anti-government speeches in which Gordon made no mention of Catholicism or relief.
64. Watson, *Lord George Gordon*, 76.
65. Treasury Solicitor's Report on the MSS of Lord George Gordon, Public Record Office 1526, TS 11–1212: Bag I, p. f. 'B2' nos. 33, 49, 60.

66. *Transactions of the Eighty-five Societies*, 20–22; *Edinburgh Advertiser*, 26–30 Nov., 30 Nov.–3 Dec. 1779. The sources give the figure of men variously as 120,000 or 150,000.
67. [Patrick Bowie] to Gordon, 3 July 1779, Public Record Office 1526, TS 11–1212: Bag I, p. f. 'B2', no. 34; David Grant to Gordon, 1 June 1779, ibid., no. 49.
68. *Protestant Packet*, 27 Oct. 1780; *Newcastle Courant*, 29 July 1780.
69. *Edinburgh Advertiser*, 14–18, 21–25 Jan.; 9–11, 22–25 Mar.; 29 Mar.–1 Apr.; 3–6, 24–27 May 1785; Miller, *Nisbet*, 82.
70. Miller, *Nisbet*, 195; *Edinburgh Advertiser*, 21–24, 24–28 May 1782. See also Adam Whyte, *Political Preaching, or the Meditations of a Well-Meaning Man . . . in a Letter . . . to the Rev. Mr. William Dun* (Glasgow, 1792).

5

THOMAS P. MILLER

Witherspoon, Blair and the Rhetoric of Civic Humanism

In the first half of the eighteenth century, the Scottish college curriculum was broadened beyond 'a decadent scholasticism' to include the study of British life and letters.[1] Francis Hutcheson and George Turnbull brought the politics and ethics of public life into the classroom, and later moral philosophers such as Adam Smith, Adam Ferguson and Thomas Reid helped to give the Scottish Enlightenment its characteristic concern for the social sources and implications of intellectual enquiry. As part of this reorientation, early eighteenth-century professors of logic like John Stevenson turned from the syllogistic reasonings of scholasticism to the inductive enquiries of Locke. The next generation of reformers, including Stevenson's students John Witherspoon and Hugh Blair, went on to establish the study of the contemporary idiom as a regular part of the curriculum in Scotland and America. These developments were closely related. Locke provided a method of enquiry for investigating individual experience; moral philosophy applied this method to the ethics and political economy of contemporary life; and rhetoricians like Blair and Witherspoon taught students how to speak to public audiences. In addition to being important public leaders, Blair and Witherspoon were the first significant professors of rhetoric and belles lettres in Scotland and America, and a comparative study of their rhetorical theory and practice offers useful insights into how the new educational philosophy was put into social practice in Scotland and America.

In response to Lockean empiricism, eighteenth-century British rhetoricians developed a new conception of the classical art of persuasion. According to Wilbur Samuel Howell, the 'new' rhetoric broadened its focus beyond persuasion to include all scientific and literary discourse; it adopted the inductive modes of enquiry of the new science; and it replaced the elaborate formal theories of classical rhetoric with an emphasis on the plain style.[2] The majority of the major British rhetoricians were in fact Scotsmen, including Adam Smith, George Campbell, Hugh Blair and

John Witherspoon. The most influential of them was Hugh Blair, Regius professor of rhetoric and belles lettres at Edinburgh from 1762 to 1784. His *Lectures on Rhetoric and Belles Lettres* was studied by 'half the educated English-speaking world in its day', and it remained the standard text in American colleges until the middle of the nineteenth century.[3] Blair was the first influential professor of English, and his belletristic approach laid the groundwork for the establishment of modern literary studies in America.[4] Witherspoon, who emigrated in 1768 to become president of the College of New Jersey at Princeton, is regarded as the first important rhetorical theorist in America. He also helped to introduce common sense moral philosophy, which exercised a dominant influence on American education until the Civil War. Unlike Blair, who aligned the new rhetoric with the study of English literature, Witherspoon maintained the close classical ties between rhetoric and moral philosophy. Witherspoon himself taught both subjects, and when his lectures were published posthumously in 'the first complete American rhetoric' in 1810, the work included his lectures on moral philosophy along with those on rhetoric.[5]

The difference between the approaches of Blair and Witherspoon has broad historical significance because the introduction of English studies was a central part of a major transition in higher education. In England classical languages were the core of higher education into the nineteenth century because the established universities educated upper-class gentry whose cultural traditions and social roles were relatively stable, but Scottish students and professors came from a middle class faced with basic challenges to traditional values and assumptions.[6] The traditional scholastic education depended on a clearly defined set of shared assumptions from which to deduce conclusions, and without them it came to be seen as mere logomachy, mere quarrelling about words that generated no new knowledge because it reasoned from less certain universal premises to more certain particular experiences.[7] In late eighteenth-century America, too, a new educational philosophy concerned with the logic and language of public life began to emerge at less established institutions like the colleges of New Jersey (Princeton) and of Philadelphia, where Scottish moral philosophy and rhetoric were first introduced.[8] On both sides of the Atlantic, middle-class provincials seeking to master the taste and idiom of the dominant culture were quite receptive to the new emphasis on rhetoric and belles lettres, and the nature of rhetoric itself made it responsive to such changing public needs. Rhetoric is both a practical art and an intellectual discipline, and this dual character has historically made it more sensitive to social change than purely academic disciplines.

Despite such contemporary influences, eighteenth-century rhetoric still owed much to the classical sources that first established it at the core of humanities. In their studies at Edinburgh, Blair and Witherspoon read

Aristotle and Cicero as well as Locke, and the common sense philosophy that Witherspoon brought to America had basic continuities with classical moral philosophy.[9] Such continuities are not surprising given the pervasive influence of classical thought in the eighteenth century; nonetheless, the fact that Aristotle and Cicero were the classical sources of major traditions in both rhetoric and moral philosophy is no accident. Rhetoric is today related to politics and ethics only in a pejorative sense, but for Aristotle and Cicero the good man speaking well was a political and ethical ideal as well as the abiding goal of rhetorical study. These civic humanists based their social philosophy on the ideal of the virtuous citizen with the practical wisdom and ethical awareness to say the right thing at the right time in order to serve the common interest, and they emphasised a broad liberal arts education centred on the study of rhetoric and moral philosophy to prepare such citizens for public life. Classical civic humanism is a useful place to begin a discussion of the first influential professors of English rhetoric in Scotland and America because the Scots' educational reforms represented a new civic philosophy that reinterpreted some of the basic assumptions of civic humanism to respond to changing social conditions. These reforms led to the foundation of new traditions in rhetoric and moral philosophy because the Scots were interested in both understanding and speaking to contemporary public life.

The influence of classical concepts of civic virtue and political economy on eighteenth-century political and ethical theory has recently attracted scholarly attention, but the significance of rhetoric within the social philosophy of classical civic humanism has been largely ignored.[10] Classical rhetoricians like Aristotle developed a civic humanism that emphasised *phronesis*, practical wisdom or prudence, as an alternative both to the speculative philosophy of Plato, which they considered inapplicable to the uncertainties of public life, and to the sophists' political *techne*, which lacked a strong moral component. Aristotle distinguishes practical wisdom from theoretical and technical knowledge to argue that political practice is guided by knowledge in context, knowledge that cannot be understood in abstract terms, nor merely methodically applied, but must be gained from political involvement with the means and ends of human action.[11] According to Aristotle's *Politics*, human nature is itself fundamentally political, but education is necessary to form a mere plurality into a community.[12] Aristotle's *Rhetoric*, which developed out of his own teaching at the Lyceum, treats rhetoric as the art of reasoned discourse, an art that is basic to the origins of civilised communities and essential to the public citizen. Other Greek civic rhetoricians like Isocrates reasoned from the same assumptions to establish a liberal arts tradition centred on rhetoric in order to educate public orators capable of speaking for the shared practical wisdom of the political community.[13]

Even today rhetoricians are widely influenced by Aristotle's rhetorical theory and by the broad educational and political philosophy that first made rhetoric a humanistic discipline, but it is Cicero who has historically personified the practical ideal of the complete orator. Cicero was concerned with maintaining the republic in practice as well as theory; and in *De Oratore* (3.19) he criticised Plato for separating the study of political arts like rhetoric from philosophy, because wisdom without the ability to make it persuasive has little impact on public life. For Cicero, as for Aristotle and Isocrates, the ability to speak for the public interest and place it before the private interest is exemplified by the ideal of the complete orator, the good man speaking well on issues of public importance, and Cicero adopted Polybius's theory of the mixed constitution to provide the forums for such debate. Cicero himself personified this ideal for well over a thousand years. However, the historical image of Cicero has two faces, the public political orator and the master stylist of polite literature, and various periods have emphasised the role that best suited their particular social context. When public political debate declined with the disintegration of the classical political world, Cicero was studied more as a man of letters and less as a practising political orator. He thus became a practical moralist without a practical political voice. By the eighteenth century Ciceronianism had become enshrouded in a stylistic rhetoric that gave more emphasis to the elaborate style of a dead language than to public political life, but Cicero's moral philosophy nonetheless influenced such seminal figures as Hutcheson and Hume.[14]

Blair and Witherspoon would also have been quite familiar with classical rhetoric and moral philosophy from their studies at Edinburgh University. John Pringle was lecturing specifically on Cicero's moral philosophy in 1741, when Blair and Witherspoon were studying divinity at Edinburgh.[15] There is also considerable evidence that they studied the civic rhetoric of Aristotle, Cicero and Quintilian in John Stevenson's logic class. Both Blair and Witherspoon matriculated under Stevenson, who was professor of logic and metaphysics at Edinburgh from 1730 to 1777; and their biographers have stated that he was the major source for their rhetorical theories.[16] Like Hutcheson at Glasgow, Stevenson made two crucial educational reforms. He ended the complete dominance of classical languages by lecturing largely in English; and he was one of the first professors in Scotland to make Locke a central part of the study of logic.[17] According to Alexander Carlyle, who was a classmate with Blair and Witherspoon, Stevenson lectured on contemporary English and French criticism, Locke's *Essay concerning Understanding*, Aristotle's *Poetics*, Longinus's *On the Sublime* and other classical texts. Other contemporary accounts refer to Stevenson's discussions of the rhetorical theory of Cicero and Quintilian.[18] Stevenson applied these classical sources to composition in the contemporary idiom, for he started the custom of having students compose essays in English as well as Latin.[19] About half of the essays that remain from Stevenson's class are in English, and their belletristic orientation suggests that Stevenson gave considerable emphasis to such topics as taste.

Stevenson's students were evidently quite anxious to improve their mastery of English composition and taste in order to overcome the limitations of their provincial dialect. As one of Stevenson's students wrote, 'the History of our own Country' shows that one must master the 'art of making himself agreeable by the charms of a well regulated conversation', which is 'the most natural and certain method of rising in the world and making one's fortune.' Along with this desire for polite improvement came an aversion to heated controversy as divisive and impolite: 'We should further be carefull how far we enter into disputes, especially upon delicate subjects where our religious, or even political principles may too far interest our positions in the argument.'[20] Other student essays also suggest that Stevenson emphasised taste and the polite style of the man of letters who stands aloof from heated public controversies. Many of these students would show this same concern for polite, disinterested sensibility when they left Stevenson's class and continued to work to eradicate their Scots dialect in literary clubs like the Select Society and Aberdeen Philosophical Society, where political and religious debate was specifically proscribed. In those societies, as in Stevenson's class, the models for study were Dryden, Pope and Addison – the belletristic models that Blair would later establish as standards of taste.

Blair and Witherspoon showed their interest in the Ciceronian strain of Stevenson's teaching in the Latin M.A. theses they wrote in 1739. Blair's thesis argues that the natural law that is the source of goodness can be discovered without revelation. Such 'Ciceronian academics' would become 'the very touchstone of "Moderate" preaching'.[21] Witherspoon's thesis also shows the Ciceronian sources for some of his later positions, particularly the common sense philosophy of his *Lectures on Moral Philosophy*. The thesis, which includes more references to Cicero than to any other source, opens with the Stoic dictum that before we can understand the world we must first 'know ourselves'. Witherspoon refers several times to 'natural ideas' that are 'general among all races and almost all men'. Such references suggest a broad continuity between the Stoics' concept of natural reason and Scottish moral philosophers' concern for common sense. Witherspoon makes six final points, including the ideas that matter, space and time are philosophical certainties and that 'men are by nature free'.[22] By basing his belief in the existence of the world on common sense, Witherspoon foreshadows the response that Scottish moral philosophers would take to Hume. His inclusion of natural rights as similarly self-evident is significant because it shows his early familiarity with the traditional view that natural rights are an integral part of the larger natural order. Witherspoon's attention to some of the basic concepts shared by classical and Scottish moral philosophy and his interest in the political implications of these concepts foreshadow some of the fundamental concerns of his later works.

Soon after graduation Blair and Witherspoon were drawn into sharp opposition. Blair was a Moderate, and Witherspoon a traditional Calvinist opponent of the spread of polite secular culture in Scotland. In *Ecclesiastical Characteristics* (1753) Witherspoon attacked both the political practices of the Moderates and the 'good-of-the-whole' philosophy of Shaftesbury and Hutcheson because he viewed the Moderates' politics as 'a transcript in miniature' of Shaftesbury and Hutcheson's aestheticism (*WJW*, 3:210). For Witherspoon, this line of thought defined human nature as 'a little glorious piece of clockwork, a wheel within a wheel', and described politics and morality with terms like 'beauty, order, proportion, harmony' (*WJW*, 3:233, 215). Such premises led the Moderates to conclude that 'an illustrious and noble end sanctifies the means of attaining it' and to suppress dissenting views because 'the principles of moderation being so very evident to reason, it is a demonstration, that none but unreasonable men can resist their influence' (*WJW*, 3:241, 251). From the beginning of his public career, then, Witherspoon rejected the aesthetic conception of political and moral issues because he thought it led politely educated people to assume that their critical acumen gave them superior moral and political authority.

Despite their public differences, the rhetorical theories of Witherspoon and Blair drew on the basic assumptions of classical civic rhetoric, particularly the classical ideal of the complete orator of public virtue and practical wisdom. Both agreed that the unrivalled accomplishments of classical rhetoric could be attributed to the fact that classical democracy provided political forums where the orator could speak for the public interest. What distinguishes the approach of Blair and Witherspoon is their different understanding of the contemporary significance of classical civic humanism. In his *Lectures on Rhetoric and Belles Lettres* (1783) and his *Critical Dissertation on the Poems of Ossian* (1763), Blair reasoned that society had changed since the heated political oratory and unrefined primitive genius of the ancients, and what was now needed was good taste and polite style. In both works he compares the advance of social history to the progression of 'age in man', which moves from the fervent imaginings of youth to the cool, dispassionate reasonings of adulthood.[23] According to this comparison, in the more mature stages of society the scope of the imagination, and the heated persuasive oratory that inflames it, are far more limited. To 'cultivate' the polite sensibility, he devotes most of his lectures not to political rhetoric but to a stylistic analysis of belletristic essays.

Though Blair's *Lectures on Rhetoric and Belles Lettres* does address contemporary public forums (the bar, the pulpit and 'popular assemblies'), his comments on 'popular' politics show how his rhetorical theory was limited by his own practical political experience. According to Blair, persuasive eloquence is no longer so 'powerful an instrument' as it has been in classical politics, not only because a 'correct turn of thinking' puts one on 'guard against the flowers of Elocution' but also because 'ministerial influence has generally prevailed in political assemblies' like parliament (Blair, 2:41–43). Such comments are striking when one considers that Blair's own time was a golden age of political oratory, but Blair recognised from his own career as a courtier of patronage that political issues were often decided not by public debate but by private deals. As one Scottish member of parliament put it, looking back on a long political career, 'I have heard many arguments which convinced my judgment, but never one which influenced my vote.'[24] In any case, Blair refers not to Burke or Pitt but to classical models, and he devotes only one lecture to political discourse while spending four on the *Spectator* and twelve on other belletristic genres.

Blair's *Lectures on Rhetoric and Belles Lettres* gives most emphasis to polite style and the psychology of the aesthetic response. When he treats the process of composing discourses, his concern for the genius of the creative imagination leads him to reject the classical attention to the creation of discourse and to focus instead on editing and the critique of style. His emphasis on the sublimity of the aesthetic experience supports his defence of the morality of literary studies, and his theory of primitive genius shapes his general understanding of the social implications of language. This theory also involved him in the Ossian controversy. In fact, it is unclear whether his theory was developed to explain *Fingal*, or *Fingal* written to document his theory. The manuscripts of Blair's *Lectures* show that he was developing his concept of primitive genius when he met Macpherson, whom he guided through the process of 'translating' *Fingal*. Blair was one of the earliest and best known defenders of the Ossianic poems, and he originally intended to publish the *Critical Dissertation* in his *Lectures*.[25] Ironically, Scotland's first English professor ended up enshrining a fake epic as a model of Scotland's sublime past while ignoring the living poetic traditions of the time.

In order to suit his audience, Blair subordinates rhetoric in its classical sense of political discourse to the study of polite literature. He defines his audience as not just those who intend to write and speak for the public but also those far more numerous readers who 'without any prospect of this kind, may wish only to improve their taste with respect to writing and discourse, and to acquire principles which will enable them to judge for themselves in that part of literature called the Belles Lettres.' For this latter audience, 'rhetoric is not so much a practical art as a speculative science; and the same instruction which assists others in composing will assist them in discerning and relishing the beauties of composition' (Blair, 1:8). Blair thus recognises that many of his readers are private, not public citizens, and he redefines the civic humanists' concern for rhetoric as a political art in terms that suit a private reading audience. This shift from the composition of public political discourse to the psychology of the private literary response reflects the expansion of the contemporary middle-class reading public. That expansion is clearly evident in the success of Blair's edition of Shakespeare (1753), his anthology of *British Poets* (1773), his *Sermons* (1777–1800) and his *Lectures on Rhetoric and Belles Lettres* (1783).

In his *Lectures on Eloquence* Witherspoon also discusses taste and style, but he gives them considerably less emphasis because he does not accept the basic idea that political rhetoric had become less important than it had been in classical society. Witherspoon's lectures are more concerned with the composition than the reception of discourse, and he gives particular emphasis to political oratory because 'oratory has its chief power in promiscuous assemblies, and there it reigned of old, and reigns still, by its visible effect' (*WJW*, 3:511). To support his argument that public oratory is politically powerful, Witherspoon does not shy away from citing such controversial figures as William Pitt and George Whitefield, the most important public evangelist of the Great Awakening, whom Witherspoon praises as a model of 'a power of elocution, and natural talents for public speaking, superior by far to any . . . on earth' (*WJW*, 3:575). While Blair would have been repelled by the idea of using an evangelist as a model, Witherspoon's praise for the oratory of controversial political and religious leaders of the day is significant because it gives a practical political base to his idealisation of rhetoric and democracy. Though both Blair and Witherspoon identified rhetoric with the idealised history of classical democracy, only Witherspoon applied rhetoric to contemporary political debate.

Witherspoon's discussions of taste and style are also more concerned with practical applications than with abstract speculations about the aesthetics of sublimity, primitive genius and the poetic imagination. Witherspoon states that the orator who speaks in the pulpit, at the bar and in political assemblies must have a liberal education and good taste, but he does not discuss taste in any systematic way until his final lecture. There he advises his students that too much attention to taste is 'not only undesirable, but contemptible' because 'when a person applies his attention so much to a matter of no great moment, it occasions a necessary neglect of other things of much greater value' (*WJW*, 3:592). The continuity between his Calvinist aversion to frivolous refinements and his practical ideal of the public citizen is evident throughout the *Lectures*: 'Persons of the middle degrees of capacity, do also, perhaps generally, fill the most useful and important stations in human life. A very great genius, is often like a very fine flower, to be wondered at, but of little service either for food or medicine' (*WJW*, 3:482). Witherspoon also de-emphasises taste and genius because they are unsuited to his social ideal, which is not the polite man of letters but the practical public citizen, who fills 'the most useful and important stations in human life'.

The specific differences between Blair and Witherspoon are less significant than the basic fact that Blair identified the study of rhetoric with the criticism of belletristic discourse, whereas Witherspoon reasserted the classical connexion between rhetoric and moral philosophy. At Princeton he delivered his lectures on eloquence along with his lectures on moral philosophy to both third- and fourth-year students, and he established a rigorous programme of public speaking and composition exercises that frequently addressed contemporary political issues. In his *Lectures on Moral Philosophy* Witherspoon refers his students to the sources that connect classical civic humanism with eighteenth-century political theory and practice: Aristotle, Cicero, Grotius, Pufendorf, Machiavelli, Harrington, Sydney and Montesquieu as well as Kames, Ferguson and especially Hutcheson. Witherspoon argues that the social contract bestows inalienable rights on the individual: 'From this view of society as a voluntary compact, results this principle, that men are originally and by nature equal, and consequently free.' He further argues that a mixed form of government best ensures the protection of these natural rights (*WJW*, 3:511, 437). Witherspoon draws heavily on Hutcheson's discussions of natural rights, the social contract and the right to rebel against unjust governments, but he rejects Hutcheson's aesthetic model of social polity and the basic idea that a moral sense is integral to an aesthetic sensibility. He accepts Hutcheson's discussion of the opposition of personal and public interests in terms of 'selfish or benevolent, public or private' affections (*WJW*, 3:375), but he does not accept these as an adequate basis for civic ethics and stresses instead feelings of moral obligation arising from conscience. While he thus accepted many of Hutcheson's basic political concepts, Witherspoon retained the ambivalence towards Hutcheson's moral sense philosophy that was evident in the *Ecclesiastical Characteristics*.

Witherspoon's *Lectures on Moral Philosophy* is also important because it helped to introduce Scottish common sense philosophy to America. Against Hume's assault 'upon cause and effect, upon personal identity, and the idea of power', Witherspoon supports 'some late writers' of Scotland who argue for 'the dictates of common sense, which are either simple perceptions, or seen with intuitive evidence. These are the foundation of all reasoning, and without them, to reason is a word without meaning' (*WJW*, 3:395). As the whole tenor of Scottish common sense philosophy makes clear, such sceptical reasonings would be 'without meaning' because they would have no reference to the shared understandings that shape public life. This communitarian aspect of common sense philosophy is evident in Reid's statement that 'in things that are within the reach of every man's understanding, and upon which the whole conduct of human life turns, the philosopher must follow the multitude.'[26] This concern for the shared understandings of public life was as basic to the tradition of civic humanism as it was to Scottish common sense philosophy.

Witherspoon follows in the civic humanist tradition that had defined rhetoric and moral philosophy as comprising the political arts essential to the public citizen. Accordingly, for Witherspoon moral philosophy's 'importance is manifest from this circumstance, that it not only points out personal duty; but is related to the whole business of active life. The languages, and even mathematical and natural knowledge, are but handmaids to this superior science' (*WJW*, 3:470).[27] In his *Lectures on Eloquence* Witherspoon shows that his social philosophy was based on the rhetorical ideal of the good man speaking well on issues of public importance. Witherspoon in fact educated some of the figures whose speeches and writings would shape American public life, including James Madison, who stayed on after graduation to pursue his studies with Witherspoon. In his *Federalist* essays Madison not only drew on the political and rhetorical theories he encountered in Witherspoon's teaching but also put them into practice by helping to build an American political consensus based on the idea of balancing competing interests to protect the shared interest. The *Federalist* presents a major practical example of the potential of eighteenth-century civic rhetoric. The *Federalist* is also a strong counterpoint to Blair's idealisation of the *Spectator* as a belletristic model for the polite man of letters. Nonetheless, the rhetorical theories of both Blair and Witherspoon had important political implications, as can be seen by examining their rhetorical practice as public leaders.

Blair's *Sermons* exemplify the ideal polite man of letters that he praised in his *Lectures on Rhetoric and Belles Lettres*. Blair preached a practical morality that suited an educated public tired of the dark orthodoxies of traditional Calvinism. In sermons like 'On Sensibility' and 'On Moderation', Blair praises the polite refinement that characterised the Moderate literati. When one considers the emphasis that Blair had given to the impassioned imagination in his discussions of poetic genius, his sermonising on the coolly moderate sensibility initially seems odd: 'there is no passion in human nature but what has, of itself, a tendency to run into excess. For all passion implies a violent emotion of mind', and 'moments of passion are always moments of delusion'.[28] However, what such comments make clear is that poetic passion was acceptable, but a passion for social and religious causes was not. Such sermons highlight the political role that the polite man of letters played, for while Blair was subtly advising his students to avoid the controversies of contemporary politics, he was himself manouevring behind the scenes to secure the ruling political powers' support for the Moderate cause. His correspondence contains many letters to influential gentry on behalf of his own advancement and that of other Moderate clergy. A letter to Lord Glasgow asking to be relieved of the duty of composing 'my Lord's speeches for him' provides a particularly apt example of how the Moderates spoke for the status quo.[29]

One need not rely on such private correspondence to see how the disinterested sensibility of the Moderate literati served the ruling political interest because the political message of sermons like 'On the Love of Our Country' is quite straightforward. On the national fast day appointed by the government in 1793, Blair praised the war with France and condemned public flirtations with republican values: 'Is it not much to be lamented that there should have sprung up among us an unaccountable spirit of discontent and disaffection, feeding itself with ideal grievances and visionary projects of reformation, til it has gone nigh to light up the torch of sedition?'[30] These sermons helped shape Scottish public opinion according to John Hill, a young Moderate of the time:

> Many, who could not judge correctly upon political subjects, were ready to be directed by him, whose sentiments upon religious topics they believed so unerring. He declared from his pulpit, that no man could be a good Christian that was a bad subject. The opinions of those French philosophers, who wished to destroy subordination, and to loosen the restraints of law, he rejected with abhorrence. . . . Sentiments like these from the mouth of such a man, and spoken at such a time, could not fail to be productive of the happiest effects on the public mind.[31]

In the pulpit and the classroom Blair spoke for the cultural ideology of the polite man of letters. This philosophy defined the study of polite culture as the means to improve the individual and promote political stability, while simultaneously justifying the cultural authority of the politely educated as the spokesmen for the public interest.[32]

In his own public career, Witherspoon opposed the literati's belief that they had the right to speak for the common interest. He criticised the Moderates' social philosophy and practice in *Ecclesiastical Characteristics* and in the pamphlet that he wrote with several other orthodox opponents of the Moderates in 1752, 'Answers to the Reasons of Dissent'. Witherspoon resisted the Moderates' efforts to silence congregations resisting the settlement of clergy chosen by the ruling political faction and local gentry. He asserts that individuals have both 'a right' and 'an indespensable duty' to follow their conscience because it speaks from God, a higher power than any civil authority. On this assumption he rests the '*self-evident* maxim' that 'no man is to be constructed an open transgressor of the laws of Christ, *merely* for not obeying the commands of any Assembly of fallible men'. According to Witherspoon, the Moderates' efforts to assume absolute authority and thus 'destroy *liberty of conscience*' are politically unacceptable because the Glorious Revolution had placed limits on the power of even the highest civil authorities.[33] This line of reasoning shows that Witherspoon understood the continuity between the commonwealthman tradition and his own faith in the primacy of the individual's relationship to God. In his defence of dissent he argues that the Moderates' philosophical systems and polite refinement do not make them any less fallible than anyone else, and that all societies must therefore recognise the inalienable right to act on conscience.

In his criticisms of the Moderates' politics in *Ecclesiastical Characteristics*, Witherspoon returns again and again to the irony that the Moderates attacked orthodoxy for spreading factionalism in the church at the same time that they were establishing themselves as the ruling faction. Witherspoon also devotes considerable attention to the Moderates' attempt to gain the support of the upper classes, touching on it in four of the twelve maxims of *Ecclesiastical Characteristics*. Witherspoon could not understand how a church could serve God if it alienated the public because he viewed the church as a social force for public piety, not polite refinement. According to his satirical critique in *Ecclesiastical Characteristics*, Moderate Christianity would be perfected only when it became a patrician religion, 'when we shall have driven away the whole common people to the Seceders, who alone are fit for them, and captivated the hearts of the gentry to a love of our solitary temples' (*WJW*, 3:259). This gentrification of the church would be accomplished by securing the patronage of the upper classes and by preaching the comforting message of polite refinement.

Differences between the general perspectives of Blair and Witherspoon become even clearer when one considers the latter's public career in America after he emigrated in 1768. The political orientation of his *Lectures on Eloquence* reflects the political views that first developed out of his conflicts with the Moderates, and were reinforced by his experience as the most politically involved religious and educational leader in Revolutionary America. Witherspoon's developing commitment to the American cause is evident in early writings like the 'Letter Sent to Scotland for the *Scots Magazine*' (1771), where he defends himself against charges that his support for Scottish emigration was unpatriotic (*WJW*, 4:281–89). He argues that the public interest is the national interest, and he implicitly rejects the mercantilist belief that a nation is made prosperous by keeping the public poor, and hence industrious. In his later writings Witherspoon moved steadily towards thinking of America's public interest as distinct from Britain's, and he soon became an active supporter of independence, first in a local correspondence society, then as head of the most radical delegation to the New Jersey Assembly that deposed the royal governor, and finally as a vocal advocate for the Declaration of Independence in the Continental Congress.

The contrast between Blair's public role as a preacher of polite values and Witherspoon's political career shows how the different social contexts of 'North Britain' and Revolutionary America shaped the reinterpretation of the civic humanist ideal of the good man speaking well on issues of public importance. While the Scots developed a new civic humanism centred on the study of the logic and language of public life, their practical political sensitivities were limited by their own marginal political status. These limitations are exemplified by the ideal of the polite disinterested sensibility, which reflects the Moderate literati's dislocation from their own public culture. When Blair and the other literati praised the impartial observer who sits back and criticises the aesthetic harmony of the political economy, they showed their own inability to become fully engaged with the political conflicts of public life. Although they occasionally spoke out when they believed they were being denied their rights as North Britons, the literati largely negotiated social power by preaching the cultural values that strengthened their social status rather than by becoming directly involved in public politics. In America, where the compelling social question was not how to adapt to being North Britons but how to create a national consciousness, civic rhetoric was put to more broad-based political purposes, and it directly contributed to the establishment of a national political consensus. In response to their differing social contexts, Blair and Witherspoon drew on two different strains of civic humanism: Blair stood for the traditional ideal of the polite man of letters, Witherspoon for the ideal of the civic orator. As a result, Blair developed a civic humanism that defined the educated individual primarily by his membership in the republic of letters, whereas Witherspoon and his students helped to create the American republic.

NOTES

1. Roger L. Emerson, 'Scottish Universities in the Eighteenth Century, 1690–1800', *SVEC* 167 (1977): 466.
2. Wilbur Samuel Howell, *Eighteenth-Century British Logic and Rhetoric* (Princeton, 1971), 441–47.
3. Robert Morrell Schmitz, *Hugh Blair* (New York, 1948), 3; see also Andrew Hook, *Scotland and America: A Study of Cultural Relations, 1750–1835* (Glasgow, 1975), 79–81.
4. Blair was preceded by John Lawson, professor in oratory and history at Trinity College, Dublin, from 1753 to 1758, but Lawson's lectures were all but ignored when published in 1758 according to 'Introduction', *Lectures Concerning Oratory*, ed. E. Neal Claussen and Karl R.

Wallace (Carbondale and Edwardsville, Ill., 1972). For Blair's influence on the modern college English studies in America, see James A. Berlin, *Writing Instruction in Nineteenth-Century American Colleges* (Carbondale and Edwardsville, Ill., 1984).

5. Warren Guthrie, 'Rhetorical Theory in Colonial America', in *History of Speech Education in America: Background Studies*, ed. Karl R. Wallace (New York, 1954), 56; see also Howell, *Logic and Rhetoric*, 671–91.
6. A comparative picture of the social backgrounds of Scottish and English college students is provided in Nicholas A. Hans, *New Trends in Education in the Eighteenth Century* (London, 1951). A good example of the middle class response to the traditional curriculum is William Thom's criticism of the Glasgow curriculum in *The Defects of an University Education, and Its Unsuitableness to a Commercial People* (London, 1762).
7. A typical criticism of scholastic reasoning is included in George Campbell, *The Philosophy of Rhetoric*, ed. Lloyd F. Bitzer (Carbondale and Edwardsville, Ill., 1988), 61–70.
8. The best study of Scottish influence on the colonial colleges is Sloan. An account of Witherspoon's impact on American education is included in the introduction to *Selected Writings of John Witherspoon*, ed. Thomas P. Miller (Carbondale and Edwardsville, Ill., 1990). The teaching of Francis Alison, a Scottish-educated professor at the College of Philadelphia, is discussed in David Fate Norton, 'Francis Hutcheson in America', *SVEC* 154 (1976): 1547–68.
9. Nicholas Phillipson has discussed the Ciceronian sources of eighteenth-century Scottish moral philosophy in 'The Pursuit of Virtue in Scottish University Education: Dugald Stewart and Scottish Moral Philosophy in the Enlightenment', in *Universities, Society, and the Future*, ed. Nicholas Phillipson (Edinburgh, 1983), 82–101.
10. J.G.A. Pocock traces the influence of classical civic humanism on the political theory of the Renaissance and the commonwealthman tradition in *The Machiavellian Moment: Florentine Political Thought and the Atlantic Republican Tradition* (Princeton, 1975) and *Politics, Language, and Time: Essays on Political Thought and History* (New York, 1971). John Dwyer argues that civic humanism, Stoicism and sensibility were the three principal sources of Scottish moral discourse in *Virtuous Discourse: Sensibility and Community in Late Eighteenth-Century Scotland* (Edinburgh, 1987).
11. The significance of this distinction is discussed in Hans-Georg Gadamer, *Truth and Method*, ed. Garrett Barden and John Cumming (New York, 1975), and Alasdair MacIntyre, *After Virtue: A Study in Moral Theory* (Notre Dame, Ind., 1981).
12. Aristotle, *Politics*, trans. H. Rackham, Loeb Classical Library (Cambridge, Mass., 1950), 12636.36.
13. Henry I. Marrou, *A History of Education in Antiquity* (London, 1956).
14. The influence of Cicero is discussed in Peter Jones, *Hume's Sentiments: Their Ciceronian and French Context* (Edinburgh, 1982) and William Robert Scott, *Francis Hutcheson: His Life, Teaching and Position in the History of Philosophy* (1900; rpt. New York, 1966).
15. The manuscript of John Pringle's 'Lectures from Cicero' (1741, EUL MS Gen. 74D) documents the strong continuities between Cicero and

Scottish moral sense philosophy. Pringle moves easily from explicating Cicero to developing one of the basic themes of Scottish moral philosophy: social virtue is based in a moral sense that gives us pleasure when we respond with approbation to disinterested 'benevolence' in others.

16. Varnum Lansing Collins, *President Witherspoon*, 2 vols. (Princeton, 1925), 1:14; Schmitz, *Hugh Blair*, 11.
17. Alexander Bower, *The History of the University of Edinburgh*, 3 vols. (Edinburgh, 1817–30), 2:279.
18. Alexander Carlyle, *The Autobiography of Dr. Alexander Carlyle of Inveresk, 1722–1805*, ed. John Hill Burton, new ed. (London and Edinburgh, 1910), 47–48; [Robert Henderson], 'A Short Account of the University of Edinburgh', *SM* 3 (Aug. 1741): 373.
19. Bower, *University of Edinburgh*, 2:280.
20. George Drummond, 'Rules of Conversation', in 'Book of Essays Written by Students in the Class of John Stevenson', 16–5–1740, EUL MS Dc.4.54: 101, 107.
21. Schmitz, *Hugh Blair*, 15.
22. Witherspoon's thesis is translated in George Eugene Rich, 'John Witherspoon: His Scottish Intellectual Background' (Ph.D. diss., Syracuse University, 1964), 158, 166, 168.
23. Hugh Blair, *A Critical Dissertation on the Poems of Ossian, the Son of Fingal*, 2nd ed. (London, 1765), 3; Blair, 1:124.
24. Quoted in Thomas Johnston, *A History of the Working Classes in Scotland* (Glasgow, 1920), 215.
25. Hugh Blair to Thomas Caddell, 20 June 1782, NLS MS 3408:1.
26. *WTR*, 1:521. For a discussion of the democratic implications of Reid's common sense philosophy, see Shannon Stimson, chap. 11 below.
27. The worst typographical error in the American editions of Witherspoon's *Works* is the replacement of 'hard words' for 'handmaids'. 'Handmaids' appears in the manuscripts of the lectures, including Princeton University Library MS AM12800:299, and 'hard words' makes these important lines nonsensical.
28. Hugh Blair, *Sermons*, 5 vols. (Edinburgh, 1819), 3:233–34.
29. Hugh Blair to Lord Glasgow, 12 May 1768, NLS MS 3464:24.
30. Blair, *Sermons*, 5:110.
31. John Hill, *An Account of the Life and Writings of Hugh Blair* (Edinburgh, 1807), 191–92.
32. As Jeffrey Smitten shows in chap. 9 below, the strategies of deferment and compromise that characterise the disinterested rhetoric of Moderates like Robertson and Blair could not really come to terms with the rhetorical situation posed by the Revolutionary period. For a reading of Blair's rhetoric and its political implications that is rather different from mine, see the essay by David Daiches, chap. 12 below.
33. 'Answers to the Reasons of Dissent', in *Annals of the General Assembly of the Church of Scotland, 1739–1766*, ed. Nathaniel Morren, 2 vols. (Edinburgh, 1838–40), 1:244.

6

PETER J. DIAMOND

Witherspoon, William Smith and the Scottish Philosophy in Revolutionary America

I

According to Ashbel Green, John Witherspoon's biographer and former student, Witherspoon discovered shortly after his arrival at Princeton in 1768 that 'the Berklean system of Metaphysics was in repute in the college'. He 'first reasoned against the System, and then ridiculed it' along the lines independently followed by Thomas Reid and other common sense opponents of the ideal system, thus driving scepticism from the College of New Jersey. Witherspoon stated in Green's presence that 'before Reid and Beatty, or any other author of their views, had published any thing on the ideal system, he wrote against it, and suggested the same train of thought which they adopted, and that he published his essay in a Scotch Magazine.'[1] On the basis of Green's account, Witherspoon is now commonly thought to have rid the college of its sceptical tendencies and to have introduced Scottish common sense philosophy to America, if only 'inspirationally' by 'paraphrasing, simplifying, systematizing, [and] editing [Reid's work] philosophically and theologically'.[2] He thereby helped introduce a set of philosophical principles appealing 'to a post-Revolutionary society much more interested in preserving and conserving social and religious stability than in pursuing further radical change in new directions.'[3]

This is not an erroneous view, but the monocausal explanation that connects the appearance of common sense philosophy in the New World with Witherspoon's arrival is simplistic for two reasons. First, it neglects those modes of Scottish thought available to colonial élites at mid-century that derived from the ethical writings of Francis Hutcheson, George Turnbull and David Fordyce. The writings of these 'moral sense' philosophers (antedating by a generation the common sense philosophy of Reid and his followers) met the ideological needs of a provincial society concerned with engendering among its citizens a practical morality that would enable them to cultivate those virtues deemed useful, as Hutcheson put it, 'for every honourable office in life, and quench that manly and laudable thirst . . . after knowledge.'[4] To be sure, the moral sense philosophy of Hutcheson and his followers exercised a profound influence on the writings of Reid and others concerned with the psychological underpinning of a casuistical science of man. Both perspectives relied on the existence of a natural moral faculty that purportedly supplied immediate knowledge of right and wrong. Both placed immense confidence in the moral judgements of ordinary persons, provided they did not allow their moral faculty to become corrupted (in Hutcheson's words) by 'the present Confusion of human Affairs'. It was this Hutchesonian universe of discourse, devoted to the academic pursuit of moral and civic virtue, that informed the educational thought of William Smith, the Aberdonian provost of the College of Philadelphia, and, a decade later, guided Witherspoon's efforts to shape the Princeton curriculum. The Reidian common sense philosophy, dominating the curricula of America's colleges by the turn of the nineteenth century, emerged from within the same philosophical and rhetorical milieu. Only by attending to these continuities can we fully appreciate American moralists' reliance upon the Scottish philosophy in the decade prior to Witherspoon's arrival.

Second, attempts to delineate common sense thought as a product of Scotland's 'counterenlightenment', as an essentially antisceptical, conservative philosophy adopted by New Side Presbyterians, neglect the extent to which common sense was understood, in the words of Samuel Stanhope Smith, as a 'science of moral philosophy [capable of providing] such general *principles* as may enable a rational and reflecting mind to deduce the point of duty for itself, on every case as it arises in practice.'[5] Smith fully shared Reid's optimism that an experimental science of human nature, proceeding according to the inductive method, would inform men accurately and with confidence of the nature and limits of their intellectual powers and so equip them for the task of moral improvement. Unfortunately, the broad agreement among moral sense and common sense philosophers over the nature and nurturing of the moral faculty has prompted scholars to conflate the two perspectives,[6] and so to neglect the rationalism of common sense philosophy. For Hutcheson's account of the moral sense was regarded by many, the common sense philosophers among them, as having failed to provide an adequate account of that faculty's ability to perceive the truth of moral propositions. When at the end of the eighteenth century Reid's common sense philosophy did take root in the curricula of the nation's universities, it offered a more rationalist and a more progressive view of the human mind's active principles than had been revealed by Hutcheson's philosophy. Efforts to depict common sense thought as a manifestation of a conservative counterenlightenment suffer from the whiggish practice of associating 'enlightenment' merely with philosophical scepticism. But 'improvement', to use a contemporary term, was often understood by both sceptics and their opponents to depend upon establishing a science of human nature. Religious conservatism was not incompatible with this agenda, nor should it be treated as a decisive consideration in depicting the age. John Witherspoon, for example, had little difficulty shifting from the anti-Moderate sarcasm of his *Ecclesiastical Characteristics* to regarding religion in terms congenial to Moderatism as 'the great polisher of the common people' (*WJW*, 4:146).

Thus we are apt to remain unclear about the role played by Scottish philosophy in the intellectual life of Revolutionary America as long as we fail to distinguish among modes of contemporary Scottish thought. It is this problem of definition I wish to address. For many, the philosophical movement associated with Reid is virtually synonymous with 'the Scottish Philosophy'. But this is at best an unhelpful conflation of terms. 'The Scottish Philosophy' came into currency in 1875 with James McCosh's book by that name, which was designed to express McCosh's commitment to 'the *common sense* principles of the Scottish School of Philosophy', principles constituting 'a body of fundamental truth, which can never be shaken, but which shall stand as a bulwark in philosophy, morals, and theology, as long as time endures.'[7] From McCosh's perspective, though Reid 'was not the founder, he is the fit representative of the Scottish philosophy', having 'enunciated in a plain manner an immense body of important truth which' – despite his 'defect of critical analysis' – 'can be shown to have the sanction of intuitive reason' (192, 220). This is not a sophisticated reading of Reid's philosophy, but it does express a prevalent view of common sense thought as a reactionary philosophy designed to refute the scepticism produced by Hume's theory of ideas and to assert the indubitable nature of common sense principles in its place.

This view of Reid's thought is also whiggish, the result of interpreting the work of Reid in the light of those who transformed his ideas to suit their own, largely conservative, purposes. For example, James Oswald wrote *An Appeal to Common Sense in Behalf of Religion* (1766–72) to combat the growing tendency among Presbyterian clergy to cultivate a polite preaching style. Indeed, Oswald's willingness to evoke the language of common sense to denounce 'the corruption of manners peculiar to this age' and to support religious truths[8] must be understood in the context of his opposition to the Moderates within the Church of Scotland. For Oswald, 'common sense' was a deliberately ambiguous term referring to nothing more specific than the beauty and simplicity of the gospel message.[9] Similarly, James Beattie's very popular *Essay on the Nature and Immutability of Truth* (1770) was designed to destroy the moral scepticism of Edinburgh society and win for its author the fame he had long craved.[10] To read Beattie (or Oswald) is to wonder why philosophical scepticism posed a threat to moral and religious values, for he believed that the mind perceives truth instantaneously, instinctively and irresistibly, and does not need the aid of 'progressive argumentation'.[11] Reid, who was prepared to take Hume's scepticism more seriously than either Oswald or Beattie, recognised that our belief in first principles does not necessarily constitute an ultimate philosophical warrant.

It would be historically imprudent to impose definitional criteria on common sense philosophy that would disentitle the writings of all those who failed to match Reid's philosophical acuity or who failed to manifest his range of interests. Clearly, the felicitous ambiguity of the language of common sense, which its adherents sought to exploit for a variety of reasons, militates against holding the writings of Reid's followers to a rigorous definitional standard. Nevertheless, we can discern the lineaments of Scottish moral discourse available to colonial American writers, not specific to Reid's common sense philosophy but associated generally with Hutchesonian moral sense philosophy and broadly identified in terms of the following interrelated aims and commitments. First, Scottish philosophy provided a polite rhetoric of 'sense' as a means of supporting claims deemed necessary to a moral casuistry. The concept of 'sense' was often not given a stipulative definition, but then Scottish educators in mid-eighteenth-century America were less philosophers than moral casuists. Second, Scottish philosophy was frequently cast as pneumatology (to use the Scottish term); those who adopted its language believed that the problems of practical morality were most effectively addressed by enquiring into the nature of the human mind. Third, Scottish philosophy insisted upon the inductive method of reasoning as the only proper approach for discovering the principles of human nature.

We can identify the robust account of common sense thought found in Reid's philosophy by noting that it was propounded in opposition to the theory of ideas (the view that impressions and ideas are the only objects of thought) which, as Reid put it, 'hath produced a system of scepticism that seems to triumph over all science, and even over the dictates of common sense' (*WTR*, 1:98). Reid's common sense may also be distinguished by its heightened devotion to the inductive method of reasoning. This commitment was less a substantive move than a rhetorical ploy. At the same time that he vilified the use of hypotheses with some regularity and regarded analogical reasoning as apt to mislead philosophers from the careful observation of the mind's operations, he allowed that hypotheses and analogies have a limited role to play in philosophy. For Reid, as for many eighteenth-century figures sometimes labelled 'Newtonians' (such as Hume), pledges of allegiance to Bacon or Newton primarily signified a commitment to establishing first principles – in this case respecting the human mind – and secondarily referred to more or less specific methodological claims. Drawing attention to the methods associated with Bacon and Newton and to the scientific success (expressed in terms of mathematical *principia*) attributed to those methods provided sociological reassurance to those, such as Reid, committed to propounding common sense *principia* of the human mind. Finally, Reid's common sense is to be distinguished from Hutcheson's moral sense philosophy by its rationalism. Reid perceived in Hutcheson's account of the moral faculty a tendency to neglect the role of reason (meaning judgement) in human conduct in favour of sensation. This objection was not original to Reid and is to be found (as we shall see) in the writings of others who sought to emend the subjectivist tendencies in Hutcheson's ethics and who were read during the period we are considering. But it was Reid who decisively opposed contemporary philosophical scepticism as a hindrance to scientific improvement by focusing on man's faculty of rational judgement; that is, on our native ability to 'pass sentence' over 'whatever is true or false' (*WTR*, 1:413).

As a moral casuist, Reid joined many who warned that if philosophical scepticism continued to be tolerated in polite society, 'piety, patriotism, friendship, parental affection, and private virtue, would appear as ridiculous as knight-errantry'. But Reid's warning should not be taken more seriously than it was intended. As he suggested in the *Inquiry*, philosophical scepticism cannot sustain itself against the weight of what our ordinary experience obliges us to believe (*WTR*, 1:95, 102). Of greater importance than scepticism's threat to the faith of a Christian was the danger it posed to 'the science of a philosopher, and of the prudence of a man of common understanding' (*WTR*, 1:95).[12] Reid did not espouse an especially optimistic view of man's rational or moral capacities, and his appeal to common sense was not democratically intended. As Reid would point out in the *Essays on the Intellectual Powers of Man*, 'all knowledge, and all science, must be built upon principles that are self-evident; and of such principles every man who has common sense is a competent judge, *when he conceives them distinctly*' (*WTR*, 1:422; my emphasis). Hence Reid morally enjoined philosophers, whose task it is to depict the first principles constituting a science of human nature, to frame such principles clearly and distinctly, thus enabling our common sense faculty to judge their propriety. So to understand Reid's programme is to appreciate the importance he attached to depicting the 'proper means' of doing philosophy. When conducted according to the experimental method of reasoning, Reid's science of human nature emerges as an optimistic, progressive attempt, as Reid put it, to teach men the compass of human power and to enable them to 'make great improvement, in acquiring the treasures of useful knowledge, the habits of skill in arts, the habits of wisdom, prudence, self-command, and every other virtue' (*WTR*, 2:530).

I do not mean to suggest that 'common sense philosophy' cannot be pressed into service to link Reid, Oswald and Beattie. That they have been grouped since 1774, when Joseph Priestley published his *Examination* of their works, and again in 1783 when Immanuel Kant referred to them jointly in the *Prolegomena*, suggests that their views are not just lexically similar. Nevertheless, Scottish common sense philosophy of the eighteenth century was not a monolithic system of ideas. A satisfactory depiction reflecting the historicity of its emergence in Scotland and in colonial America must take account of two of its dimensions without confining itself to either. The first concerns the use of the term itself. An appeal to 'the common sense of mankind' in support of some philosophical, moral or political statement was a bid for credibility always worth attempting. One merely risked censure from those philosophers offended by the vulgar pretensions of this device; but the threat from this quarter was not serious during an age whose literati were increasingly taken with the 'sociological reassurance'[13] an appeal to 'common sense' unfailingly provided. For 'common sense' was an inevitably social construction of reality reflecting the values and beliefs of those with whom its proponent identified. As such it had a certain buoyancy throughout the eighteenth century, reflecting the moral values espoused in the polite but not frivolous conversation of those in the middling rank. Given the 'positive ambiguity' of 'common sense',[14] an ambiguity which was seized upon by Reid and Beattie and many others in the interest of maximising the rhetorical force of their writing, this device was used repeatedly and successfully by philosophers and *litterateurs* throughout the eighteenth century. Thus Kant's attempt in 1783 to characterise the efforts of Reid, Beattie and Oswald as an appeal to the 'judgement of the crowd' was ignored in the Anglophone world during much of the nineteenth century, judging from the dominance of the common sense philosophy in American and British universities through the first half of the century. In America, for example, James Wilson relied upon the intuitively derived common sense of mankind, made manifest in the 'sensible conversation' of polite society, to counter the 'absolute skepticism' of Hume's philosophy.[15] The pamphlet warfare of 1776 represented by Thomas Paine's *Common Sense* and William Smith's *Plain Truth* also reflects the power of this rhetoric, though of course there was precious little common sense philosophy in the exchange.

The popularity of this rhetorical gesture alone suggests we ought to avoid equating common sense philosophy with the mere appearance of the words 'common sense' in the writings of an eighteenth-century author. Reid realised, at least in his post-*Inquiry* writings, that it would be necessary to stipulate a more precise definition of 'common sense' if it were to serve as a tribunal of last resort. He created this definition by coupling common sense and reason or judgement. 'Common sense', Reid argued, 'is that degree of judgment which is common to men with whom we can converse and transact business'. In fact, we do not refer to any authority beyond common sense to arbitrate the disagreements that arise in ordinary life. Instead, we refer to propositions that we hold to be self-evidently true. In this respect, he believed, reason and common sense have the same office. 'We ascribe to reason two offices, or two degrees. The first is to judge of things self-evident; the second to draw conclusions that are not self-evident from those that are. The first of these is the province, and the sole province, of common sense' (*WTR*, 1:421, 425). Reid knew that in order for his appeal to common sense to withstand the charge that all such appeals are empty, that all human judgements are relative to particular persons and to particular circumstances, he would have to elaborate a list of self-evident propositions. He would also have to provide a criterion whereby authentic first principles could be distinguished from the spurious claims of human fancy.

This second dimension of common sense thought, constituted by Reid's enumeration of necessary and contingent principles, presents a more demanding standard of identification than the mere textual presence of 'common sense'. In the *Intellectual Powers* Reid insists that a proper philosophical account justifying an appeal to common sense principles must rely upon the experimental method of reasoning. In this respect Reid's appeal must be distinguished from such contemporary, irrefragable versions of the argument as Oswald's *Appeal* and Beattie's *Essay*. Both Oswald and Beattie depicted common sense as the mind's ability to discern truth 'with a quickness, clearness, and indubitable certainty, similar if not equal, to the information conveyed by the external organs of sense'.[16] Neither writer admitted the need, let alone the possibility, of a corrective to the deliverances of the common sense faculty. Reid's account differs by supplying just that: although his principles of common sense were designed to reassert those principles and powers that characterise human existence and enable the pursuit of moral and civic virtue, his approach placed immense importance on the ratiocinative quality of everyday human action (*WTR*, 1:446–52).[17] In contrast to the widely influential moral sense philosophy of Shaftesbury and Hutcheson, which Reid believed 'degraded the senses too much' by not recognising their power of judging right from wrong (*WTR*, 2:589–90), he argued that men must be able to reflect critically upon their own endeavours if they are to improve themselves. Our ability to apprehend a chain of consequences, to perceive the relation of cause to effect, to make analogies and to connect the present with the future and, consequently, our ability to make choices respecting our good on the whole and what appears to be our duty, depends upon the development of our rational faculties. Reid's argument in favour of common sense was intended to show that any theory placing reason in a subservient role to the passions fails to account adequately for man's capacity for self-improvement (*WTR*, 2:529–30). For Reid, Hume's science of man had jeopardised 'the proper exercise of this gift of God' by introducing the threat of a wholly unmitigated scepticism into the calculus of human improvement.

Examining the educational writings of two of the most prominent Scots educators in Revolutionary America, William Smith and John Witherspoon, one discovers that they, too, adopted the language of common sense to elaborate a commitment to moral and civic improvement. But they did *not* rely directly upon Reid's philosophy, which did not dominate American thought until the end of the eighteenth century, when circumstances allowed a more reflective look at the problems of human improvement. Although Smith and Witherspoon were in rival political and religious camps, they nevertheless found the rhetoric of common sense to be eminently suited to the demands of moral pedagogy.

II

William Smith's writings on education indicate that he learned to share the preoccupations of the most capable minds affiliated with Aberdeen's two colleges, King's (where he was a student from 1743–47) and, especially, Marischal. Most directly, Smith's *General Idea of the College of Mirania* (1753) was indebted to David Fordyce's *Dialogues concerning Education* (1745) and to the curriculum reforms instituted at Marischal and largely copied by King's in 1753, which were inspired by Fordyce and implemented (at Marischal) by his pupil Alexander Gerard and by Thomas Blackwell the younger, the brilliant classicist and principal of Marischal. Smith's *College of Mirania* embodied many of the Aberdeen reforms respecting the supervision of students and the ordering of subjects. Marischal and Mirania both adopted the professorial system, and both preserved the sustained personal guidance of students that characterised the regenting system by appointing a professor to supervise each year's course of study.[18] Smith also adopted Marischal's intention 'to render the study of the sciences more natural and progressive, and to fit their students to be more *useful in life*' by ridding the curriculum of 'the sophisticated Distinctions and idle Jargon of School-Logic', which, Smith believed, lumbered the teaching of logic and metaphysics. What does not emerge from a mere comparison of the two curricula is the extent to which Smith's Mirania reflected the academic and political culture of Aberdeen. The literati of Aberdeen were intensely aware of the importance of education in refining the moral sense and in acquainting the understanding with 'just notions of liberty and virtue' in order to make men good and useful citizens. Turnbull's *Principles of Moral Philosophy* (1740) and

Observations upon Liberal Education (1742), Fordyce's *Dialogues* and *Elements of Moral Philosophy* (1754) and Alexander Gerard's *Plan of Education in the Marischal College and University of Aberdeen* (1755) all testify to the broadly Hutchesonian temper of Aberdeen's educationists.

Although Fordyce's lectures and writings closely followed Hutcheson's moral sense philosophy, Turnbull and Gerard adopted a more explicitly rationalist line than Hutcheson by locating the foundation of morality in an active, reasoning faculty capable of judging the truth of moral propositions. To be sure, neither explicitly took exception to Hutcheson's moral sense theory, but neither confined himself to the antirationalist language of moral *feeling*, thus avoiding the inference that a person's ideas of morality are merely subjective. We have no reason to suppose that either Turnbull or Gerard doubted that Hutcheson was a moral realist. But their willingness to depict the moral sense as a judgemental faculty enabling the mind to perceive and to correct moral propositions suggests that they sought to avoid the subjectivist tendencies some contemporaries believed (whether mistakenly or not) afflicted Hutcheson's theory. This willingness may help to explain their determination to teach by examples taken chiefly from history and nature before embarking on the study of morals, a programme aptly expressed in Turnbull's avowal that 'true philosophy teaches the order of nature, and the order of human life'. Otherwise, 'how abstruse, how abstract, dry and laborious will lectures [in moral philosophy] be, till youth have been led by real examples to the knowledge of moral facts and their causes?'[19] Such education has both a substantive and an instrumental aim. Substantively, Turnbull and his Aberdeen successors presumed that history, geography, chronology, natural history, mathematics and natural philosophy (to draw from the Marischal arts curriculum of 1753) would 'fit students to be more useful in life'. Instrumentally, the study of natural philosophy was intended, as Turnbull explained, to provide 'repeated views of [the] harmony, wisdom and goodness in all the works of nature' and so to 'rivet firmly upon the mind a fixed conviction' of the absolute goodness of God. 'Nothing', Turnbull added, 'can have a more sweetening influence upon the mind.'[20] This was an essentially (and explicitly) Ciceronian perspective brought into conformity with the principles of natural religion and Bacon's *Novum Organum*. Even Fordyce, one of the less methodologically self-conscious Aberdonians, recognised that an adequate moral casuistry 'depends on observation, and builds its Reasonings on plain uncontroverted Experiments, as upon the fullest Induction of Particulars of which the Subject will admit'.[21]

Smith's educational thought embodied much the same agenda. Although he was not preoccupied with the pneumatological or methodological underpinnings of his moral casuistry, his project was unmistakably

Aberdonian. Smith assumed the existence of a rational moral sense, justified by God's providential ordering of man and nature, and his sights were (in his educational writings) steadfastly focused on 'the easiest, simplest, and most natural method of forming youth to the knowledge and exercise of private and public virtue'. Such education, Smith maintained, rejects the merely 'superfluous and hypothetical', and 'mount[s] directly up to fundamental principles, and endeavor[s] to ascertain the relations in which we stand, that we may sustain . . . the rank assigned us among intellectual natures'. The task of inculcating these principles

> requires no such depth of understanding, no such subtle reasonings and tedious researches, as some would persuade us. For, besides his revealed will, God has given intimations of his will to us, by appealing to our senses in the constitution of our nature, and the constitution and harmony of the material universe. We have only to reason by analogy, and correct our reasonings by these holy oracles.[22]

Smith was heading in the direction that Reid would take about a decade later. Smith did adopt a rhetoric of common sense to help legitimate his educational proposals. For in addition to adopting the moral sense psychology of his teachers he argued that the Miranian curriculum was itself the product of 'the unbiased dictates of their own good sense, conscious that, though they could not project an unexceptionable, far less a perfect plan', they could still devise one 'in a condition of being improved as often as circumstances might alter, and experience discover defects in' (179). That curriculum, as well as the one Smith managed to implement at the College of Philadelphia, also reflected an Aberdonian commitment to cultivating man's power of moral reasoning. Hence the instrumental value Smith attached to giving his students, even those enrolled in the Miranian 'mechanic's school' and not destined for the learned professions, an extensive acquaintance with mathematics, which he regarded as the best means of expanding his students' mental faculties (180–81).

Smith was in several respects a tragic figure. A man of great passion and even greater ambition, he left the confines of Aberdeen farther behind than most who fled the poverty and isolation of the Northeast, arriving in New York in 1751. Shortly afterwards he wrote of his desire 'to be thought a good Englishman' in suggesting that a college be erected in the province.[23] The following year he repeated the proposal in much greater detail by publishing his *College of Mirania*. Although he was unsuccessful in that venture he was resourceful enough to send copies of the pamphlet to a number of potentially interested parties, including Benjamin Franklin, then president of the board of trustees of the Academy and Charitable School of Philadelphia. Franklin and the board, who planned to add a college to the foundation, offered Smith a post 'upon Trial' teaching logic, rhetoric, ethics and natural philosophy, while the necessary funds were raised. Smith in turn undertook to solicit funds in England, no doubt with the expectation that he would be offered the provostship of the college once the charter was secured. While abroad, Smith took orders in the Anglican church and managed to attract the favourable notice of Thomas Herring, archbishop of Canterbury, and Thomas Penn, the colony's proprietor. It was Smith's willingness to do the two men's bidding in Pennsylvania – frequently with considerable ruthlessness – that earned him the animosity of Franklin and the Pennsylvania Assembly.[24]

Smith's politics were self-serving, but they were not always unprincipled. Politically conservative, he wrote often and eloquently of the importance of education in 'contriv[ing] and execut[ing] a proper scheme for forming a succession of sober, virtuous, industrious citizens, and checking the course of growing luxury'. Smith's Miranians knew 'that the best laws are little better than *verba minantia*, and would often be infringed by powerful villainy; that the magistrate can at best but frighten vice into a corner, and that it is education alone which can mend and rectify the heart'.[25] Thus the language of civic humanism taught by Hutcheson and his Aberdeen followers served Smith well: he couched his proposals for erecting a college in New York in terms of ridding the colonies of its dangerous dependency, not on Britain, but on luxury. 'If we neglect this favourable Opportunity of purging the Fountain', Smith wrote of this plan,

> by making a last Provision for educating a Succession of true Patriots and Citizens, it may soon be too late; and tho' there was no Danger of being surprised in this State of Indolence, we ourselves will soon be in no Capacity even to think of a Reformation of Manners; for let us remember, that if once Corruption, which treads close on the Heels of Luxury, gets Footing amongst us, all the Art of Man cannot, and Heaven will not, *save us*.[26]

Smith also called for an extensive religious liberty (while he advanced the cause of the Anglican church in the College of Philadelphia at the expense of Francis Alison's Old Side Presbyterians). But unlike Alison and Witherspoon, who employed a rhetoric of civic virtue in favour of American independence, Smith's jeremiad was voiced in favour of British national unity. He was also the principal author of *Plain Truth*, a hastily conceived attempt to fling Montesquieu and Hume into the teeth of Paine's *Common Sense*. *Plain Truth* managed to employ the same down-to-earth language as *Common Sense* (both pamphlets exploited the rhetoric of common sense) while arguing against democracy and for the continuance of commerce between Great Britain and its American colonies. Smith's theme was the familiar one of trade refining and moderating behaviour, of making men polite, which from his perspective was entirely consistent with nurturing the moral sense. The task of making men polite was both a political and a moral matter, to be carried on by government (by promoting trade) and by schools. 'I am far from thinking it necessary', Smith wrote in *Some Thoughts on Education*, his 1752 proposal for erecting a college in New York,

> that our Youth should be Masters of all the insipid Punctilios of French Politesse, nor is there any Danger of this in our Country; but there is an artificial Manner of softening our natural Roughness, which distinguishes the Man from the Savage; and a certain Easiness of Behavior, which is the Characteristic of the Gentleman; – this I could wish to see every one Master of, who acts in any higher Sphere, it being the peculiar Ornament of a public Station.(12)

The connexion between politeness and the moral or common sense faculty would be made even more clearly over a decade later by another Scot transplanted to Philadelphia, James Wilson.[27]

For the most part, Smith's politics were not inconsistent with his educational views and the philosophical commitments that informed them. Clearly, the moral sense doctrine upon which Smith relied did not entail revolutionary politics. Although there are good reasons to assume, with David Fate Norton, that there was a strong connexion between Hutcheson's moral and political views and the revolutionary politics of Alison and Witherspoon,[28] Smith (as we have noted) did not scrupulously adhere to Hutcheson's account of the moral sense. It does not follow that Smith's politics were determined by his moral sense views any more than the political actions of Alison and Witherspoon followed directly from their close adherence to Hutcheson's philosophy. But some light may be shed on the role of Scottish philosophy during the Revolutionary period by attending to the logic of their arguments. T.D. Campbell has contended that it was Hutcheson's confidence in the moral sense of the average citizen that enabled him to look on the prospect of revolutionary action 'with an equanimity that would be irrational on more pessimistic assumptions'.[29] We cannot now pursue this suggestion with respect to the political thought of Alison and Witherspoon beyond pointing to their well-known use of Hutcheson's moral philosophy in their own lectures. But if Norton's contention is correct with respect to Alison and Witherspoon, then Smith's more rationalistic view of the moral sense may help to account for his conservative political views. Smith's Anglicanism and his political ties to the Penn family no doubt had much to do with his politics, which may well have found expression in his somewhat rationalistic conception of the moral sense. Smith was willing to rely on the moral judgements of ordinary persons, but he believed, more readily perhaps than his contemporaries, that those judgements stood in need of rational correction. Smith's early interest in the education of the lower class, his efforts to educate the German-speaking Pennsylvanians into a condition of cultural homogeneity with their Anglophone neighbours, his commitment to the study of history as a foundation for ethics evident in the Mirania plan and in the Philadelphia curriculum so reminiscent of Turnbull's educational writings, his preoccupation with mathematics 'as the best system of logic that can be given to youth' (leading to the comprehensive mathematics programme at the College of Philadelphia), his ambition to teach students to be self-conscious about their own nature:[30] all these manifest his concern with cultivating a person's ability to 'principle' the mind and to deliberate, a concern to be reflected no less strongly and for similar reasons in the common sense philosophy of Thomas Reid. It may be alleged that a similar set of preoccupations was not nearly as much in evidence in the more democratically oriented Presbyterianism of Alison and Witherspoon.

It was perhaps a pity that Smith's politics (and the manner in which he conducted them) led to his dismissal from the College of Philadelphia during the Revolution and effectively deprived him of the American bishopric he long sought. But Smith's political conservatism should not be allowed to obscure his contribution to Philadelphia society: 'the most concentrated centre of enlightened thinking' in America.[31] Smith's talents lay squarely in the realm of 'natural and experimental philosophy'. He was a distinguished astronomer who, with David Rittenhouse and John Lukens, observed the transit of Venus of 1769 for the American Philosophical Society, a body he helped found. He eventually served as the college's professor of astronomy. By all accounts he was a teacher of immense influence, nurturing the careers of a number of colonial luminaries.

In 1757 he began editing the *American Magazine*, an impressively wide-ranging periodical meant to be 'a work of general use for all the *British* colonies, and not confined to the affairs of a few particular ones'. Intended as a vehicle for the promotion of British unity, Smith's *American Magazine* commented on European politics; it provided a 'Philosophical Miscellany, containing the newest discoveries and improvements in any of the branches of philosophy, natural history, agriculture, mathematics or the mechanic arts'; and it published essays in prose and verse, including a monthly submission from Smith called 'The Hermit' (a curious title from a writer devoted to cultivating the sociable virtues) intended to warn that the practice of religion in a liberal society must be freed from controversy to be civilly and morally useful. Smith spent more than four months of 1758 in Philadelphia's Newgate jail, arrested by the Quaker-dominated assembly for publishing 'a seditious libel' against that body, a fact that perhaps helps explain the Hermit's perspective, though Smith began the series before his imprisonment.

Thus Smith was neither an ideologue nor an abstract thinker. He was principally an educator who adopted the language of his Aberdeen teachers to the extent that it helped define and lend coherence to his many projects. He did not slavishly adhere to Hutcheson's moral sense philosophy but modified it, much as his Aberdeen teachers had done and Reid would do, in order to emphasise the rational and hence improvable aspects of the moral faculty. Although Smith may be regarded as conservative both politically (considering his loyalist sympathies on the eve of the Revolution) and morally (if we choose to regard his efforts to cultivate the 'good sense' of ordinary persons as an implicitly antisceptical endeavour), we must also credit him with having fostered an ethos of polite virtuosity bent upon moral, civic and especially scientific improvement.

A similar point may be made with respect to Witherspoon's career at the College of New Jersey. He came to America with the reputation of an educator of considerable ability, not merely that of an evangelical firebrand. Scholars have focused on the former and have taken the latter for granted, making Witherspoon's enlightened presidency 'ironic' if not puzzling. But few of those who knew Witherspoon believed him to be merely a polemicist. The trustees regarded him as someone who would enhance the teaching of science and religion in the college, and Francis Alison thought of Witherspoon's appointment as 'a way to unite' New Side and Old Side factions. Witherspoon's conduct becomes clearer still when one considers his commitment to pursuing a moral casuistry suited to the needs of ordinary Americans. He, too, employed a rhetoric of common sense to that end, but unlike Smith he did not rely directly on its Aberdonian rendition.

To be sure, Witherspoon revised the curriculum in a recognisably Scottish manner, establishing a sequence of courses including mathematics and natural and moral philosophy. He did not possess Smith's facility in natural philosophy, nor did his curriculum manifest the same mathematical bent found in the College of Philadelphia. For Witherspoon, the key to moral and civic improvement was the teaching of religion, an emphasis he shared with James Oswald, fellow leader of the Popular party in the kirk. Despite their opposition to Hutchesonian polite preaching, both men were broadly reliant upon Hutcheson's philosophy in assuming the existence of a natural moral faculty that provided immediate knowledge of right and wrong, recognising as well that the pursuit of virtue depends upon a well-cultivated moral sense. Witherspoon (to a larger extent than Oswald) shared Hutcheson's confidence in the 'good sense' of ordinary persons (*WJW*, 4:446–57), though he accorded reason a greater share of the burden of establishing moral principles than Hutcheson allowed (*WJW*, 3:378–83). Just as Smith and

Reid and others emphasised the rationality of the moral sense (Jean-Jacques Burlamaqui's *Principles of Natural and Political Law* was also prominent among the revisionist sources, as Morton White reminds us[32]), Witherspoon emended Hutcheson in order to provide a better account of how and why a moral casuistry is necessary.

We should be wary of any claim that Witherspoon substantially moderated his views while at Princeton.[33] He relied on Hutcheson's moral philosophy in his lectures to explain how men make moral judgements and why a moral casuistry is a necessary part of moral and civic improvement. But philosophical principles do not necessarily entail specific modes of moral discourse. Considering Witherspoon's opposition to Hutchesonian academic preaching as one such mode, his (unacknowledged) debt to Hutcheson's *System of Moral Philosophy* simply reflects his determination, as a practical moralist, to equip his students with as full and true an account of the principles of morality as possible. In America he abandoned the lampooning rhetoric of the *Ecclesiastical Characteristics* in favour of more polite modes of discourse, realising that rhetoric and the context of one's utterances play an important role in reforming manners (*WJW*, 4:307, 311, 314).[34] Thus as a peacemaker between Old Side and New Side Presbyterians, as an educator intent upon 'improv[ing] the temper and morals' of his readership during a period of political crisis, and as a belletrist concerned with purging the English language in America of 'errors in grammar, improprieties and vulgarisms' in order to improve the conversation and hence the manners of its people (*WJW*, 4:458–75), Witherspoon recognised that the pursuit of virtue requires the cultivation of a *sensible* politeness. 'If . . . fine sense does not differ essentially from common sense', he explained, 'and the first is nothing more than a certain brightness or polish given to the last, it would seem as if by common sense we ought to understand the rational powers in general, and the *capacity* of improvement' (*WJW*, 4:449).

Similarly, Oswald appealed to common sense to discredit the 'Moderate Men' who had come to dominate the Church of Scotland in the late 1750s. These 'men of conversation', who 'picked up somewhat of the English language [and] can read another man's sermon with a becoming grace', were, to Oswald's mind, insufficiently acquainted 'with the real sentiments' of ordinary men. To encourage young ministers to preach the gospel in language their congregations could understand, Oswald proposed that the 'men of sense and breeding' in a congregation be given the opportunity of deciding upon a minister's fitness.[35] Witherspoon adopted much the same rhetoric, arguing that promoting 'true religion' (meaning a tolerant Christianity) is necessary to the perfection of 'true politeness' (*WJW*, 4:145). He repeatedly borrowed from and invoked the authority of Montesquieu (*WJW*, 3:447–55, 472; 4:294, 385, 430) to urge the civic and economic importance of improving the temper and morals of the public. 'The want of public spirit, in those who retain any sense of religion', he claimed in his 'Prayer for National Prosperity', 'is an evidence of its low and languishing state. When it is lively, it will always be communicative. Love to God and love to man, the two great branches of practical religion, necessarily imply a concern for its progress' (*WJW*, 2:473).

By appealing to common sense and its cognates, Oswald and Witherspoon deployed a rhetoric of practical morality designed to teach that the pursuit of virtue entails a pious and sensible politeness. Witherspoon's aims were not primarily philosophic, and it is slightly misleading to contend that he introduced Scottish common sense philosophy to America, for his writings were little more reliant upon Reid's thought than were William Smith's later works. Neither his 1753 letter to the *Scots Magazine*, in which he sought to refute the Berkeleian idealism he believed underlay Lord Kames's necessitarianism, nor his *Lectures on Moral Philosophy*, penned almost two decades later, had much in common with Reid's philosophy besides their opposition to philosophical scepticism and a commitment to moral improvement. Witherspoon recognised, with Smith and others schooled in the philosophy of Hutcheson and his followers, that American prosperity depended primarily upon the proper cultivation of moral sensibilities.

NOTES

1. Ashbel Green, *The Life of the Revd John Witherspoon*, ed. Henry Lyttleton Savage (Princeton, 1973), 132. The essay referred to appeared in *SM* in 1753.
2. Nicholas Phillipson, 'The Export of Enlightenment', *Times Literary Supplement*, 2 July 1976, 823.
3. Andrew Hook, 'Scotland and America Revisited', in *SEAR*, 87.
4. Francis Hutcheson, *A Short Introduction to Moral Philosophy* (Glasgow, 1747), iv.
5. Samuel Stanhope Smith, *The Lectures . . . in the College of New Jersey on the Subjects of Moral and Political Philosophy*, 2 vols. (Trenton, N.J., 1812), 1:24.
6. See Gladys Bryson, *Man and Society: The Scottish Inquiry of the Eighteenth Century* (Princeton, 1945), 10–11, and Jay Fliegelman, *Prodigals and Pilgrims: The American Revolution against Patriarchal Authority, 1750–1810* (Cambridge, 1982), 23–24.
7. James McCosh, *The Scottish Philosophy* (New York, 1875), 11. The phrase 'the *common sense* principles of the Scottish School of Philosophy' appears in McCosh's application for the Edinburgh chair of moral philosophy in 1852 (quoted in Nicholas Phillipson, 'Evangelists of Common Sense', *Times Literary Supplement*, 23 Oct. 1981, 1245).
8. James Oswald, *Sermon, Preached at the Opening of the General Assembly*

of the Church of Scotland . . . to Which Are Annexed, Letters on Some Points of Importance Contained in the Sermon (Edinburgh, 1766), 28. See also his *Appeal to Common Sense in Behalf of Religion*, 2 vols. (Edinburgh, 1766–72), 1:24–25, 66–67, 36, 41, 257–58, 274, 322; 2:35.

9. Oswald, *Appeal*, 1:40.
10. See Nicholas Phillipson, 'James Beattie and the Defence of Common Sense', in *Festschrift für Rainer Gruenter*, ed. Bernhard Fabian (Heidelberg, 1978), 145–54.
11. James Beattie, *An Essay on the Nature and Immutability of Truth*, in his *Essays* (1776; rpt. New York, 1971), 26–27.
12. Reid's claim 'that absolute scepticism *is not more destructive* [my emphasis] of the faith of a Christian than of the science of a philosopher, and of the prudence of a man of common understanding' is a notable understatement, considering the energy he devoted to depicting and practising the science of philosophy as the key to human improvement.
13. The phrase is taken from John Dunn's 'From Applied Theology to Social Analysis', in *WV*, 120, where it is used to describe the thought of Hume and Smith.
14. See Hans-Georg Gadamer, *Truth and Method*, ed. Garrett Barden and John Cumming (New York, 1975), 20.
15. For further discussion of common sense philosophy in Wilson, see Shannon Stimson's contribution to this volume, chap. 11 below.
16. Oswald, *Appeal*, 1:8.
17. See especially the sixth and eighth through eleventh of Reid's 'first principles of contingent truths'.
18. Sloan, 160, 84–85.
19. George Turnbull, *Observations upon Liberal Education* (London, 1742), 379.
20. Ibid., 353–54; see also John Stewart, *Sir Isaac Newton's Two Treatises of the Quadrature of Curves . . . Explained* (London, 1745), vi–x, 478–79.
21. David Fordyce, *The Elements of Moral Philosophy* (London, 1754), 7–8.
22. *The Works of William Smith*, 2 vols. (Philadelphia, 1803), 1:176–78.
23. William Smith, *Some Thoughts on Education* (New York, 1752), viii.
24. Thomas Firth Jones, *A Pair of Lawn Sleeves: A Biography of William Smith* (Philadelphia, 1972), 1–20.
25. Smith, *Works*, 1:175.
26. Smith, *Some Thoughts*, vii.
27. Stephen Conrad, 'Polite Foundation: Citizenship and Common Sense in James Wilson's Republican Theory', in *The Supreme Court Review 1984*, ed. Philip B. Kurland et al. (Chicago, 1985), 364–65. For a contemporary critique of such common sense discourse, see Benjamin Rush, *Essays Literary, Moral and Philosophical* (Philadelphia, 1798), 249–56.
28. David Fate Norton, 'Francis Hutcheson in America', *SVEC* 154 (1976): 1547–68.
29. T.D. Campbell, 'Francis Hutcheson: "Father" of the Scottish Enlightenment', in *The Origins and Nature of the Scottish Enlightenment*, ed. R.H. Campbell and Andrew S. Skinner (Edinburgh, 1982), 182.
30. *SM* 12 (1750): 489; Sloan, 84.
31. J.R. Pole, 'Enlightenment and the Politics of American Culture', in

The Enlightenment in National Context, ed. Roy Porter and Mikuláš Teich (Cambridge, 1981), 199.

32. Morton White, *The Philosophy of the American Revolution* (New York, 1978), 37–41, 107–13.
33. On the essential unity of Witherspoon's career, see Ned Landsman's essay, chap. 1 above.
34. Witherspoon certainly changed his rhetorical style in the years following his move from Scotland to America, the clearest example being his renunciation of satire in favour of simple and direct communication. In his *Lectures on Moral Philosophy* Witherspoon argued in opposition to Shaftesbury that ridicule is not a test of truth because it appeals to the imagination and not to reason (*WJW*, 3:380). Elsewhere he disparaged parody as a form of writing, preferring (in the circumstances of 1776) that men be fully informed of events rather than merely entertained (*WJW*, 4:307, 311, 426–27).
35. James Oswald, *Letters concerning the Present State of the Church of Scotland* (Edinburgh, 1767), 13–15, 23–24, 27.

II. Philosophers and Founding Fathers

7

DONALD W. LIVINGSTON

Hume, English Barbarism and American Independence

The last decade of Hume's life was filled with momentous political events, beginning with the repeal of the Stamp Act in 1766, extending through the 'Wilkes and Liberty' riots and ending 20 August 1776, when the *Caledonian Mercury* published the American Declaration of Independence just five days before his death. Hume's letters of this period abound with insistent judgements about contemporary events. Some have found them paradoxical, if not inconsistent, for although Hume supported independence for the American colonies, he bitterly rejected efforts to move the constitution in a more republican direction. J.Y.T. Greig puts the perplexity this way: 'How could the same man, and at the same time, be both Edmund Burke and George III? How could he defend the Colonists in North America for their resistance to the arbitrary power of King, ministers, and venal House of Commons, and yet attack the Old Whigs, the Patriots, the Wilkites, and democratic radicals of every sort, for trying to resist the same agencies at home?'[1] But Hume was neither Burke nor George III. The politics of the letters of the last decade of his life reflect a coherent criticism of British social and political order already stated in his philosophical and historical writings. Indeed, the letters are significant because they bring into focus important aspects of these writings that have been overlooked.

In 1769 Hume wrote to William Strahan that it had been his misfortune to write in 'the Language of the most stupid and factious Barbarians in the World' (*HL*, 2:209). Writing to Benjamin Franklin in 1772, he again complained about English factionalism and prejudice, observing that 'I fancy that I must have recourse to America for justice' (*HL*, 2:258). Hume supported American independence as early as 1768, and he maintained that position throughout the rest of his life. But his conception of the American crisis and his reasons for supporting American independence cannot be understood without appreciating what he means, in the letters, by the charge that the English are a barbarous nation. In what follows, I shall explore Hume's reasons for favouring American independence in the context of the broader theme of English barbarism.

I

In at least thirty of the letters the English are described as 'barbarians' or the same under other names. Hume despairs at the 'Madness and Wickedness of the English', who are 'sunk in Stupidity and Barbarism and Faction' (*HL*, 2:226, 269). The English are a 'deluded People' who have 'given themselves up to barbarous and absurd Faction' (*HL*, 2:215, 310). Much of this is a reaction to anti-Scottish prejudice, strong in England at this time, and the sting of which can be gathered from a reply to Gilbert Elliot's refusal to take seriously Hume's plan of leaving England permanently for France: 'Can you seriously talk of my continuing an Englishman? Am I, or are you, an Englishman? Will they allow us to be so? Do they not treat with Derision our Pretensions to that Name, and with Hatred our just Pretensions to surpass & to govern them?' (*HL*, 1:470). But there is more to Hume's metaphorical ascriptions of barbarism to the English than the fury of a provincial's injured pride. Here I wish to develop one theme: the sense in which the English are 'barbarous' because they are 'a stupid, factious Nation'.

'Factious' and 'barbarous' are often coupled in the letters as if they were virtually synonymous. In 'Of Parties in General', Hume distinguished three sorts of political faction or party, those of affection, interest and principle. Each is a menace to the public good, but the first two are the most excusable because they pursue a limited good that is empirically identifiable and can be the object of negotiation. The last, however, is singled out as especially noxious and as an evil peculiar to modern times: 'Parties from *principle*, especially abstract speculative principle, are known only to modern times, and are, perhaps, the most extraordinary and unaccountable *phænomenon*, that has yet appeared in human affairs' (*E*, 60). Parties of principle are parties of *theory*, and the reason they are so dangerous is that, if not handled properly, theoretical thinking can distort reality as well as illuminate it. As a philosopher, Hume had explored, in the *Treatise of Human Nature*, the process whereby misplaced theoretical thinking can invert experience, transforming realities into illusions and illusions into what are thought to be realities. Writing of philosophers in 'The Sceptic', Hume says that 'there is one mistake, to which they seem liable, almost without exception; . . . When a philosopher has once laid hold of a favourite principle, which perhaps accounts for many natural effects, he extends the same principle over the whole creation, and reduces to it every phœnomenon, though by the most violent and absurd reasoning' (*E*, 159). The history of thought abounds with examples that illustrate Hume's point. Thales discovered that everything is really just water; Zeno that nothing moves; Hobbes that all acts of benevolence are really acts of self-love; Locke that no government is legitimate that is not based on consent; Marx that all history is the story of class struggle, and so on. In all these cases, one part of common life, through theoretical reflection, magically transforms the rest into itself, yielding a profound alienation in the thinker's own existence. Hume describes the process as 'philosophical chymistry' and likens it to alchemy and black magic (*EM*, 297; *E*, 161).

In the passage quoted above, 'philosophy' should not be taken to refer to metaphysical theory as distinct from scientific theory. For Hume, 'philosophy' refers indifferently to all theoretical activity, and his point is that theorising of any kind is dangerous; there is a tendency to 'philosophical chymistry' in all theory, and it must be handled with great care.

Furthermore, there is a tendency of the theoretical intellect to seek dominion over others: 'such is the nature of the human mind, that it always lays hold on every mind that approaches it; and . . . so is it shocked and disturbed by any contrariety' (*E*, 60–61). The tendency of the theoretical intellect to 'philosophical chymistry' and to dominion over the minds of others could be disastrous if ever brought to inform political parties. When he wrote the *Treatise*, Hume thought that theoretical activity, being cultivated only by a few in their closets, could not be much of a threat to social and political stability. The real threat was religion: 'Generally speaking, the errors in religion are dangerous; those in philosophy only ridiculous' (*THN*, 272). Yet Hume described his own age as 'this philosophic age', that is, an age in which theoretical activity had begun to filter down to the populace (*EM*, 197n.). In 'Of Essay Writing', published in 1742, Hume characterised his role as an essayist as that of an 'ambassador' between the world of theory and the everyday world of conversation. In 'Of the Original Contract', published in 1748, he frankly admitted that theorising had become an established part of modern politics: 'no party, in the present age, can well support itself, without a philosophical or speculative system of principles, annexed to its political or practical one . . . to protect and cover that scheme of actions, which it pursues' (*E*, 465). One could not expect the refined restraints on theorising that Hume had worked out in the *Treatise*, in his distinction between true and false philosophy, to restrain the populace in a philosophic age: 'The people being commonly very rude builders, especially in this speculative way, and more especially still, when actuated by party-zeal; it is natural to imagine, that their workmanship must be a little unshapely, and discover evident marks of that violence and hurry, in which it was raised' (*E*, 466).

By the middle of the century, Hume saw that the tendency of the theoretical intellect to dominion and to philosophical chemistry had become a potentially explosive part of English politics. The explosion occurred in the late 1760s with the 'Wilkes and Liberty' riots and the drift of the country towards civil war. The ferment was about something called 'liberty'. It seemed to Hume that the English were captured by a false theory of liberty which prevented them from understanding and improving the liberal order they actually enjoyed. Theory had created a world of its own, and in trying to carry out the dictates of this dream world the English seemed to be destroying their own liberal political order.

The barbarian destroys out of ignorance a civilised world he cannot understand. But Hume was witnessing a barbarism, not of ignorance, but of critical reflection. Here was something new: a special sort of barbarism possible only in a civilised age, where misplaced theoretical reflection had created a kind of self-imposed ignorance and stupidity that could destroy a liberal order in the name of 'liberty'. When Hume says the English are sunk in 'Barbarism and Faction', he means the worst sort of faction, not factions of affection or interest, but those that are 'known only to modern times', namely factions of 'principle'. The barbarism can be said to be *English* because the distorting theory has become part of English self-professed national identity. I turn now to an examination of the theory and Hume's criticism of it.

II

Bernard Bailyn observes that 'it would be difficult to exaggerate the keenness of eighteenth-century Britons' sense of their multifarious accomplishments and world eminence and their distinctiveness in the achievement of liberty'.[2] There was a theory as to how this achievement had come about. Greatly simplified it was this. The greatness of Britain is due to her constitution, the end of which is liberty. The constitution is a balance of three estates, king, lords and commons, representing in parliament the three classical forms of government (monarchy, aristocracy and democracy) as well as the three functions of government (executive, judicial and legislative). As a balance of these estates and functions, the constitution is perfect. Moreover, the constitution is not the creation of philosophers but is rooted in English national character and pre-exists the modern world. Indeed, some thought it existed in greater perfection prior to the Norman Conquest. English history, therefore, has been the story of preserving the balance of the constitution from the encroachments of kings and unpatriotic factions. In modern times the great threat has come from the Scottish Stuart kings, but in the Glorious Revolution of 1688 the English nation asserted its rights and restored the ancient constitution. It is this restoration that accounts for Britain's present greatness. More radical versions of the theory held that the Revolution settlement made clear what was all along understood in the constitution, that legitimate government is by consent of the people, a doctrine given philosophical expression in Locke's contract theory.

We may call this theory the Revolution ideology because it grew out of an attempt to justify the Glorious Revolution of 1688 and because, like that Revolution itself, it was accepted by almost everyone, George III as well as the Rockingham Whigs. As Bailyn has especially made clear, it was a theory that provided the rationale for an unreal, conspiratorial style in politics.[3] Since the constitution is a perfect balance of estates and functions, any great distress must be the result of some dark faction seeking to undo the balance for its own interests. Thus Catharine Macaulay could write that 'a faction has ever existed in this state, from the earliest period of our constitution' to 'remove the limitations necessary to render monarchy consistent with liberty'.[4] But, equally, George III could and did think there was a faction in the House of Commons and ministry making it impossible for him to carry out his constitutional responsibilities as executive.

Hume agreed with much of the Revolution panygeric literature: 'during these last sixty years', he wrote in the mid-eighteenth century, '. . . public liberty, with internal peace and order, has flourished almost without interruption: Trade and manufactures, and agriculture, have encreased: The arts, and sciences, and philosophy, have been cultivated', and, he added, 'nor is there another instance in the whole history of mankind, that so many millions of people have, during such a space of time, been held together, in a manner so free, so rational, and so suitable to the dignity of human nature' (*E*, 508). But Hume's explanation of this marvel was completely different from that of Revolution ideology.

To begin with, Hume did not conceive of the constitution as a timeless substance. For Hume, the human world is an order of evolving conventions. Such conventions are not the result of a contract or of any conscious planning. Like a natural language, they evolve spontaneously over time to satisfy human needs. The moral and legal rules of a political constitution are like the rules of English grammar: a formal expression of what has evolved unreflectively over time and is open to still further evolution. From this position, Hume was able to argue that the English constitution was not a re-enactment of an ancient constitution that had been successfully handed down despite attacks by unpatriotic factions. In the *History* he showed that the constitution had been in constant flux and that there had been four discernable constitutions in English history. And so Hume could speak of the 'wisdom of the English constitution, or rather the concurrence of accidents'.[5]

Given the spontaneous and evolutionary character of all political constitutions, it follows that the legitimacy of government is not founded on anything that could be called a contract. The idea, however, is a compelling one and, if taken seriously, powerfully distorts political experience. Hume thought the theory had become, over time, a part of English political consciousness, and he regretted that something of it had infected the first volume of his *History*, which was 'too full of those foolish English Prejudices, which all Nations and all Ages disavow' (*HL*, 2:216). Indeed, as a popular view of political reality, it is rejected, he says, 'in every place but this single kingdom' (*E*, 487).

III

Revolution ideology, whether employed by the opposition or by George III, construed the political world in moralistic and legalistic terms. In such a world, all issues were issues of 'rights' and conspiracies against rights. Such an outlook made it virtually impossible to understand how the constitution actually worked. Viewing rights as the formal expression of social utilities in evolving conventions, Hume was able to achieve a deeper understanding of how the constitution functioned. Much was made in the eighteenth century, but especially by Rockingham Whigs, of how the crown, by virtue of its right to fill and create offices, was corrupting the independence of parliament by the power of patronage. In 'Of the Independency of Parliament' Hume argued that the Revolution settlement had left parliament virtually all powerful. If, according to Revolution ideology, the crown was to 'balance' the commons and lords, much less carry out the executive function, some influence in parliament was necessary. Hume saw clearly that the doctrine of three independent estates corresponding to three separate functions of government was a distortion. The parts of the constitution never were and never could be in 'balance'. The interests, property and constitutional functions of each intertwined in a way that could be understood only by careful historical and causal analysis of how the convention of the constitution had evolved and what utilities it served. Montesquieu had made popular a picture of the English constitution as having separated the executive, legislative and judicial functions of government. Hume admired his work but deplored 'its false Refinements and its rash and crude Positions' (*HL*, 2:133).

Although Hume agreed that the English enjoy 'the most entire system of liberty, that ever was known amongst mankind',[6] he did not think this was due to an ancient, balanced and perfect constitution that was a unique possession of the English and that framed their national character. This was a cardinal point in Revolution ideology and, for Hume, one of its most absurd aspects. Viewed as a historical process, liberty (as the rule of law) is not unique to the English but is part of a larger civilising process of economic and social forces that includes most of the nations of Europe. These civilising forces have established to some degree the ideal and much of the practice of civil liberty even in monarchies. Life and property are as secure in the absolute monarchy of France as in England (*E*, 93–94).

The English chauvinism in Revolution ideology helps to explain anti-

Scottish attitudes. If liberty is tied to an ancient *English* constitution, then since the Union of Scottish and English parliaments occurred in 1707, the Scots are newcomers and participate in the constitution, as it were, by courtesy and not by nature. Moreover, the Scottish political mind reveals an authoritarian cast like that of the French, as is manifest from the threat to liberty posed by the Stuart kings and the Jacobite rebellions of 1715 and 1745.

Revolution chauvinism prevented the English not only from seeing their own enjoyment of liberty as the tip of the iceberg of a larger civilising process going on in Europe but also from appreciating the superior cultural achievements of France. The French were regularly described as 'Turkish slaves' and their culture as corrupting and effeminate. Catharine Macaulay complained about how 'what is called the tour of Europe' corrupts English youths, who, being 'caught with the gaudy tinsel of a superb court, the frolic levity of unreflecting slaves, and thus deceived by appearances, are riveted in a taste for servitude'. This corruption 'is the finishing stroke that renders them useless to all the good purposes of preserving the birthright of an Englishman'.[7]

In 'My Own Life' Hume complained that Revolution ideology, throughout his lifetime, had not only captured the state but politicised literature as well: 'the Whig Party were in possession of bestowing all places, both in the State and in Literature' (*HL*, 1:5). His judgement is corroborated by Bailyn, who observes that from 'the end of the war in 1713 until the crisis over America' the triumph of Britain in commerce, war and liberty 'was the constant theme not only of formal state pronouncements and of political essays, tracts, and orations but of belles-lettres as well'.[8] In a letter to Tobias Smollett, 1768, Hume remarks on 'the indifference of ministers towards literature, which has been long, and indeed always, the case in England' (*HL*, 2:186). And, as already noted, he complained to Strahan in 1769 that it had been his 'Misfortune to write in the Language of the most stupid and factious Barbarians in the World' (*HL*, 2:209). In 1773 Hume told Strahan that finding an English author of merit would be unlikely: 'For as to any Englishman, that Nation is so sunk in Stupidity and Barbarism and Faction that you may as well think of Lapland for an Author'. He thought that the best book written by an 'Englishman these thirty years (for Dr. Franklyn is an American) is Tristram Shandy, bad as it is' (*HL*, 2:269). Three years later Hume expressed his surprise to Gibbon, upon receiving a copy of his *Decline and Fall*, that such a work could have come from an Englishman: 'You may smile at this Sentiment; but as it seems to me that your Countrymen, for almost a whole Generation, have given themselves up to barbarous and absurd Faction, and have totally neglected all polite Letters, I no longer expected any valuable Production ever to come from them' (*HL*, 2:310).

The politicisation of literature was for Hume a serious matter. The failure to cultivate polite letters was a failure to cultivate the mind. 'I am only sorry to see', he wrote to Thomas Percy in 1773, 'that the great Decline, if we ought not rather to say, the total Extinction of Literature in England, prognosticates a very short Duration of all our other Improvements, and threatens a new and a sudden Inroad of Ignorance, Superstition and Barbarism.'[9] A sudden inroad of barbarism had in fact occurred, Hume thought, with the 'Wilkes and Liberty' riots and demonstrations that flared up throughout the nation and indeed the empire during the years 1768–71, and it was continuous with the civil war with the colonists that erupted in the spring of 1775.

IV

John Wilkes fled the country in 1763, refusing to stand trial for seditious libel, and was declared an outlaw. He returned in 1768, presenting himself as the victim of a corrupt ministry, and was elected to parliament from the county of Middlesex. He immediately stood trial for his old offence and was sentenced to twenty-two months imprisonment and fined £1,000. He was expelled from the House of Commons in February 1769. While still in prison, he was elected three more times and expelled three times. This farcical struggle between parliament and the electors led to a three-year period of riots and demonstrations throughout Britain and the empire. The riots in London were often savage: houses were set afire, ministers assaulted (on one occasion Lord North just escaped with his life) and the king insulted. At least 500 constables were reported necessary to escort the king to the House of Lords in 1771. In March 1770 the City of London drew up a remonstrance asking the king to dissolve parliament and remove corrupt ministers. This action seemed to be a direct challenge to the independence of parliament and hence to the rule of law. It seemed to many that Britain was on the verge of civil war. Hume wrote to Strahan in November 1769: 'I wish only the Army may be faithful, and the Militia quiet' (*HL*, 2:211–12). Had Wilkes and Pitt been revolutionaries a civil war could have erupted, with both sides fighting over different interpretations of 'liberty'.

What Hume found remarkable about the affair was its unreal, ideological character. The slogan 'Wilkes and Liberty' was being chanted by men of all classes and ranks in London, throughout Britain, in India, the West Indies and North America. But none of this added up to a coherent criticism of government that could be corrected by reform. Writing to Turgot in 1768, Hume rejects his notion that society is capable of perpetual progress and points to the 'Wilkes and Liberty' riots as confirmation: 'Here is a People thrown into Disorders . . . merely from the Abuse of Liberty . . . without any Grievance, I do not only say, real, but even imaginary; and without any of them being able to tell one Circumstance of Government which they wish to have corrected' (*HL*, 2:180). Two generations of Revolution ideology had planted firmly in the minds of Britons throughout the empire the idea that their constitutional liberties were threatened by conspiratorial forces. The political world was a world of victims and conspirators. Wilkes became a symbol for this feeling of threatened victimisation. With the 'Wilkes and Liberty' affair, Revolution ideology ceased to be merely a false and self-deceptive interpretation of British political order and became a cause of mass passions. 'They roar Liberty', Hume said, 'tho' they have apparently more Liberty than any People in the World' (*HL*, 2:180). In a strange kind of madness men could ardently seek (while at the same time destroying) what they already possessed.

It was like the distortions of political reality brought on by religious fanaticism that Hume had explored in the volumes of the *History* covering the English Civil War. But the distortion of reality in the 'Wilkes and Liberty' affair was not due to religion but to secular theory. Hume observes to Strahan in 1771 that political 'factious prejudices are more prevalent in England than religious ones' (*HL*, 2:233). Writing to Hugh Blair in 1769, he says: 'This Madness about Wilkes . . . exceeds the Absurdity of Titus Oates and the popish Plot; and is so much more disgraceful to the Nation, as the former Folly, being derivd from Religion, flow'd from a Source, which has, from uniform Prescription, acquird a Right to impose Nonsense on all Nations & all Ages: But the present Extravagance is peculiar to Ourselves, and quite risible' (*HL*, 2:197). Here and elsewhere Hume suggests that the distortion of political reality is due to Revolution ideology, which has become a settled part of English political consciousness and should not be confused with the erratic behaviour of a London mob. Writing to Strahan in 1770, he says: 'The Madness and Wickedness of the English (for do not say, the Scum of London) appear astonishing, even after all the Experience we have had. It must end fatally either to the King or Constitution or to both' (*HL*, 2:226).

The 'Wilkes and Liberty' affair demonstrated not only the power of Revolution ideology to generate mass passions but also the great power of the commercial interests centred in London. It was to the merchants, professionals and craftsmen that Wilkes had played the victim. And this same extraparliamentary power supported Pitt's policy of dominating world trade through the supremacy of sea power, a policy brilliantly successful in the Seven Years' War, which left Britain with a vast empire of trade in the East and West. Through Revolution ideology Pitt had been able to rouse nationalist passions and to lift mere wars of commerce to the level of moral grandeur and glory.

It seemed to Hume that forces were in play that were shifting the constitution in the direction of a republic and, indeed, of a mercantile republican empire. This was alarming for a number of reasons. In 'Whether the British Government Inclines More to Absolute Monarchy, or to a Republic', published in 1741, he argued that although the constitution had evolved into what was virtually a republic, there were signs that it might (and Hume hoped it would) develop into a civilised absolute monarchy. Although Hume always held to the republican ideal of government and even wrote an essay describing what an ideal republic would look like (*E*, 512–29), he thought monarchy a better form of government under modern conditions. Modern civilised monarchies were less factious and more stable; they tended to encourage the arts and sciences; and they were better at controlling the tendency of all modern governments to accumulate a public debt.

Similarly, in 'Of Public Credit' he argued that one pernicious effect of national debt is that it enriches the power and privileges of cities at the expense of the provinces and, in the case of a republic or a limited monarchy, tends to instability. Hume took London as an example: the 'immense greatness' of which, 'under a government which admits not of discretionary power, renders the people factious, mutinous, seditious, and even perhaps rebellious' (*E*, 355). These remarks were published in 1752, four years before the outbreak of the Seven Years' War. At the conclusion of the war in 1763, the nation was left with an unprecedented national debt and a vast mercantile empire to protect against a humiliated and revengeful France and Spain, meaning further wars and more debt. The expanding empire had increased the power of London beyond what Hume had imagined in 1752 when he said that 'the head is undoubtedly too large for the body'. In its challenge to parliament during the Wilkes affair, the City of London revealed itself capable of open rebellion. And although after three years the government had muddled through, Hume wondered whether the authority of government had not been fundamentally weakened: 'if in a case, where popular Complaints had not the smallest Shadow of Pretence, the King and Parliament have prevaild after a long Struggle and with much Difficulty, what must it be, where there is some plausible Appearance, and perhaps some real Ground of Complaint, such as it is natural to expect in all Governments?' (*HL*, 2:221).

Britain seemed to be moving towards a republic dominated by London as the hub of a vast commercial empire. Given historical circumstances, Hume thought that a republican Britain meant anarchy and a restoration of some latter-day Cromwell and the consequent loss of liberty. As he explained to his nephew in 1775: 'Such Fools are they, who perpetually cry out Liberty: [and think to] augment it, by shaking off the Monarchy' (*HL*, 2:306).

V

We are now in a position to understand how, when the American crisis arose, Hume could so quickly support independence for the colonies. The Stamp Act was repealed in 1766. Hume argued for independence as early as 22 July 1768, and he maintained that position until his death. Few Americans thought of independence by 1768, and Hume appears alone among the British in supporting it that early. Even those statesmen known as 'the friends of America' – Burke, Fox, Shelburne, Dartmouth, Barré and Pitt – refused to take independence seriously until after the capture of Bourgoyne's forces at Saratoga in 1777. And even then most sought to establish some sort of tie with Britain. Hume's position, however, was for complete separation.

Hume's view was in even starker contrast to the Scottish literary and political establishment, which was against independence and for strong measures against the Americans. Hume's friends Hugh Blair, William Robertson, John Home, Adam Ferguson, Allan Ramsay and Thomas Blacklock were strongly pro-government, and the latter four wrote pamphlets supporting that position.[10] War began in the spring of 1775; by the autumn loyal addresses from the freeholders of counties across the country were pouring in. Lord Home had asked Hume to write such an address, and he had refused. Hume's good friend and fellow Scot William Strahan was shocked at Hume's position: 'I am really surprised you are of a different opinion' (*HL*, 2:301n.). Baron Mure may have felt much the same way. He had written asking Hume to write a loyal address on behalf of the freeholders of Renfrewshire. Hume's reply of 27 October 1775 expresses the uncomfortable feeling that he is becoming a disappointment to his friends: 'Oh! Dear Baron, you have thrown me into Agonies and almost into Convulsions by your Request. You ask what seems reasonable, what seems a mere trifle; yet am I so unfit for it, that it is almost impossible for me to comply. . . . I am an American in my Principles, and wish we woud let them alone to govern or misgovern themselves as they think proper: The Affair is of no Consequence, or of little Consequence to us' (*HL*, 2:302–3).

Although Hume was 'an American' in his principles, he was not pro-American in thinking colonial constitutional arguments superior to those of the government. Hume's conception of the conflict was of a different order from that in which the colonists and government argued. Both accepted the Revolution ideology of the ancient, balanced and perfect constitution. Both appealed to the same constitution, and so the conflict is best thought of as a civil war (similar to the secession of the southern states from the United States in the American Civil War) rather than as a colonial war of national independence in the twentieth-century sense. As we have seen, Revolution ideology inclined towards a conspiracy mode of explaining political troubles. The colonists saw a conspiracy of the ministry to enslave them and appealed to the king for redress. When, after some years, it became obvious that the king supported the ministry, they found themselves adrift from constitutional discourse and appealed to natural right to reconstitute themselves.

Since Hume was free from the grip of this ideology and saw it as part of the cause of English barbarism, he could have no sympathy with American versions of the same thing. In a letter to John Home, 8 February 1776, he wonders how far 'the frenzies of the people' in America will go (*HL*, 2:308). And in the letter to Mure, mentioned above, he speaks of 'the poor infatuated Americans'. Hume considered it a defect of his friend Franklin's character that he was 'a very factious man, and Faction, next to Fanaticism, is, of all passions, the most destructive of Morality' (*HL*, 2:286).

Hume rejected the entire question of rights as understood within the framework of Revolution ideology in favour of a causal analysis of an ever-changing constitution. Support for American independence is linked to his criticism of a London-dominated republican empire in the grip of a bellicose nationalist ideology, and all that meant in the loss of liberty and culture. In 'That Politics May Be Reduced to a Science', published in 1741, Hume laid it down as a maxim that republican empires are more oppressive than monarchical ones. Monarchs tend to view the colonial subjects of their dominions as having the same status, but 'a free state necessarily makes a great distinction. . . . The conquerors, in such a government, are all legislators, and will be sure to contrive matters, by restrictions on trade, and by taxes, so as to draw some private, as well as public, advantage from their conquests. Provincial governors have also a better chance, in a republic, to escape with their plunder, by means of bribery or intrigue; and their fellow-citizens, . . . enriched by the spoils of the subject provinces, will be the more inclined to tolerate such abuses' (*E*, 19). England is treated in the essay as a virtual republic, and its oppressive treatment of Ireland is contrasted with the more liberal treatment that the absolute monarchy of France extends to its colonies. As if to confirm this thesis, Hume informed Strahan in 1772 that the idea of a parliamentary enquiry into the activities of the East India Company 'did not originally proceed from the Ministry, but from the King himself, who was shockd with the Accounts he receivd of the Oppressions exercisd over the poor Natives, and demanded a Remedy. I wish it may be possible to provide any, that will be durable' (*HL*, 2:260).

It is interesting that the Americans at first appealed to the crown for protection, arguing that they were subjects of the king not of the House of Commons. Even after war broke out in 1775, George Washington regularly described his opponent as 'the ministerial army'. But the colonial appeal made no sense within the structure of Revolution ideology as interpreted at home, for it implied compromising the independence of parliament and increasing the prerogative of the king. After the Stamp Act controversy and the emergence of Grenville's 'republican' model of empire as an orbit of subordinate satellites serving the interests of the centre, Hume (like the Americans) saw the colonies swept out of the protection of monarchy into the oppression of a mercantile republican empire governed by London.

In a letter to Sir Gilbert Elliot, 22 July 1768, when the second round of 'Wilkes and Liberty' was just beginning, Hume entertained a fantasy that ties together all the themes discussed above: 'These are fine doings in America. O! how I long to see America and the East Indies revolted totally & finally, the Revenue reduc'd to half, public Credit fully discredited by Bankruptcy, the third of London in Ruins, and the rascally Mob subdu'd' (*HL*, 2:184). Over a year later the same fantasy appears in a letter to Strahan: 'Notwithstanding my Age, I hope to see a public Bankruptcy, the total Revolt of America, the Expulsion of the English from the East Indies, the Diminution of London to less than a half, and the Restoration of the Government to the King, Nobility, and Gentry of this Realm' (*HL*, 2:210). Hume's support for American independence transcends entirely the question of 'rights' as determined by Revolution ideology and relies instead on causal judgements about the pernicious effects the trend to a republic is likely to have on the nation and the provinces: judgements rooted in views published early in his career on the nature of republics, monarchies, public credit, the British constitution and empire.

Hume also believed in free trade and hated the belligerent mercantile system of Pitt. Writing to Strahan in 1775, Hume observed that 'a forced and every day more precarious Monopoly of about 6 or 700,000 Pounds a year of Manufactures, was not worth contending for' and 'that we shoud preserve the greater part of this Trade even if the Ports of America were open to all Nations' (*HL*, 2:300). But quite apart from whatever economic value the colonies might have, Hume was convinced that the war to keep them could not be won, and to lose them in defeat might undermine an already weakened government: '*the worst Effect of the Loss of America, will not be the Detriment to our Manufactures, which will be a mere trifle, . . . but to the Credit and Reputation of Government, which has already but too little Authority. You will probably see a Scene of Anarchy and Confusion open'd at home*' (*HL*, 2:304–5).

Revolution ideology, with its world of conspiracies and threatened rights, distorted and hardened the outlook of colonists and the government and prevented them from an imaginative understanding of their differences. Not restricted by these barriers, Hume offered a causal analysis of the conflict that enabled him to have a more imaginative grasp of the colonists' position, if not of the government's. In the *History* Hume observed that the colonies in America were founded on a self-conception of liberty and independence unique in history: 'What chiefly renders the reign of James memorable, is the commencement of the English colonies in America; colonies established on the noblest footing that has been known in any age or nation . . . The spirit of independency, which was reviving in England, here shone forth in its full lustre, and received new accession from the aspiring character of those, who, being discontented with the established church and monarchy, had sought for freedom amidst those savage desarts'.[11] The colonists were animated from the first with the spirit of political autonomy, and Hume noted during the time he was working on the *Treatise* that 'the Charter Governments in America are almost entirely independent of England'.[12]

Hume's judgement was that a new order of political societies had spontaneously evolved in America that would have to be recognised on pain of a war that could not be won or, if it could, of a reign of terror to keep the colonies in subjection, which a liberty-loving regime such as Britain could not stomach, much less afford financially (*HL*, 2:300–301). It was a question not of prescriptive or natural rights but of the causal nature of things. In 1771 Hume wrote: 'our Union with America . . . in the Nature of things, cannot long subsist' (*HL*, 2:237). In October 1775 he urged that 'both Fleet and Army be withdrawn from America, and these Colonists be left entirely to themselves. . . . this Measure only anticipates the necessary Course of Events a few Years'. He concluded by saying: 'Let us, therefore, lay aside all Anger; shake hands, and part Friends. Or if we retain any anger, let it only be against ourselves for our past Folly; and against that wicked Madman, Pitt; who has reducd us to our present Condition' (*HL*, 2:300–301). Again, Hume's judgement is causal, not moralistic or legalistic; 'our past Folly' refers to bad causal judgements about what was, is and will be – judgements distorted in large part by Revolution ideology.

VI

Hume took seriously his early essay 'That Politics May Be Reduced to a Science'. One great discovery of that science is that all political order is constituted by opinion. From this it follows that a disorder in opinion can distort not only thought about political reality but the reality itself. In his philosophical works Hume explored the religious mind, showing how enthusiasm and superstition distort experience. In the *History* he exposed the role of religious ideology in bringing on the English Civil War. In the letters of the last decade of his life he saw the power of purely secular ideology to distort experience. Revolution ideology was secular, containing a historical theory of the English constitution and a philosophical theory of the legitimacy of the state. But it was able to generate mass passions and a special sort of bigotry peculiar to the critical intellect itself, the equal, in its way, of any absurdity produced by religion.

At the beginning of his career Hume had taught that, generally, the errors of religion are dangerous, those of philosophy merely ridiculous: a maxim expressing the confidence and innocence of the Enlightenment. He died catching a glimpse of a world in which almost the opposite would be true. Religion was contained by the watchful eye of the civil magistrate. But philosophical reflection was becoming a mass phenomenon, and the new vulgar philosophers had left off fighting the priests to fight among themselves. A new and unexpected form of darkness had appeared within the critical intellect itself. The end of the Enlightenment was at hand.

NOTES

1. J.Y.T. Greig, *David Hume* (London, 1931), 375–76.
2. Bernard Bailyn, *The Origins of American Politics* (New York, 1968), 17.
3. Ibid., chap. 1, and the general introduction to *Pamphlets of the American Revolution, 1750–1776*, ed. Bernard Bailyn (Cambridge, Mass., 1965).
4. Catharine Macaulay, *The History of England* (London, 1763), xi.
5. David Hume, *The History of England, from the Invasion of Julius Caesar to The Revolution in 1688*, 6 vols. (1778 ed.; Indianapolis, 1983), 5:569.
6. Ibid., 6:531.
7. Macaulay, *History of England*, xv–xvi.
8. Bailyn, *Origins of American Politics*, 17–18.
9. *New Letters of David Hume*, ed. Raymond Klibansky and Ernest C. Mossner (Oxford, 1954), 199.
10. For a discussion of the pro-government stance of the Moderate clergy in Edinburgh, see Sher, chap. 7.
11. Hume, *History of England*, 5:146–47.
12. Ernest C. Mossner, 'Hume's Early Memoranda, 1729–1740: The Complete Text', *Journal of the History of Ideas* 9 (1948): 504.

8

ANDREW S. SKINNER

Adam Smith and America: The Political Economy of Conflict

Every student of Adam Smith is familiar with his reference to the 'abilities and Virtues of the never to be forgotten Dr Hutcheson'.[1] Hutcheson was a great teacher whose work on ethics, jurisprudence and economics exerted a powerful influence on his famous pupil. There were of course disagreements, perhaps none more marked than in the field of political theory, where Hutcheson appeared as an advocate of the contract theory of government, in the manner of John Locke, and of the associated doctrine of the right to resist when the purpose of the original agreement is thought to have been violated.

Caroline Robbins has reminded us that the latter doctrine applies not only to the relationship between a people and a government but also to the relationship between colonies and a mother country.[2] The same theme has been taken up in David Fate Norton's examination of the dissemination of Hutcheson's political ideas (including the critique of slavery), notably by Witherspoon and Francis Alison. Norton's contention, indeed, is 'that Hutcheson's political philosophy provided a foundation for revolution and independence, and that, through the teaching and preaching of his disciple, Francis Alison, he was a contributing cause of the American War of Independence'.[3]

Adam Smith, in contrast, was no advocate of the contract theory (following Hume) and far less of the right to revolution.[4] Yet it has to be noted that his long analysis of the American question in the *Wealth of Nations* was designed to introduce major changes in British policy. Smith's brand of radicalism is distinctive in the sense that he addressed the American question from the standpoint of a political *economist*. In particular, Smith set out to demonstrate that the policy behind the Navigation Acts was fundamentally flawed. He supported this thesis by offering his readers a model cast in the classical mould of exercises in philosophical history as manifested, for example, in the essay on astronomy and in the treatment of the origins of the 'present establishments' in Europe (*WN*, III).

In the case of America, he began the account by outlining the legislative environment before illustrating the impact it would have on growth rates in Britain and America.[5] The argument prompts the conclusion that the quantitative development of productive forces must at some stage impinge upon the legislative environment itself, at least if actual conflict is to be avoided.

Looked at from one point of view, the analysis seems designed to confirm the importance of economic factors in political life. As such, it constitutes a powerful exhibition of Smith's capacity for systematic economic thought, here placed in a setting of high political drama. It can also be seen as further support for freedom of trade or, alternatively, as a means of preserving that position of political dominance which had followed the peace of 1763 and which at the same time had been rendered less secure by it.[6]

I

In describing the objectives of colonial policy, Smith concentrated mainly on its economic aspects and duly reported on the extensive range of restrictions Britain had imposed on trade and manufactures, domestic as well as American. To begin with, the Navigation Acts required trade between the colonies and Great Britain to be carried on in British ships, and certain classes of commodities were to be confined initially to the market of the mother country. The so-called 'enumerated' goods were of two types: those that were either the peculiar produce of America or were not produced in Britain and, secondly, those that were produced in Britain but in insufficient quantities to meet domestic demand. Examples of the first type were sugar, coffee and tobacco; of the second, naval stores, masts, pig iron and copper.

The first broad category of goods could not harm British industry; and here the object of policy, as reported by Smith, was to ensure that British merchants could buy cheaper in the colonies with a view to supplying other countries at higher prices and at the same time establishing a useful carrying trade. In the second case, the objectives were to ensure essential supplies and, through the careful use of duties, to discourage imports from other countries with which the balance of trade was supposed to be unfavourable.

Smith also took notice of another feature of British policy, namely that the production of the more 'advanced or more refined manufactures' was discouraged in the colonies (*WN*, IV.vii.b.40). Thus woollen manufactures were forbidden; and although the colonists were encouraged to export pig iron, they were prevented from erecting slitt mills, which might have led ultimately to the development of manufactures competitive with those of Great Britain.

There was a certain ingenuity in these arrangements (no doubt, as Smith suggests, as much the product of accident as design) in that the colonial relationship could be seen to benefit both parties at least in the short run. The relationship with the colonies, as defined by the Navigation Acts, had the effect of creating a self-supporting economic unit whose main components provided complementary markets for each others' products and in addition helped to minimise gold flows abroad (*WN*, IV.viii.15). By the same token, the colonial relationship gave Britain access to strategic materials and thus contributed to national defence (*WN*, IV.ii.30), through the encouragement given to the mercantile marine.

Smith argued that there were considerable opportunities for economic growth within the framework of the colonial relationship. He placed most emphasis on American experience and drew attention to five factors that helped to explain America's rapid rate of expansion. First, Smith isolated what may be described as 'institutional' forces in pointing out that the colonies possessed political institutions derived from the British model, which encouraged economic activity by guaranteeing the security of the individual (*WN*, IV.vii.b.51).

Second, he pointed out that the colonists had brought to an under-developed territory the habit of subordination and a 'knowledge of agriculture and of other useful arts' (*WN*, IV.vii.b.2), the legacy of the more developed economies from which they had often come. Smith also emphasised that certain features slowing the rate of growth in Europe were absent from the colonies: for example, high rents, tithes and taxes, together with legal arrangements such as laws of entail, which hindered the sale of lands to those whose object was to improve them.[7]

Third, he drew attention to the economic situation of the colonial territories: 'A new colony must always for some time be more under-stocked in proportion to the extent of its territory, and more under-peopled in proportion to the extent of its stock, than the greater part of other countries' (*WN*, I.ix.11). This meant that the rates of both wages and profits were likely to be high, thus contributing to a level of activity that explained the 'continual complaint of the scarcity of hands in North America. The demand for labourers, the funds destined for maintaining them, increase, it seems, still faster than they can find labourers to employ' (*WN*, I.viii.23).

Fourth, Smith argued that the legislative arrangements governing trade with the mother country had contributed most materially to colonial development, even though that had not always been the motive behind them. He drew attention to the fact that 'the most perfect freedom of trade is permitted between the British colonies of America and the West Indies', thus providing a 'great internal market' for their products (*WN* IV.vii.b.39).

In addition, the relative freedom of trade in non-enumerated commodities provided a further market for the primary products involved, while Britain also gave preferential treatment to American goods that were confined to its own domestic market. Again, Britain provided a large European market (albeit indirectly) for the enumerated items; for example, goods like tobacco that were largely re-exported.

Taken as a whole, the colonial policy had the effect of encouraging agriculture, which Smith considered 'the proper business of all new colonies; a business which the cheapness of land renders more advantageous than any other' (*WN*, IV.vii.c.51). This point is of great importance since, on Smith's argument, agriculture was the most productive of all forms of investment, capable of generating large surpluses that could sustain further growth.

Indeed, Smith argued that the restrictions imposed on the introduction of manufactures had *benefited* the colonies by ensuring that they bought from the cheaper European markets and therefore avoided diverting any part of the available capital into less productive employments. He concluded:

> Unjust, however, as such prohibitions may be, they have not hitherto been very hurtful to the colonies. Land is still so cheap, and, consequently, labour so dear among them, that they can import from the mother country, almost all the more refined or more advanced manufactures cheaper than they could make them for themselves. Though they had not, therefore, been prohibited from establishing such manufactures, yet in their present state of improvement, a regard to their own interest would, probably, have prevented them from doing so. (*WN*, IV.vii.b.44)

There is no doubt as to the buoyancy of Smith's tone in describing the growth rate of North America: 'though North America is not yet so rich as England, it is much more thriving, and advancing with much greater rapidity to the further acquisition of riches' (*WN*, I.viii.23).

Yet it cannot be said that Smith minimised the benefits to Britain from the standpoint of economic growth. He pointed out that Britain (together with its neighbours) had as a matter of fact acquired, through the control of the colonies, a 'new and inexhaustible market' that had given occasion to 'new divisions of labour and improvement of art'. Smith's assertion of benefit accruing to Great Britain as a result of the colonial relationship reflects his own grasp of the gains from trade (*WN*, IV.i.31).

Taken as a whole, Smith's argument seems designed to suggest that for a time at least the colonial relationship had contributed to, and proved compatible with, a relatively high rate of growth in both the colonies and the mother country. The relationship between mother country and colonies is represented as beneficial to the two parties, regarding both the politico-economic objectives of the Navigation Acts and the stimulus given to economic growth.

But Smith believed that there were contradictions inherent in the colonial relationship which must begin to manifest themselves over time. For example, while he took pains to emphasise the great stimulus given to economic growth in the colonies, he also pointed out that the high and rapid rate of growth they had attained must ultimately conflict with the restrictions imposed on colonial trade and manufactures, restrictions that could be regarded as the 'principal badge of their dependency' (*WN*, IV.vii.c.64) and as a 'manifest violation of one of the most sacred rights of mankind'. He also pointed out: 'In their present state of improvement, those prohibitions, perhaps, without cramping their industry, or restraining it from any employment to which it would have gone of its own accord, are only impertinent badges of slavery. . . . In a more advanced state they might be really oppressive and insupportable' (*WN*, IV.vii.b.44). Smith believed that in the long run some change must come in the colonial relationship for the reason just stated, although he did place most emphasis on the more immediate problems faced by Britain itself.

So far as Great Britain was concerned, Smith contended that although 'the colony trade' was 'upon the whole beneficial, and greatly beneficial' (*WN*, IV.vii.c.47), the rate of growth was necessarily less than it would have been in the absence of the Navigation Acts. He believed that 'if the manufactures of Great Britain . . . have been advanced, as they certainly have, by the colony trade, it has not been by means of the monopoly of that trade, but in spite of the monopoly' (*WN*, IV.vii.c.55).

Smith advanced a number of points in support of this contention. First, he suggested that the monopoly of the colony trade had inevitably increased the volume of business to be done by a relatively limited amount of British capital and, therefore, the prevailing rate of profit. He argued that high rates of profit would affect the improvement of land and the frugality of the merchant classes, while also ensuring that available capital would be partly drawn, and partly driven, from those trades where Britain lacked the monopoly (that is, drawn by the higher profits available in the colony trade and driven from them by a poorer competitive position).

Smith especially emphasised that the pattern of British trade had been altered in such a way that its manufactures, 'instead of being suited, as before the act of navigation, to the neighbouring market of Europe, or to the more distant one of the countries which lie round the Mediterranean sea, have, the greater part of them, been accommodated to the still more distant one of the colonies' (*WN*, IV.vii.c.22). Smith's point was that the existing legislation had drawn capital from trades carried on with a near market (Europe) and diverted it to trade carried on with a distant market (America), while forcing a certain amount of capital from a direct to an indirect foreign trade: all with consequent effects on the rate of return, the employment of productive labour and, therefore, the rate of economic growth.

Smith added that the pattern of British trade had been altered in such a way as to make her unduly dependent on a single (though large) market:

> Her commerce, instead of running in a great number of small channels, has been taught to run principally in one great channel. But the whole system of her industry and commerce has thereby been rendered less secure; the whole state of her body politick less healthful, than it otherwise would have been. In her present condition, Great Britain resembles one of those unwholesome bodies in which some of the vital parts are overgrown, and which, upon that account, are liable to many dangerous disorders scarce incident to those in which all the parts are more properly proportioned. (*WN*, IV.vii.c.43)

In sum, the colonial relationship was compatible with a high rate of growth in America, but also produced a sub-optimal rate of growth as far as Great Britain was concerned. Smith roundly asserted that 'the present system of management' ensured that Britain derived nothing but loss from the dominion assumed over the colonies and that *current* costs exceeded the profits actually gained. Looked at from this point of view, the colonial policy emerged as essentially contradictory, at least in the long run, and as attractive only to the 'undiscerning eye of giddy ambition' (*WN*, IV.vii.c.85).

Smith's account of the problem currently facing Great Britain was largely dominated by fiscal need. In Smith's opinion Britain's needs seemed to be growing more rapidly than its resources, and he noted in this connexion that by January 1775 the national debt had reached the then astronomical figure of £130 millions (absorbing £4.5 millions in interest charges), much of which was due to the acquisition of the colonial territories. This was a matter of some moment. It meant that a country whose rate of growth had been adversely affected by the colonial relationship had to face a large and probably growing tax burden, which would itself affect the rate of economic expansion, and thus compound the problem.

The mercantile approach to the colonial relationship was thus fundamentally flawed. *In the long run* the colonies would have to confront the restraints imposed upon their manufactures, while at the same time Great Britain would have to confront the consequences of a sub-optimal rate of growth. Smith laid the blame for British policies of the period on the merchant groups: 'We must not wonder, therefore, if, in the greater part of them, their interest has been more considered than either that of the colonies or that of the mother country' (*WN*, IV.vii.b.49). As he remarked in one of the most famous passages in the *Wealth of Nations* (which may have caught the eye of Napoleon):

> To found a great empire for the sole purpose of raising up a people of customers, may at first sight appear a project fit only for a nation of shopkeepers. It is, however, a project altogether unfit for a nation of shopkeepers; but extremely fit for a nation whose government is influenced by shopkeepers. (*WN*, IV.vii.c.63)

As this passage implies, government, too, had fallen into a trap set by 'the groundless jealousy of the merchants and manufacturers of the mother country' (*WN*, IV.vii.b.44), compounded by the emotional considerations of national pride:

> The rulers of Great Britain have, for more than a century past, amused the people with the imagination that they possessed a great empire on the west side of the Atlantic. This empire, however, has hitherto existed in imagination only. It has hitherto been, not an empire, but the project of an empire. . . . If the project cannot be compleated, it ought to be given up. If any of the provinces of the British empire cannot be made to contribute towards the support of the whole empire, it is surely time that Great Britain should . . . endeavour to accommodate her future views and designs to the real mediocrity of her circumstances. (*WN*, V.iii.92)

Yet Smith believed that the project of empire could be completed. He also believed that Britain both could and should tax the colonies, partly as a means of relief from the growing burden of the national debt and partly as a means of making the colonies pay for the benefits received from the imperial connexion. It is worth noting that Smith did not defend colonial taxation on the ground that Britain had planted the colonies; on the contrary, he pointed out that they had been originally peopled largely as the result of religious persecution (*WN*, IV.vii.b.61). Nor did he suggest that taxation was justified on the ground that the mother country had originally invested in their improvement; rather, he insisted that policy to regulate the colonies had been implemented only after the original colonists had made significant economic progress (*WN*, IV.vii.b.63). He simply argued:

> It is not contrary to justice that both Ireland and America should contribute towards the discharge of the publick debt of Great Britain. That debt has been contracted in support of the government established by the Revolution, a government to which the protestants of Ireland owe, not only the whole authority which they at present enjoy in their own country, but every security which they possess for their

> liberty, their property, and their religion; a government to which several of the colonies of America owe their present charters, and consequently their present constitution, and to which all the colonies of America owe the liberty, security, and property which they have ever since enjoyed. That publick debt has been contracted in the defence, not of Great Britain alone, but of all the different provinces of the empire; the immense debt contracted in the late war in particular, and a great part of that contracted in the war before, were both properly contracted in defence of America. (*WN*, V.iii.88)

Smith concluded that the British government should extend the British system of taxation to all the colonies. The concluding sections of the *Wealth of Nations* are largely concerned with the technical problems of this aspect of harmonisation, and Smith saw no reason to suppose that the major British taxes (land tax, stamp duties, customs and excise) could not be successfully applied to both America and Ireland. He added that such a change of policy should be accompanied by freedom of trade between all parts of the empire and, most dramatically, that it would require a form of union which would give the colonies representation in the British Parliament and in effect create a single state:

> This, however, could scarce, perhaps, be done, consistently with the principles of the British constitution, without admitting into the British parliament, or if you will into the states-general of the British Empire, a fair and equal representation of all those different provinces, that of each province bearing the same proportion to the produce of its taxes, as the representation of Great Britain might bear to the produce of the taxes levied upon Great Britain. (*WN*, V.iii.68)[8]

Indeed Smith believed that

> there is not the least probability that the British constitution would be hurt by the union of Great Britain with her colonies. That constitution, on the contrary, would be completed by it, and seems to be imperfect without it. The assembly which deliberates and decides concerning the affairs of every part of the empire, in order to be properly informed, ought certainly to have representatives from every part of it. (*WN*, IV.vii.c.77)

Union, at least in the sense in which it has been discussed so far, represented for Smith the *logical* solution to the economic and constitutional difficulties of mercantile policy. But union had to be discussed in the context of options actually open to the British government at the time, as Smith was well aware. His published views on the subject probably led Alexander Wedderburn, solicitor general in Lord North's administration, to seek Smith's advice in the aftermath of Saratoga.[9] Wedderburn, it may be recalled, had been responsible for the hostile examination of Benjamin Franklin before the privy council in 1774, an exchange that moved Hume to remark in a letter to Smith that Wedderburn's treatment of the distinguished (and initially sympathetic) colonist had been 'most cruel' (*CAS*, 171).

One of the possible, and at one stage practicable, solutions in Smith's view was consistent with his general position, namely an incorporating union. By the time Smith published the *Wealth of Nations*, however, the opportunity had been lost: 'We, on this side of the water, are afraid lest the multitude of American representatives should overturn the balance of the constitution', whereas those 'on the other side of the water are afraid lest their distance from the seat of government might expose them to many oppressions' (*WN*, IV.vii.c.78,79). His tone had hardened further in his *Memorandum* of 1778: 'in their present elevation of spirits,' he advised Wedderburn, 'the ulcerated minds of the Americans are not likely to consent to any union even upon terms the most advantageous to themselves' (*CAS*, 381). In Britain, he wrote, the plan of union 'seems not to be agreeable to any considerable party of men'. He sadly concluded: 'The plan which, if it could be executed, would certainly tend most to the prosperity, to the splendour, and to the duration of the empire, if you except here and there a solitary philosopher like myself, seems scarce to have a single advocate' (*CAS*, 382).

A second possible solution was military victory and the restoration of existing institutional arrangements. But as Smith wryly pointed out, the difficulty in such a solution 'arises altogether from the resistance of America' (*CAS*, 381). He had already noted in the *Wealth of Nations* that while a professional standing army like Great Britain's was always likely to be the superior of a militia, experience suggested that this was not always true when the latter was long in the field: 'Should the war in America drag out through another campaign, the American militia may become in every respect a match for that standing army, of which the valour appeared, in the last war, at least not inferior to that of the hardiest veterans of France and Spain' (*WN*, V.i.a.27). Yet even if victory were possible, the outcome, he advised, would still be basically unworkable.[10] A military government, he wrote, 'is what, of all others, the Americans hate and dread the most. While they are able to keep the field they never will submit to it; and if, in spite of their utmost resistance, it should be established, they will, for more than a century to come, be at all times ready to take arms in order to overturn it' (*CAS*, 381).

A third option was simplicity itself: voluntary withdrawal from the conflict and recognition of America as a separate state. The advantages of such a bold course were, in Smith's opinion, considerable. At one stroke, Britain would be free of the crushing burden of expenditure needed to defend the colonies and could avoid further conflict with France and Spain, at least in the New World. As Smith wrote in the *Wealth of Nations*:

'By thus parting good friends, the natural affection of the colonies to the mother country, which, perhaps, our late dissensions have well nigh extinguished, would quickly revive'. Yet withdrawal from the conflict was unlikely: 'Such sacrifices, though they might frequently be agreeable to the interest, are always mortifying to the pride of every nation, and what is perhaps of still greater consequence, they are always contrary to the private interest of the governing part of it' (*WN*, IV.vii.c.66).[11]

Nor was Smith above a little Machiavellian intrigue, in the popular sense of that term, in suggesting that Britain might also consider restoring Canada to France and Florida to Spain, thus making 'our colonies the natural enemies of those two monarchies and consequently the natural allies of Great Britain' (*CAS*, 383). But for Smith the most likely outcome was also the most expensive: partial military defeat that would mean the loss of some or all of the 'thirteen united colonies' and the retention of Canada. The *Memorandum* must have made bleak reading for the solicitor general, but it would have seemed bleaker still had he known how accurately Smith had forecast the events of 1783.

II

Despite his reading of the situation in 1778, Smith offers essentially an economic rather than a political analysis of the American problem, an analysis that may be seen as the centrepiece of his critique of the mercantile system. Certainly Smith encouraged this view, writing as he did in the third edition and in the year of peace with America: 'It is unnecessary, I apprehend, at present to say anything further, in order to expose the folly of a system, which fatal experience has now sufficiently exposed' (*WN*, IV.viii.15).[12]

But what had actually been exposed? Arguably the most important single cause of the 'disturbances' was to be found in the widening gulf between the British and colonial interpretation of the law of the constitution. There was a classic confrontation between Franklin's view 'that one of the privileges of English subjects is, that they are not to be taxed but with their common consent' and the British assertion of parliamentary sovereignty as contained in the Declaratory Act of 1766 which, while repealing the Stamp Act, took occasion to note that the king in parliament 'had, hath, and of right ought have, full power and authority to make laws and statutes of sufficient force and validity to bind the colonies and people of America, subjects of the Crown of Great Britain, in all cases whatsoever'. It could well be argued, therefore, that the immediate cause of the 'disturbances' revealed a contradiction inherent in the dogma of parliamentary sovereignty: what the British perceived to be an affirmation of freedom from absolutism the Americans interpreted as a symbol of tyranny.[13]

Moreover, it has to be noted that while the Navigation Acts were central to the problem of differential rates of growth, they were not actually the *cause* of the 'present disturbances', a fact that Smith's exposition tends to obscure. He conceals the point that the colonists were not in fact objecting to mercantile regulations, that such regulations did not figure in such key documents as the Declaration of Rights and Grievances (1774), the Olive Branch Petition (1775) or even the Declaration of Independence (1776), which contained an otherwise comprehensive indictment of British policy. The point is nicely put in Resolve No. 4 of the Suffolk Resolves, where it is stated that 'we cheerfully consent to the regulating of our external commerce, for the purpose of securing the commercial advantages of the whole empire to the mother country, and the commercial benefits of its respective members'.[14]

It should also be observed that Smith's analysis depends upon his treatment of the natural progress of opulence and upon the ranking of the productivities of different areas of investment. It also depends crucially on his belief that any interference with the natural balance of industry must slow down the rate of growth, as he argued had been the case with Great Britain.

Yet there is remarkably little offered by way of empirical support for the analytical concepts central to the case, leading Governor Pownall to remark that Smith was using theses established in one part of his book as proven principles in another.[15] The governor recognised the importance of Smith's views on the productivity of investment but noted: 'In that part, however, which explains the different effect of different employment of capital . . . I will beg to arrest your steps for a moment, while we examine the ground whereon we tread; and the more so, as I find these propositions used in the second part of your work as data; whence you endeavour to prove, that the monopoly of the colony trade is a disadvantageous commercial institution' (*CAS*, 354).

The governor also drew attention to the style of Smith's argument:

> It strikes me as material, and I am sure, therefore, you will excuse me making, in this place, one remark *on the manner* of your argument, and how *you stretch your reasoning nicely*. You in words advance upon the ground of *probable reasons for believing* only, you prove by probable suppositions only; yet most people who read your book, will think you mean to set up an absolute proof, and your conclusion is drawn as though you had. (*CAS*, 369)[16]

As Richard Koebner has observed, Smith often presents views on the colonial issue in such a way that they appear as 'unavoidable inferences' from his argument as a whole.[17]

But equally it has to be noted that criticism or rejection of Smith's formal explanation for the phenomenon of differential rates of growth refutes neither the empirical statement that the rates of growth were different nor the argument that this phenomenon must lead, eventually, to a change in the nature of the relationship between the colonies and the mother country. It was in this context, as we have seen, that Smith advocated an incorporating union which would include Ireland. The idea was hardly novel, dating back as it does to Benjamin Franklin's Albany Plan of 1754. Twenty years later, the first Continental Congress debated, and narrowly defeated, Joseph Galloway's 'proposal for a grand legislative union'. But Smith's advocacy of union is still a notable contribution to the debate, and interesting, too, in that it reveals the preferences of the 'solitary philosopher'. As David Stevens has noted, 'Smith was interested in the welfare of the empire and particularly the mother country'.[18] There seems little doubt that the judgement is accurate: Smith would have preferred to see the empire left intact through the creation in effect of an Atlantic Economic Community that would have preserved the position of global dominance established by the defeat of France in 1763. An enormous opportunity had been lost.

The case for union depended on Smith's acceptance of the constitutional 'rule' that there should be no taxation without representation,[19] but it is chiefly remarkable for its basis in economic factors. This emphasis also affected Smith's judgement as to the future course of events. In Smith's view the progress of the colonies had been, and would continue to be, such that

> in the course of little more than a century, perhaps, the produce of American might exceed that of British taxation. The seat of the empire would then naturally remove itself to that part of the empire which contributed most to the general defence and support of the whole. (*WN*, IV.vii.c.79)

Thomas Pownall offered a similar prediction, in commenting on the future of his own proposal for a 'grand marine dominion'. Even without union, the logic of the argument served to suggest that America would in due course become the dominant power. The point was caught exactly by Franklin, writing to Lord Kames in 1767:

> Scotland and Ireland are differently circumstanc'd. Confin'd by the Sea, they can scarcely increase in Numbers, Wealth and Strength so as to overbalance England. But America, an immense Territory, favour'd by Nature with all Advantages of Climate, Soil, great navigable Rivers, and Lakes &c. must become a great Country, populous and mighty; and will in a less time than is generally conceiv'd, be able to shake off any Shackles that may be impos'd on her, and perhaps place them on the Imposers.[20]

But if Smith contemplated the loss of the colonies with regret, he also did so with some equanimity. Writing very much in the manner of Josiah

Tucker, he recognised that in the long run it would be in America's interest to maintain and further to develop trade links with Great Britain.[21] Indeed, he looked forward to a special relationship based upon a similarity of language and manners (*CAS*, 383). Writing in the same vein he was able to assure William Eden in December 1783 that there was little to fear in the long run despite present inconveniences (*CAS*, 271).

As Bailyn has noted, Smith 'understood the economic power that America would soon create and the political dominance that that would eventually entail, and while his political solution, a consolidated union between the two peoples, was impractical, his economic solution, free trade and the open development of American manufactures, was not.'[22] This is the key issue and the feature of Smith's work that enabled later generations of Americans to recognise in it what Stevens has aptly described as a 'compatible philosophy'.[23] Nor, in view of the remarks made earlier about Francis Hutcheson, should one forget the fundamental principles inherent in this 'philosophy'. Throughout the critique of the colonial relationship, Smith defended not only the concept of empire but also the basic issue of freedom on economic, political and above all moral grounds.[24] His objection to all the expedients of the mercantile system was that they were impolitic and unjust, involving as they did an abuse of political power and a violation of natural liberty, one of the most sacred rights of mankind.

If Hutcheson's work was used by Scottish emigrants to America like Francis Alison and John Witherspoon in order to justify revolution, Smith apparently found no difficulty in assimilating its implications so as to express the same 'warm love of liberty' that had been so marked a feature of his master's character and teaching.

NOTES

The present writer's views are elaborated in 'Mercantilist Policy: The American Colonies', in *A System of Social Science: Papers Relating to Adam Smith* (Oxford, 1979), 184–208, and 'Adam Smith: The Demise of the Colonial Relationship', in *The Treaty of Paris (1783) in a Changing State System*, ed. Prosser Gifford (Washington, 1985), 23–43.

1. Smith to Archibald Davidson, 16 Nov. 1787, in *CAS*, 309.
2. Caroline Robbins, ' "When Is It That Colonies May Turn Independent": An Analysis of the Environment and Politics of Francis Hutcheson ', *WMQ*, 214–51. See also the same author's *The Eighteenth-Century Commonwealthman* (Cambridge, Mass., 1959), chap. 6.
3. David Fate Norton, 'Francis Hutcheson in America', *SVEC* 154 (1976): 1548.

4. Donald Winch, *Adam Smith's Politics: A Study in Historiographic Revision* (Cambridge, 1978), 52. Josiah Tucker, whose analysis of the American problem agrees in many respects with that of Smith, was also at one with him in regard to this problem. In 1775 'he declared that Locke's principles of government, if carried out as the Americans construed them, would destroy every government on Earth'. Quoted in Robert Livingston Schuyler, *Josiah Tucker: A Selection from His Economic and Political Writings* (New York, 1931), 41.
5. The critical role played by rates of growth in America and Great Britain is a prominent feature of Bernard Bailyn, '1776: A Year of Challenge — A World Transformed', *Journal of Law and Economics* 19 (1976): 437–66. Richard Koebner, *Empire* (Cambridge, 1961), and Donald Winch, *Classical Political Economy and the Colonies* (London, 1965) are particularly helpful for the economic aspects of Smith's analysis.
6. As Josiah Tucker observed: 'For an undoubted Fact it is, that from the moment in which *Canada* came into the Possession of the *English*, an end was put to the Sovereignty of the Mother-Country over her Colonies. They had nothing then to fear from a Foreign Enemy'. *The True Interest of Great Britain Set Forth in Regard to the Colonies* (1774), in Schuyler, *Josiah Tucker*, 337–38.
7. But see Stanley N. Katz, 'Thomas Jefferson and the Right to Property in Revolutionary America', *Journal of Law and Economics* 19 (1976): 467–88.
8. Smith accepted the 'rule' that there should be no taxation without representation, but see H.L.A. Hart, 'Bentham and the United States of America', *Journal of Law and Economics* 19 (1976): 547–67.
9. 'Smith's Thoughts on the State of the Contest with America, February 1778' was first edited by G.H. Gutteridge and published in the *American Historical Review* 38 (1932–33): 714–20. The edition used here was prepared by David Stevens and is presented in *CAS* as appendix B, 377–85. It is cited hereafter as *Memorandum*.
10. The point was further elaborated in the *Memorandum*, 383. Josiah Tucker offers a similar assessment in *True Interest of Great Britain*, 324–25, 355. One of Smith's friends, the distinguished French economist A.R.J. Turgot, expressed the hope that the British would win precisely because victory would exhaust her resources in policing an unruly country, thus freeing France from the attentions of her tormentor. See R.R. Palmer, 'Turgot: Paragon of the Continental Enlightenment', *Journal of Law and Economics* 19 (1976): 612.
11. As Smith noted in the *Memorandum*, 'tho' this termination of the war might be really advantageous, it would not, in the eyes of Europe appear honourable to Great Britain' (383). He added that the government would have much to fear from the 'rage and indignation' of the electorate at the 'public disgrace and calamity, for such they would suppose it to be, of thus dismembering the empire'. Tucker also advocated this radical solution, following a careful review of the options open to the British Government in 1774 (*True Interest of Great Britain*, 359).
12. The present writer has argued that this passage suggests that Smith's purpose was at least in part rhetorical. See Skinner, *System of Social Science* 208.

13. See especially Max Beloff, *The Debate on the American Revolution, 1763–1783*, 2nd ed. (Cambridge, 1960), and Hart, 'Bentham and the United States'. The problems of the eighteenth century find an interesting echo in Geoffrey Marshall, *Parliamentary Sovereignty and the Commonwealth* (Oxford, 1957). It is interesting to note that Tucker argued strongly at the time of the Stamp Act for the unlimited authority of parliament (Schuyler, *Josiah Tucker*, 25).
14. Quoted in David Stevens, 'Adam Smith and the Colonial Disturbances', in *Essays on Adam Smith*, ed. Andrew S. Skinner and Thomas Wilson (Oxford, 1975), 213.
15. *A Letter from Governor Pownall to Adam Smith* (London, 1776), in *CAS*, appendix A.
16. This is a telling comment on Smith's argument. In a letter to Andreas Holt dated 26 October 1780, Smith stated that he had 'obviated all the objections of Governor Pownal' in the second edition of *WN* (CAS, 250). In fact he had not.
17. Koebner, *Empire*, 227.
18. Stevens, 'Colonial Disturbances', 214.
19. But see Hart, 'Bentham and the United States'.
20. Franklin, 14:69–70.
21. As Schuyler has noted, the 'doctrine of self-interest explains . . . Tucker's confident and happy prediction that the loss of the colonies would not result in a decline of British trade' (*Josiah Tucker*, 35–36).
22. Bailyn, '1776: A Year of Challenge', 465–66.
23. Stevens, 'Colonial Disturbances', 217.
24. On this topic see Richard F. Teichgraeber III, *'Free Trade' and Moral Philosophy: Rethinking the Sources of Adam Smith's 'Wealth of Nations'* (Durham, N.C., 1986).

9

JEFFREY R. SMITTEN

Moderatism and History: William Robertson's Unfinished History of British America

Over a decade ago George Shepperson called for detailed study of Scottish attitudes towards the American Revolution, arguing that we still need a wealth of detail documenting Scottish-American relations during this period.[1] William Robertson, principal of Edinburgh University from 1762 to 1793, is a case in point. Shepperson, in fact, cites him as an example of the sort of neglected figure whose attitudes may add significantly to the total picture; and today, in the wake of Richard B. Sher's *Church and University in the Scottish Enlightenment*, there can be no doubt about the importance of Robertson's views on politics and history. As the leading spokesman for the Moderates, he was at the centre of one of the most powerful groups comprising the Scottish Enlightenment; and his personal dilemmas may well have representative significance.

The few previous studies of Robertson's attitudes towards America address two apparently unrelated issues. First, it would seem that he became increasingly conservative and critical of American actions between the time of the Stamp Act and the Declaration of Independence. Initially, the argument goes, Robertson welcomed American resistance to the Stamp Act, implicitly recognising the vast potential of America; but he ultimately backed away from claims of full independence. Dalphy I. Fagerstrom, the main proponent of this view, even suggests that Robertson seems 'to have submitted to government views at the expense of earlier sympathies.'[2] Second, there is the problem of Robertson's unfinished history of British America. He had hoped to write a full history of colonisation in North and South America, including particularly the settlements of the Spanish, the Portuguese and the British; however, by the summer of 1776 he felt compelled to publish the Spanish portion separately and to put the British portion aside. He reached this decision because, as he told Sir Robert Murray Keith: 'It is impossible to give any description of . . . [the British colonies'] political or commercial situation, or to venture upon any speculation concerning them while the contest between us remains undecided.'[3] But no one has asked why Robertson was unable to write in this situation. R.A. Humphreys merely observes that 'true Scot that he was, Robertson preferred to postpone his discussion of the British colonies until he should know what was going to happen to them.'[4] Sher only remarks that Robertson felt his history was 'inappropriate' under the circumstances.[5]

This chapter addresses these two issues, showing that Robertson's attitudes did not shift between 1766 and 1776 (and after) but rather remained fundamentally consistent. It also offers an explanation for Robertson's abandonment of his history of British America. I will suggest that these two apparently unrelated issues, Robertson's conservatism and his inability to finish his history, are connected. In other words, Robertson's views on America, considered in light of changing British opinion, prevented him from completing his American history, the work he had intended to be his magnum opus.[6]

I

In establishing the conservatism of Robertson's views, Fagerstrom showed that Robertson accepted the principle of British supremacy in America. What he failed to recognise, however, is that Robertson applied this principle consistently over time. Robertson concurred with popular writers such as Thomas Pownall that Britain had to be the centre of its colonial system. But that meant incorporating the colonies into a larger whole, not merely subjugating them to British power. For example, Pownall referred to George Grenville as a minister 'who, convinced that the mother country has a just and natural right to govern the colonies, will yet so administer the power of that government in the genuine spirit of laws and equity to that true and constitutional obedience, which is their real liberty.'[7] However fitting such a tribute to the author of the Stamp Act may be, Pownall nonetheless saw the constitution as providing the terms that mediate the relations of mother country and colonies. Yet there can be no doubt about the central position of the mother country: 'Great Britain, as the center of this system, must be the center of attraction, to which these colonies, in the administration of every power of their government, in the exercise of their judicial powers, and the execution of their laws, and in every operation of their trade must tend' (36). Pownall's main interest was not simply to establish lines of authority but to lay the foundation for a commercial empire, one in which 'subordination to the government of the mother country' is blended with 'a temper and spirit which remember that these are our people, our brethren, faithful, good and beneficial subjects, and free-born Englishmen, or by adoption, possessing all the right of freedom' (38). British supremacy and American rights were inseparably connected.

Robertson knew Pownall's book as early as 1769 and consulted it when he worked on his history of British America;[8] but from his earliest speculations, perhaps even before he had read Pownall, he held a very similar position, endorsing British supremacy, while allowing for a harmonious union of mother country and colonies. Thus, in 1766, when writing to William Strahan about the repeal of the Stamp Act, Robertson declares:

> I am glad to hear the determination of the house of commons concerning the stamp-act. I rejoice, from my love of the human species, that a million of men in America have some chance of running the same great career which other free people have held before them. I do not apprehend revolution or independence sooner than these must and should come. A very little skill and attention in the art of governing may preserve the supremacy of Britain as long as it ought to be preserved.[9]

Although Robertson endorses repeal of the Stamp Act on the grounds of human liberty, he sets this endorsement in the context of British supremacy in America. The colonial pursuit of liberty must take place under the aegis of British control. But when revolution and independence did in fact come 'sooner than these must and should', Robertson thought, consistently enough, that no amount of pressure should abrogate British supremacy in America. Thus, when he wrote to Strahan concerning American affairs a decade later, his fundamental position had not changed. The colonists, he declares, will one day attain full independence,

> but not just now, if there be any degree of political wisdom or vigour remaining. At the same time one cannot but regret that prosperous growing states should be checked in their career. As a lover of mankind, I bewail it; but as a subject of Great Britain, I must wish that their dependence on it should continue. If the wisdom of government can terminate the contest with honour instantly, that would be the most desirable issue. This, however, I take to be *now* impossible; and I will venture to foretel, that if our leaders do not at once exert the power of the British empire in its full force, the struggle will be long, dubious, and disgraceful. We are past the hour of lenitives and half exertions.[10]

By advocating military action against the colonies, Robertson does not reject general sympathy with independence but simply extends his assumption about the necessity of British supremacy to achieve it properly. Independence is a worthy goal, but for the present it is in the empire's best interest, according to Robertson, that the colonies remain part of the whole; and military action must be taken to ensure the empire's balance, unity and coherence.[11]

Robertson may well have agreed with Pownall's views on the colonies because they harmonised with some of his deepest assumptions as a Moderate. Robertson understood the colonial situation in the same general terms that he had developed during the 1750s and 1760s to deal with Scottish ecclesiastical and political affairs. Ian D.L. Clark has described the basis of this Moderate view-point:

> The guiding principle of Moderatism was *balance*. . . . The Moderates as a party appear to have been consciously concerned to break down the sharp antitheses which had grown up within the framework of Calvinism in Scotland in the 17th century, and it was this which brought them again and again into conflict with the representatives of 'Orthodoxy'.[12]

Accordingly, Clark observes, 'one of the most noticeable features of Moderate preaching is its insistence that what God has joined man should not put asunder. Faith-and-works, revelation-and-reason, divinity-and-humanity, truth-and-charity were all units of thought rather than (as in so many Evangelical sermons) antitheses' (242). In Robertson's understanding of this idea, there is a desire to defuse and ultimately to control social, political, religious and intellectual conflict. By breaking down sharp antitheses in the church and in society, he wished to mediate, indeed to manage, conflict. He was not, of course, acting as a selfless peacemaker, for he instigated his share of intrigue and conflict during the period of Moderate supremacy in Scotland. Instead, with this strategy of balance and *discordia concors* he presented himself and the Moderates as impartial arbiters of a divided society, as men under whose guidance religious and political conflict could be transformed into more peaceable social dialogue.

Style, in both oratory and writing, was an important part of this managerial strategy. To combat the opposition directly would be merely to create antitheses. The better tactic, in Robertson's view, would be to balance opposing ideas in order to reach an apparently impartial, mutually acceptable conclusion. If opposing sides believed they had been heard, then presumably they would accept the conclusion to which they had both contributed. Robertson was an acknowledged master of this style of discourse and debate, as we learn from Henry Mackenzie, who knew the effect Robertson could create and understood its intent. In social situations, he noted, Robertson 'spoke, as became him, a good deal; but there was nothing assuming or authoritative either in the manner or the matter of his discourse. He took every opportunity of calling on his hearers for their share of the dialogue'. This manner 'is always flattering to the person we address, because it seems to call for the favour of his information.'[13] Robertson, in other words, brought his listener into the discourse and made him a part of it through an air of deference. In the more formal circumstances of public oratory, Robertson also appeared deferential, creating a kind of dialogue by balancing opinions:

> Dr. Robertson has a power of speaking in a manner admirably calculated for his situation as a leader of what was called the Moderate Party of the Church, temperate, conciliating, and candid; he generally wound up the debate with a concise and impartial view of the opposite arguments, and frequently brought the opposite parties to an amicable settlement, by proposing some resolution which allowed to both a portion of what they had contended for, and did not trench on any of the principles which they considered as fixed, and not to be departed from. (1:61–62)

Making allowance for Mackenzie's adulation, it is clear that Robertson's rhetorical strategy, characteristic of his Moderate stance, is to practise deference to the opinions of others and deferral of his own judgements: he aims to draw opponents into his discourse by balancing opposed views, to steer a middle course between opposites, to remain detached and impartial in the face of conflict and to postpone final decisions, all in an effort to defuse opposition and maintain control.

In his written work, Robertson created an exact analogy of his oratory, and very much for the same purpose. A suitably polite style was nowhere considered more important than in history, a field directly relevant to social and religious change and one dominated by party advocates.[14] Although we do not know the precise form in which Robertson intended to publish his history of British America, his characteristic style is apparent in the broad structure of the unfinished narrative as well as in the conduct of argument and the handling of sources.

Robertson organises the narrative of his British history around a contrast with the closing chapter of the *History of America*, describing the highly centralised Spanish colonial empire. The dominant feature of Spanish America, he writes, is that 'authority of every species centres in the crown' (*WWR*, 7:358), and the story he tells is one of very slow liberalisation of such rigid authority by the mid-eighteenth century. By contrast, the dominant feature of British America is a failure to organise authority, a theme established early in the history:

> During the course of two centuries [from approximately the fourteenth to the sixteenth century], while industry and commerce were making gradual progress, both in the south and north of Europe, the English continued so blind to the advantages of their situation, that they hardly began to bend their thoughts towards those objects and pursuits, to which they are indebted for their present opulence and power. (*WWR*, 8:6)

The disparity Robertson observes in these early colonial efforts reappears through the fragment. The British managed their colonies with very little attention to planning or administration; yet by the eighteenth century the nation had come to benefit from the colonies enormously (see *WWR*, 8:11, 16, 36). Thus, as the Spanish were tentatively liberalising their empire, the British were just as tentatively exerting authority over theirs. These contrasting stories neatly embody Robertson's own middle-of-the-road position between the endorsement of liberty on the one hand and the assertion of British supremacy on the other. By linking the Spanish and British histories, he shows the virtues and defects of each kind of colonial experience, creating a sense of completeness and impartial balance in his rendering of the subject.

Within the history of British America itself, a further contrast operates to organise the narrative. Rather than give a colony-by-colony account organised spatially, as most previous historians had done, Robertson shows the historical development of the colonies over time. Accordingly, he chooses the two original areas of colonisation, Virginia and New England, as the subject of detailed narrative, with the others to be noticed briefly. As the twin foundations of the colonial empire, these embody the two spirits driving emigration to the New World: commerce and religion. The history of Virginia is primarily a history of commerce, and here Robertson sounds most like Adam Smith, deploring needless restrictions on trade and praising the growth of steady application, industry and self-sufficiency (see the narrative of the establishment of Jamestown, *WWR*, 8:41–43). When he turns to New England, however, he introduces a different animating principle:

> But what mere attention to private emolument or to national utility could not effect, was accomplished by the operation of a higher principle. Religion had gradually excited among a great body of the people a spirit that fitted them remarkably for encountering the dangers, and surmounting the obstacles, which had hitherto rendered abortive the schemes of colonization in that part of America allotted to the company of Plymouth. As the various settlements in New England are indebted for their origin to this spirit, as in the course of our narrative we shall discern its influence mingling in all their transactions, and giving a peculiar tincture to the character of the people, as well as to their institutions, both civil and ecclesiastical, it becomes necessary to trace its rise and progress with attention and accuracy. (*WWR*, 8:87)

As a corollary of this new spirit, Robertson is concerned with religious fanaticism, and now appears to be very critical of claims to independence because they often seem to arise from this distempered base. Thus, once more, he has balanced opposed ideas, setting commerce against religion and independence against fanaticism. The effect is to imply (not state) a middle position that is detached from the extremes and that gives both sides their due, a position that acknowledges both the commercial and the religious basis of British America as well as the virtues of independence and the necessity of firm governance.

A few examples will indicate how these broad contrasts are reflected in some of the details of the history. Although Robertson praises industry and commercial success, he avoids taking an immediate stand (at least in the extant portion of the history) on the Navigation Acts. Instead of laying down at the outset an authoritative position on economic policy, Robertson characteristically defers final judgement:

> By these successive regulations, the plan of securing to England a monopoly of the commerce with its colonies, and of shutting up every other channel into which it might be diverted, was perfected and reduced into complete system. On one side of the Atlantic these regulations have been extolled as an extraordinary effort of political sagacity, and have been considered as the great charter of national commerce, to which the parent state is indebted for all its opulence and power. On the other they have been execrated as a code of oppression, more suited to the illiberality of mercantile ideas, than to extensive views of legislative wisdom. Which of these opinions is best founded I shall examine at large in another part of this work. (*WWR*, 8:77)

As I shall explain later, circumstances may have made it impossible for Robertson to reach what would be for him a satisfactory conclusion on such an issue. It is only necessary to observe here Robertson's polite style, how deliberately he weighs contrary views so as to incorporate both sides into his conclusion through deference, and how he defers stating his own views until all sides have established their positions.

Robertson is equally polite in the handling of his sources. He typically balances differing points of view, especially in book 10 (on New England), where he weighs pro-American and pro-Puritan views against more sceptical, secular viewpoints. For instance, when he reports the extraordinary coincidence in which Charles I prevents Haselrig, Hampden and Cromwell from emigrating to America, Robertson writes: 'By order of council, an embargo was laid on these when on the point of sailing; and Charles, far from suspecting that the future revolutions in his kingdoms were to be excited and directed by persons in such a humble sphere of life, forcibly detained the men destined to overturn his throne, and to terminate his days by a violent death' (*WWR*, 8:123). Supporting his point, Robertson cites Cotton Mather, Daniel Neal and George Chalmers, who represent a variety of perspectives on this event. Mather relishes it: 'There were especially Three Famous Persons, whom I suppose their Adversaries would not have so studiously detained at Home, if they had *forseen* Events; those were *Oliver Cromwell*, and Mr. *Hampden*, and Sir *Arthur Haselrig*: Nevertheless, this is not the only Instance *of Persecuting Churchmens* not having the *Spirit of Prophecy*.' Chalmers, on the contrary, seems sympathetic to Charles: 'Happy perhaps would it have been, for himself at least, had the misguided Charles suffered those vessels to have sailed, that they might have transported passengers beyond the Atlantic, who afterwards proved so fatal to him!' Neal, however, barely registers the irony at all, observing that he only mentions the incident 'because it confirms what has been reported by several Historians, that Mr. *Pym*, Mr. *Hampden*, Mr. *Pelham*, and other great Men in the Long Parliament, were about to remove to *New-England* before the Altercations which happened at home kept them here.' Robertson, as the passage indicates, accepts the irony but from a balanced perspective, clearing away strong partisan connotations and steering a middle course among his sources by registering both irony and sympathy.[15]

Even when Robertson's attitude towards events is openly declared, he manages to distance himself so as to avoid the suggestion of strong feeling. His stance on the dispute over the standard of St George in the Massachusetts Bay colony is clear: 'After a long controversy, carried on by both parties with that heat and zeal which in trivial disputes supply the want of argument, the contest was terminated by a compromise' (*WWR*, 8:112). In documenting the incident, however, Robertson moderates his stance, citing not only Neal and Chalmers, his more sceptical guides, but also Thomas Hutchinson, who is somewhat more favourable. Although Hutchinson mentions the episode in a single sentence, he adds of Roger Williams that 'a writer of the history of those times questions whether his zeal would have carried him so far, as to refuse to receive the King's coin because of the cross upon it.' Both Neal and Chalmers narrate the incident at some length. The latter is forthright in dismissing it: 'Nothing can demonstrate more clearly the dark fanaticism of the times and of the people than this singular dispute.' The former narrates the incident to illustrate the 'seditious Tendency of Mr. *Williams*'s Principles'. Robertson's stance here is typical of that which he adopts throughout the history: although he is critical of Williams, his language works to diminish the importance of the event. Chalmers and Neal hurl charges of fanaticism and sedition, but Robertson uses less loaded language, scaling down and defusing the episode by mentioning only heat, zeal and triviality. He also emphasises the successful compromise solution, giving the story a more agreeable flavour than do his sources. By politely refusing a passionate engagement with events, he subdues and controls them.[16]

II

The history of British America shows Robertson at the height of his powers as a historian as well as a rhetorician. Moreover, in the 1770s he was at the peak of his reputation, and he was working on a narrative that he believed was of great importance and to which he had a longstanding commitment. Why, then, did he abandon his project? Humphreys, in the remark quoted earlier, is correct in saying that Robertson needed to know how the conflict would end in order to complete his history. But not any ending would do: he had to be on the winning side, and the issue to be explained is why. Although the evidence is sketchy and speculative, it is probable that Robertson abandoned the project because he could not maintain his polite stance with respect to events in America. To be sure, the illness that afflicted him in the later 1770s and early 1780s played a role in his decision, and his still unexplained resignation from church leadership in 1780 may have had a bearing on his historical work.[17] But his Moderatism, with its reliance on deference and deferral as instruments of control, was at odds with the intensely polemical atmosphere prevailing in British society during the Revolutionary period. Edmund Burke described this situation in his *Letter to the Sheriffs of Bristol* (1777), lamenting that in discussions of the Revolution 'moderation . . . is a sort of treason'.[18]

Likewise, a historian like Chalmers was acutely aware of the divisive atmosphere in which he wrote in 1779. In the preface to the *Political Annals*, he complains of the contentiousness of previous discussions of the Revolution, alleging 'that almost every capital fact had been controverted; that every principle of public law had been disputed; that a shade had been thrown over the whole, either by the inattention of former writers or the misrepresentations of the present.' The result was that Chalmers had to weigh historical claims just as a lawyer would sift facts in preparing to argue a case: 'When ancient privileges were said to have been invaded, it seemed of the greatest importance to investigate, with precision, what immunities the colonists were originally entitled to possess; when chartered rights were said to have been infringed, it was deemed of use to ascertain what the charters really contained; when it was zealously contended that a different rule of colonial administration had been adopted soon after the peace of *1763*, it became necessary to exhibit the genuine spirit of every government, whether of kings, or parliaments, or protectors, antecedent to the present reign' (sig. Av; original italicised). In the midst of such contentious legalism, where deferral and deferment are powerless to arbitrate, it would be almost impossible for Robertson to adopt the stance with which he was most comfortable. If he were to write the history of British America, he could not be an impartial arbitrator; he would have to become a combatant defending one side or the other.

Moreover, for someone like Robertson, committed by position to ministerial support and by conviction to British supremacy, it was less and less possible in Scotland to adopt a position that would not be seen as merely an apology for a failed ministry. Modern historians have noted a change in Scottish opinion during the last half of the 1770s that suggests the increasing isolation of defenders of ministerial policy in America. Fagerstrom has shown that before the war and in its early stages, there was a good deal of support for the ministry; but towards the end of the 1770s and the beginning of the 1780s, disillusionment grew. By 1780 'those who asserted the old attitude of unquestioning loyalty were on the defensive, and it was their letters [to the newspapers] which occasioned numerous replies demonstrating the fallibility of the ministry and decrying uncritical loyalty. The remaining months of the war confirmed the failure of the ministry and correspondingly strengthened Scottish opposition sentiment.'[19] In such an atmosphere, Robertson's work would not have been understood in the way he wished it to be.

A sign of the difficulties in Robertson's position appears in the national fast day sermon he delivered on 26 February 1778, which (apart from a few letters) is virtually the only substantive comment by him on American affairs in the late 1770s. The actual text of the sermon does not survive, but we do have notes apparently taken by someone in the congregation. The sermon was evidently preached in London.[20] Its tone and emphasis generally follow those of the general assembly's loyal addresses (especially for 1777 and 1778), condemning the American Revolution as unnatural and praising the conciliatory temper of George III in the face of such hostility. But Robertson also stresses the nonpolitical, reminding his listeners that they do not have much governmental influence and urging them to remember their moral ties with the Americans. Thus, he opens the sermon with the claim that 'in private virtue alone lyes the security of a people', shifting the ground of discussion from the public to the private sphere, where greater conciliation may be found. Likewise, he closes with a strong plea for compassion:

> But while animated with a Zeal for our own cause, let us with humanity pity those of our Ennemies who have fallen by the exertions we were obliged to make for our own safety, Let us remember that they are a People of the same faith Nation and Lineage, and let us devoutly Pray that they may return to their Duty – that the Hands and the Feet, may no longer Rise up against the Head, that peace may once more smile upon us and the Sword be returned into its Scabbard.[21]

More conciliatory than other Moderates who addressed American affairs in their sermons,[22] Robertson asks his audience to transcend political issues in an act of Christian pity and forgiveness. He has managed to assume his preferred role as mediator in this sermon, but he has done so by setting aside history and politics in favour of religion, a clear indication of his difficulty in writing a narrative history of the British colonies.

The rhythm of Robertson's work on the history appears to reflect his shifting awareness of his situation. After putting the manuscript aside in the summer of 1776, he did not touch it again for four years. His general attitude is well expressed in a letter to Robert Waddilove of July 1778, shortly after his return from London:

> The state of our affairs in North America is not such as to invite me to go on with my history of the New World. I must wait for times of greater tranquillity, when I can write and the public read with more impartiality and better information than at present. Every person with whom I conversed in London confirmed me in my resolution of making a pause for a little, until it shall be known in what manner the ferment will subside.

In January 1778 William Strahan had suggested that in lieu of his American history Robertson write a history of England from William to Anne that would serve as a continuation of Hume's narrative. Robertson thought about the project, discussing it with his London friends and examining papers. But he was again very sensitive to his rhetorical situation, as he confided to Waddilove:

> I know that I shall get upon dangerous ground, and must relate events concerning which our political factions entertain very different sentiments. But I am little alarmed with this. I flatter myself that I have temper enough to judge with impartiality; and if, after examining with candour, I do give offense, there is no man whose situation is more independent.

Nothing more, however, is heard of this project. It is possible that it, too, fell victim to the increasingly polemical and even violent atmosphere surrounding Robertson at the decade's end, as illustrated by the anti-Catholic riots of 1779 (in which he was a main object of attack), the rhetorical assaults of Gilbert Stuart and the political pressures behind his resignation from church leadership.[23]

Despite this atmosphere, Robertson resumed work on the history on 15 August 1780, making extensive revisions in the light of Chalmers's recent account and adding new material. It is possible only to speculate on what prompted him to take up the project again. Of course, having resigned as leader of the Moderates, he now had more time for writing. Perhaps even more important, Cornwallis's victories in the South raised the prospect of an honourable end to the war. A letter in the *Caledonian Mercury* of 31 July 1780 declared: '1780 is likely to stand memorable in the British annals, for having put a concluding stroke to a formidable rebellion of seven years growth, and giving the House of Bourbon that chastisement which is due to insolence and perfidy.' Still more emphatic was the humble address from the town council of Montrose printed in the *Caledonian Mercury* on 5 August 1780:

> We beg leave to express before you the joy we feel from the late distinguished success of your Majesty's arms, in the reduction of the capital and province of South Carolina. We entertain the hope, that this important event will have a doubly good effect; to intimidate and overawe the remains of that desperate and republican faction, from which has originated the rebellion in America, and all the miseries consequent on it; and to stimulate the well-affected through all the Colonies to unite in sentiment and effort with your Majesty's servants, for terminating the reign of democracy, tyranny, and confusion; for accomplishing the re-union of America with the parent state, and all the blessings which flow from its orderly and free constitution, governed by your Majesty with so much justice, paternal care, and moderation.[24]

Robertson, accordingly, may have been encouraged to resume his history because of its close connexion to British supremacy in America.

Robertson soon saw, however, that the empire in America was lost, and he stopped work on his revision on 2 November 1780. He picked it up again for a week in mid-April 1781, but that was the last time he worked on it. The tide of events was now resolutely against the British in America. At home Robertson also found himself under considerable pressure. Some indication of how Robertson was perceived by his public may be found in a poem published in London probably in September 1781, just a few months after he had finally abandoned his manuscript. The anonymous poem is titled *A Poetical Epistle to the Reverend Dr. Robertson Occasioned by His History of America*,[25] and it is based, flatteringly enough, on a comparison of Robertson and Livy. However, the advertisement to the poem makes clear that although both historians are excellent prose writers, what is really at stake is the 'cause of liberty'. Livy, argues the author, is eminent for his attachment to the cause:

> Nor is there any reason to apprehend, from the writings of the English historian, that his principles are opposite. Yet the history he has promised of British America, is, in this respect, become exceedingly critical. Therefore the Author of the following Epistle, anxious for the fame of a Writer whom he respects, and for a cause which he thinks equitable, hopes he has not transgressed against propriety, in hazarding what has the appearance of an admonition. (sig. B; original italicised)

The first half of the poem commends the history of Spanish America, though in the author's view Robertson is too accepting of slavery and the Spanish treatment of the Indians. The second half turns to the proposed history of British America, acknowledging the difficulty of treating a civil conflict but concluding:

> As thou would'st prize immortal fame
> Be careful of their growing name;
> Else will the Muse lament – for dear
> Is freedom to the Muse – that e'er
> She fed thee with ambrosial showers,
> Receiv'd thee in her blissful bowers,
> And gave thee of the blooms that blow
> Where Aganippe's fountains flow:
> Or may with rigorous command
> Reclaim from thy reluctant hand,
> Her gift misus'd, the golden key
> That opes the fount of melody. (16)

For the sake of his reputation, in other words, Robertson simply must give proper recognition to the American side. But whatever he has to say, the poem clearly implies, will be assessed in resolutely partisan terms.

Looking back on his unfinished history in 1784, Robertson wrote to a correspondent:

> I laboured beyond my strength, [during] the time of publishing the History of America. This brought upon me a violent Rheumatick fever, which shattered my constitution so much that it cost me three years attention, & three journeys to Buxton, to re-establish my health. As I had written between two and three hundred pages of *excellent* History of the British Colonies in North America, I long flattered myself that the war might terminate so favourably for G. Britain, that I might go on with my work. But alas America is now lost to the Empire & to me, & what would have been a good introduction to the settlement of British Colonies, will suit very ill the establishment of Independant States.[26]

Robertson here acknowledges for the last time the role of his rhetorical situation in his failure to complete the history. To be sure, he makes much of his ill-health (as he did repeatedly throughout his life); but he points directly to the fact that his history is not properly adapted to the current state of affairs. Robertson's polite style could not successfully cope with the loss of empire in America or its associated polemics at home. Although his most unusual historical work, the *Disquisition on India*, was still to come in 1791, it is the work of a man in retirement from public affairs. His failure to complete the history of British America marks the end of the major phase of the Moderates' hegemony, and it illustrates the impact the American Revolution had on Moderate thought in the Scottish Enlightenment.

NOTES

1. George Shepperson, 'The American Revolution in Scotland', *Scotia* 1 (1977): 3–17. See also *SEAR*, 129–38.
2. Dalphy I. Fagerstrom, 'Scottish Opinion and the American Revolution', *WMQ*, 258.
3. 26 Aug. 1776, BL MS 35,350:60. BL tentatively names the recipient of this letter as the earl of Hardwicke; however, I believe this letter is the one written to Keith that is referred to in BL MS 35,511:21–22.
4. R.A. Humphreys, *William Robertson and His History of America: A Lecture Delivered at Canning House on 11 June 1954* (London, 1954), 13.
5. Sher, 275.
6. Robertson's interest in Spanish colonisation grew inevitably from his work on *Charles V*. But he appears to have had a long-standing interest in British America as well. Space does not permit a full description of Robertson's ties to America; however, the importance he attached to it appears in the remark recorded by Henry Marchant in 1771: Robertson, he wrote, 'fully imagines America must in some future Period be the Seat of a Mighty Empire' (quoted in J. Bennett Nolan, *Benjamin Franklin in Scotland and Ireland, 1759 and 1771* [Philadelphia, 1938], 176). In keeping with this keen interest, Robertson intended to publish a comprehensive work dealing with British, as well as Spanish and Portuguese, exploration and colonisation of America. But his decision in summer 1776 to publish the Spanish portion separately left in doubt just what form the British and Portuguese segments would take. Would they now be continuations or separate histories? His son William may have been acting on a sense of his father's intentions when he offered the manuscript to Andrew Strahan in 1795, requesting that it be published as an independent work under the title 'The History of British America: A Fragment'. Under pressure from Strahan, however, William reluctantly agreed to publish it as part of the *History of America*, agreeing as well to John Playfair's division of the narrative into two books (labelled IX and X) that make it, in effect, simply a continuation of the Spanish history. *WWR*, 6:iii, 8:iii–iv; the letter to Keith cited in n. 3 above; and the correspondence between William Robertson *secundus* and Andrew Strahan, NLS MS 3944:169–70, 181–83, 189–91, 197.
7. Thomas Pownall, *The Administration of the Colonies* (London, 1765), sig. Av.
8. According to borrowing registers of EUL (MS Da. 2.2–4), Robertson withdrew the book on 4 October 1769, 12 October 1775, and 24 October 1780. He had evidently begun research on his American history in 1769, withdrawing a number of other books pertinent to the subject along with Pownall's during the year. He worked primarily on the Spanish history until autumn 1775 when he withdrew a large number of books on British America, again including Pownall's. A major portion of the holograph manuscript of the British history survives (NLS MS 3965), and Robertson's practice of dating the manuscript each time he wrote provides a record of his progress. Because the first 15–30 pages are missing, we do not know exactly when Robertson began writing; however, we

can assume it was summer or very early autumn 1775 because the first extant installment, apparently concluding an extended period of writing, is dated 4 November 1775 (f. 287). Subsequent periods of composition were 9–29 Apr. 1776 (ff. 288–301); 29 June–8 July 1776 (ff. 302–6); 15 Aug.–2 Nov. 1780 (ff. 306–35); 10–16 Apr. 1781 (ff. 336–39).

9. In Dugald Stewart, *Account of the Life and Writings of William Robertson*, in *WWR*, 1:liii.
10. 6 Oct. 1775, in Stewart, *Account*, 1:lii.
11. It may be objected that this description of Robertson's colonial views omits his proclaimed agreement with Adam Smith – and Smith, of course, had argued extensively against Pownall (see *WN*, IV.vii.c. 63–66; and *A Letter from Governor Pownall to Adam Smith* [London, 1776], *CAS*, appendix A). Robertson had written to Smith on the appearance of the *Wealth of Nations*: 'I shall often follow you as my Guide and instructor. I am happy to find my own ideas concerning the absurdity of the limitations upon the Colony trade established much better than I could have done myself' (8 Apr. 1776, in *CAS*, 192). Yet the discrepancy may be more apparent than real. Both Pownall and Smith argue positions opposed to the highly restricted system of colonial trade that dominated the Spanish empire, and the Spanish system was probably Robertson's immediate frame of reference in 1775–76. Thus, for Robertson sound policy lay somewhere between narrow restriction and free trade. In the *History of America* he endorsed the liberal policy of Charles III, who in 1774 had authorised free trade among four of Spain's largest colonies (*WWR*, 7:399); but he did so cautiously. Pownall, of course, had argued that no such trade among colonies ought to be permitted, but Smith had urged the benefits of free trade. In a typical gesture of Moderate compromise, Robertson seems to wish to combine the benefits of imperial control with those of freer trade, thus steering a middle course between opposed points of view. In light of Andrew Skinner's chapter on Smith above, Robertson's compromise gesture also shares something with Smith's balanced views on the benefits and liabilities of the colonial relationship to the Americans.
12. Ian D.L. Clark, 'Moderatism and the Moderate Party in the Church of Scotland, 1752–1805' (Ph.D. diss., Cambridge University, 1964), ix.
13. 'Life of John Home', in *Works of John Home*, ed. Henry Mackenzie. 3 vols. (Edinburgh, 1822), 1:55–56.
14. Previous critics have often contrasted Robertson's polite style, with its apparent impartiality, to that of more obviously polemical party historians. See, for example, Manfred Schlenke, 'Aus der Frühzeit des englischen Historismus: William Robertsons Beitrag zür methodischen Grundlegung der Geschichtswissenschaft im 18. Jahrhundert', *Saeculum* 7 (1956): 107–25, and Douglas Duncan, *Thomas Ruddiman: A Study in Scottish Scholarship of the Early Eighteenth Century* (Edinburgh, 1965), 122–44. David J. Womersley, 'The Historical Writings of William Robertson', *Journal of the History of Ideas* 47 (1986): 497–506, has also stressed Robertson's openness to his historical data. Without denying the apparent impartiality and openness of Robertson's style by comparison to others, I nonetheless wish to claim that his stance has (inescapably) ideological implica-

tions and purposes. Thomas Miller's discussion in chap. 5 above explores some of the implications of this Moderate rhetoric.

15. Cotton Mather, *Magnalia Christi Americana* (London, 1702), 23; George Chalmers, *Political Annals of the Present United Colonies* (London, 1780), 161; Daniel Neal, *History of New-England*, 2 vols. (London, 1747), 1:166.
16. Thomas Hutchinson, *History of the Colony and Province of Massachusetts-Bay*, ed. Lawrence Shaw Mayo, 3 vols. (Cambridge, Mass., 1936), 1:35; Chalmers, *Political Annals*, 156; Neal, *History of New-England*, 1:159.
17. These issues are summarised in Clark, 'Moderatism', 401–11.
18. In Edmund Burke, *Writings and Speeches*, 12 vols. (New York, 1901), 2:210. Robertson admired Burke's stance on American affairs, and he had received a copy of the *Letter* from Burke before delivering his fast day sermon discussed below. See Robertson to Burke, 5 June 1777, Sheffield City Libraries, Fitzwilliam MSS WWM bk 1/973; Burke to Robertson, 9 June 1777, in *The Correspondence of Edmund Burke*, ed. T.W. Copeland et al., 9 vols. (Cambridge, 1958–70), 3:350–52.
19. Dalphy I. Fagerstrom, 'The American Revolution in Scottish Opinion, 1763–83' (Ph.D. diss., University of Edinburgh, 1951), 339.
20. There is strong circumstantial evidence for this claim. Mrs Montagu's memoranda for February 1778 say Robertson was to dine with her in London on 'thursday', which must have been before the Thursday fast day at the end of the month (*Mrs. Montagu, 'Queen of the Blues': Her Letters and Friendships from 1762 to 1800*, ed. Reginald Blunt, 2 vols. [London, 1923], 2:42). Robertson remained in London at least through April in order to gather materials for his proposed continuation of Hume's *History of England.*
21. NLS MS 5003:92–93.
22. The views of the Moderates are summarised by Sher, 262–76, though he does not discuss Robertson's fast day sermon. Compare Robertson's stance to the more belligerent one in Alexander Carlyle's *The Justice and Necessity of the War with our American Colonies Examined* (Edinburgh, 1777) and especially Alexander Gerard's *Liberty the Cloke of Maliciousness, Both in the American Rebellion and in the Manners of the Times* (Aberdeen, 1778).
23. See Robertson to Waddilove, July 1778, in Stewart, *Account*, 1:liii–liv; Strahan to Robertson, 8 Jan. 1778, NLS MS 3943:59; *SM* 41 (1779): 409–15; William J. Zachs, 'The Life and Works of Gilbert Stuart, 1743–86: A Social and Literary Study (Ph.D. diss., University of Edinburgh, 1988), 217–27; Clark, 'Moderatism', 401–11. Strahan's effort to persuade Robertson to write a history of England echoes similar ones made in 1759. See Stewart, *Account*, 1:xxviii–xxxii; R.B. Sher and M.A. Stewart, 'William Robertson and David Hume: Three Letters', *Hume Studies: Tenth Anniversary Issue* (1985), 79–80.
24. Fagerstrom ('American Revolution in Scottish Opinion', 339–40) claims that with the coming of autumn 1780 public opinion in Scotland began to recognise the hopelessness of the British situation in America. Robertson worked from August to November, exactly spanning this swing in the public's mood.

25. The poem was first noticed in the October 1781 number of the *Monthly Review*. I am grateful to Richard Sher for providing a copy of the poem.
26. BL Add. MS 35,350:70. BL tentatively identifies the recipient as the earl of Hardwicke; however, I believe the letter is to Sir Robert Murray Keith, who was at this time inquiring about the progress of Robertson's history (see Robert Arbuthnot to Keith, 12 Jan. 1784, BL Add. MS 35,531:18–19). I am indebted to Jeremy Black for calling my attention to Arbuthnot's letter.

10

BRUCE P. LENMAN

Aristocratic 'Country' Whiggery in Scotland and the American Revolution

After 1763, with the Jacobite threat an irrelevance and New France conquered, the Atlantic-divided British world was made entirely safe for triumphant Whigs and their political traditions deriving from the Glorious Revolution of 1688. However, those traditions ranged over a wide spectrum, and the nature of the dominant version of Whiggery was liable to be very different in different parts of this vast state-complex. If 'country' ideologies stressing the need for participation and positive civic virtue to guard liberties hard-won in 1688 (and ever-threatened by executive aggression and corruption) flourished in the American provinces, creating the climate that made the American Revolution possible, then Scotland appears to be a province at the opposite extreme, dominated by 'court' Whiggery anxious to curry favour by serving the absolutist pretensions of the Westminster parliament and to limit the concept of freedom to mere consumer rights. Though there was considerable sympathy, there was little effective pro-American agitation in Scotland after 1775, and many of the Scots nobility, and especially the ex-Jacobite nobility, fell over themselves to raise troops to put down American rebels.[1] Nevertheless, in no British province in the eighteenth century was there total subservience to the claims of Westminster. Even in Scotland there was a distinguished strand of aristocratic pro-American 'country' Whiggery.

The Scottish Enlightenment was never part of Peter Gay's international conspiracy of liberal anticlericals.[2] The majority of its secular scholars were as conservative as the society they lived in, and its single most important structure was a national network of conservative, if urbanely cosmopolitan, Presbyterian clergymen known as the Moderates.[3] In the great antipathy between court and country, the Scottish Whig establishment was undoubtedly an extreme example of that ultraconservative court Whiggery, with its exaltation of the executive and minimalist views of the Glorious Revolution, which H.T. Dickinson has taught us to see as the normal political stance of the eighteenth-century British establishment.[4] Scotland is also, arguably, an extreme example of the proposition that there never was the slightest possibility of serious social revolution in early modern British society.[5]

However, the fact is that nearly all active Jacobites were militantly country in their views. With what degree of sincerity James VII and II adhered to a country concept of monarchy after 1694 may be a matter of debate, but even James' bid for the country constituency, with its deep distrust of an irresponsible, overarmed, tax-raising centralised executive. It was precisely the ability of the Jacobite cause to mobilise a whole range of regional and national economic, religious and political grievances behind its banners that made it such a formidable force in Scotland for so long.[6] The central issues in British politics in the eighteenth century were not the electoral minutiae beloved of the Namierites. They were issues of foreign policy, peace and war and, above all, a whole range of crises between court and country, core and periphery, Westminster and its subjects. Nor were Jacobites the only, let alone the most enduring, spokesmen for country views in Scotland.

Scottish Whiggery after 1688 contained both a court and a country strand, as well as men who occupied the ambiguous centre of the Whig spectrum. Gilbert Burnet, the Presbyterian divine who became bishop of Salisbury, was the exponent of a theory of forfeiture of the crown by King James that justified resistance without denying that the monarch was independent of his legislatures and indeed supreme within the legal constitution. Burnet's *An Enquiry into Measures of Submission*, published in Holland in 1687, was distributed by the thousands in England by William as a semi-official view.[7]

Scotland also boasted one of the outstanding spokesmen for the true Whig or commonwealthman position: Andrew Fletcher of Saltoun, 'the Patriot Laird'. He was descended on his mother's side from Robert the Bruce, and his father's family had a distinguished legal tradition. As minister of Saltoun, Gilbert Burnet, the future bishop, had been tutor to the young Andrew Fletcher. It is important not to see Andrew Fletcher simply as 'an early Scottish nationalist'. He was a member of a very British circle associated with the commonwealthman par excellence, the Irishman Robert, Viscount Molesworth. Scots were always a smallish element in this London-based group, which for nearly forty years after the Revolution tried to secure it and extend its benefits.[8] Fletcher was a defender of civic liberty and that civic virtue without which it cannot flourish. In 1689, when he had hopes of a radical overhaul of English institutions and feared a counterrevolution in Scotland, he had been willing to contemplate union with England to safeguard Revolution principles. He opposed the Union of 1707 because he saw it, rightly, as a sellout to court influences of a disturbing and reactionary kind.[9]

It requires only a glance at an issue like the Massacre of Glencoe to realise how the court versus country divide could transcend the Jacobite versus Whig split. The brief, botched punitive strike against the MacIains or MacDonalds of Glencoe in February 1692 was one of the less competent exercises in bloodletting in Highland history. Thirty-eight people died. The wee clan was not destroyed, far from it, for it survived to send 100 swordsmen to the Jacobite standard in both the Fifteen and the Forty-Five. The whole episode was a gift to Jacobite propaganda and has attracted historians, in numbers wholly disproportionate to its significance, ranging from a self-styled 'Moderate' (i.e., a Tory M.P.) to a neo-Marxist professional writer to a clever blend of photographer and journalist.[10] None of them seems to grasp what it was that caused the contemporary stir, which was not a clash of Highland against Lowland, Campbell versus MacDonald or even Whig versus Jacobite. It was the abuse of arbitrary power by an effectively irresponsible executive, coupled with the 'Scottish Watergate' that ensued as a stubborn monarch tried to obscure the truth and protect his tarnished instruments, such as Sir James Dalrymple, Master of Stair and later second viscount.

Fletcher was icily clear about the true issues raised by Glencoe. He believed – correctly, modern scholarship would say – that the government of King James had deliberately fomented and used violence in the Highlands for its own sordid political ends.[11] Sir James Dalrymple had been a member of that government. Now Dalrymple sat in the Williamite regime, supposedly raised on 'Revolution Principles', and nothing seemed to have changed. As Fletcher said in his *First Discourse Concerning the Affairs of Scotland* (1698):

> Is it not enough, that the punishment of those who endeavored to enslave us under the late reigns has been delayed till now? Because they have renewed the same practices under this, must it still be delayed, to the end that (as they have already done in the affair of Glencoe) that they may continue to give his majesty the same bad counsel with which the late kings were poisoned?[12]

There was the issue: the abuse of executive power. Most modern historians have preferred to stress almost any other aspect of the Massacre of Glencoe. It is only very recently that simple facts about the episode, such as its incomprehensibility except in the frame of reference of an on-going war in the Highlands and the fact that the Glencoe people were victims of a last-minute retargeting of a government punitive strike, have been established. The 'real' Whig or country tradition foundered in the face of the rise of the executive under such tough, high-handed management as that of Sir Robert Walpole. Nor was the country cause in Britain helped by the failure of a whole series of Jacobite rebellions. Only in the American provinces of the English nation did the rhetoric of the Whig opposition survive to become the accepted norm of political discussion and therefore one of the foundations of American national identity after 1775.[13]

Scotland moved in the opposite direction after 1746. Its ruling class on the whole accepted that the only viable political option was an unconditional subservience to the court in exchange for office and other financial and political favours;[14] and if a Scottish group of burghs could be a difficult seat to manage, this was because of the aggressive self-interest of the few voters rather than the strength of their principles.[15]

George Dempster of Dunnichen was an exception. He was a member of parliament for many years yet occupied no office, save the small and poorly paid one of secretary to the Order of the Thistle. To his close friend Sir Adam Fergusson he once remarked: 'It is almost impossible for a man to acquire consideration without embracing the popular side, or power without betraying it.'[16] In September 1774 he told Sir Adam: 'the impropriety of continuing in Parliament with so small a fortune as mine frequently comes across me, and but that it would be equally foolish to relinquish an interest which no body seems disposed to contest with me I should be at no loss to take my resolution'.[17] Dempster was never taken to the bosom of any Whig opposition groups because they never knew how he was going to vote. He had been one of the minority of forty-nine who had voted against the first reading of the Stamp Act in February 1765. In January 1775, as storm clouds piled up ominously on the Anglo-American horizon, Dempster told Fergusson that his views remained unchanged since 1765 and commented, most significantly:

> The ministry are, I see, determined to adhere to their system, the Americans to their natural rights. God knows how it may end. I foretell it will begin with bloodshed in America and end with a change of ministers and measures in England.[18]

George Dempster was an Angus laird with banking and other business interests.[19] A large proportion of his income came from his holdings of East India Company stock. As early as 1764 he was a noted supporter of Laurence Sulivan's party in the titanic battle for control of the company between Sulivan and Robert Clive. Elected a director in 1769 and again in 1772, Dempster later resigned because of the depth of his hostility to the creation of a great British territorial empire in India, which he saw as likely in the long run to have the same corrosive effect on British government that the acquisition of an Asian empire once had on the Roman Republic.[20] Dempster was returned very easily indeed for the Perth burghs (Perth, Dundee, St Andrews, Forfar and Cupar) in 1780. He was acutely conscious of 'the ridicule of an individual offering advice to administration', especially when that advice was the unpalatable message that, having provoked and lost an American war, Westminster would have to acknowledge the independence of the United States if it wished to escape greater disasters.[24] So he devoted the later 1770s and early 1780s to a meandering grand tour of Europe. Dempster clearly saw himself at times as a voice calling in the wilderness, but it is obvious that he was not a socially isolated man, and his political ideas, though often unpalatable to the administration of the day, were rooted in civic humanist platitudes that few contemporaries would be prepared to deny *in toto*, at least in public, though an extreme conservative like John Ramsay of Ochtertyre could privately express hostility to central tenets of that tradition, such as the desirability of a citizen militia.[22]

Andrew Fletcher of Saltoun had expressed the classic Whig distrust of an executive monopoly of armed force in his *Discourse of Government with Relation to Militias* (1697). Despite the apparently total failure of his political career, his name lived on because of the lucidity with which he articulated ideas which, if shocking to some in authority, struck others as just plain common sense. The psychological and political reasons that made it necessary for a large part of the English ruling class to adhere to the absurd view that the Old Pretender was not the true son of King James but a supposititious child may be set beside Fletcher's delightful remark, in a letter from Paris in February 1716, that the sheer incompetence with which the Pretender was leading the dying rebellion in Scotland 'convinces everybody who formerly did not believe it that he is of the Family'.[23]

There was always an audience for Fletcher's writings in England as well as Scotland. They were reprinted in London in 1732 with an 'Advertisement' stating: 'Mr. Fletcher never wrote for a party; and his writings therefore ought to last: Being scarce, they are collected with that regard which is due to his great judgement and sincerity'.[24] The posthumous career of Andrew Fletcher of Saltoun is a neglected subject. Not only were his writings collected and reprinted, but he was also cited as an accepted historical source,[25] and his name retained sufficient authority at the time of the agitation for what was to become the Reform Act of 1832 to be enrolled among the supporters of that measure[26] (which, we may be sure, he would have been quick to point out was a mere rejigging of the franchise and no reform of British government at all).

Not least among the reasons for this capacity for survival was the breadth of Fletcher's appeal. It was always an appeal to a minority, but that minority was composed of a set of minorities spread across the literate orders of British society. Fletcher could appeal as easily to a belted earl as to a self-improving weaver. It is no accident that the archfuglemen for the great lurch to the right in late eighteenth-century Britain tended to be socially insecure bourgeois. In 1792 David Stuart, earl of Buchan, remarked in the introduction to his essays on Fletcher and the poet James

Thomson, author of a lengthy poem on Liberty: 'I am sensible that the very sound and sight of the word Liberty had become disagreeable, if not terrible, to the fashionable world in Britain.'[27] Buchan was referring to the panic-stricken revulsion against the development of the French Revolution. His own failure to share in that revulsion cost him dearly, for dyed-in-the-wool reactionaries like Walter Scott were careful to leave for posterity an image of Buchan that stressed his eccentricities while skating over his principled opposition to the forging of an authoritarian and reactionary official culture, literary as well as political. Buchan sympathised with the American Revolution and always held a very high opinion of General George Washington, but he also opposed the very successful campaign by Samuel Johnson, that firm foe of American rebels, to create a pantheon for English literature that would enshrine writers like Shakespeare and Dryden (and, indeed, Johnson himself), all men of staunchly reactionary and authoritarian views. It is no accident that Johnson came from a neo-Jacobite background and admired to distraction the courtier and Jacobite Dryden. Milton, whom Johnson described as 'an acrimonious and surly Republican', was always rather a problem for Johnson, which he sidled round by arguing, absurdly, that in Milton there was no connexion between the man and the poet.[28]

The earl of Buchan had no illusions as to the lack of sympathy with which the literary dictator of the day would approach poems like Thomson's *Liberty*. Thomson had been an admirer of modern republics such as Geneva and a leading spokesman for the opposition in the great war of the 1730s between Walpole and the wits. Buchan talked bluntly of 'the brutal Johnson', but then Johnson was swimming with the tide of authoritarian opinion, which began to set in very markedly with the reconciliation of the High Tories and ex-Jacobites with the regime of George III after 1760, while Buchan was a man of firm country views very close to those articulated in Thomson's circle. To the earl of Chatham, the somewhat shopsoiled hero of those deeply suspicious of the court and executive, Buchan had said in 1766 that he feared for the future of 'poor England, that doats on the imperfections of her pretended constitution'.[29]

There was always a living tradition of country politics in the eighteenth-century Scottish aristocracy, not least because the old Scots pre-Union peerage deemed itself slighted by the arrangements for the representation of their order in the post-Union state. Buchan's grandfather, David Erskine, Lord Cardross and subsequently earl of Buchan, had been deprived at one stage of all his offices under the crown because of his fierce protest against the Treaty of Union for allowing only sixteen elected representative peers to represent their order at Westminster. Having demonstrated his Hanoverian loyalties during the Fifteen, he was, in fact, elected a representative peer and remained one from 1715 to 1734.[30] Of course, the more important Scots peers had hoped to reach Westminster on the back of their English or United Kingdom peerages, and the decision of the House of Lords in 1712 to ban such a mode of entry was not only bad law but also politically provocative, for it left the Scots peers scrabbling for a few places in elections notoriously and blatantly 'fixed' by the government.[31] The dukes of Hamilton and Queensbury did make unsuccessful attempts to claim entry to the House of Lords in 1712 and 1719 respectively under their English titles of duke of Brandon and duke of Dover. The duke ofArgyll never tried, despite his English title after the Fifteen as duke of Greenwich, but then Argyll could usually manipulate the election.[32]

Even so, Argyll was prepared privately to defend an eventually unsuccessful proposal to close the House of Lords to new creations by the crown (as distinct from replacements of extinct peerages), and to replace the Scottish representative peers by a number of hereditary family representatives, on the grounds that the elections for representative peers were a farce dominated by the court anyway.[33] This farce suited the needs of the executive very well, as is shown by the grovelling relationship between the impoverished scapegrace James, second earl of Rosebery and Sir Robert Walpole, whom Rosebery touched for a few pounds now and again in exchange for the only asset he had worth selling: his vote at representative peer elections. Such an offensively corrupt racket was just too valuable for government willingly ever to abandon, but it was also something even the most arrogant of court Whigs preferred not to discuss in public. In 1719 the secretary of state for Scotland, the duke of Montrose, told his closest associate that only a total time-server could be a representative peer.[34] The remark was only slightly exaggerated.

The unofficial canvass of the electors was, in the case of a successful candidate, usually more like a lap of honour than a race. There were always a certain number of peers who refused to have anything at all to do with the procedure (itself a sobering comment on the system), but others made no bones about the all-important role of 'our managers', described more precisely as 'them who either had, or pretended to have the Queen's pleasure lodged with them'. It was not deemed offensive to congratulate a candidate on the grounds that 'our managers' were making a choice above and beyond their usual dismal level.[35] It is worth recalling that Lord George Murray, the outstanding Jacobite general of the Forty-Five, considered the degradation of the Scots peerage to be the greatest political grievance of his native land. The firm but elastic political conventions of the day could and did allow a shifting balance of power within the elements of the central élite. The problem lay in gaining access to that élite.

It is, therefore, scarcely surprising that there was always an active country tradition among the Scots aristocracy. More surprising is the failure of historians to recognise it. One reason for this failure is the influence of Henry Cockburn's Edinburgh-centric *Memorials of His Time*, which concentrates on the period after 1800 and exaggerates the role of 'a few lawyers' in leading opposition to executive policies. Only casually does Cockburn admit that a Whig lawyer like Robert Cullen did his best work for an active Whig nobleman, Lord Daer.[36] Because of modern historians' insistence on some sort of incipient social revolution behind any 'serious' opposition, the opposition of several Scots lairds and peers to the War of American Independence has just been ignored. The Stamp Act crisis does appear to have used up what little reserves of sympathy for American grievances existed in the parliamentary élite in Great Britain, and the Scots office-holding élites, lay and clerical, took their lead from Westminster in 1775. Dunbar Hamilton Douglas, fourth earl of Selkirk did nothing of the sort, but then he never had. A noted agricultural improver upon his Galloway estates, he was a man of conspicuously independent mind (earning him the reputation of near insanity in the British Establishment). In the notorious Douglas cause over the right of succession to the vast Douglas estates, Selkirk flew in the face of much pseudo-radical opinion by expressing (extremely well-founded) scepticism about the parentage of Archibald Douglas, who managed to cling to the estates, if not the title, by the skin of his teeth and with massive help from a wave of nostalgic hysteria whipped up by, among others, a young advocate called James Boswell. In 1770 and 1774 Lord Selkirk was prominent in an ineffective, but to the government of Lord North unforgivably embarrassing, series of protests against government interference and skulduggery in peerage elections. Selkirk gave vent to several ringing assertions of true Whig principles, which might be ignored in practice but which still stung Westminster in theory. Logically enough, the fourth earl of Selkirk went on to be a public critic of the government's policies towards the American colonies, writing: 'with regard to the King's Ministers, I neither have nor can have any interest with them, as particular of almost their whole conduct in the unhappy and ill-judged American War'.[37]

These attitudes did not spare the Selkirk mansion a raid by sailors from John Paul Jones's flotilla. The noble host was not at home to be kidnapped, and Jones later returned the family silver. Selkirk was sensible enough to see that he could not change official attitudes, and he lived very quietly for most of the period of the American War. As its failure became ever more apparent, he joined in 1782 the Society for Constitutional Information, founded by Christopher Wyvill and John Cartwright, thus committing himself not only to parliamentary reform but also to reform proposals much influenced by a very shrewd distrust of the Westminster parliament. In his fierce political battles, which culminated in his finally smashing through the barriers of ministerial hostility and securing election as a representative peer in 1787, the fourth earl of Selkirk was staunchly supported by his son and heir, Basil William, Lord Daer. Presumably all this activity totally failed to impress Lyon King Sir James Balfour Paul, who in the seventh volume of his *Scots Peerage* records that Lord Selkirk had strongly supported the government during the Forty-Five but otherwise 'did not take much active part in public life'.[38]

Scottish gentlemen could and did oppose Lord North's policies towards the American colonies on sound conservative grounds. Of course, many more of them supported the creation of a more powerful Westminster-based executive because they hoped it would shower patronage on them. Nevertheless, the young James Boswell had the courage to reject the fiercely pro-executive views of his mentor Samuel Johnson, maintaining a moderately but firmly pro-American view throughout the war. The propagandist of Corsican independence could scarcely do less. Boswell even broke into (sadly mediocre) verse over the so-called 'Intolerable Acts' designed to punish Boston for the Tea Party episode. Those acts involved the arbitrary breach of chartered right, making Boswell consistent (for once) in criticising, in his 1783 *A Letter to the People of Scotland*, Burke and Fox's India Bill. Not only did it involve arbitrary confiscation of the East India Company charter, but it also posed a direct challenge to the mixed pattern of government by seeking to transfer extensive patronage to the prime minister, in defiance of the royal prerogative.[39]

Boswell seems to have been steadied by his instinctive acceptance of the classic Whig doctrines about the sacredness of property rights and the desirability of an active monarch within the pattern of mixed government, hardly surprising in a man who, after entering the University of Edinburgh in the academic session 1753–54, attended arts and then law classes there for the next six years.[40] The Scottish universities, all of which had at various points been purged of Jacobite sympathisers, were nothing if not Whig in tone. The fourth earl of Selkirk had sat at the feet of Francis Hutcheson, professor of moral philosophy in the University of Glasgow and an associate, as befitted an Ulsterman and a true Whig, of the Molesworth circle. Hutcheson was in a sense the archetypal Presbyterian clergyman-academic admired by the conservative Moderate faction dominating the Church of Scotland in the 1750s, but his politics were far less acquiescent than theirs, extending even to a consideration of when colonies might reasonably become independent. There was always a strand of Hutchesonian radicalism among educated upper-class Scots in the second half of the eighteenth century. One example is John Maclaurin, Lord Dreghorn, a senator of the College of Justice who came from an impeccably Whig family with a good anti-Jacobite record but who opposed the attempt to crush the American colonies, rejoiced in their independence and regarded the conservative powers' invasion of republican France as 'unjust and impolitic', as well as counterproductive. It is no accident that his reverend uncle was a clergyman opposed to the Moderate party's attempt to subvert all popular rights in the Church of Scotland.[41]

James Maitland, eighth earl of Lauderdale, is perhaps the most striking example of a liberal Scots nobleman permanently affected by his university experience. Educated at the High School and University of Edinburgh, he was much influenced by a remarkable tutor, the classicist Andrew Dalzel, a man of firm if moderately-stated Whig views. James Maitland spent only a term at Trinity College, Oxford, before wisely moving north to the University of Glasgow, where he attended John Millar's lectures on civil law. A member of the Faculty of Advocates in Edinburgh and a student of Lincoln's Inn, Maitland entered the House of Commons for a Cornish burgh in 1780. In 1781 he opposed the continuation of the American War, arguing that its ministerial authors were hostile to British as well as to American liberties.[42] In 1791 Lauderdale even fought a (fortunately bloodless) duel with a man whom he deemed a traitor to American liberty – Benedict Arnold.

Lauderdale, an eminent political economist, was so influenced by the experience of the American War of Independence that he could not grasp that the French Revolutionary War would not follow the pattern of the American one, when fiscal and logistical pressures combined with political discouragement had reached a point where it became impossible for the Westminster government to continue to fight. In 1798 Lauderdale published a pamphlet in which he said of 'the general situation and state of the country' that it was 'such as no one can contemplate with satisfaction, few without the deepest regret'.[43] His political opponents were, however, already gleefully pointing out that the vigour of the British economy was such that it could stand indefinitely a prolongation of the war. Pitt could and did raise credit on reasonable terms, and the other crucial indicators were quite exceptionally healthy. For example, navy bills (the Royal Navy's own public debt), which had accumulated at the end of the American Revolutionary War to the then vast sum of £27,000,000 and stood at the unheard of discount of 20 percent, had been far more successfully handled by Pitt. Lauderdale exaggerated the financial crisis.[44]

'Country' Whiggery, always a vocal minority view among the Scottish aristocracy, died in the late 1790s. Hope could not be deferred indefinitely, and hope withered. The slow but steady expansion of an imperial executive based on Westminster could and did absorb men like the fifth earl of Selkirk, the younger brother of Lord Daer, whose residual radicalism was channelled into plans to use organised emigration from the Highlands not only to better the lot of Highlanders but also to hold the imperial frontier in Canada against the threat of American republicanism.[45] The great leap by a significant section of the lower orders into violent loyalism from 1791 severely shook the hopes of men like Lauderdale, who had obviously expected, indeed who more or less told George III to his face, that rising prices and especially rising grain prices would make the war unpopular.[46] Above all, the fact that repeated military failure during the French wars did not generate the sort of political pressures on British government that had occurred at the end of the War of American Independence deprived them of any chance of entering office and securing policy reversals.

The Lords Lauderdale, Selkirk and Buchan, who were contemporary with and admirers of the American Revolution, were gentlemen of the Enlightenment rather than nineteenth-century rabble-rousers. So were George Dempster, James Boswell and John Maclaurin. It is ironic that Lauderdale's most important work in economics was much drawn on by subsequent socialist thinkers.[47] It is doubtful if he and his Scots political allies would have had much time for the wilder demagogues of the American Whig tradition, but they closely resembled the Virginia gentlemen George Washington and Thomas Jefferson, whose achievements they admired and, like them, they deserve to be remembered with pride by their fellow countrymen.

NOTES

1. Dalphy I. Fagerstrom, 'Scottish Opinion and the American Revolution', *WMQ*, 252–75; Bruce P. Lenman, *The Jacobite Clans of the Great Glen 1650–1784* (London, 1984), esp. chap. 9.
2. Peter Gay, *The Enlightenment: An Interpretation*, 2 vols. (London, 1966–69).
3. Bruce P. Lenman, *Integration, Enlightenment and Industrialisation: Scotland, 1746–1832* (London, 1981); Sher.
4. H.T. Dickinson, *Liberty and Property: Political Ideology in Eighteenth-Century Britain* (London, 1977).
5. J.C.D. Clark, *English Society, 1688–1832* (Cambridge, 1985).
6. Bruce P. Lenman, *The Jacobite Risings in Britain, 1689–1746* (London, 1984).
7. Julian H. Franklin, *John Locke and the Theory of Sovereignty* (Cambridge, 1981), 98–100.
8. Caroline Robbins, *The Eighteenth-Century Commonwealthman* (Cambridge, Mass., 1959), esp. chap. 4.
9. William Ferguson, *Scotland's Relations with England: A Survey to 1707* (Edinburgh, 1977), 170–72.

10. Respectively, John Buchan, *The Massacre of Glencoe* (London, 1933); John Prebble, *Glencoe* (London, 1966); Magnus Linklater, with photographs by Anthony Gascoigne, *Massacre: The Story of Glencoe* (London, 1982).
11. Allan I. Macinnes, 'Repression and Conciliation: The Highland Dimension, 1660–1688', *Scottish Historical Review* 65 (1986): 167–95.
12. In *Andrew Fletcher of Saltoun: Selected Political Writings and Speeches*, ed. David Daiches (Edinburgh, 1979), 44.
13. On the background of the massacre, see Paul Hopkins, *Glencoe and the End of the Highland War* (Edinburgh, 1986); on the rhetoric of opposition, see Bernard Bailyn, *The Ideological Origins of the American Revolution* (Cambridge, Mass., 1967).
14. Alexander Murdoch, *'The People Above': Politics and Administration in Mid-Eighteenth-Century Scotland* (Edinburgh, 1980); John Stuart Shaw, *The Management of Scottish Society, 1701–1764: Power, Nobles, Lawyers, Edinburgh Agents and English Influences* (Edinburgh, 1983).
15. Ronald M. Sunter, *Patronage and Politics in Scotland, 1704–1832* (Edinburgh, 1986).
16. *Letters of George Dempster to Sir Adam Fergusson, 1756–1813*, ed. James Fergusson (London, 1934), xvii.
17. Dempster to Fergusson, 12 Sept. 1774, ibid., 82.
18. Dempster to Fergusson, 26 Jan. 1775, ibid., 85–86.
19. C.W. Boase, *A Century of Banking in Dundee . . . from 1764 to 1864* (Edinburgh, 1867).
20. *Letters of George Dempster*, 73.
21. Dempster to Fergusson, 4 Feb. 1778, ibid., 93–95.
22. John Ramsay, *Scotland and Scotsmen in the Eighteenth Century*, ed. Alexander Allardyce, 2 vols. (Edinburgh, 1888), 1:332–35.
23. Andrew Fletcher to his namesake and nephew, 20 Feb. 1716 (N.S.), in *Miscellany 10*, Scottish History Society Publications, 4th ser., (Edinburgh, 1965), 2:155–56.
24. *The Political Works of Andrew Fletcher, Esq.* (London, 1732), sig. A2r.
25. Fletcher's *Works* are extensively cited in, for example, vol. 5 of *The History of Scotland Translated from the Latin of George Buchanan with Notes and a Continuation to the Present Time*, ed. James Aikman (Edinburgh, 1827).
26. Notably in the 'Preface by the Editor of the Present Edition' in the misascribed *An Historical Account of the Ancient Rights and Power of the Parliament of Scotland by Andrew Fletcher of Saltoun* (Aberdeen, 1823).
27. David Stuart, earl of Buchan, *Essays on the Lives and Writings of Fletcher of Saltoun and the Poet Thomson* (London, 1792), sig. B^{r}.
28. James Boswell, *The Life of Samuel Johnson*, ed. G.B. Hill, rev. L.F. Powell, 6 vols. (Oxford, 1934), 4:42.
29. Buchan, *Essays*, 215. The conversation with Chatham is dated 'eighteen years after Thomson's death', which occurred in 1748. For Thomson's politics, see Douglas Grant, *James Thomson: Poet of 'The Seasons'* (London, 1951).
30. *The Scots Peerage*, ed. Sir James Balfour Paul, 9 vols. (Edinburgh, 1904–14), 2:275.
31. Sir James Ferguson, *The Sixteen Peers of Scotland* (Oxford, 1960).
32. See copies from House of Lords records in 'Peers Elections', Scottish Record Office PE 18/21–22, Hannay Papers.

33. Duke of Argyll and Greenwich to Lord Grange, 25 May 1721, in *Historical Manuscripts Commission: Report on the Manuscripts of the Earl of Mar and Kellie* (London, 1904), 522–23. For the proposal to close the peerage, see *The British Aristocracy and the Peerage Bill of 1719*, ed. John F. Naylor (New York, 1968).
34. Bruce P. Lenman, 'A Client Society: Scotland between the '15 and the '45', in *Britain in the Age of Walpole*, ed. Jeremy Black (London, 1984), 82–83.
35. Correspondence resulting from the earl of Findlater's successful candidacy at a by-election in 1712 in Scottish Record Office GS248/561 (1–49), Seafield Papers. The blunt remarks cited are from a letter by Patrick, third Lord Kinnaird, 26 July 1712, item 24 in the bundle. Lord Kinnaird voted against the Union in 1707 and lived quietly but perceptively until he died early in 1715.
36. Henry Cockburn, *Memorials of His Time*, ed. James Thin (Edinburgh, 1971), 86, 144.
37. For the career of the fourth earl of Selkirk, by far the best source is the introduction to *The Collected Writings of Lord Selkirk, 1799–1809*, ed. J.M. Bumstead, Manitoba Record Society Publications, no. 7 (Winnipeg, 1984).
38. *Scots Peerage*, ed. Paul, 7:521.
39. Frank Brady, *James Boswell: The Later Years, 1769–1795* (London, 1984), 93, 110, 126, 183, 249–51, 403.
40. Frederick A. Pottle, *James Boswell: The Earlier Years, 1740–1769* (London, 1966), 23.
41. For a study of Hutcheson's politics, see Caroline Robbins, ' "When It Is That Colonies May Turn Independent:" An Analysis of the Environment and Politics of Francis Hutcheson (1694–1746)', *WMQ*, 214–51. *The Works of the Late John Maclaurin, Esq., of Dreghorn*, 2 vols. (Edinburgh, 1798) shows a man of stature who merits further study. For his clerical uncle's views on kirk politics, see John Maclaurin, *The Terms of Ministerial and Christian Communion Imposed on the Church of Scotland by a Prevailing Party in the General Assembly, in Opposition to the Great Bulk Both of Office-Bearers and Private Christians, Considered* (Glasgow, 1753).
42. There are useful introductory biographies of both Dalzel and Lauderdale in the *Dictionary of National Biography*.
43. Earl of Lauderdale, *A Letter on the Present Measures of Finance* (London, 1797).
44. Daniel Wakefield, *Observations on the Credit and Finances of Great Britain* (London, 1797).
45. John Morgan Gray, *Lord Selkirk of Red River* (London, 1963).
46. Duke of Portland to George III, 16 Nov. 1795, in *The Later Correspondence of George III*, ed. Arthur Aspinall, 5 vols. (Cambridge, 1962–70), 2:425–26.
47. Earl of Lauderdale, *An Inquiry into the Nature and Origin of Public Wealth and into the Means and Causes of Its Increase* (Edinburgh, 1804). I am indebted to Istvan Hont for the valuable insight into Lauderdale's influence on subsequent socialist thought.

11

SHANNON C. STIMSON

'A Jury of the Country': Common Sense Philosophy and the Jurisprudence of James Wilson

> A judge is the blessing, or he is the curse of society.
>
> There is not in the whole science of politicks a more solid or more important maxim than this – that of all governments, those are the best, which, by the natural effect of their constitutions, are frequently renewed or drawn back to their first principles.
>
> James Wilson

This chapter examines the democratic implications of Scottish common sense thought, particularly that of Thomas Reid, in the political and jurisprudential thought of James Wilson. Of all the American founding fathers, Wilson is perhaps the least well understood. To some his was the most consistent voice of political democracy to be heard at the Federal Convention of 1787.[1] His revolutionary advocacy of a 'supreme, absolute and uncontrollable' sovereignty residing in the people, as well as his consistent support at the Constitutional Convention for proportional representation and the direct election of the president and the members of the national House and Senate, certainly outstripped the popular impulse of Madison.[2] This democratic tendency also expressed itself in Wilson's rejection of Blackstone's common law jurisprudence, which posited a source of law 'superior' to the people. Wilson claimed instead that the principles underlying American law were 'materially different' from those underpinning the laws of England (*WJasW*, 1:74–78, 104–6, 168–71).[3] Yet it is indisputably true that prior to, during and after the Constitutional Convention Wilson emerged as the pre-eminent spokesman for a degree of wide-ranging judicial power at the national level that many would consider intrinsically antidemocratic.[4] One might, of course, merely note the presence of these apparently contradictory tendencies and explore the political incongruities to which they give rise. But that would be to leave Wilson's argument at the very point at which his original contribution actually took shape. A better understanding of Wilson's jurisprudential thought recognises that this contribution begins with an effort to reconcile the apparent incongruity between popular sovereignty and a constitutional supreme court by providing a new view of law and courts, one deriving from the democratic first principles of Reid's common sense philosophy.

To demonstrate this reconciliation I begin with a brief examination of the elements of Reid's common sense epistemology and moral theory, which Wilson self-consciously employed to lay the democratic foundations of his jurisprudence 'deep and solid' (*WJasW*, 1:103). I then examine how Wilson extended and developed Reid's common sense theory into his own argument for a new American theory of jurisprudence and judicial institutions.

I

Reid's claim for the general epistemological equality of men, particularly for the equal status of philosophers and common men as 'knowers', lies at the heart of his challenge to Hume's scepticism: 'The judgments grounded upon the evidence of sense, of memory, and consciousness, put all men upon a level. The philosopher, with regard to these, has no prerogative above the illiterate, or even above the savage' (*WTR*, 1:415). Hume, of course, had argued in both his *Treatise of Human Nature* and his two *Enquiries* that a moderate, philosophical scepticism about man's certain knowledge was the appropriate reaction to a world in which it is 'universally allow'd by philosophers, and is besides pretty obvious of itself, that nothing is ever really present with the mind but its perceptions or impressions and ideas, and that external objects become known to us only by those perceptions they occasion' (*THN*, 67). Hume was confident that custom, imagination and what he termed 'natural beliefs' worked on the psychology of man both to impose order on the world and to nullify the potentially debilitating effects of the radical philosophical scepticism fully warranted by the results of his investigations. If sustained, such radical sceptical doubts 'subverted all conviction' and left man in 'the most deplorable condition imaginable, inviron'd with the deepest darkness, and utterly depriv'd of the use of every member and faculty' (*THN*, 187, 269). Were men universally willing and able to reflect philosophically on the radical limits of their understanding, 'all discourse, all action would immediately cease; and men remain in a total lethargy, till the necessities of nature, unsatisfied, put an end to their miserable existence' (*EM*, 160).

Fortunately, or rather naturally, men were neither universally willing nor able to reflect philosophically. Radical scepticism was countered by nature, and 'the greater part of mankind' were naturally an ignorant multitude, who are always 'clamorous' and dogmatical, even in the nicest questions (*EM*, 161, 40–41). Hume recognised that his own analysis projected an unresolvable tension between the ostensibly unblinkered reality uncovered by philosophers such as himself and the necessary deceptions of common men and common life: philosophical enquiry destroys our natural beliefs; the pursuit of common life undercuts the force of philosophical enquiry and its sceptical conclusions. Hume therefore questioned whether a philosophical enquiry into the narrow bounds of human understanding could have any practical impact on common life, or whether it simply forced men, and particularly the philosophical few, to live a 'mixed kind of life'. 'Be a philosopher; but, amidst all your philosophy, be still a man' (*EM*, 9).

Hume concluded that there was a practical good which a moderate or 'mitigated' scepticism might serve when applied to the 'action', 'employment' and 'occupation of common life'. This good would be to moderate the opinion of the greater part of dogmatic and obstinate mankind by example and instruction. The 'small tincture' of scepticism introduced by philosophers such as Hume himself might then serve to 'inspire them with more modesty and reserve, and diminish their fond opinion of themselves, and their prejudice against antagonists' (*EM*, 161). In the face of the religious zeal that Hume thought plagued his age, and against which he pitted his *Enquiries*, it seems an admirably modest goal.

For Reid, however, neither Hume's epistemological scepticism nor his conclusions about its potential to serve a positive social function when applied in moderate doses was acceptable. In his philosophical writings, Reid meticulously dissected Hume's examination of the basis of rational belief about such things as personal identity, the objective existence of an external world, causation and the source and character of moral rules, declaring them philosophically unsustainable and morally corruptive.

His philosophical response to Hume's characterisation of personal identity, based on what Reid considered a suspect theory of ideas and conceived of as no more than a stream of unconnected sense perceptions, was that it collapsed under logical scrutiny. How could Hume (or before him Descartes) posit the existence of such a stream of perceptions without first assuming the real existence of the personal perceiver – the 'I'? Reid further objected to the philosopher's 'fleeting' characterisation of persons on the ground that it diminished the individual status of men, made it possible to isolate or elevate what was shared or common in men and generally made Reid 'ashamed of my frame. . . . I see myself and the whole frame of nature, shrink into fleeting ideas, which like Epicurus' atoms, dance about in emptiness' (*WTR*, 1:103).

Indeed, the bulk of Reid's critique of Hume is a profoundly democratic challenge to the superiority of philosophy in the study of man and to its privileged status as a mode of discourse about epistemology and morals.

'I despise Philosophy, and renounce its guidance', wrote Reid; 'let my soul dwell with Common Sense' (*WTR*, 1:101; *WJasW*, 1:212). Reid's might be considered both a democratic and a sceptical challenge to Hume's scepticism: why reject the beliefs common to mankind in order to accept the arguments of philosophy? Rather than produce a moderate sceptical corrective to dogmatic beliefs, Reid thought the social function of Hume's challenge to reason was to undermine the principles of understanding, prudence and judgement that all men know to be true by a common or shared sense.

Reid argued that the first principles of human understanding were antecedent to reason, or more properly reasoning, but such principles need not be relegated to the status of Hume's psychologically necessary hunches. The first principles of knowledge were intuitively known and, like our elemental five senses, perceived directly and self-evidently. The ground of such self-evidence was an appeal to universal opinion, since by common sense Reid means little more than *common* sense or judgement. 'We ought', Reid argues,

> . . . to take for granted, as first principles, things wherein we find an universal agreement, among the learned and unlearned, in the different nations and ages of the world. A consent of ages and nations, of the learned and the vulgar, ought, at least, to have great authority, unless we can shew some prejudice as universal as that consent is, which might be the cause of it. (*WTR*, 1:233)[5]

This appeal to universal agreement is at once the democratic and the common sense core of Reid's thought.

From this initial claim, Reid challenged the superiority of philosophical discourse to ordinary language as the medium through which to discuss moral and social issues: 'The meaning of a common word is not to be ascertained by philosophical theory, but by common usage' (*WTR*, 2:674). Through the analysis of ordinary language, Reid placed an active 'power' for reason within the reach of common men. He promoted loose, ordinary language definitions, attempting to demonstrate that the terms 'sense', 'judgement' and 'reasonable' are analogous, at least in their extended senses:

> In common language, sense always implies judgment. A man of good sense is a man of judgment. Good sense is good judgment. Nonsense is what is evidently contrary to right judgment. Common sense is that degree of judgment which is common to men with whom we can converse and transact business. (*WTR* 1:421)

Perhaps most fundamental to his disagreement with Hume and to the democratic implications of his thought was Reid's retrieval of a rational component for the 'power' of judgement in moral decision-making, and his claim for the capacity of all men to exercise this power. By rarely using the term 'judgement' in discussing moral decisions, preferring instead the emotive term 'pronouncements', Hume suggested that morality was 'more properly felt than judg'd of' (*THN*, 470). Feeling and not reason was at work in our initial moral perceptions. At the same time Hume claimed that the vast majority of our moral rules were not (could not be) supplied by our nonrational moral sense but must be supplied by long chains of reasoning and demonstration, in which 'nice distinctions be made, just conclusions drawn, distant comparisons formed, complicated relations examined, and general facts fixed and ascertained' (*EM*, 173).[6] Such a position easily placed the claim to moral knowledge well out of the reach of common men, who must rely on others to extrapolate for them.

Reid countered that it was absurd to conceive of an opposition between reason and men's intuitive moral judgements:

> We ascribe to reason two offices, or two degrees. The first is to judge of things self-evident; the second to draw conclusions that are not self-evident from those that are. The first of these is the province, and the sole province, of common sense; and, therefore, it coincides with reason in its whole extent, and is only another name for one branch or one degree of reason. (*WTR*, 1:425)

Contrary to Hume's claim, Reid argued that in the moral sphere comprising 'the common occurrences of life . . . the cases that require reasoning are few, compared with those that require none'. In fact the common man, whom Reid identifies as the 'man of integrity', 'sees his duty without reasoning, as he sees the highway'. If indeed the rules of virtue required the demonstrative reasoning Hume suggests, Reid concludes that 'sad would be the condition of the far greater part of men', who lack significant powers to this kind of reasoning (*WTR*, 1:481). Thus, Reid argues backwards from common experience to suggest that while few men are strong demonstrative reasoners, most do know and follow moral rules. This clinches what may be termed the democratic element of his epistemology and moral theory:

> To judge of first principles, requires no more than a sound mind free from prejudice, and a distinct conception of the question. The learned and the unlearned, the philosopher and the day-labourer, are upon a level, and will pass the same judgment, when they are not misled by some bias, or taught to renounce their understanding from some mistaken religious principle. (*WTR*, 1:438)

Critics of Reid's common sense theory have argued that it merely assumes the very scheme that scepticism and empiricism called into question — the merging or conflation of sense and reason, feeling and judgement, psychology and metaphysics.[7] Certainly it inspired the view that intellect and feeling were not to be kept distinct. The more unsettling criticism is that Reid's ordinary language analysis of judgement permits the conflation of psychological certainty and certain knowledge, of 'unavoidable *doxa* with *episteme*', by supposing that the terms 'unavoidable beliefs' and 'known to be true' have the same extension.[8] Reid at least recognised the problem of error and the evidence of experience: 'Men may, to the end of life, be ignorant of self-evident truths. They may, to the end of life, entertain gross absurdities.' But such errors were due to partiality, interest, affection, fashion or even social isolation (*WTR*, 2:641). Common judgement might thus be 'perverted, by education, by authority, by party zeal' (*WTR*, 1:438). However, Reid believed the 'active' power of reason and judging could be improved through early 'instruction' of habits and the experience and development of voluntary rational reflection (*WTR*, 2:641, 941). Finally, the measure of truth in Reid's thought was not simply the strength of unavoidable belief but the universality of the opinion as well. Although Reid does not propose it, such universality could be measured through democratic discussion and debate.

II

> To believe in our senses – to give credit to human testimony, has been considered an unphilosophical, and consequently, irrational, if not absurd. The connexion on the subject, between the principles law, of philosophy, and human nature has never . . . been sufficiently traced and examined.
>
> James Wilson

All the democratic elements implicit in Reid's common sense epistemology and moral sense judgement are explicitly developed in Wilson's work, particularly in his *Lectures on Law*.[9] Indeed, what is evident is less accurately termed the 'influence' of Reid's thought than it is, in many instances, the verbatim transposition of text (or nearly so) from Reid's work into Wilson's discussions of the nature of man, society, government and law. The contribution of any other thinker on Wilson suffers by comparison to the number and centrality of Reidian arguments interwoven into Wilson's own texts.[10]

Four Reidian elements are central to Wilson's democratic thought: (1) the rejection of scepticism; (2) the preference for an ordinary language conflation of sense, judgement and reason; (3) the interaction of feeling and intellect in judgement; (4) the social resolution of the problem of error. As a point of departure for his analysis of the scope and limits of knowledge, Wilson simply paraphrased Reid's reaction to scepticism and the theory of ideas: 'Such degenerate philosophy let us abandon: let us renounce its instruction: let us embrace the philosophy which dwells with common sense' (*WJasW*, 1:212; *WTR*, 1:101). From the introductory advertisement to his first article (written in 1768 but not published until

1774) to his final lectures on American law, Wilson relied on a common sense epistemology of law. He employed Reidian arguments on knowledge to secure a more confident rendering of Locke's 'revolution principle', that the people (in this case American colonists) might judge for themselves which laws they were obliged to obey (*WJasW*, 1:77–78). Wilson's argument in the 1768 'Considerations on the Nature and Extent of the Legislative Authority of the British Parliament' is in many ways similar to other imperial federal arguments made at the time, recognising that Americans and Britons 'are fellow subjects; they are under allegiance to the same prince; and this union of allegiance naturally produces a union of hearts' (*WJasW*, 2:745). Nevertheless, Wilson advances considerably beyond these arguments when he claims that the application of parliamentary statutes (such as the dreaded non-importation laws) should be challenged as 'repugnant to the essential maxims of jurisprudence, to the ultimate end of all governments, and to the genius of the British constitution, and the liberty and happiness of the colonies'. According to Wilson's argument, what is 'repugnant' to the essential maxims of jurisprudence is nothing less than the whole of Blackstonian common law. Wilson labels this theory 'despotic' for two reasons: because it rests on a sceptical foundation of knowledge without confidence in the 'power' of reason of the people; and because this scepticism underpins the view that there can be no law without a 'superior' (*WJasW*, 2:735, 1:374, 221, 103, 212).

Against a Blackstonian argument for 'superiority' as the ground of obedience, Wilson pitted the democratic common sense principle of validity by consent and common opinion: 'All men are, by nature, equal and free: no one has a right to any authority over another without his consent: all lawful government is founded on the consent of those who are subject to it' (*WJasW*, 2:723). By tying obligation to consent, and consent to direct rather than virtual representation, Wilson shows that the American people cannot be considered legally bound by the authority of a parliament to whose laws they have not consented. Their continued allegiance is no more than a 'duty founded on principles of gratitude'. Wilson's argument, however, moves well beyond the issue of inadequate representation in parliament. Americans, he claims, have a right to judge for themselves which British laws they will obey because they are capable of knowing which laws (within their own colonies) custom has rendered applicable to their circumstances and therefore worthy of incorporation (*WJasW*, 2:735, 2:744, 1:105, 1:102, 2:738). No appeal to heaven is made to verify natural law. On Wilson's argument, colonial dependence on the superiority of parliament was uncommon and uncustomary: 'The dependence of the colonies in America on the parliament of England seems to have been a doctrine altogether unknown and even unsuspected by the colonists who emigrated. . . . It seems not, for a long time, to have been a doctrine known to the parliament itself' (*WJasW*, 1:364).

In contrast to Blackstone's defence of a parliamentary claim to theoretical and historical supremacy, Wilson offers evidence of the process by which the assemblies and legislatures of the American colonies in the seventeenth century had selectively incorporated only those English common law and statutory enactments that, in the words of one such legislature (Maryland), were not judged 'inconsistent with the condition of the colony' (*WJasW*, 1:361).[11] Even rules of common law having the force of 'experience and custom' in England were, Wilson notes, purposely withdrawn by conscious 'discontinuance and disuse' within the colonies (*WJasW*, 1:362).[12] Such modified legislative independence, established as custom on the principle that the American colonists knew and could judge for themselves which laws were appropriate for their own conditions, provided the common sense grounding for Wilson's 1775 resolution, before the Pennsylvania Convention, that they judge the offending British laws to be unconstitutional.

> That the act of the British parliament for altering the charter and constitution of the colony of Massachusetts Bay, and those 'for the impartial administration of justice' in that colony, for shutting the port of Boston, and for quartering soldiers on the inhabitants of the colonies, are unconstitutional and void; and can confer no authority upon those who act under colour of them. . . . [A]ll attempts to alter the said charter or constitution, unless by the authority of the legislature of that colony, are . . . illegal. (*WJasW*, 2:752–53).

Wilson argued it was not necessary to prove by elaborate or demonstrative reasoning that such acts were unconstitutional. Their unconstitutionality rested upon 'plain and indubitable truths' of common sense: 'We do not send members to the British parliament: we have parliaments (it is immaterial what name they go by) of our own' (*WJasW*, 2:753).

As is seen in his discussions of 'custom' or 'common' law, Wilson followed Reid's ordinary language identification of common sense with the judgements common to ordinary men (*WJasW*, 1:209). In the *Lectures on Law* he transposed Reid's arguments nearly verbatim to his own consideration of 'man, as an individual': 'In common language, and in the writings of the best authors, sense always implies judgment: a man of sense is a man of judgment: common sense is that degree of judgment, which is to be expected in men of common education and common understanding' (*WJasW*, 1:209). There is much in Wilson's writings, however, to suggest that he extended the ordinary language application of common sense epistemology and moral theory to questions of politics and law Reid never considered. This extension supported and shaped his positions on both democratic lawmaking and the role of juries in post-

Revolutionary America at both the state and national level. Finally, it provides the key to understanding Wilson's unrivalled advocacy for the institution which, on an understanding different from his own, has come to be identified as paradigmatically antidemocratic: the Supreme Court with judicial review.

III

Wilson has been called an 'unequivocal advocate' of majority rule, and certainly his common sense epistemology underpins an argument for the widest possible implementation of popular sovereignty in the form of constitutional government, direct and actual representation, widespread suffrage and majority rule by 'the people'. Wilson contends, however, that absolute sovereignty always resides in the people even after government has been formed, making the American constitution 'materially different' from and 'better' than the British (*WJasW*, 1:77, 2:771). Because sovereignty resides in the people, it 'should be exercised by them in person, if that could be done with convenience' (*WJasW*, 1:405). Representation is thus less desirable than direct participation as a mode of self-rule and, as he informed participants at the Constitutional Convention, 'representative' legislatures 'ought to be the most exact transcript of the whole Society' since 'representation is made necessary only because it is impossible for the people to act collectively'.[13] The common sense principle that a 'universally held opinion' has a status of law suggests a legitimating forum larger than the majority of the members of the legislature: majority rule is but a 'practical principle' (*WJasW*, 1:387–88).

As early as 1779, Wilson challenged the 'democratic' theory contained in the Pennsylvania constitution of 1776, which established the principle of majority rule within a unicameral legislature and justified all governmental measures by reference to this majority's will. Throughout the next three years, Wilson engaged in a fierce public debate (frequently carried forward in the local newspapers) with the radicals of western Pennsylvania over whether a bicameral legislature was necessary to democratic rule. But Wilson's support for bicameralism, which garnered him a reputation as an antidemocrat, was couched neither in the Madisonian terms of encouraging necessary counterfactions nor in the more 'élitist' language of John Adams's 'mixed Government' and the need for incorporating aristocractic or intellectual groups within the legislature. Instead, Wilson sided with his opponents from the West in insisting that representatives in both houses be popularly elected: 'May merit and the unbiassed voice of the people be the only title to distinction ever known in Pennsylvania.'[14] The purpose of Wilson's two houses was to reduce error in reproducing the common sense of the people by encouraging public discussion. It was not simply to 'restrain' but to 'inform'. Hasty and impetuous acion, unreflective of the reason as well as the feeling involved in the common sense judgement of the public, could be reduced if the two houses of representatives were made to discuss publicly and 'to justify their conduct in the judgment of their constitutents upon whom they are equally dependent'.[15] One political implication of democratic epistemology was that ordinary men not only were capable of knowing the law but also had a strong political need to know it. Wilson recognised the 'fury of legislative tempests' consequent to democratic rule: 'Kings are not the only tyrants' (*WJasW*, 1:133–37, 291–308, 318–19, 2:728).

On Wilson's argument, then, one way ordinary men come to know, to shape and thus to admire the law is through their participation on juries. The jury is Wilson's model of political participation and democratic epistemology in action. When Wilson asks who can and should know the law, the answer is that 'the science of law should, in some measure, and in some degree, be the study of every free citizen, and of every free man'. It is this knowledge that enables men to be both just and independent. Such knowledge is possible because of the makeup of man and of the law: 'The knowledge of those rational principles on which the law is founded, ought, especially in a free government, to be diffused over the whole community' (*WJasW*, 1:72–73). Juries, by diffusing common understanding of the law, serve this function:

> The rights and the duties of jurors, in the United States, are great and extensive. No punishment can be inflicted without the intervention of one – in much the greater number of cases, without the intervention of more than one jury. . . . Is it not, then, of immense consequence to both [the public and individuals], that jurors should possess the spirit of just discernment, to discriminate between the innocent and the guilty? This spirit of just discernment requires knowledge of, at least, the general principles of the law, as well as knowledge of the minute particulars concerning the facts. (*WJasW*, 1:74)

Wilson believed the powers of American juries were considerably more expansive, and better, than those of their English counterparts. Significantly, he saw no clear separation of powers between judges and juries over the determination of law and facts. The province of factual determination was clearly the jury's to decide. In matters of law, however, Wilson's common sense theory militated against the English common law position that the judge alone has knowledge of the law. After all, Wilson noted, 'in many respectable courts within the United States, the judges are not, and, for a long time, cannot be gentlemen of professional acquirements' (*WJasW*, 1:74). In other words, on practical grounds alone there may be cause to argue that juries know the law as well as judges. However,

Wilson's argument for the expansive powers of juries rests on deeper theoretical commitments. For example, in matters of criminal law (and here, issues of treason and sedition are his constant referents) juries are the final authority in 'judging' the law regardless of the qualifications of the judge. Wilson notes: 'It is true, that, in matters of law, jurors are entitled to the assistance of the judges; but it is also true, that, after they receive it, they have the right of judging for themselves.' In those instances, where the fundamental principles of the country must be known and applied, the jury becomes the key democratic institution – 'the selected body who act for the country'. Such a jury, judging in criminal trials in which the commonly held political principles of the country have been challenged, Wilson calls 'a jury of the country' (*WJasW*, 2:529, 547, 1:74). In contrast to the deep distrust of crown-appointed judges during the Revolutionary era that supported an expansive colonial claim for jury powers, Wilson's role for juries is underpinned by common sense and a presumption of jural cooperation. He speaks of juries and judges cooperating in a dialogue of 'mutual assistance' as well as 'mutual check' (*WJasW*, 2:542). The aim throughout is mutual balance rather than functional separation of the component parts of common sense judging – reason and feeling – which *both* share. Their aim is cooperation in avoiding error in law to which judges as well as juries are susceptible.

Wilson's most direct challenge to Blackstone's jurisprudence concerned the legal knowledge that the common people could be presumed to have. Blackstone had claimed not only that the powers of parliament are 'transcendent and absolute' but also that in parliament the House of Lords served a judicial as well as a legislative function, uttering *final judgements* on the validity of its own laws. Blackstone argued that the law of parliament was 'to be sought by all, unknown by many, and known by few'.[16] Judges, accordingly, were assumed to possess a knowledge of the law superior to that of juries and, by the same token, parliament held legal authority superior to that of the people. Wilson challenged the first claim in his discussion of juries. He challenged the second in his proposals at the Constitutional Convention (and after) for a national 'council of revision' and for a supreme court with judicial review.

In response to Blackstone's claims for the supreme judicial function of parliament, Wilson argued there was 'nothing in the formation of the House of Lords; nor in the education, habits, character, or professions of the members who compose it; nor in the mode of their appointment, or the right, by which they succeed to their places, that suggests any intelligible fitness, in the nature of this regulation' (*WJasW*, 1:323). The same argument militated against leaving the power to determine law, without a mechanism of review, in state or national legislatures. Sovereignty lay in the people, and Wilson wanted to dispel the notion that the legislative power alone was the 'people's representative' (*WJasW*, 1:293). Not surprisingly, Wilson's initial vision of the judicial institution to which the people may attach themselves took the form of a jury.

In the *Lectures on Law* Wilson's discussion of the history of English judicial institutions of relevance to America ends at a period 'at which others generally begin theirs' (*WJasW*, 2:453). He examined the role of a thirteenth-century institution, the *aula regis*, an 'institutional antiquity' that Wilson believed had been incorporated with some revision in the Supreme Court of Pennsylvania. The *aula regis* had originated as a council of advisers, serving both a jural and judicial function for the king, with the power of deciding cases and reviewing the decisions of inferior jurisdictions. The experience of the lack of a national judiciary in the Confederation period, culminating in Wilson's participation in the formation of a national 'jury' at the Trenton Trial (1782) to weigh the legal claims of two competing states, raised the call for some comparable body under the new national Constitution (*WJasW*, 2:454, 450).[17] Wilson reiterated the need for a national 'jury' on the law at the Constitutional Convention, where he supported (together with Madison) the creation of a 'Council of revision' in which the executive and the judiciary could exercise power of review over legislative acts.[18] As proposed, the powers of this council extended to a revisory as well as review power because, as Wilson claimed: 'Laws may be unjust, may be unwise, may be dangerous, may be destructive; and yet not be so unconstitutional as to justify the Judges in refusing to give them effect.'[19] By permitting participation by members of a national judiciary in this 'Revisionary power', Wilson argued for the power of 'opinion' to counteract or correct 'improper' views of the legislature.

When the convention rejected the council, Wilson proposed a separately conceived power of judicial review of both state laws and acts of the national legislature (*WJasW*, 2:455–56). Wilson's proposal for a power of judicial review was supported at the convention by Madison as well as a significant number of delegates who held otherwise widely divergent views.[20] However, for both the council of revision and its successor in a supreme court with judicial review, Wilson alone offered a theoretical understanding congruent with the common sense theory of democratic judgement.

The function of judicial review in Wilson's account was neither to 'disparage the legislative authority', nor to 'confer upon the judicial department a power superiour, in its general nature'. It was to avoid the errors that may arise in legislation, perhaps not in the immediate perception of basic political principles, but in the legislative reasoning that constitutes their development under a government by discussion. Judicial review, like Wilson's common sense revision of Locke's 'revolution principle', was intended not to be a principle of 'discord, rancour, or war' but rather of 'melioration'. The balance of the court, the legislature and the people in the achievement of justice would require 'much discussion and inquiry' if the errors of judgement produced by Reidian bias and partiality and by 'jealousies and attachments' were to be exposed 'in order to be avoided'. Wilson was confident, however, that when properly considered, such balancing of feeling and reason in the common sense politics of ordinary men would be viewed in a favourable light by the legislature itself (*WJasW*, 1:330, 79–80, 290–91). To support the power of judicial review in the *Lectures on Law*, Wilson quoted Elias Boudinot's statement from the House debates on the judiciary, which summarises nicely the revisionary power Wilson projected for judicial review:

> It has been objected . . . that, by adopting the bill before us, we expose the measure to be considered and defeated by the judiciary of the United States, who may adjudge it to be contrary to the constitution, and therefore void, and not lend their aid to carry it into execution. This gives me no uneasiness. I am so far from controverting this right in the judiciary, that it is my boast and my confidence. It leads me to greater decision on all subjects of a constitutional nature, when I reflect, that, if from inattention, want of precision, or any other defect, I should do wrong, there is a power in the government, which can constitutionally prevent the operation of a wrong measure from affecting my constituents. I am legislating for a nation, and for thousands yet unborn; and it is the glory of the constitution, that there is a remedy for the failures even of the legislature itself. (*WJasW*, 1:330–31)

In Wilson's vision, the Supreme Court with judicial review functioned on the model and the principles of the jury of the country, as 'the selected body who act for the country'. The common sense judgement of the people was vested in it, yet Wilson never treated this power as analogous to sovereignty. Sovereignty, even over the Constitution itself, remained with the people, who were at liberty to correct even the mistaken judgements of the high court through constitutional amendment – the 'revolution principle' – when such judgements did not stand the test of 'universal opinion'.

Wilson's most extensive opinion delivered while on the Supreme Court, *Chisholm v. Georgia* (1793), is prefaced by a quotation from Reid, suggesting that innovation cannot be made in the philosophy of men's common life 'without using new words and phrases, or giving a different meaning to those that are received'. Wilson proceeds to give new meanings to the terms 'state' and 'Sovereign' that faithfully follow the democratic theory he had developed over the course of his career. A 'state' is 'a complete body of free persons united together for their common benefit, to enjoy what is peacefully their own, and to do justice to others. It is an artificial person.'[21] Accordingly, Wilson concludes that the citizens of Georgia had a constitutional right to sue their state and to have their claims adjudicated. The response to the decision followed true to Wilson's Reidian principles and the melioration of error, but it could hardly have been the result Wilson expected. Proponents of 'state sovereignty' reacted immediately against what they believed to be a 'perversion' of common language and opinion. They accused Wilson of political 'partiality' in the cause of the national Federalists against their 'states' rights' opponents. Within a year Congress passed a resolution employing the 'revolution principle' to amend the Constitution in order to secure a meaning of the 'sovereignty' of states that would prevent individual citizens from pressing a legal suit against them. The eleventh amendment was ratified in 1798, the year of Wilson's death.

One can make a parallel move from the jurisprudence of James Wilson to that of John Marshall. There is much they share, and in at least one respect *Chisholm* clearly prefigures *Marbury*, the decision commonly referred to as having established (even originated) judicial review. What can readily be seen in the opinions of Marshall is Wilson's democratic, ordinary language put into practice. Marshall's jurisprudence has been characterised as 'the perfect model and logical extension of the need to speak a contemporary language that all Americans could understand and heed'. Marshall was dismissive of case law, preferring instead in his five greatest opinions as chief justice not to cite even the previous decisions of the Supreme Court as authority.[22] He grounded each opinion instead on appeals to the 'self-evident principles' he insisted all Americans shared. Wilson first envisioned judicial review in America as an institution carrying forward the jurisprudential implications of Reid's common sense theories of epistemology and morals. Marshall *re*invented judicial review for the Supreme Court, not as the exercise of common sense judgement in which feeling and intellect comingle but as an 'oracle' of reason that once again set sense and judgement at opposite poles of jurisprudential discourse, juxtaposed popular sentiment and court 'reason' and launched a debate over the competing roles of the Supreme Court and the Congress that persists in America today.

NOTES

The author wishes to thank Ned Landsman, Murray Milgate, J. Russell Muirhead, Jeffrey Smitten and Cheryl B. Weich for helpful comments on an earlier draft of this chapter.

1. *WJasW*, 2:770. Robert McCloskey was the first to argue for the con-

sistency of Wilson's democratic vision. Gordon Wood, however, has persuasively suggested that Wilson's attachment to strong national government led him to support Federalist arguments encouraging participation in government by the 'best' men in the community. But to characterise such support as unqualified 'élitism' – and consequently to label Wilson anti-democratic in spirit, if not in practice – is perhaps to impose too stringent criteria for 'democratic' thought in the eighteenth century (or any other) and certainly requires us to set aside the greater number of Wilson's statements explicitly supporting popular sovereignty and the widest possible suffrage. See Wood, *The Creation of the American Republic, 1776–1787* (Chapel Hill, N.C., 1969), 492–93. See also Hannah Arendt, *On Revolution* (New York, 1963), 236. It should be noted that Arendt's conclusion that Wilson was anti-democratic stems from a highly selective and a-contextual reading of a quotation taken secondhand from William Seal Carpenter, *The Development of American Political Thought* (Princeton, 1930), 93–94.

2. *The Records of the Federal Convention of 1787*, ed. Max Farrand, 3 vols. (New Haven, Conn., 1911), 1: 52, 69, 132–33, 405–6; 2:56. On proportional representation, see ibid., 1:179, 483; *WJasW*, 1:406, 312. Wilson was critical of the unequal representation of the House of Commons, in which the will of the people could be expressed only 'very feebly and imperfectly' because a majority of the Commons was elected by a minority of the population. Wilson's arguments for equal representation were later cited in support of the 'one man one vote' decisions of the Supreme Court in *Wesberry v. Sanders*, 376 U.S. 1, 17 (1964) and *Reynolds v. Sims*, 377 U.S. 533, 564, n. 41 (1964).
3. Wilson claims Blackstone was not 'a votary of despotic power' in 'making an artful use of "superiority" in politics' but rather was led to this conclusion from unsound and 'sceptical' principles of knowledge.
4. Wilson's views on judicial review are found in *Records*, ed. Farrand, 2:73, 391; at the Pennsylvania Ratifying Convention, in *Debates in the Several State Conventions, in the Adoption of the Federal Constitution*, 4 vols. (Washington, D.C., 1854), 2: 445, 478, 489; and *WJasW*, 2:445–56. For a more fully developed account of Wilson's contribution to the development of American jurisprudence and to the theoretical origins of judicial review, see Shannon C. Stimson, *The American Revolution in the Law: Perspectives on Anglo-American Jurisprudence before John Marshall* (London, 1990). For an earlier discussion of Wilson's legal thought, see Randolph C. Adams, 'The Legal Theories of James Wilson', *University of Pennsylvania Law Review and Law Register* 68 (1919): 337–55.
5. Reid and Wilson argued not for the rejection of philosophy, but rather for what both considered the 'metaphysical lunacy' of some philosophical doctrines. See *WTR*, 1:209.
6. Reid's suggestion of self-evidence contained a justifying appeal to providential naturalism. The ground of such self-evidence was an appeal to universal opinion: 'If man had not the faculty given him by God of perceiving certain things in conduct to be right, and others to be wrong, and of perceiving his obligation to do what is right,

and not to do what is wrong, he would not be a moral and accountable being' (*WTR*, 1:479).

7. Arnaud B. Leavelle, 'James Wilson and the Relation of the Scottish Metaphysics to American Political Thought', *Political Science Quarterly* 57 (1942): 394–410.
8. David Fate Norton, *David Hume: Common-Sense Moralist, Sceptical Metaphysician* (Princeton, 1982), 201.
9. My claim here is not that Reid's moral epistemology is in fact democratic or that it must be so conceived, but rather that Wilson himself perceived it to have broadly democratic implications when properly understood and explicitly developed in his own work.
10. At least one commentator on Wilson has argued that 'although Wilson followed Thomas Reid on many matters, he departed from him on the subject of the Moral Sense' and accepted instead a view influenced by Hume. See Morton White, *Science and Sentiment in America* (New York, 1972), 68. According to White, Wilson followed Hume in imputing a purely emotive origin to moral sense. This claim seems too strong. Consider the following unattributed parallel textual references to Reid in Wilson: *WJasW*, 1:137–38 (*WTR*, 1:481); *WJasW*, 1:205, 225 (*WTR*, 1:100); *WJasW*, 1:203–6 (*WTR*, 1:441–52, 339–46, 360–68); *WJasW*, 1:379–82 (*WTR*, 1:117–19); *WJasW*, 1:223 (*WTR*, 1:230); *WJasW*, 1:213 (*WTR*, 1:425); *WJasW*, 1:212 (*WTR*, 1:101). Wilson cites Reid to criticise Hume in *WJasW*, 1:205. I am grateful to J. Russell Muirhead for calling my attention to several of these parallel citations.
11. Wilson cites a famous navigation act made by parliament that met with opposition in Massachusetts (*WJasW,* 1:367).
12. Wilson cites Blackstone for having recognised this. For an examination of this selective incorporation, see Elizabeth Gaspar Brown, *British Statutes in American Law, 1776–1836* (Ann Arbor, Mich., 1964), 4–5.
13. *Records,* ed. Farrand, 1:132–33.
14. *Pennsylvania Gazette,* 24 March 1779.
15. *Pennsylvania Journal and Weekly Advertiser,* 7 July 1784. Wilson won this argument in 1790.
16. Sir William Blackstone, *Commentaries on the Laws of England* (Philadelphia, 1894), 2 vols., 1:124 (chap. 2, sec. 5).
17. The Trenton Trial of 1782 is discussed in Jefferson, 6:474ff.
18. *Records*, ed. Farrand, 1:94, 104.
19. Ibid., 2:73.
20. At least six others can be named: Elbridge Gerry, Rufus King, Roger Sherman, Gouverneur Morris, Luther Martin and George Mason. Hamilton and Marshall clearly supported it after the fact. See Forrest McDonald, *Novus Ordo Seclorum: The Intellectual Origins of the Constitution* (Lawrence, Kan., 1985), 254–55.
21. 2 *United States Reports* (Dallas), 454–55 (1793).
22. Robert A. Ferguson, *Law and Letters in American Culture* (Cambridge, Mass., 1984), 23.

12

DAVID DAICHES

STYLE PÉRIODIQUE *and* STYLE COUPÉ:
Hugh Blair and the Scottish Rhetoric of American Independence

The Founding Fathers of the United States of America were much concerned with rhetoric. They knew the classical authorities on the subject, especially Aristotle, Cicero and Quintilian. They knew that Plato had been suspicious of rhetoric for having no necessary concern with the discovery of truth and that Aristotle had taken a more neutral position, pointing out that the argument that rhetoric can be used to do harm 'applies equally to all good things except virtue, and above all to those things which are most useful, such as strength, health, wealth, generalship; for as these things, rightly used, may be of the greatest benefit, so, wrongly used, they may do an equal amount of harm.'[1] Above all, they were familiar with Cicero's view of the civic importance of the tools of persuasion:

> There is to my mind no more excellent thing than the power, by means of oratory, to get a hold on assemblies of men, win their good will, direct their inclinations wherever the speaker wishes . . . In every free nation, and most of all in communities which have attained the enjoyment of peace and tranquillity, this one art has always flourished above the rest . . . the wise control of the complete orator is that which chiefly upholds not only his own dignity, but the safety of countless individuals and of the entire state.[2]

And they had read Quintilian, who had also insisted on rhetoric's civic function: 'The man who can really play his part as a citizen and is capable of meeting the demands both of public and private business, the man who can guide a state by his counsels, give it a firm basis by his legislation and purge its vices by his decisions as a judge, is assuredly no other than the orator of our quest.'[3]

It was, however, among the writers of the Scottish Enlightenment that interest in rhetoric as a civic virtue rose to its height, and it was Scottish teachers who brought this renewed interest to America during the period when the debate on American independence was under way. The reason for the special Scottish interest in rhetoric lay partly in the view of many eighteenth-century Scotsmen that their own version of the English language was, in David Hume's words, 'very corrupt',[4] making them anxious to write an elegant, formal, persuasive and 'correct' English. Accordingly, Edinburgh had a chair of English (for that is what Hugh Blair's unsalaried chair of 'Rhetoric' of 1760 – upgraded to a Regius chair of 'Rhetoric and Belles Lettres' in 1762 – essentially was) a century and a half before Oxford or Cambridge. The Roman student studied Greek; the English student studied Latin; the Scottish student studied English. The Scots, conscious of being in some sense on the periphery of English literary culture, as in a rather different but parallel sense the Americans were also, studied English style and rhetoric as the English did not. And so did the Americans. The proliferation of professors of English in American universities long before they were found in England need not therefore surprise us.

Of the Scottish teachers bringing renewed interest in rhetoric to America during the age of the Enlightenment, by far the most influential was Hugh Blair. By the time the American Constitution was being drafted in the late 1780s, large numbers of college-educated Americans had read his two-volume *Lectures on Rhetoric and Belles Lettres*. That book was published at London in June 1783, a year before Blair's retirement from active teaching. Numerous further editions followed, including one at Philadelphia in 1784 and some three dozen subsequent American editions.[5] It was introduced as a textbook at Yale in 1785 and at Harvard in 1788. Equally important, Blair noted in the preface to his *Lectures* that 'imperfect Copies of them, in Manuscript, from notes taken by Students who heard them read, were first privately handed about; and afterwards frequently exposed to public sale.' Since the preface implied that the lectures had remained fundamentally the same since they were first delivered in the 1759–60 academic year, it is safe to assume that their influence in Britain, and possibly also in America, predated their publication by many years.[6] A manuscript copy of Blair's lectures may even have found its way into the hands of John Witherspoon before his emigration to Princeton in 1768, for the latter's student and biographer Ashbel Green noted that 'a striking similarity, in their General views and leading thoughts, has been observed between the lectures of Dr. Blair on Belles Lettres, and those of Dr. Witherspoon on Composition, taste and criticism'.[7]

When confronted with this embarrassing observation by his friend, Witherspoon denied 'the interchange [with Blair] of a single thought on these subjects'. Green himself attributed the similarity to the fact that both men had 'studied under the same teachers, and thus derived their original traits of thinking on the subjects in question from a common source'.[8] This argument is not entirely convincing, but it is certainly true that Blair's *Lectures* drew substantially on earlier Scottish ideas about rhetoric and belles lettres. When Blair and Witherspoon were students at Edinburgh University in the 1730s, the professor of logic, John Stevenson, gave rhetoric lectures of a rather old-fashioned kind, combining Aristotle and Longinus with some of the ideas of John Locke. Another student from that era, Alexander Carlyle, recalled Stevenson's class in a memoir intended for publication:

> In my second year at the College, November 1736 . . . I went to the Logic class, taught by Mr. John Stevenson, who, though he had no pretensions to superiority in point of learning and genius, yet was the most popular of all the Professors on account of his civility and even kindness to his students, and at the same time the most useful; for being a man of sense and industry, he had made a judicious selection from the French and English critics, which he gave at the morning hour of eight, when he read with us Aristotle's *Poetics* and Longinus *On the Sublime*. At eleven he read Heineccius' *Logic*, and an abridgement of Locke's *Essay*; and in the afternoon at two . . . he read to us a compendious history of the ancient philosophers, and an account of their tenets.[9]

In a briefer memoir that was *not* intended for publication, Carlyle was more critical, observing that Stevenson's teaching had been generally overrated by former students.[10] Nevertheless, in abandoning the old logic of the sixteenth-century French humanist Petrus Ramus, with its division of persuasive speech into invention (dealing with notion and definition) and judgement (including judgement proper, syllogism and method), which had been standard in the Scottish universities, and introducing Locke into university teaching, Stevenson was an important pioneer.

In his *Lectures* Blair made no mention of Stevenson, but he acknowledged the influence of 'a manuscript treatise on rhetoric . . . by the learned and ingenious Author, Dr. Adam Smith' (Blair, 1:381n.). Smith had delivered private rhetoric lectures at Edinburgh from 1748 to 1751, chiefly to students of law and theology, and he built on these lectures as professor of logic and then of moral philosophy at the University of Glasgow. These lectures were never published by Smith, though a set of student notes from his 1762-63 session appeared in 1963.[11] We know from Smith's student John Millar, the brilliant Glasgow law professor and author, just how Smith proceeded and what his intentions were: 'The best method of explaining and illustrating the various powers of the human mind, the most useful part of metaphysics, arises from an examination of the several ways of communicating our thoughts by speech, and from an attention to the principles of those literary compositions which contribute to persuasion or entertainment.'[12] When Smith moved to Glasgow, his lecture course was continued at Edinburgh by Robert Watson, until his appointment to the chair of logic, rhetoric and metaphysics at St Andrews University in 1756. Thus, when Blair gave his first Edinburgh lectures on rhetoric in December 1759 (several months before the foundation of his chair), he was following a tradition of private rhetoric teaching pioneered by Smith and developed by Watson.

Smith, Watson and Blair differed from Stevenson in viewing rhetoric, drawn from a study of particular literary examples, as a study in its own right and not merely a branch of logic. They had for a principal aim the replacement of the old medieval tradition of rhetoric, which had degenerated into innumerable lists and classifications of rhetorical figures and devices, as well as of the Renaissance humanist rhetoric that succeeded it, by a useful modern study that would help in both the appreciation and production of literary styles suitable to – and effective on – appropriate occasions. 'Our words must . . . be put in such order that the meaning of the sentence shall be quite plain and not depend upon the accuracy of the printer in placing the points, or of the readers in laying the emphasis on any certain word', Smith told his students in his *Lectures* (5). This was a rhetoric for the literati of the Scottish Enlightenment, bent on exploring and clarifying their views of man and nature, as it was a rhetoric for the men of the American Revolution, bent on explaining, clarifying and justifying the objectives of their revolutionary activity.[13]

Given this general similarity in outlook, it is not surprising that Blair was especially congenial to the Founding Fathers. Blair's attraction was further enhanced by his explicitly associating eloquence with freedom. 'It is an observation made by several writers,' he notes in lecture 25, on 'Eloquence, or Public Speaking', 'that Eloquence is to be looked for only in free states. . . . Liberty, [Longinus] remarks, is the nurse of true genius; it animates the spirit, and invigorates the hopes of men; excites honourable emulation, and a desire of excelling in every Art' (Blair, 2:8). Later in this lecture he asserts: 'Wherever man can acquire most power over man by means of reason and discourse, which certainly is under a free state of government, there we may naturally expect that true Eloquence will be best understood, and carried to the greatest height' (Blair, 2:9).

In addition, Blair made the highest civic claims for the study of rhetoric and belles lettres: 'The elevated sentiments and high examples which poetry, eloquence and history are often bringing under our view, naturally tend to nourish in our minds publick spirit, the love of glory, contempt of external fortune, and the admiration of what is truly illustrious and great' (Blair, 1:13). And the most effective orator must be a good man:

> Without possessing the virtuous affections in a strong degree, no man can attain eminence in the sublime parts of eloquence. He must feel what a good man feels, if he expects greatly to move or to interest

> mankind. They are the ardent sentiments of honour, virtue, magnanimity, and publick spirit. (Blair, 1:13–14)

Later Blair spelled out the character traits he considered 'particularly requisite' for an orator to cultivate: 'The love of justice and order, and indignation at insolence and oppression; the love of honesty and truth, and detestation of fraud, meanness, and corruption; magnanimity of spirit; the love of liberty, of their country and the public; zeal for all great and noble designs, and reverence for all worthy and heroic characters' (Blair, 2:232).

The association of eloquence with freedom and virtue (two separate kinds of association that tended to fuse in eighteenth-century discussions of the subject) became firmly implanted in the American mind during the great debate on American independence, and we find this view expressed as representing common knowledge of the subject for a long while afterwards. When John Quincy Adams, son of an American president and himself later to become president, delivered his lectures as the first Boylston professor of rhetoric and oratory at Harvard in 1806–9, he drew on Blair, among others, to give his students what might be called the standard view of the subject that had developed in America in the last third of the eighteenth century:

> The art of speaking must be most eagerly sought, where it is found to be most useful. It must be most useful, where it is capable of producing the greatest effects; and that can be done in no other state of things, than where the power of persuasion operates upon the will, and prompts the actions of other men. The only birth of eloquence therefore must be a free state. Under military governments, where the lot is cast upon one man to command, and upon all the rest to obey; where the despot, like the Roman centurion, has only to say to one go, and he goeth, and to another come, and he cometh, persuasion is of no avail. Between authority and obedience there can be no deliberation; and wheresoever submission is the principle of government in a nation, eloquence can never arise. Eloquence is the child of liberty, and can descend from no other stock.[14]

But to appreciate Blair's influence more specifically, we should observe how his ideas illuminate the style of the American Constitution itself. For Blair, literature was essentially communication, and if not properly received by audience or reader it did not serve its function. In his tenth lecture, on perspicuity and precision in style, he writes:

> If we are obliged to follow a writer with much care, to pause, and to read over his sentences a second time, in order to comprehend them fully, he will never please us long. . . . Authors sometimes plead the difficulty of their subject, as an excuse for the want of Perspicuity. But the excuse can rarely, if ever, be sustained. For whatever a man

> conceives clearly, that, it is in his power, if he will be at the trouble, to put into distinct propositions, or to express clearly to others: and upon no subject ought any man to write, where he cannot think clearly. (Blair, 1:185–86)

In the same lecture, Blair deprecates 'the pomp and parade of language' and 'the dress of state and majesty' aspired to by some writers. He objects also to circumlocution and that 'loose style' marked by 'the injudicious use of those words termed Synonymous'. There are few if any true synonyms, he argues: words often deemed synonymous have each their own shade of meaning, and a good writer chooses words in order to take advantage of that special shade. Those who confound words with each other and 'employ them carelessly, merely for the sake of filling up a period, or of rounding and diversifying the Language' only produce 'a certain mist, and indistinctness' in style (Blair, 1:195).

Blair's insistence on the need for precision and his suspicion of the pomp and parade of language do not mean that he advocated only simple and brief sentences. He saw a proper place both for the *style périodique* and the *style coupé*. The former is 'where the sentences are composed of several members linked together, and hanging upon one another, so that the sense of the whole is not brought out till the close.' He calls this 'the most pompous, musical, and oratorical manner of composing' and refers to Cicero's frequent use of it (Blair, 1: 206). It is true that Ciceronian Latin, with its deferring of the principal verb or verbal phrase to the end of a long periodic sentence, does produce a style that can be called 'pompous, musical, and oratorical'. (In this sense 'pompous' is not used pejoratively by Blair.) Part of the genius of the Latin language exploited by Cicero was the ability to defer the clinching element in the meaning of a sentence to the end (as Renaissance German scholars contrived to make German do and as it has done ever since). But one can use the deferred crux of meaning equally well in less elaborate prose. The opening sentence or preamble of the American Constitution conforms exactly to Blair's definition of the *style périodique*: 'We, the People of the United States, in order to form a more perfect union, establish justice, insure domestic tranquillity, provide for the common defence, promote the general welfare, and secure the blessings of liberty to ourselves and our posterity, do ordain and establish this Constitution for the United States of America.'[15] The main verbs here ('do ordain and establish') come in the final clause of the sentence: one does not know what the intention of the sentence is until these verbs are reached. But the two verbs, in conformity with Blair's rule, are not synonyms: 'ordain' and 'establish' are distinct words, with the meaning of each equally essential to the intention of the sentence. To ordain is to enact, and to establish is to found or institute – the consequence of ordaining.

There is another way in which the preamble of the Constitution conforms exactly to Blair's definition of the *style périodique*. This is in the periodic parallel phrases that come between the opening phrase 'We, the People of the United States' and the final verbal clause: 'in order to form a more perfect union, establish justice, insure domestic tranquillity, provide for the common defence, promote the general welfare, and secure the blessings of liberty to ourselves and our posterity . . .' The purpose of what they are about to do is given before what they are going to do is stated, in true Ciceronian style, and that purpose is presented in a series of parallel phrases, each of which defines precisely a different aspect of the purpose. Blair gives as a typical example of the *style périodique* a sentence from a letter by Sir William Temple: ' "If you look about you, and consider the lives of others as well as your own; if you think how few are born with honour, and how many die without name or children; how little beauty we see, and how few friends we hear of; how many diseases, and how much poverty there is in the world; you will fall down upon your knees, and, instead of repining at one affliction, will admire so many blessings which you have received from the hand of God." ' (Blair, 1:206). The structure here, in spite of its being more elaborate, is precisely that of the preamble of the Constitution, with its marching parallel phrases leading towards the concluding principal clause.

The preamble provides a revealing glimpse into the process of stylistic revision at the Constitutional Convention. The significance of stylistic considerations is clear from the very fact that on 8 September 1787 the convention charged a 'committee of style' with putting the final touches on the language agreed upon by its 'committee of detail'. Here is the version of the preamble that the former committee inherited from the latter: 'We the people of the States of New Hampshire, Massachusetts, Rhode-Island and Providence Plantations, Connecticut, New-York, New-Jersey, Pennsylvania, Delaware, Maryland, Virginia, North-Carolina, South-Carolina, and Georgia, do ordain, declare and establish the following Constitution for the government of ourselves and our posterity.' The most impressive accomplishment of the committee of style was to transform this flat, plodding sentence into the striking preamble with which we are familiar. James Madison must have had this achievement in mind when he credited Gouverneur Morris, the committee of style's leading member, with furnishing 'the *finish*' to the Constitution's style'. Besides reducing the tedious list of individual states to a single entity, Morris and the committee shortened and sharpened the final verbal clause, eliminating the unnecessary verb 'declare' and reinforcing the opening emphasis on the primacy and unity of the 'United States of America'. They also inserted the critically important crescendo of parallel phrases building to a dramatic climax, which transformed the preamble into a powerful instance of the *style périodique*.[16]

The actual articles of the Constitution are for the most part written in

Blair's *style coupé*, 'where the sense is formed into short independent propositions, each complete within itself' (Blair, 1:206). The independent propositions tend to be connected simply by 'and' or 'but' or by a relative pronoun.

> All legislative powers herein granted shall be vested in a Congress of the United States, which shall consist of a Senate and House of Representatives. . . .
>
> The House of Representatives shall be composed of members chosen every second year by the people of the several states, and the electors in each state shall have the qualifications requisite for the electors of the most numerous branch of the state legislature. . . .
>
> The number of representatives shall not exceed one for every thirty thousand, but each state shall have at least one representative; and until such enumeration shall be made, the state of New-Hampshire shall be entitled to choose three, Massachusetts eight, Rhode-Island and Providence Plantations one, . . . (ART. 1, SEC. 2)

In such sentences there is a minimum of delay before the meaning is conveyed, and the meaning is conveyed cumulatively rather than by suspension until a final verbal clause clears everything up. This, of course, is the natural language of legal enactment. Precise communication of intention and lack of dependence on punctuation are necessities of legal documents: indeed, in many legal documents such as wills it is deemed an advantage to have no punctuation at all except periods at the ends of sentences, so that everything must be made explicit in the actual words and their order without any dependence on rhetorical pauses.

Is it possible to go further in defining the language of the American Constitution in the light of Blair's teaching? Although the dry particularities of the specific articles of the Constitution tend to be legal in phraseology, dependent on no obvious rhetorical devices, set out in successive clauses that follow each other with simple conjunctions or relative pronouns, Blair's *style coupé* rather than his *style périodique*, yet even in the specific articles there sometimes emerges a certain rising eloquence, often the result of a cumulative list in which categories are both enlarged and distinguished.

> The judicial power shall extend to all cases, in law and equity, arising under this constitution, the laws of the United States, and treaties made, or which shall be made, under their authority; to all cases affecting ambassadors, other public ministers and consuls; to all cases of admiralty and maritime jurisdiction; to controversies to which the United States shall be a party, to controversies between two or more States, between a state and citizens of another state, between citizens of different States, between citizens of the same state claiming lands under grants of different States, and between a state,

> or the citizens thereof, and foreign States, citizens or subjects. (ART. 3, SEC. 2)

The rising repetitions and changing of terms – 'to all cases affecting ambassadors . . .; to all cases of admiralty and maritime jurisdiction; to controversies to which . . . to controversies between . . .; between . . ., between . . ., and between . . .'– produces its own kind of eloquence.

'In every composition, of whatever kind,' Blair announced in his eleventh lecture,

> some degree of unity is required. . . . But most of all, in a single sentence, is required the strictest unity. For the very nature of a sentence implies one proposition to be expressed. It may consist of parts, indeed; but these parts must be so closely bound together, as to make the impression upon the mind, of one object, not of many. (Blair, 1:216–17)

The sentence just quoted from the Constitution is a perfect application of Blair's rule. A single point is being made, the extent of the judicial power of the United States, but the point 'consists of parts' and these are 'so closely bound together, as to make the impression upon the mind, of one object, not of many.' The judicial power of the United States extends to cover various categories, but that breadth of coverage is a definition of the strength and unity of that power. It may further be noted that the clauses in this sentence are not connected by 'and'. In his twelfth lecture Blair discusses the use of 'a connecting particle' and when it is helpful to reduce such conjunctions to a minimum. It is, he says, 'a remarkable particularity in Language, that the omission of a connecting particle should sometimes serve to make objects appear more closely connected; and that the repetition of it should distinguish and separate them, in some measure, from each other' (Blair, 1:232). This is precisely what happens in the sentence from the Constitution. The balanced list of cases to which the judicial power of the United States extends rolls on without conjunctions to give an impressive effect of a unifying power, the only use of 'and' being to connect minor categories within the larger ones.

There are not many articles of the Constitution that repay an analysis of this kind, for the utilitarian purpose of defining a function, which is generally the prime consideration, usually demands a simple string of associated clauses. Take, for example, the definition of the powers of the president:

> The president shall be commander in chief of the army and navy of the United States, and of the militia of the several States, when called into the actual service of the United States; he may require the opinion, in writing, of the principal officer in each of the executive departments, upon any subject relating to the duties of their respective offices, and he shall have power to grant reprieves and pardons

> for offences against the United States, except in cases of impeachment.
>
> He shall have power, by and with the advice and consent of the senate, to make treaties, provided two-thirds of the senators present concur; and he shall nominate, and by and with the advice and consent of the senate, shall appoint ambassadors, other public ministers and consuls, judges of the supreme court, and all other officers of the United States, whose appointments are not herein otherwise provided for, and which shall be established by law. But the Congress may by law invest the appointment of such inferior officers, as they think proper, in the president alone, in the courts of law, or in the heads of departments.
>
> The president shall have power to fill up all vacancies that may happen during the recess of the senate, by granting commissions which shall expire at the end of their next session. (ART. 2, SEC. 2)

'The president shall be. . . . He shall have power . . . and he shall nominate. . . . But the Congress may. . . .' This is the style of prescriptive declaration, and only the most general of Blair's observations, such as his insistence on 'clearness and precision', are here relevant. However, when we come to the letter, signed by George Washington, accompanying the submission of the Constitution to Congress, we find a more rhetorically wrought style with just that intermixing of the *style coupé* and the *style périodique* that Blair recommends in his eleventh lecture. The opening sentence is short and to the point: 'We have now the honor to submit to the consideration of the United States in Congress assembled, that Constitution which has appeared to us the most adviseable'. This is followed by a more elaborately wrought paragraph:

> The friends of our country have long seen and desired, that the power of making war, peace and treaties, that of levying money and regulating commerce, and the correspondent executive and judicial authorities, should be fully and generally vested in the general government of the Union: but the impropriety of delegating such executive trust to one body is evident – Hence results the necessity of a different organization.

The opening phrase, 'the friends of our country', has an emotive ring; it is followed by a phrase which includes two verbs that are parallel but distinct (reminding us of Blair's views of synonyms), 'have long seen and desired', and then the operative verbal phrase 'should be fully and effectually vested in the general government of the Union' is postponed until the objects of what should be so vested ('the power of making war', etc.) have been listed. Then comes a qualification, heralded by 'but', and the resulting conclusion: 'Hence results the necessity of a different organization.' This is not the direct *style coupé* of the individual articles and the opening sentence of the letter: it is an artful combination of rhetoric and logic in a *style périodique* which arouses the emotions before introducting the logic.

The next paragraph of the letter consists of three sentences – or perhaps four, depending on whether you consider the dash to be the equivalent of a colon or of a period. It would seem to be, both here and at the end of the preceding paragraph, more in the nature of a colon, separating a significant clause of the sentence rather than indicating the close of one sentence and the opening of another. So we may consider the paragraph to consist of three sentences, of which the second is brief and pointed and at the same time carefully balanced:

> It is obviously impracticable in the fœderal government of these States, to secure all rights of independent sovereignty to each, and yet provide for the interest and safety of all – Individuals entering into society, must give up a share of liberty to preserve the rest. The magnitude of the sacrifice must depend as well on situation and circumstance, as on the object to be obtained. It is at all times difficult to draw with precision the line between those rights which must be surrendered, and those which may be reserved; and on the present occasion this difficulty was encreased by a difference among the several States as to their situation, extent, habits, and particular interests.

The whole paragraph is a balancing act, and the balance is echoed by successive pairs of phrases: 'to secure all rights of independent sovereignty to each, and yet provide for the interest and safety of all'; 'Individuals . . . the rest'; 'those rights which must be surrendered, and those which may be reserved' (note *must* be surrendered but *may* be reserved).

The following paragraph contains further emotive phrases ('every true American', 'the consolidation of our Union') and a fine rising list of objectives ('our prosperity, felicity, safety, perhaps our national existence'):

> In all our deliberations on this subject we kept steadily in our view, that which appears to us the greatest interest of every true American, the consolidation of our Union, in which is involved our prosperity, felicity, safety, perhaps our national existence. This important consideration, seriously and deeply impressed on our minds, led each State in the Convention to be less rigid on points of inferior magnitude, than might have been otherwise expected; and thus the Constitution, which we now present, is the result of a spirit of amity, and of that mutual deference and concession which the peculiarity of our political situation rendered indispensible.

'In the construction of sentences,' wrote Blair in his eleventh lecture,

> one of the first things to be attended to, is, the marshalling of the

> words in such order as shall most clearly mark the relation of the several parts of the sentence to one another; particularly, that adverbs shall always be made to adhere closely to the words which they are intended to qualify; that, where a circumstance is thrown in, it shall never hang loose in the midst of a period, but be determined by its place to one or other member of it; and that every relative word which is used, shall instantly present its antecedent to the mind of the reader, without the least obscurity. (Blair, 1:214–15)

The placing of the phrase 'seriously and deeply impressed on our minds' at a crucial point in the paragraph adds significantly to the weight of the argument being adduced. Note the actual flow of the argument: 'In all our deliberations. . . . This important consideration . . . and thus the Constitution. . . .' The 'marshalling of the words' here is skilfully done. The use of relative pronouns ('in which is involved our prosperity', 'the Constitution, which we now present', 'which the peculiarity of our political situation rendered indispensable'), the coupling of adverbs ('seriously and deeply impressed on our minds', adverbs of parallel but distinct meaning), the balancing of nouns ('mutual deference and concession') may not be the result of a deliberate following of Blair's prescription for the proper construction of sentences, but they certainly meet his criteria.

The concluding paragraph of the letter has the most balanced rise and fall of all and is a clear example of a skilful use of the *style périodique*:

> That it will meet the full and entire approbation of every State is not perhaps to be expected; but each will doubtless consider, that had her interests been alone consulted, the consequences might have been particularly disagreeable or injurious to others; that it is liable to as few exceptions as could reasonably have been expected, we hope and believe; that it may promote the lasting welfare of that country so dear to us all, and secure her freedom and happiness, is our most ardent wish.

The rise and fall of the phrases here echo the parallel structure of the argument in an almost Ciceronian fashion, or rather in the Ciceronian fashion as adapted by that most sententious of eighteenth-century prose stylists, Dr Johnson. The cadence is similar to that of Johnson's famous letter to Lord Chesterfield: 'The notice which you have been pleased to take of my labours, had it been early, had been kind; but it has been delayed till I am indifferent, and cannot enjoy it; till I am solitary, and cannot impart it; till I am known, and do not want it.' In general the final paragraph of the letter accompanying the submission of the Constitution is a fine example of late eighteenth-century rhetoric. The parallel clauses separated by semicolons, the listing of considerations each beginning with 'that' ('that had her interests been alone consulted', 'that it is liable to as few exceptions', 'that it may promote the lasting welfare of that country so dear to us all'), the ringing phrase 'freedom and happiness', the resting on the culminating phrase 'is our most ardent wish', make a suitable rhetorical conclusion to what the authors knew to be a historic document. It is in the heightened language of this conclusion that the sense of history most strongly emerges.

Moving away from the Constitution, we can trace the effects of the *style périodique* and the *style coupé* at large in the writings of the Founding Fathers. Once again, Blair's ideas help to illuminate the sense of language in their work, complementing their sense of history. For instance, Jefferson's draft of instructions to the Virginia delegates in the Continental Congress well illustrates the balanced *style périodique* characteristic of his more passionate style:

> That thus have we hastened thro' the reigns which preceded his majesty's, during which the violation of our rights were less alarming, because repeated at more distant intervals, than that rapid and bold succession of injuries which is likely to distinguish the present from all other periods of American story. Scarcely have our minds been able to emerge from the astonishment into which one stroke of parliamentary thunder has involved us, before another more heavy and more alarming is fallen on us. Single acts of tyranny may be ascribed to the accidental opinion of a day; but a series of oppressions begun at a distinguished period, and pursued unalterably thro' every change of ministers, too plainly prove a deliberate, systematical plan of reducing us to slavery. (Jefferson, 1:125)

The cadence of the final sentence, with its balancing of 'single acts of tyranny' against 'a series of oppressions' and the rise to the final punch, 'a deliberate, systematical plan of reducing us to slavery', shows an artful deployment of rhetorical skill. The slap of the final word 'slavery', which is the climax of this part of the argument, is almost physical in its force.

Jefferson's original draft of the Declaration of Independence has in parts a more consciously rhetorical ring than the final version as amended by Congress. He liked to link associated words in rhythmic pairs. 'We hold these truths to be sacred & undeniable; that all men are created equal & independant, that from that equal creation they derive rights inherent & inalienable' (Jefferson, 1:423). Jefferson's colleagues evidently thought these swinging pairs – 'sacred and undeniable', 'equal and independent', 'inherent and inalienable' – too declamatory, for they changed this sentence to read: 'We hold these truths to be self-evident, that all men are created equal, that they are endowed by their Creator with certain unalienable Rights' (Jefferson, 1:429).

The most declamatory passage in Jefferson's draft, in which he gave free vent to his rhetorical artfulness, was deleted by Congress altogether (and not only for stylistic reasons):

> He [King George] has waged cruel war against human nature itself, violating it's most sacred rights of life & liberty in the persons of a distant people who never offended him, captivating & carrying them into slavery in another hemisphere, or to incur miserable death in their transportation thither, this piratical warfare, the opprobrium of *infidel* powers, is the warfare of the CHRISTIAN king of Great Britain. Determined to keep open a market where MEN should be bought & sold, he has prostituted his negative for suppressing every legislative attempt to prohibit or to restrain this execrable commerce: and that this assemblage of horrors might want no fact of distinguished die, he is now exciting those very people to rise in arms among us, and to purchase that liberty of which *he* has deprived them, by murdering the people upon whom *he* has obtruded them; thus paying off former crimes against the *liberties* of one people, with crimes which he urges them to commit against the *lives* of another. (Jefferson, 1:426)

Though Jefferson was not a great orator, as for example James Wilson was, his written words can have the ring of spoken oratory, and this passage, with its capitals and italics, clearly reflects a passionate inner voice that Jefferson heard as he penned the lines. Congress also eliminated Jefferson's oratorical conclusion to his list of the king's misdeeds: 'future ages will scarce believe that the hardiness of one man, adventured within the short compass of 12 years only, on so many acts of tyranny without a mask, over a people fostered & fixed in principles of liberty' (Jefferson, 1:426).

James Madison, whose hand and voice are so clearly discernible in the American Constitution, was from his earliest years interested in rhetoric. At the age of eight he copied from the July 1758 issue of *The American Magazine and Monthly Chronicle for the British Colonies* a poem entitled 'Upon the Tropes of Rhetoric'.[17] His period of study with Witherspoon at the College of New Jersey must have encouraged his interest in rhetoric and in literary style in general. In a letter to William Bradford in August 1774 he says: 'I have seen the instructions of your committee to your representatives & greatly admire the wisdom of the advice & the elegance and cogency of the diction.'[18] 'Elegance and cogency' is very much a Witherspoon phrase, as it is also a Hugh Blair idea. (Blair talks of 'perspicuity, strength, neatness and simplicity' as beauties of style to be aimed at, together with 'grace and dignity'.) Consciously or not, Madison's characteristic style is that 'intermixing' of the *style périodique* and the *style coupé* recommended by Blair. In August 1785 he wrote to James Monroe:

> If Congress as they are now constituted, can not be trusted with the

> power of digesting and enforcing this opinion [i.e., 'the opinion of a reasonable majority of the States' concerning the regulation of navigation and commerce], let them be otherwise constituted: let their numbers be encreased, let them be chosen oftener, and let their period of service be shortned; or if any better medium than Congress can be proposed, by which the wills of the States may be concentered, let it be substituted; or lastly let no regulation of trade adopted by Congress be in force untill it shall have been ratified by a certain proportion of the States. But let us not sacrifice the end to the means: let us not rush on certain ruin in order to avoid a possible danger.[19]

The *style périodique* – 'let them be . . . let their numbers be . . . let them be . . . let their period of service be . . . let it be . . . let no regulation . . . be . . .' — is followed by the short, clinching 'But let us not sacrifice the end to the means'. Again, writing to Monroe in June 1786 against the Jay-Gardoqui proposal to give up the American demand for Mississippi navigation in exchange for a treaty of commerce with Spain:

> Again can there be a more shortsighted or dishonorable policy than to concur with Spain in frustrating the benevolent views of nature to sell the affections of our ultramontane breathr[en], to depreciate the richest fund we possess, to distrust an ally [France] whom we know to be able to befriend us and to have an interest in doing it against the only na[tion] whose enmity we can dread, and at the same time to court by the most precious sacrifices the alliance of a nation whose impotency is notorious, who has given no proof of regard for us and the genius of whose government religion & manners unfit them, of all the nations in Christendom for a coalition with this country.[20]

This is a good example of one kind of *style périodique* – not the Ciceronian, where the qualifications and objectives come before the principal clause that gives the whole sentence meaning – but the cumulative, listing, with a succession of infinitive verbs, the errors of the policy criticised, and ending with an eloquently contemptuous dismissal of the government, manners and religion of the nation with whom his opponents want an alliance.

Madison's characteristic style, however, does not employ a long sentence of this kind but prefers a cogent brevity of the kind praised by Hugh Blair as most likely to achieve clarity and precision. His famous tenth *Federalist* paper (in which he develops an idea put forward by David Hume in his 'Idea of a Perfect Commonwealth') begins with three sentences in Blair's *style coupé*:

> Among the numerous advantages promised by a well-constructed Union, none deserves to be more accurately developed than its tendency to break and control the violence of faction. The friend of popular governments never finds himself so much alarmed for their

> character and fate as when he contemplates their propensity to this dangerous vice. He will not fail, therefore, to set a due value on any plan which, without violating the principles to which he is attached, provides a proper cure for it.[21]

This is not the high rhetoric of an impassioned pleader of a cause, but the quietly reasonable tone of someone who is discussing the means to an agreed end. After American independence was established, and especially after the Constitution was adopted by Congress, the need for such high rhetoric was less urgent. Calmly logical persuasion was what was now required if the individual states were to be successfully argued into ratifying the Constitution. Hamilton in particular, in his contributions to the *Federalist Papers*, uses the language of reasonable discussion:

> From these observations this conclusion results: that the trial by jury in civil cases would not be abolished; and that the use attempted to be made of the maxims which have been quoted is contrary to reason and common sense, and therefore not admissable. . . .
>
> Having now seen that the maxims relied upon will not bear the use made of them, let us endeavor to ascertain their proper use and true meaning. This will be best done by examples.[22]

John Jay, too, in his contributions to *The Federalist*, uses for the most part the language of calm legal argument, although his tendency to break out into generalisations as well as the occasional histrionic outburst, such as that at the end of his first contribution,[23] can add a certain rhetorical variety to his articles. What might be called the true rhetoric of the American Revolution is found in the speeches and pamphlets preceding the Declaration of Independence, in the Declaration itself, in the preamble to the Constitution and the letter of transmission and in the self-congratulatory element found in celebrations of victory both in the field and in the council chamber. It was this last element that American political rhetoric was to develop in the next century.

But these considerations lead in another direction. I have been concerned in this chapter with just one aspect of the much larger subject of the rhetoric of American independence. My interest in studying connexions between Scottish rhetoric, as embodied in Blair's *Lectures*, and American political language derives from a conviction that there were some common factors in the Scottish and American situations in the eighteenth century that made Americans especially receptive to Scottish concern with language, and more especially with the language of political persuasion. Blair, I believe, is a telling case in point. These common factors, moreover, suggest yet deeper bonds. The quality of a culture can be illuminated by a study of the language in which it states its political ideals and presuppositions. Political rhetoric can, therefore, get us close to the heart of a people – closer, perhaps, than the ideological content it is intended to communicate. Hugh Blair opposed the American Revolution and preached against it from his Edinburgh pulpit, but the principles he laid down for a rhetoric of freedom and virtue, varying the *style périodique* and *style coupé* to achieve the best possible balance of factual clarity and dramatic effect, informed the political rhetoric of the American Founding Fathers and their offspring for generations to come.

NOTES

1. Plato, *Gorgias,* passim; Aristotle, *The 'Art' of Rhetoric*, trans. John Henry Freese, Loeb Classical Library (Cambridge, Mass., 1926), 1.1.13.
2. Cicero, *De Oratore*, trans. E.W. Sutton and H. Rackham, 2 vols., Loeb Classical Library (Cambridge, Mass., 1942), 1.7.30.
3. Quintilian, *Institution Oratoria*, trans. H.E. Butler, 4 vols., Loeb Classical Library (Cambridge, Mass., 1921), 1.Pr.10.
4. Hume to Gilbert Elliot of Minto, 2 July 1757, in *HL*, 1:255.
5. See the bibliography in Robert Morrell Schmitz, *Hugh Blair* (New York, 1948), 139–45. The 1784 Philadelphia edition was published by the Scotsman Robert Aitken, supposedly on the advice of John Witherspoon (Ashbel Green, *The Life of the Revd John Witherspoon*, ed. Henry Lyttleton Savage [Princeton, 1973], 128, n. 6).
6. The preface began: 'The following Lectures were read in the University of Edinburgh, for Twenty-four years' (i.e., 1759–60 through 1782–83). Later Blair wrote: 'as such a length of time has elapsed since the first Composition of [the author's] Lectures' (v).
7. Green, *Life of Witherspoon*, 128–29.
8. Ibid., 129.
9. *The Autobiography of Dr. Alexander Carlyle of Inveresk, 1722–1805*, ed. John Hill Burton , new ed. (London and Edinburgh, 1910), 47–48.
10. Alexander Carlyle, 'Recollections', NLS MS 3463.
11. The latest edition is Adam Smith, *Lectures on Rhetoric and Belles Lettres*, ed. J.C. Bryce (Oxford, 1983).
12. John Millar, quoted in Dugald Stewart, *Account of the Life and Writings of Adam Smith, LL.D.*, ed. I.S. Ross, in Adam Smith, *Essays on Philosophical Subjects*, ed. W.P.D. Wightman and J.C. Bryce (Oxford, 1980), 274.
13. While Thomas Miller, in his article in this volume, rightly points to the difference between Blair's emphasis on the 'polite' use of rhetoric and Witherspoon's emphasis on its political use, it must not be forgotten that Witherspoon shared Blair's interest in correct and elegant style and in the 'general principles of taste and criticism' (*WJW*, 3:592) and that Blair was, like Witherspoon, in the Ciceronian tradition that saw rhetoric as a public moral force. There are many passages in Witherspoon's lectures on eloquence (e.g. his praise, on stylistic grounds, of Addison and Swift and even of the Moderate Robertson and the infidel Hume) that read like Blair (*WJW*, 3:485). While Miller is clearly right to contrast Blair's political conservatism with the political position developed by

Witherspoon, I would suggest that the contradictions in the political stance of the literati are more complicated than he indicates: Robert Burns, a passionate egalitarian, supported the Moderate position ecclesiastically even on the patronage question, and the theologically conservative Calvinist 'high flyers', opposed by both Burns and the Moderates, were (like those who supported the Great Awakening in America) radical reformers in politics.

14. John Quincy Adams, *Lectures on Rhetoric and Oratory*, 2 vols. (Cambridge, Mass., 1810), 1:68.
15. All quotations from the Constitution and the letter accompanying it are taken from a photocopy of the original printing by Dunlop and Claypoole, in the collections of the Manuscript Division of the Library of Congress. I am grateful to the former Librarian of Congress, Daniel T. Boorstin, for sending me this.
16. Clinton Rossiter, *1787: The Grand Convention* (New York and London, 1966), 224–25, 229; Madison to Jared Sparks, 8 Apr. 1831, in Sparks, *The Life of Gouverneur Morris*, 3 vols. (Boston, 1892), 1:284–85.
17. Ralph Ketcham, *James Madison: A Biography* (New York, 1971), 19.
18. In *James Madison: A Biography in His Own Words*, ed. Merrill D. Peterson (New York, 1974), 32.
19. Ibid., 97–98.
20. Ibid., 101.
21. *The Federalist Papers*, ed. Clinton Rossiter (New York, 1961), 101.
22. Ibid., 497.
23. Ibid., 41.

III. Scottish Thought and Culture in Early Philadelphia

13

ANDREW HOOK

Philadelphia, Edinburgh and the Scottish Enlightenment

In an essay originally published in 1977, Carl Bridenbaugh asked some searching questions about the export of the European Enlightenment to eighteenth-century Philadelphia: 'By whom were the Enlightened ideas and programs chosen, and how did they make the selection? What auxiliary ideas and programs were sent off at the same time? How and when did they cross the ocean?' And was the Enlightenment 'being exported in any organized or institutional forms, or was the transit to America merely a series of random occurrences or the chance work of a few individuals?'[1] Bridenbaugh did not attempt to answer all these questions – and it would be easy enough to add others to his list – but merely by asking them he indicated the kinds of problems facing anyone interested in how cultural and intellectual values are transmitted from one society to another. The difficulty is not just in finding answers to the questions raised; it is in agreeing on what might be seen as the 'evidence' upon which an answer could be based. Facts and statistics are hard to come by in this field; and even those that seem to be available tend to lose credibility the closer they are examined. In the eighteenth century large numbers of Europeans, including many from Scotland, left their own countries and settled in America, not a few of them in Philadelphia. Every one of them was potentially a source of cultural influence, but immigration statistics hardly amount to proof that in fact they were. Even books, including the Scottish books that were readily available to readers in eighteenth-century Philadelphia, are less reliable evidence than they seem. Books certainly contain ideas, but for those ideas to exert any influence the books have not only to be available but also to be read, and read in a receptive frame of mind. The 'facts' of cultural history once again seem to raise more questions than they answer.

To write on the cultural history of Philadelphia in the eighteenth century is thus no simple matter. That the city was a primary focus of American intellectual life in the colonial and Revolutionary periods is not disputed:

the evidence is there in Philadelphia's institutions designed to encourage intellectual enquiry and development, in the achievements and publications of its writers and thinkers and in the contributions of its leading citizens to every aspect of America's developing cultural life. Philadelphia was a city receptive to ideas, a place where the life of the mind was seen to be important. Given its intellectual pre-eminence, Philadelphia could not be other than the major transatlantic recipient of the exciting configuration of ideas that constituted the eighteenth-century Enlightenment in Europe. In so far as Scotland in the eighteenth century participated in, and in no minor way contributed to, that European Enlightenment, it would not be unreasonable to suggest that Philadelphia was influenced by the Scottish Enlightenment. I am convinced it was. But the evidence, however substantial it may appear, has to be seen for what it is: an interpretation of the past rather than an assembly of incontrovertible facts.

The difficulty in identifying a specifically Scottish contribution to the Philadelphia Enlightenment is demonstrated by the fact that in 1977 Bridenbaugh recognised no need to allude to any such contribution. In attempting to provide an answer to the important questions he had begun by raising, he drew attention solely to the dissenting, anti-Establishment tradition within the Enlightenment in Great Britain, arguing that this tradition provided a distinctive coloration to the forms of Enlightenment exported to Philadelphia. Seen in this perspective, the Scots, rather than making any distinctive contribution of their own, are simply to be assimilated within this dissenting tradition: as Presbyterians, they are assumed to share the radical Protestantism of the English dissenters and so, like them, to have contributed to 'the industrial, educational, and humanitarian, and scientific activities' of the Enlightenment in Great Britain.[2] The problems with such an account are obvious enough. The Church of Scotland was the established church in Scotland; the Scots, unlike the dissenters, were not debarred from their own country's universities or from public office. Nor was the Scottish Enlightenment wholly the preserve of Presbyterians: from the end of the seventeenth until well into the eighteenth century, the Scottish Episcopal Church was a significant force in the country's intellectual and cultural life.[3]

Yet Bridenbaugh's analysis does help to explain why the Enlightenment ideas exported to Philadelphia might well have had a distinctive Scottish coloration. He notes the dominant place occupied by dissenters in the English merchant class trading with America. Hence dissenters 'owned and freighted most of the ships that transported people, books, news, letters, ideas, and sentiments to colonial seaports, and especially, after 1720, to Philadelphia; they also controlled most of the news coming in from their counterparts in the New World.'[4] Such a reminder will almost inevitably trigger a sympathetic response from those of us who have long seen in the Scottish-American trading link a highly significant circumstance for the transmission of Scottish ideas across the Atlantic. Analysing Glasgow's rise to dominance in the tobacco trade with the American colonies, Jacob Price, as long ago as 1954, assessed the significance of this Scots-American connexion in terms very similar to those of Bridenbaugh. Of the Scottish mercantile community in the Chesapeake Bay area, he wrote: 'they were there, and twice a year their ships came to them from the Clyde – ships as numerous as those from all Britain besides. For many a Virginian, this must have meant that mail, news, reading matter, ideas, religion, politics came to him via Glasgow.'[5] It is true that Scottish merchants never dominated Philadelphia as they did the tobacco-exporting ports to the south, but Philadelphia was nonetheless part of the close-knit network of Scottish trading activities stretching from New York down the entire seaboard of the mid-Atlantic colonies. Hence Bridenbaugh's analysis, just as much as Price's, indicates that Philadelphia was almost ideally placed to be a potential recipient of those enlightened ideas that formed a central part of Scotland's cultural exports from the mid-eighteenth century onwards. The realisation of that potentiality is well illustrated by a single image: the well known portrait of Benjamin Rush by Charles Willson Peale. In the background of this painting appear a number of scholarly volumes, including the *Essay on Truth* by James Beattie. That Rush, one of Philadelphia's leading intellectuals, should choose to associate himself with a work in which an Aberdeen moral philosopher tried to combat the dangerous scepticism of David Hume clearly demonstrates how the concerns of the Scottish Enlightenment came to inform Philadelphia's intellectual life in the late eighteenth century.

I

But how had it happened? Why should Philadelphia have taken an interest in the concerns of the Enlightenment and of the Scottish Enlightenment in particular? If, as I have suggested, Scottish trading links with the eastern seaboard of America provided a viable means for the transmission of Scottish ideas to Philadelphia, why should Philadelphians have been willing to absorb such ideas? What factors might have inclined Philadelphia to pay attention to Enlightenment ideas originating in Scotland?

Of first importance are the cultural parallels between Philadelphia and a Scottish city such as Edinburgh. Both Philadelphia and Edinburgh in the eighteenth century were provincial cities, and it has been frequently noted that the European Enlightenment flourished in provincial cities such as Dublin, Bordeaux and Naples almost as readily as in metropolitan capitals. Thus, it is no cause for surprise that at least some of the attitudes and values associated with the Enlightenment began to emerge within the societies of Edinburgh and Philadelphia at roughly the same time. But in fact

Philadelphia had rather more in common with Edinburgh than with the other provincial cities just mentioned, and it is this common ground that may help most in explaining the American city's responsiveness to the Scottish Enlightenment. The nature of these cities' shared experience may be identified and explained in two ways: one sociopolitical, the other sociopsychological. The sociopolitical explanation draws in particular on the work of Nicholas Phillipson, who has argued that the Enlightenment provided the social and intellectual élites of provincial societies with an ideology affording them identity and coherence of purpose.[6] The parallel sociopsychological explanation simply takes over the older Clive and Bailyn thesis on the similarities between the provincial cultures of Scotland and America and applies it to the particular circumstances of Philadelphia and Edinburgh.[7]

Obviously, for most of the eighteenth century Philadelphia's cultural situation was more like Edinburgh's than that of metropolitan London. Neither provincial city was a centre of ultimate political authority, yet both had developed institutions and assemblies that wielded very considerable power, were locally run and usually enjoyed considerable freedom from outside interference. Both cities could and did support an important and powerful ruling élite that had a more or less free hand in determining the direction of their growth and development. In Philadelphia's case one suspects that this sense of being in a position to shape and guide, even to create, the city's destiny must often have seemed particularly strong and clear. In this situation what the Enlightenment provided was a direction in which to go, a road to follow. The sign-posts were marked with words such as 'progress', 'improvement' or 'politeness', and these were accepted as the desirable destinations. Both Edinburgh and Philadelphia aimed to create a society that was modern and progressive, at least in the eyes of significant sections of their controlling élites, rather than provincial and backward — a society that might in the end command the approval, rather than the disdain, of the metropolitan capital that remained the standard of a mature and civilised culture. The very smallness and compactness of the intellectual society in cities such as Philadelphia and Edinburgh made such a coherence of purpose and sharing of aims easier to achieve. Throughout the eighteenth century Edinburgh's population was substantially larger than that of Philadelphia: in the 1790s, for example, Edinburgh's total was well over eighty thousand while Philadelphia's was just over forty thousand. Nonetheless, neither city was large enough to sustain a series of separate intellectual groups; the pattern in both was rather for the same range of individuals to be involved in a variety of intellectual and cultural activities.

The best evidence of this latter similarity is the prevalence in both cities of clubs or societies, and other corporate and civic institutions, which became major agencies for advancing the kinds of progressive change that signal the spread of Enlightenment values. As is well known, Philadelphia's first public effort in this area proved abortive: Franklin's American Philosophic Society of 1744 survived for only a year or two. But even this Philadelphian failure suggests an Edinburgh parallel: the *Edinburgh Review* of 1755 proved equally short-lived, despite the fact that its contributors included such distinguished literati as Hugh Blair, Adam Smith and William Robertson. The year 1766 saw the rebirth of Franklin's Philosophic Society as the American Society for Promoting and Propagating Useful Knowledge, Held in Philadelphia. Whereas Franklin's original society had concentrated mainly on scientific observation, the new society emphasised invention and agricultural improvement. The focus of a rival organisation founded three years later – the American Philosophical Society – was the study of pure science and astronomy. But it was not long before the two organisations, in a move characteristic of the impulse towards unity in the city's intellectual life, amalgamated under the title American Philosophical Society Held at Philadelphia for Promoting Useful Knowledge. Thus was created the single most important organisation for the development of science in America both before and after the Revolution.[8]

Of course, by the end of the 1760s some of Edinburgh's most famous societies had been in existence for several decades: the Rankenian Club had been formed as early as 1716, and the Philosophical Society of Edinburgh (forerunner of the Royal Society of Edinburgh of 1783) had first met in 1737. The Select Society, however, bringing together nearly all of Edinburgh's literati, was not founded until 1754. And in the 1760s the impulse to create clubs and societies as a focus of intellectual debate and enquiry was as strong as ever: the Poker Club, the Tuesday Club and the vitally important Speculative Society were all founded in that decade. Of special significance is the emphasis placed by all these organisations, both in Edinburgh and Philadelphia, on 'useful knowledge'. The Scottish Enlightenment had always been characterised by a strong emphasis on the practical, social benefits of progress and improvement: the Scottish clubs and societies mentioned had their social, convivial side, but rather than the pursuit of knowledge for its own sake they frequently had quite specific, practical aims. Self-improvement and civic advancement seemed to go hand-in-hand. No emphasis could have been more to the taste of the Philadelphia improvers. From the earliest days of the Junto, in 1727, Franklin had been emphatic on this point: the Junto was 'a Club for Mutual Improvement'. The parallel with Allan Ramsay's Easy Club, founded in Edinburgh in 1712 'in order that by a Mutual Improvement in Conversation' its members might 'become more adapted for fellowship with the politer part of mankind and learn also from one anothers happy observations', is almost exact. And Franklin's later comment – 'what signifies Philosophy that does not apply to some Use?' – could well stand as a motto for the advancement of the intellectual life of both Edinburgh and Philadelphia.[9] That Edinburgh's Society for Improvement in the Knowledge of Agriculture should thus be matched by Philadelphia's Society for the Promotion of Agriculture hardly comes as a surprise.

The social structures of the intellectual life of Philadelphia and Edinburgh clearly had much in common; but how are we to understand the similar emphasis on the need for knowledge to be useful? Bridenbaugh probably provides the correct answer. Of the citizens of Philadelphia he says: 'Progress for them was not an idea, not a dream; it was a visible reality.'[10] The remark could apply equally to the citizens of Edinburgh. At the end of the eighteenth century Edinburgh, just as much as Philadelphia, was a dramatically new city. At the beginning of the century, when Philadelphia was just beginning to grow, Edinburgh was the capital of one of the poorest, most backward and least familiar countries in Europe; by the end of the eighteenth century Edinburgh and Philadelphia had both become capitals of thriving, progressive countries, increasingly more than holding their own as contributors to Western culture. Enlightenment values had been given tangible social and civic embodiment in the development of both cities.

II

These parallels between Edinburgh and Philadelphia go some way towards explaining why both cities should have shared an active interest in Enlightenment values. The economic tie between Scotland and the American colonies provided an accessible route whereby Scottish ideas could be exported across the Atlantic. But there remains the question of receptiveness: why should Philadelphians have been open to influence from the Scottish dimension of the European Enlightenment? The Clive and Bailyn thesis provides part of an answer to this question. By the middle of the eighteenth century, at a time when the intellectual life of Philadelphia was still in the process of formation, Edinburgh was already making some of its most significant contributions to the wider world of the Enlightenment. There is no question as to which city was more likely to learn from the other. But by allowing us to see that Edinburgh and Philadelphia may have shared a complex sense of intellectual and cultural inferiority (a consequence of their provincial status in relation to standard-setting London), Clive and Bailyn help us to understand why some Philadelphians at least, like Americans elsewhere, might have been particularly interested in Scottish responses and solutions to shared problems.

It is these 'shared problems' that need to be emphasised. There is no evidence that Philadelphians regarded Scottish culture itself as in any sense 'inferior'; on the contrary, respect and admiration for Scotland's cultural achievements clearly continued to grow in Philadelphia throughout the eighteenth century. In other words, it is not primarily an awareness of its provincial status that explains Philadelphian responsiveness to the Scottish Enlightenment; a shared sense of 'cultural provincialism' could only have been a single dimension of that wider pattern of similarities between Philadelphia and Edinburgh, already alluded to, which ensured a Philadelphian interest in Scottish cultural progress.

There remains the question of evidence in support of the theoretical Philadelphian response to the Scottish Enlightenment. In my view the area of intellectual activity most relevant is education, and the decisive period the 1740s. Specific Scottish contributions to education in Philadelphia were the result of two factors: influential Scottish educators present in the city on the one hand, Philadelphians travelling to Scotland for educational purposes on the other. In the first category the key figure is William Smith, Episcopal clergyman and graduate of King's College, Aberdeen. But Smith's appointments, first as head of the Philadelphia Academy in 1753 and, two years later, as provost of the College of Philadelphia, into which the academy developed, are themselves to be seen as the consequence of increasing Scottish influence in Philadelphia around mid-century. By the 1740s the old Quaker hegemony over most aspects of Philadelphia's political and social life had broken down and, as Henry F. May argues, the powerful Presbyterian element in the city was simultaneously split over the issues created by the Great Awakening. In the consequent power vacuum it was, in May's view, the largely upper-class Episcopalian party that benefited the most: Smith's appointment is thus evidence of their rise to a position of dominance in Philadelphia life and culture.[11]

But Smith's Scottishness may have mattered as much as his Episcopalianism. The 1740s had seen a consolidation of Scottish influence in Philadelphia. In 1747 the St Andrews Society of Philadelphia had been founded, thus providing all the Scots in the city with a meeting-ground that was almost certainly used for purposes extending beyond the purely charitable aims of the organisation. The society's original membership of twenty-five included Thomas Graeme, a physician from Perthshire who was the St Andrews Society's first president and also a founding member of the American Philosophical Society; James Hamilton, lieutenant governor of Pennsylvania, the society's second president and subsequently also president of the American Philosophical Society; Alexander Alexander, who later taught at the College of Philadelphia; Alexander Barclay, comptroller of customs in Philadelphia; and Franklin's business partner David Hall. It is true that the Scots were caught up in the debate over the Great Awakening and its consequences, but the resurgence of evangelical Scottish Presbyterianism should not be allowed to obscure the significance of the Scottish Episcopalian tradition that a man like Smith represents. Thus, the coincidence of the founding of the St Andrews Society and the rise to dominance of the Anglican faction suggests a potential increase in Scottish influence on Philadelphia's intellectual and cultural life.

What is the nature of that influence as defined by the appointment of William Smith? Franklin was largely responsible for securing Smith's initial appointment, so perhaps the question should be rephrased to ask what it was about Smith that appealed to Franklin. The answer probably is that Smith appealed as a new man, with innovative enlightened and progressive ideas, who would nonetheless be entirely acceptable to upholders of conventional moral and religious orthodoxies. Smith had set out his educational theories in *A General Idea of the College of Mirania*, first published in New York in 1753. Among the distinctive features of his programme were its recognition that a college need not be seen only as a school for clergymen, and its emphasis on the need for the future leaders of civic society to be trained in the arts and graces of polite living as well as in the traditional scholarly disciplines. The main point here is that Smith's programme, as Peter J. Diamond has shown in chapter 6 above, derives from his experiences as a student at Aberdeen, and particularly from the changes introduced there in the 1740s.

Franklin's sympathy for an educational programme such as Smith's was guaranteed. In his own *Proposals for the Education of Youth* (1749) he had in fact drawn largely upon the very same Aberdonian tradition that Smith represented. In the writings of the Aberdeen regents George Turnbull and David Fordyce, and perhaps also in Alexander Gerard, Franklin had found an educational ideology that exactly suited his own predilections.[12] This ideology can be defined as a vision of a liberal university education, dedicated to the promotion of civic virtue and the protection of liberty. The ideal polite academy would further these aims by including in its pattern of education first the old commonwealthman Whig tradition of Toland and Molesworth, which had always emphasised virtue and liberty as primary aims of education; second, an emphasis on the superiority of the empirical, Baconian method over older scholastic traditions; and third, Shaftesbury and Molesworth's desire to bring out the moral and aesthetic faculties inherent in human nature.[13] These were the kinds of educational objectives that Franklin himself sought to promote, and it is therefore easy to understand his support for Smith, who in *Mirania* agreed with Tillotson 'that the knowledge of what tends neither directly nor indirectly to make better men, or better citizens, is but a knowledge of trifles'.[14] In supporting Smith, Franklin must have believed he was taking practical steps to promote the realisation in Philadelphia of the ideals of college education to which he was committed. Hence both in theory and practice Scottish models played a highly significant role in the development of Philadelphia's major educational institution.

At the college, Smith himself taught courses in logic, rhetoric (that favourite Scottish topic) and moral and natural philosophy, all subjects he had studied at Aberdeen in the 1740s. And Smith was not without considerable additional Scottish support. Francis Alison, an Ulster Scot who had studied at Edinburgh and Glasgow Universities, had run a school in New London for nine years before becoming vice-provost of the College of Philadelphia. Alison, a classical scholar, was an Old Side Presbyterian – the college had been established on an interdenominational basis – and soon, as assistant to Robert Cross in the First Presbyterian Church, became the Old Side leader in the complex Presbyterian politics of the city. At least two other Scots, Alexander Alexander and John Beveridge, held teaching posts at the college in its early years; and James Wilson himself, after his brief initial stint as a Latin tutor, retained a teaching connexion with the college. As Shannon Stimson has demonstrated in chapter 11 above, Wilson's philosophical sympathies lay with the common sense, anti-Humean side of the Scottish Enlightenment – and this perhaps reinforces one's sense that the progressive modernism of the Scottish Enlightenment, as it was presented by Philadelphia's college, was unlikely to be too dangerously radical.

The emergence of the College of Philadelphia's medical school represented another major infusion of Scottish influence into Philadelphia's educational and intellectual life, but any understanding of this development requires a preliminary glance at Franklin's own Scottish connexions. These are sufficiently significant to justify the assertion that, even if there had been no other factors, the Scottish Enlightenment would have played some part in Philadelphia's culture through the person of the city's own leading intellectual. Franklin and Scotland were tightly linked; moreover, it was Franklin above all who brought Philadelphia and Edinburgh into a close and creative relationship. Within Philadelphian society, Franklin's Scottish friendships were numerous. David Hall, his partner in the printing business, was a Scot who had come out to Philadelphia in 1744 from the London office of William Strahan, himself a Scot and long one of Franklin's closest friends. Hall, as has been noted, was a founding member of the Philadelphia St Andrews Society and therefore closely associated with all the most influential members of the Scots colony in the city: Thomas Graeme, James Hamilton (and his father Andrew Hamilton, a leading lawyer), Alexander Alexander, Alexander Barclay and Robert Smith, the builder and architect treated more fully by Charles Peterson in chapter 16 below. When Franklin was first contemplating a trip to Scotland in 1759, he doubtless had heard much of their native land from these Philadelphian Scots, and by then, through William Strahan, he had already come into contact with nearly all the leading members of the Scottish circle in London.

More important than these encounters, however, were Franklin's actual trips to Scotland in 1759 and 1771. These visits brought Franklin into immediate personal contact with all the leading members of those intellectual groups whose joint efforts had made the Enlightenment flower in Scotland.[15] In 1759 in Edinburgh – and most of these contacts were renewed in 1771, despite the changed political circumstances – he met Hume, Kames, Sir Alexander Dick, William Robertson, Adam Ferguson; Joseph Black, William Cullen, the two Monros and Adam Smith; in Glasgow, Robert Simson, Alexander Wilson, the Foulis brothers and John Anderson (John Millar was a new contact in 1771); in St Andrews, David Gregory and Patrick Baird, a doctor who had practised for a time in Philadelphia. Such a list is practically a roll-call of the luminaries of the Scottish Enlightenment. And Franklin's respect for them is well documented. In a letter to Jonathan Potts and Benjamin Rush, young Philadelphians proposing to study medicine at Edinburgh in the 1760s, he wrote: 'You have great Advantages in going to study at Edinburgh at this Time, where there happens to be collected a Set of as truly great Men, Professors of the several Branches of Knowledge, as have ever appeared in any Age or Country.'[16]

Such a view would soon be commonplace among American intellectuals, but Franklin's position in Philadelphia's intellectual world was so central that his words gain much more than a personal significance: if in Scotland he was a kind of intellectual ambassador for his own country, then he was inevitably a channel of the most significant kind for the conveyance of almost every aspect of the Scottish Enlightenment into Philadelphia's cultural scene.

The tangible evidence of Franklin's importance is apparent in what I earlier suggested was a second specifically Scottish contribution to Philadelphia's educational life: the experience of Philadelphians who travelled to Scotland for educational purposes. In the spring of 1760 John Morgan arrived in London from Philadelphia undecided whether to pursue his medical education at Leyden or Edinburgh. A member of the first graduating class of the College of Philadelphia, Morgan applied to Franklin for advice, and Franklin, no doubt recalling his recent Scottish experience, recommended Edinburgh. Morgan did not in fact proceed to Edinburgh until the autumn of 1761; by then William Shippen, another Philadelphian and a graduate of the College of New Jersey, had already completed his first year of study at the Edinburgh Medical School. Both Morgan and Shippen arrived in Edinburgh bearing letters of introduction from Franklin to William Cullen. They were soon followed by a succession of other American medical students, among whom students from Philadelphia were always prominent: for example, Benjamin Rush, Jonathan Potts, Adam Kuhn and Hugh Williamson in the 1760s; George Logan and Thomas Parke in the 1770s. By 1800 no less than forty-one Philadelphians had studied medicine at the University of Edinburgh:[17] an educational phenomenon explored by Deborah Brunton in chapter 14 below.

How much influence their Scottish experience exerted on the intellectual lives of these students is, of course, not quantifiable. But it is very hard to believe that a period of study in Edinburgh in the late eighteenth century could have done other than produce a significant widening of intellectual horizons. When Benjamin Rush looked back on his student experience at Edinburgh, he had no doubt of the value of the 'halcyon days' spent there: 'The two years I spent in Edinburgh I consider as the most important in their influence upon my character and conduct of any period of my life.'[18] When these Edinburgh-trained doctors returned to Philadelphia, it was more or less inevitable that the Enlightenment they brought back with them should have had a distinctly Scottish dimension. Rush, for example, who had joined the Edinburgh Medical Society and probably attended meetings of the Philosophical Society, testified to the immense intellectual value of such institutions when he wrote to John Morgan in 1768 urging the advantages that would arise from the founding of a 'literary and physical society' in Philadelphia.[19] Morgan and Rush would be among the active founding members of the reactivated American Philosophical Society in Philadelphia in 1769.

By that year the Edinburgh-Philadelphia medical connexion had produced an even more tangible result. On his return from Edinburgh in 1761, William Shippen began to deliver lectures on anatomy in his father's house. When Morgan returned in 1764, he and Shippen became the founders of the first American medical school, set up in the College of Philadelphia in 1765; they were soon joined by Rush and Adam Kuhn. Inevitably the school was modelled on that of Edinburgh, and up to the end of the eighteenth century all its professors save one were Edinburgh-trained.[20] Philadelphia's medical education was very much a question of Edinburgh in America.

III

I have attempted to show how the pattern of education in Philadelphia owed a specific debt to aspects of the Scottish Enlightenment. But in assessing Philadelphia's overall debt to Scottish intellectual life, such precision, as I have already suggested, cannot be achieved. In the Revolutionary and post-Revolutionary periods, Philadelphia's debt to the

Scottish Enlightenment continued to grow. Immensely relevant here is John Witherspoon's assumption of the presidency of the College of New Jersey in 1768. No other Scot came to exercise such a profound influence over American educational, intellectual and political life. And Witherspoon's Philadelphian connexions were strong: Benjamin Rush, for example, played an important part in persuading the Scottish clergyman to accept the Princeton appointment; and once in New Jersey, Witherspoon worked closely with the Presbyterian synod in Philadelphia. Given the extraordinary speed and success with which he transformed the struggling College of New Jersey into one of America's leading educational institutions, Witherspoon's presence meant the channelling of a new wave of Scottish Enlightenment values into the cultural life of his adopted country. The only Scot, apart from James Wilson, to sign the Declaration of Independence, Witherspoon's political allegiance was never in doubt; but there was nothing revolutionary about the moral and religious philosophy he taught at Princeton. Despite the anti-Moderate tendency of his theology, he embodied in his teaching both the modernity and the moderation that characterised central aspects of the Enlightenment in Scotland. These were precisely the aspects of the Scottish Enlightenment that appealed increasingly to many Philadelphians in the late eighteenth century.

An ideology that was both modern and moderate was particularly to the taste of a Philadelphian cultural élite, one of whose characteristics had always been a successful resistance to the extremes of religious and political factionalism. In this connexion it is important to stress how far Enlightenment was bound up with questions of taste, decorum and politeness for provincial societies like those of Scotland and America. Enlightenment learning was polite learning. In Philadelphia we have already seen how this emphasis was present in William Smith's College of Philadelphia, indeed how Smith himself, minor poet and man of letters, embodied just such an ideal. But Philadelphia offers other Scottish examples.

Just like their counterparts in Edinburgh, Philadelphia's literati were not very productive in the area of creative, imaginative writing. Brockden Brown did not appear until the eighteenth century was almost over. But a respect for literature, drama, music and painting had always been present among the city's élite. Here the Scottish connexion in eighteenth-century Philadelphia is once again evident; for example, in Franklin's enthusiasm for the Scots songs sent to his family by Sir Alexander Dick's daughter in 1763, in the production in Philadelphia of John Home's *Douglas* as early as 1759, and in the influence on Philadelphia of the Edinburgh Musical Society, as discussed by Anne McClenny Krauss in chapter 15 below. Moreover, Philadelphia possessed at least one literary salon, established in the 1760s by Elizabeth Graeme Ferguson, that had much in common with later establishments in Edinburgh. Elizabeth Graeme was the daughter of Dr Thomas Graeme, and her home became a fashionable resort for those in Philadelphia, particularly in Episcopalian circles, with a taste for polite literature. William Smith himself was one of her circle; John Morgan, Benjamin Rush and William Franklin were also regular visitors.[21] But despite her strong Scottish connexions, which make one wonder whether her description of Philadelphia as 'the Athens of North America' was a conscious echo of the description of Edinburgh as 'the Athens of the North', her own minor verse suggests a greater affinity with the English Augustan poets and their Scottish imitators than with eighteenth-century Scottish vernacular writers. Several decades would have to pass before Philadelphia would share in the general American enthusiasm for Scottish writing. When that taste did develop, however, Philadelphia played a major role: in the early nineteenth century Matthew Carey's *American Museum* and Brockden Brown's *Literary Magazine* both contained frequent laudatory references to the 'Scottish literati', while Joseph Dennie's *Port Folio* was even more consistently favourable towards all aspects of Scottish literature.

In the late eighteenth century, however, the Scottish Enlightenment's linking of progress and the advancement of polite society could well have been a major source of its continuing appeal for most of Philadelphia's ruling élite. In the period of the Revolution the polite, intellectual consensus that had been successfully established in Philadelphia broke down. The ultrademocratic Pennsylvania constitution of 1776 was seen by the property-conscious, anti-radical élite as a serious threat from below: modern progressiveness carried to a revolutionary extreme. Smith's College of Philadelphia was closed as too Tory and Episcopalian; the theatres were shut down; and James Wilson's house was stoned by a mob. But in the 1780s the more conservative forces regained control of the city, and the status quo – including even Smith – was more or less restored.

But Philadelphia had had a taste of what revolutionary change could mean, not in this case for the British but for its own leading citizens. Perhaps it is not then surprising that it should have continued to be attracted by the most powerful, modern and progressive, but broadly conservative ideology available, that of the Scottish Enlightenment in its post-Humean, common sense phase. In that phase what the Scottish Enlightenment offered was above all an acceptable spirit of moderation and compromise by means of which traditional morality and progressive thinking, social order and civic development, religious faith and scientific enquiry, could all be reconciled. Such a philosophy exactly suited the progressive, tolerant but anti-revolutionary élite of America's cultural capital. Writing of Philadelphia's cultural life in the post-Revolutionary period, Henry May has suggested that 'history had produced a delicate balance between the Moderate and the Revolutionary forms of Enlightenment.'[22] Both in producing that balance and in helping to sustain it, the Scottish Enlightenment played a crucial role.

NOTES

1. Carl Bridenbaugh, 'Philosophy Put to Use: Voluntary Associations for Propagating the Enlightenment in Philadelphia, 1727–1776', in his *Early Americans* (New York, 1981), 151.
2. Ibid., 152.
3. Hugh Ouston, 'Cultural Life from the Restoration to the Union', in *The History of Scottish Literature, 1660–1800*, ed. Andrew Hook (Aberdeen, 1987), 11–30.
4. Bridenbaugh, 'Philosophy Put to Use', 152.
5. Jacob M. Price, 'The Rise of Glasgow in the Chesapeake Tobacco Trade, 1707–1775', *WMQ*, 198.
6. Nicholas T. Phillipson, 'Culture and Society in the Eighteenth Century Province: The Case of Edinburgh and the Scottish Enlightenment', in *The University in Society*, ed. Lawrence Stone, 2 vols. (Princeton, 1974), 2:407–48.
7. John Clive and Bernard Bailyn, 'England's Cultural Provinces: Scotland and America', *WMQ*, 200–13.
8. See Henry F. May, *The Enlightenment in America* (New York, 1976), 84. The American Philosophical Society soon became a focus of the cultural exchange between Philadelphia and Scotland. When the first volume of that society's *Transactions* was published, William Smith directed Franklin to send a copy to the librarian of King's College, Aberdeen. In 1786 Benjamin Rush arranged James Beattie's admission as a member of the society. See *Letters of Benjamin Rush*, ed. L.H. Butterfield, 2 vols. (Princeton, 1951), 1:394.
9. Bridenbaugh, 'Philosophy Put to Use', 150.
10. Ibid., 155.
11. May, *Enlightenment in America*, 80.
12. Caroline Robbins, *The Eighteenth-Century Commonwealthman* (Cambridge, Mass., 1959), 100.
13. See Peter Jones, 'The Polite Academy and the Presbyterians, 1720–1770', in *New Perspectives on the Politics and Culture of Early Modern Scotland*, ed. John Dwyer et al. (Edinburgh, 1982), 156–78, and 'The Scottish Professoriate and the Polite Academy, 1720–46', in *WV*, 89–117. See also M.A. Stewart, 'George Turnbull and Educational Reform', in *Aberdeen and the Enlightenment*, ed. Jennifer J. Carter and Joan H. Pittock (Aberdeen, 1987), 95–103.
14. Quoted in May, *Enlightenment in America*, 81.
15. J. Bennett Nolan, *Benjamin Franklin in Scotland and Ireland, 1759 and 1771* (Philadelphia, 1938).
16. Franklin, 15:530.

17. William R. Brock, *Scotus Americanus: A Survey of the Sources for Links between Scotland and America in the Eighteenth Century* (Edinburgh, 1982), 119.
18. *The Autobiography of Benjamin Rush*, ed. G.W. Corner (Princeton, 1948), 43.
19. *Letters of Benjamin Rush*, ed. Butterfield, 1:51.
20. Brock, *Scotus Americanus*, 119.
21. See Martha C. Slotten, 'Elizabeth Graeme Ferguson, a Poet in "The Athens of North America" ', *PMHB* 108 (1984): 259–88. In possessing a literary salon run by a woman in the 1760s, Philadelphia may well have had an edge over Edinburgh: Mrs Archibald Fletcher and Mrs Anne Grant of Laggan and their literary salons did not emerge upon the Edinburgh scene until several decades later.
22. May, *Enlightenment in America*, 198.

14

DEBORAH C. BRUNTON

The Transfer of Medical Education: Teaching at the Edinburgh and Philadelphia Medical Schools

The strong Scottish influence on American medicine during the eighteenth century has often been noted. Helen Brock and Jane Rendall have shown that many Scottish practitioners emigrated to colonial America and that large numbers of American students crossed the Atlantic to study in Scotland.[1] Both remark on the close, long-term connexions between the Edinburgh Medical School and its Philadelphia counterpart, which was founded by an Edinburgh graduate in 1765 and was dominated by Scottish-trained professors until the early nineteenth century. Yet there is little detailed scholarship on relations between the two institutions or on the history of the Philadelphia school in general.[2] Most commentators simply repeat the claim that John Morgan modelled the new medical school on the one at Edinburgh. As we shall see, this claim is true to a point: Morgan deliberately instituted an organisational structure and curriculum similar to Edinburgh's, and it is possible that he meant to adopt the semi-autonomous administrative structure of the Edinburgh school as well. But this chapter will also discuss important respects in which the influence of Edinburgh extended into areas beyond the control of Morgan and outside the reach of his founding plan. Distinctive Scottish teaching methods and medical theories were transferred across the Atlantic not only by Morgan but also by his Edinburgh-trained colleagues, who reproduced the organisation and content of their medical school courses in their own lectures at Philadelphia.

The Edinburgh Medical School was not the only force that shaped the development of the Philadelphia school. The American context also had a strong influence, driving Philadelphia away from Scottish ideas and practices. Differences in climate and epidemiology, along with post-Revolutionary nationalism, encouraged Philadelphia's professors to stop simply replicating British and European ideas and to construct a self-consciously American medicine. However, medical students on both sides of the Atlantic required a similar training in a broad range of subjects, with courses that included the latest medical knowledge and degrees that provided adequate qualifications for success in the medical profession. I will argue that these similar requirements led to continued parallel development at the Edinburgh and Philadelphia schools long after the original links between the institutions had been broken.

I

Whereas the establishment of the Philadelphia Medical School can be traced to a particular founder and date, the origins of the Edinburgh Medical School are more complex and often obscure. Attempts to introduce medical teaching in Edinburgh began in the seventeenth century; in 1676 the town council appointed James Sutherland to teach botany, and nine years later it created three chairs of medicine. These efforts were largely unsuccessful, for it is doubtful if any of the early professors actually taught within the university. The first professor known to have regularly offered classes was James Crawford, elected professor of medicine and chemistry in 1713.[3]

Regular teaching within a medical faculty began in the 1720s under the leadership of George Drummond, six times lord provost of Edinburgh and one of the city's most influential figures. Drummond saw the creation of a medical school as a means of reviving the city's declining fortunes following the Act of Union of 1707. In a minute granting life tenure to the first professor of anatomy in 1722, the town council expressed its satisfaction at 'how much this profession may tend to the advantage and honor of the city, by the small expence of the inhabitants children their education [sic], and the resort of students who have been and will be induced to come here from all the several parts of Scotland, as also from England and Ireland'.[4] Drummond and his colleagues sought to imitate the success of the University of Leyden where, under Hermann Boerhaave, the medical school had rapidly developed an international reputation and attracted large numbers of students.[5]

Edinburgh's first chair of anatomy evolved from the close ties between the town council and the Incorporation of Surgeons, one of the city's most powerful guilds. From 1705 the incorporation had elected public dissectors to teach anatomy to its apprentices. To encourage this teaching, the town council granted the incorporation the rights to bodies of suicides and executed criminals for use as dissection subjects, and appointed the incorporation's dissectors 'professors of anatomy in the city' with a salary of £15 each. In 1719 John Monro, a past president of the incorporation and one of Edinburgh's most prominent surgeons, arranged for his son Alexander to be appointed public dissector. The incorporation duly recommended that the town council appoint him city professor of anatomy. Inadvertently, or perhaps by John Monro's design, the petition described the post as professor in the 'city and college'. This wording was repeated in the minute appointing Alexander Monro, thereby turning the city post into a university position.[6] Monro taught in Surgeons' Hall to an audience largely composed of surgeons' apprentices, but instead of the occasional week-long dissections offered by his predecessors, he delivered annual courses of more than a hundred lectures running throughout the academic year. Monro gradually developed a closer relationship with the university; in 1722 he was granted life tenure and in 1725 moved his classes into the university buildings.[7]

The medical school was effectively established with the appointment of four additional professors. In 1725 four Leyden graduates – John Rutherford, Andrew Sinclair, John Innes and Andrew Plummer – began teaching private classes in medicine and chemistry. The following year they successfully petitioned the town council and were appointed professors of the theory and practice of medicine and of medicine and chemistry. The four professors seem to have taught collectively until the death of Innes in 1733, when each of the survivors took responsibility for one subject.

The curriculum was expanded steadily over the next forty years. In 1738 the old botany chair was drawn into the medical faculty, and in 1756 the post of city professor of midwifery was turned into a university position. In 1768 the faculty was completed with the creation of a new chair of materia medica.[8] By this time Edinburgh was well on its way to achieving a position as the foremost medical school in Europe. Its broad curriculum, its institution of lecturing in the vernacular rather than Latin and its high quality of teaching by Alexander Monro *secundus*, William Cullen and Joseph Black drew hundreds of students to the city – among them John Morgan.[9] Like most American medical students, Morgan came to Edinburgh to complete a comprehensive medical education, having already served an apprenticeship in Philadelphia with a local practitioner and having practised as a regimental surgeon in the Pennsylvania provincial troops. He set out for London in 1760, spending the winter at William Hunter's surgical school before travelling north to enrol at the Edinburgh Medical School the following year.

Morgan drew up plans to establish a medical school in Philadelphia while he was studying in Scotland. He first formulated a scheme with William Shippen, a fellow Philadelphian, but after Shippen graduated and returned to Philadelphia in 1762 Morgan devised a new plan to graft the proposed school onto Philadelphia's small liberal arts college. Using his letters of introduction to influential Philadelphians resident in London, Morgan set out to win support for his plan. He succeeded in obtaining the approval of Thomas Penn, the proprietor of Pennsylvania and a patron of the College of Philadelphia, as well as two visiting college trustees and his two most eminent teachers, William Hunter and William Cullen. In May

1765, shortly after his return to America, Morgan presented their recommendations and a plan for the school, which he implied was entirely his own, to the college's board of trustees. The trustees immediately accepted his proposals and appointed him the school's first professor of the theory and practice of physick.[10]

The Edinburgh Medical School was not only the inspiration for Morgan's plan but also a resource for generating public support. As Andrew Hook has observed in the previous chapter, Philadelphia already had strong intellectual connexions with Scotland. Several leading figures at the College of Philadelphia were trained there: William Smith, the provost of the college, had been educated at Aberdeen, and the vice-provost, Francis Alison, had studied at Glasgow and Edinburgh. The college's teaching methods and curriculum were drawn largely from the Scottish universities. In addition, Philadelphia's citizens shared many of the values of the Scottish Enlightenment. Morgan exploited these Scottish connexions in presenting his proposal for the new medical school. In *A Discourse upon the Institution of Medical Schools in America* he appealed to a common faith in the beneficial effects of cultivating science and 'useful knowledge' and emphasised how the new medical school would implement this ideal:

> The cultivation of Science, and the progress of arts have justly merited the regard of every age and country. I esteem myself happy, therefore, that I have an opportunity of delivering my sentiments . . . upon a subject which respects the advancement of the most useful knowledge, and the growing credit of this institution; – a subject as important as can well be imagined to employ our serious deliberation, or animate our warmest pursuit.[11]

He suggested that in the field of medical education Philadelphia should seek to emulate Edinburgh. There,

> within the space of little more than forty years, the present professorships in Medicine were first formed. . . . With countenance and support from the patrons of the university, and by the great abilities, assiduity, and experience of those gentlemen, . . . the reputation of that place is raised to such a height, that, to their immortal honor, it already rivals, if not surpasses that of every other school of Physic in Europe. (29)

The curriculum of the Philadelphia school, which exemplified the Enlightenment desire for a rational progression of knowledge, was derived from the 'so justly celebrated, school of physic at Edinburgh' (36), with medical students progressing systematically through a course of study from simple to more complex forms of knowledge. Classes in the 'basic sciences' – anatomy, botany and chemistry – preceded the more complex and specialised classes in physiology, pathology and therapeutics.

If anyone required further persuasion as to the advantages of the new school, Morgan alluded to other benefits, including pecuniary ones, that would be generated by such a large influx of students: 'There is a great resort of medical students at the university of Edinburgh, . . . [and] these bring to the university and city considerable advantages, and, in return, carry the fame of their learning and their professors to every quarter of the globe' (29). Considering Philadelphia's established community of medical practitioners, many of whom were already training apprentices, and its established college and hospital, Morgan saw no reason why a medical school in that city would not prove as prestigious and prosperous as its counterpart in Edinburgh.

Chairs in the Philadelphia school were established in accordance with Morgan's planned curriculum as suitable candidates presented themselves.[12] In spite of Morgan's snub in not consulting him over the revised plan, William Shippen applied for and obtained a professorship of anatomy in 1765. The following year Thomas Bond, one of the college trustees, began teaching clinical medicine at the Pennsylvania Hospital. Morgan and Shippen divided the remainder of the curriculum between them until 1768, when Adam Kuhn was elected professor of materia medica and botany upon completion of his studies with Carl Linné at the University of Uppsala and at the Edinburgh Medical School. The faculty was completed the following year with the appointment of a fourth Edinburgh graduate, Benjamin Rush, to a chair of chemistry.

In the *Discourse* Morgan did not discuss the administration of the new school, but in this respect, too, the Philadelphia school closely resembled that of Edinburgh. Both faculties enjoyed semiautonomous status within their respective parent institutions, the College of Philadelphia and the University of Edinburgh. As parts of larger institutional entities, the Philadelphia and Edinburgh medical schools did not have direct responsibility for maintaining buildings or for founding and filling chairs, but in both cities the medical faculties were influential in all matters pertaining to their areas of expertise, and much of the day-to-day running of the schools was left to them. Brief university regulations set degree requirements and fixed the maximum fees for classes, matriculation and graduation but otherwise exerted minimal control over medical faculty and students. Although Edinburgh's and Philadelphia's civic authorities encouraged the new schools, they provided little or no direct financial backing. Edinburgh chairs created before 1720 carried small salaries, but the remaining professors at Edinburgh and all faculty at Philadelphia drew their incomes entirely from class fees, out of which they paid the costs of demonstrations, the salaries of assistants and, in Philadelphia, the rent for use of the college classrooms.[13] The Philadelphia faculty also supervised the construction of new buildings, although the building budget was supplied by the college.[14]

Morgan's plan for the Philadelphia Medical School proved remarkably resilient, outlasting his own relatively brief teaching career that effectively ended in 1775 and surviving the institutional upheavals caused by the Revolutionary War. When the colonial College of Philadelphia was dismantled in 1779, Morgan's curriculum and organisation were adopted by its replacement, the University of the State of Pennsylvania, and were retained when the latter institution merged with the re-established College of Philadelphia to form the University of Pennsylvania in 1791. In order to accommodate all the professors from both medical schools and avoid internecine disputes, separate chairs of botany and materia medica and a new chair of the institutes of medicine and clinical medicine were then established.[15]

II

Although he played a key role, John Morgan should not be given all the credit for shaping the Philadelphia Medical School. He set the school's curriculum but had little influence over actual teaching. The form and content of courses were left entirely to individual professors, who taught courses they hoped would attract large numbers of students. For this reason the curriculum at the Philadelphia school did not always correspond to the one planned by Morgan. William Shippen, for example, included lectures on surgery and midwifery in his anatomy course, although neither subject was mentioned in Morgan's proposals. Similarly, botany teaching, which Morgan considered one of the key elements of the curriculum, was somewhat erratic: Adam Kuhn was appointed professor of materia medica and botany, but so few students took his first botany classes that he dropped the subject, and it is not clear exactly when it was revived.[16]

The similarity of teaching methods and course content at Edinburgh and Philadelphia was also less the result of Morgan's efforts than of the collective action of Philadelphia's predominantly Edinburgh-trained faculty. Ten of the school's first twelve professors had attended the Edinburgh Medical School. Under their tenure, Scottish teaching methods and ideas dominated the Philadelphia curriculum until the turn of the century. It is not difficult to see how this transfer of medical knowledge was accomplished. At Edinburgh, professors dictated lectures to students, who took detailed notes from which they later reconstructed the text of the lecture as fully as possible. A fair copy of a complete set of notes could run to several hundred pages, and manuscript copies were bought and sold as textbooks. On their return to Philadelphia, the young professors used these notes as a basis for their own courses.

Lecture notes taken by Philadelphia students show the extent of their professors' debt to Edinburgh. Courses replicated much of the technical content of Edinburgh lectures and also borrowed Scottish Enlightenment ideology. American professors praised Enlightenment virtues of rationality and progress, and adopted the 'synthetic' method of teaching that embodied these values, with lectures proceeding from general principles to specific phenomena.[17] For example, the chemistry courses taught by Joseph Black and Benjamin Rush opened with an introductory lecture emphasising the nature of chemistry as a form of polite scientific knowledge with valuable practical applications. Both professors defined chemistry as the science dealing with the effects of heat and mixture. Their courses began with a discussion of the principles of heat, elective attraction and chemical transformations and then used these principles to analyse and classify materials as salts, earths, inflammables, metals, waters and animal and vegetable substances.[18] Rush must have read his early courses from a set of Edinburgh notes, since he reproduced Black's lectures virtually word for word, but his later courses included minor changes, such as a separate section on gases. Rush's successors continued to teach courses similar to those at Edinburgh: Caspar Wistar, who trained in Edinburgh, also modelled his lectures on those of Black, whereas James Woodhouse, in a testimony to Rush's adherence to Black's syllabus, retained much of the structure and content of Edinburgh chemistry courses even though he was educated in Philadelphia and never travelled to Scotland.[19]

Medical subjects followed the same general pattern. In accordance with the model of the anatomy course given at Edinburgh by Alexander Monro *secundus*, William Shippen began with a short series of lectures on general physiology – the structure and function of blood, bones, nerves and vessels – before embarking on the anatomical description of the human body. Both professors ended their courses with lectures on surgery and midwifery in which this knowledge was put to practical use. Although they retained this syllabus, Monro and Shippen were forced to vary the order of the anatomical descriptions from year to year according to the state of preservation of the dissection subjects.[20]

The distinctive medical theories formulated and taught at Edinburgh in the 1760s and 1770s also crossed the Atlantic with the future Philadelphia professors. John Morgan's theory and practice of medicine courses were based on those of Robert Whytt, the last Edinburgh professor to follow Hermann Boerhaave's medical theories.[21] Like Whytt, Morgan taught that health depended on a qualitative and quantitative equilibrium of the body fluids and the state of tension in the fibres. These ideas were taught for only a short time at Philadelphia, not lasting beyond Morgan's tenure. His successors, Adam Kuhn, elected professor of the theory and practice of medicine in 1789, and Benjamin Smith Barton, appointed to the chair in 1813, attended Edinburgh University after Whytt's death and learned instead the theories developed by John Gregory and William

Cullen from Whytt's experimental work. Though Gregory and Cullen taught slightly different theories, both emphasised the role of the nervous system in determining health and proposed that an imbalance between excitation and individual 'sensibility' — the ability of the body to perceive and respond to stimuli — was a primary cause of disease.[22]

American students held Cullen's teaching in particularly high regard. Rush wrote: 'Dr Gregory's lectures abound with excellent practical observations, but are by no means equal to the unrivaled Dr Cullen, whose merit is beyond all praise'.[23] Kuhn and Barton chose to base their courses on Cullen's theory, exploiting its potential to provide a powerfully coherent, rationalistic explanation of disease and therapy. Following Cullen, they divided their courses among physiology, pathology and therapeutics. Courses began with a discussion of the physiology of the nervous system and its properties of irritability and sensibility, then went on to describe pathological processes as the result of excessive changes in sensibility. The bulk of their courses consisted of a catalogue of diseases arranged by class, order, genera and species according to Cullen's nosology.[24] Materia medica courses were also reformulated in accordance with Cullen's theory. If nervous dysfunction was the primary cause of disease, then drugs acted not on the fluids but on the nervous system, countering excessive or deficient levels of excitement. Kuhn's syllabus followed Cullen's classification of the materia medica with new categories of stimulants, sedatives and tonics alongside the traditional classes of evacuants.[25]

Edinburgh theories dominated the curriculum at the Philadelphia school until 1791, when Benjamin Rush began teaching his own theories from the chair of the institutes of medicine. Although championed as the first body of American medical theory, Rush's work was clearly derived from Cullen's ideas and bore a strong resemblance to the work of John Brown, another of Cullen's pupils.[26] Rush proposed that there was only one pathological state: all diseases were produced by a 'morbid excitement' caused by over-stimulation. Consequently, although it retained the synthetic form, the syllabus taught by Rush (and later by Nathaniel Chapman, John Syng Dorsey and John Redman Coxe) differed substantially from that taught by Cullen. Cullen's complex nosology, which classified diseases as discrete entities, was abandoned. Rush boasted: 'From attending these lectures, gentlemen, you will loose [sic] much more than you will gain. You will loose that immense burden of hard names contained in nosological writers, and substitute in their place observation and judgment.'[27] Rush categorised diseases according to the organs of the body principally affected. Therapy was highly simplistic: in the materia medica courses taught by Rush's followers, all drugs were classified as different types of sedative, either directly or indirectly reducing nervous excitement,[28] and this approach justified Rush's infamous use of stringent bloodletting and huge doses of evacuants.

The adoption of Rush's theories in practice of medicine and materia medica classes marked the end of the close relationship between the Edinburgh and Philadelphia medical schools. Rush's theories superseded those of Cullen in Philadelphia courses, as faculty positions were filled by professors trained primarily in America, not Edinburgh. Philip Syng Physick, appointed in 1805, was the last Philadelphia professor to hold a degree from the Edinburgh Medical School, and he had crammed all seven classes into one year of study. In the next few years he was joined on the faculty by a group of Philadelphia graduates: Thomas Chalkey James, Nathaniel Chapman, John Syng Dorsey and John Redman Coxe, most of whom had studied medicine briefly in Edinburgh but mainly in London or Paris.[29]

The reasons for the changing patterns of education among the Philadelphia faculty are complex. The Revolutionary War had only a short-term effect on students travelling to Europe. The numbers of Americans studying in Scotland dropped sharply in 1777 but rose again in 1783 and remained high until the end of the century. Perhaps more important, the relative status of the two schools shifted in the late eighteenth and early nineteenth centuries. Although student numbers continued to increase in the nineteenth century, the Edinburgh school had lost some of its most prestigious teachers with the death or retirement of Joseph Black, William Cullen and Alexander Monro *secundus*. The next generation of professors, mostly sons of the faculty, were competent teachers but never acquired the formidable reputations of their predecessors. At the same time, under Rush's leadership the prestige of the Philadelphia school increased rapidly. The impact of these developments was considerable. Like their predecessors, the new generation of professors taught classes that reflected their own education, with the result that after 1800 most lectures were based on those taught at Philadelphia, not Edinburgh. The two cities did continue to exchange ideas: the Philadelphia faculty established journals to publicise European developments in medicine, and Rush's theories were debated in Edinburgh. But the special relationship between the medical schools was never revived.

III

However close the ties between the Edinburgh and Philadelphia medical schools during the second half of the eighteenth century, the Scottish system of medical education was not transplanted wholesale but was adapted to its new national context. Like most eighteenth-century medical men, Philadelphia's professors stressed the influence of the environment, particularly climate, on disease.[30] Within a few years of the school's founding, they were teaching classes that reflected the distinctive diseases and epidemiology of the New World. Not only did Americans suffer from diseases such as malaria and yellow fever, which were rare or unknown in Britain, but familiar European complaints were said to exhibit more severe symptoms as a result of the country's peculiar physical environment. Nathaniel Chapman explained with some pride: 'Nature has cast the new world in her largest mould, and given many of its productions corresponding properties. No instance of stinted or niggardly creation exists. . . . Even our diseases partake of the same character and have a violence, which exacts for their cure, either new means, or original combinations of vigorous practice'.[31]

Students were warned not to rely on the treatment recommended by British textbooks because in America all diseases required more stringent forms of therapy. Indigenous diseases were better treated with drugs compounded from native American plants. As Adam Kuhn explained, 'Nature has supplied every Country with Remedies for the diseases which are peculiar to it. . . . In this country where the Rattlesnake is the most venomous animal we have many powerful antidotes amongst which is the Seneka Snake Root'.[32] In their classes Kuhn and his successors included American remedies alongside the drugs listed in the standard European pharmacopieas, and Benjamin Smith Barton, who published extensively on American botany, compiled a comprehensive list of indigenous medicinal plants and their therapeutic uses.

In the post-Revolutionary period these tendencies became more marked, and even esoteric medical knowledge was used as a vehicle to express nationalist concerns. In his institutes of medicine class in 1802, Rush used his own physiological theories to justify republicanism. One student recorded:

> Those [governments] dependent on the *Sovereignty of the People are the best* – the excitability and excitement are here equable; and are Kept so by the frequent occurrence of Elections. You see here, Gentlemen, say Dr. *Rush* [sic] the same Unity of Truth as elsewhere. A Physician who is not a Republican contests his own Principles. Joy acts with more force on Britons than Americans, from the accumulation of excitability, occasioned by *fear of Oppression.* Elections serve to carry off the excitability, like chimneys carry off smoke; and hence excitability is more accumulated in Britons for want of those political Chimnies – And hence their political joys and fears are more excessive and fatal.[33]

Although the political context encouraged Philadelphia's professors to construct distinctively American forms of medical knowledge, common pressures to keep up with the latest medical trends and techniques led to parallel developments at the two schools. The addition of surgical teaching to the curriculum in the first decade of the nineteenth century illustrates this point. The established faculties could literally not afford to ignore the competition as students flocked to the growing number of private schools and hospitals teaching anatomy and surgery. In London, which became the centre for surgical teaching, prominent surgeons lectured and demonstrated operations before hundreds of students in specially built theatres. Those students who could afford the additional fees for 'subjects' were given facilities to carry out their own dissections and to practise operations on cadavers.[34]

In Philadelphia Philip Syng Physick, who had taught a popular extramural class in surgery for five years, approached the faculty and suggested splitting William Shippen's chair of anatomy, surgery and midwifery. Shippen, who was nearing the end of his teaching career, raised no objection, and Physick was duly appointed the school's first professor of surgery in 1805.[35] In Edinburgh the medical school faced even stronger competition from the anatomy schools of John Bell and John Barclay and the lecture courses offered by the Incorporation of Surgeons (now the Royal College of Surgeons), but attempts to establish a university chair of surgery were blocked by the anatomy professors, who saw the creation of a chair of surgery as a threat to their livelihood. In 1777 Alexander Monro *secundus* persuaded the town council to grant him a new commission as professor of anatomy and surgery, providing a monopoly on surgical teaching within the university. Although the council acceded to Monro's request in recognition of his considerable contributions to the school, it was aware of the demand for surgical teaching and reserved the right to divide the chair after his death. In the early nineteenth century, under renewed pressure for reform, the council compromised by creating a chair in the specialist area of clinical surgery. In 1802 James Russell was appointed its first incumbent, while Monro, now conjoint professor with his son Alexander Monro *tertius*, retained his right to teach general surgery. Four years later a Regius chair of military surgery was created by the crown over the heads of the university authorities, but it was another twenty-five years before a chair of general surgery was established.[36]

IV

Similarities between the Edinburgh and Philadelphia medical schools were not limited to the transfer of ideas and personnel. Changing attitudes towards courses, curriculum and degree regulations, all of which were shaped by the need to attract students and provide an education that would serve them well once they set up in practice, suggest that the development of the medical profession in America – so far little studied – paralleled that of Britain.

In late eighteenth-century Britain, the medieval divisions of practice among physicians, surgeons and apothecaries were theoretically still in effect. A small, élite group of physicians, distinguished by possession of the M.D. degree, diagnosed and prescribed for internal disease while apprentice-trained surgeons performed manual operations and apothecaries dispensed medicines. These monopolies of practice were enforced by the colleges of physicians, which prosecuted practitioners straying outside their proper spheres. In practice, divisions were observed only in large towns and cities; in rural areas medical men acted as general practitioners. In America, however, the British tripartite division was not introduced, and all practitioners practised all branches of medicine. John Morgan, who held an expensive European degree, condemned American medical men for acting as general practitioners. He himself attempted to set up in practice as a physician and envisaged the Philadelphia Medical School as the basis for establishing a tripartite division. In 1766 Morgan asked Thomas Penn for a charter creating a college of physicians in Philadelphia with powers similar to those of the London college. His request was rejected, partly through strong opposition from local practitioners, and partly on the advice of John Fothergill, a London physician who pointed out that the divisions were outdated and that the London college no longer acted as a licensing body. When the College of Physicians of Philadelphia was finally instituted in 1787, it had no licensing powers and served only as a forum for the exchange of ideas.[37]

Although the formal structures of the profession in Britain and America differed, in principle if not in practice, the Edinburgh and Philadelphia medical schools attracted a similar audience of students. Both drew a small number of students intending to earn the M.D. degree, who studied for two or three years, taking most or all of the classes offered. However, students were free to attend as many or as few classes as they wished, and the majority entered with no plans to graduate. Most had already completed an apprenticeship and spent a year or two at the school to finish their medical education. They attended only two or three classes, anatomy, chemistry and practice of medicine being the most popular choices.[38]

During the late eighteenth and early nineteenth centuries, both schools instituted and enforced more and more rigorous degree requirements, making the degree an increasingly long and expensive undertaking. Edinburgh's first regulations, set in 1767, required degree candidates to attend the medical school for two years. A prescribed programme of study was established in 1777; thereafter students had to take classes in anatomy, chemistry, botany, materia medica and the theory and practice of medicine before they could sit the degree examinations. In 1783 the required period of study was extended to three years. During its early days, when its faculty was small, the Philadelphia Medical School tried to preserve the status of the M.D. degree by instituting quite different degree requirements from those at Edinburgh. The college offered two degrees. Students who attended all three classes offered by the new faculty, and passed a sequence of written and oral examinations similar to those at Edinburgh, were awarded a bachelor of medicine degree. To obtain the M.D., graduates had to practise medicine for three years, then return to present a Latin thesis. In addition, all degree candidates had to have served a 'sufficient apprenticeship to some reputable Practitioner in Physic' and to be proficient in Latin, mathematics and natural philosophy. With the expansion of the Philadelphia faculty in 1791, the bachelor of medicine degree and the entrance requirements were dropped, and thereafter the trustees adopted the same degree requirements as Edinburgh.[39]

At the same time, although degrees took longer and were more expensive, an increasing proportion of students at both schools chose to take them. In the mid-eighteenth century only a dozen or so students graduated each year from the Edinburgh Medical School, even though particular classes attracted well over a hundred students. By 1790 the proportion taking the M.D. degree had more than doubled to about twenty percent.[40] The records of the Philadelphia school are incomplete but show a similar pattern. Fewer than ten students graduated each year from 1768 until the 1790s, but numbers rose rapidly after 1800, increasing to more than fifty per annum by 1808. Between 1810 (the first year for which matriculation records are available) and 1840, the proportion of students passing the M.D. examinations increased from approximately fourteen percent to almost thirty-three percent.

Clearly, medical students in Edinburgh and Philadelphia regarded the M.D. as an increasingly valuable qualification in their professional careers, and by the mid-nineteenth century a large proportion of practitioners held the degree. Both schools were also eager to ensure that their graduates received a comprehensive medical education, even though their degrees had no formal status as a license to practise medicine.

V

The transfer of knowledge and teaching methods between the Edinburgh and Philadelphia medical schools was not a unique phenomenon, and John Morgan's attempts to model the Philadelphia faculty on that of Edinburgh are best understood as part of a much broader pattern of educational exchanges. The organisation and curriculum he copied from Edinburgh were themselves originally based on those of the University of Leyden, and the continuing reliance of the Philadelphia school on the Edinburgh faculty was characteristic of the strong influence of the Scottish universities on many eighteenth-century American colleges.

In reproducing the Edinburgh curriculum and course content, Morgan and his colleagues were simply drawing on a highly successful formula. As young men they had been attracted to Edinburgh by the wide range of subjects and innovative theories taught at the medical school. In Philadelphia this combination proved equally successful for attracting large numbers of American students. The process of replicating successful courses was not confined to the early years of the Philadelphia school, when the faculty had close personal ties to Edinburgh. It continued until the emergence in the early nineteenth century of a Philadelphia-trained professoriate, who modelled their classes on those they had attended as students in America rather than Scotland.

Ultimately, the main factor affecting the Philadelphia school was its ability to draw fee-paying students. The Edinburgh Medical School exerted a strong and lasting influence because its curriculum fulfilled the need among American students for a broad-based, up-to-date medical education. When Edinburgh's medical teaching no longer embodied the most innovative knowledge, the Philadelphia professors began to look elsewhere for inspiration, and modified the Edinburgh curriculum in order to continue attracting students. In this way the Philadelphia Medical School finally emerged from the shadow of its Edinburgh counterpart as a distinctive institution, competing for students on its own terms and adjusting successfully to new developments in medical theory and practice within the context of the young American republic.

NOTES

1. Helen Brock, 'Scotland and American Medicine', in William H. Brock, *Scotus Americanus: A Survey of the Sources for Links between Scotland and America in the Eighteenth Century* (Edinburgh, 1982), 118–19; J. Rendall, 'The Influence of the Edinburgh Medical School on America in the Eighteenth Century', in *The Early Years of the Edinburgh Medical School*, ed. R.G.W. Anderson and A.D.C. Simpson (Edinburgh, 1976), 95–124. These works contain references to most of the earlier literature in this field.
2. William Corner, *Two Centuries of Medicine: A History of the School of Medicine at the University of Pennsylvania* (Philadelphia, 1965) appeared as part of the school's bicentennial celebrations, but the most detailed history of the Philadelphia Medical School is still Joseph Carson, *A History of the Medical Department of the University of Pennsylvania* (Philadelphia, 1869). Accounts of the early years of the Philadelphia school may also be found in biographies of three of its original professors: Whitfield J. Bell, Jr, *John Morgan, Continental Doctor* (Philadelphia, 1965); Betsy Copping Corner, *William Shippen, Jr: Pioneer in American Medicine* (Philadelphia, 1951); Nathan G. Goodman, *Benjamin Rush: Physician and Citizen, 1746–1813* (Philadelphia,

1934); C.A.L. Binger, *Revolutionary Doctor: Benjamin Rush, 1746–1813* (New York, 1966); and David Freeman Hawke, *Benjamin Rush: Revolutionary Gadfly* (Indianapolis, 1971).

3. J.B. Morrell, 'The Edinburgh Town Council and Its University', in *Early Years of the Edinburgh Medical School*, ed. Anderson and Simpson, 46–65; Roger L. Emerson, 'Scottish Universities in the Eighteenth Century, 1690–1800', *SVEC* 167 (1977): 453–74.
4. Quoted in Alexander Bower, *The History of the University of Edinburgh*, 3 vols. (Edinburgh, 1817–30), 2:181.
5. W.R.O. Goslings, 'Leiden and Edinburgh: The Seed, the Soil and the Climate', in *Early Years of the Edinburgh Medical School*, ed. Anderson and Simpson, 1–18, as well as other essays in that volume.
6. Bower, *University of Edinburgh*, 2:166–67.
7. Rex Wright-St Clair, *Doctors Monro: A Medical Saga* (London, 1964), 20–37.
8. John D. Comrie, *A History of Scottish Medicine*, 2nd ed., 2 vols. (London, 1932), 1:297–304.
9. Bell, *John Morgan*, 25–75.
10. Ibid., 106–18.
11. John Morgan, *A Discourse upon the Institution of Medical Schools in America* (Philadelphia, 1765), 1.
12. Carson, *History of the Medical Department*, 55–56, 61–65, 72–75.
13. J.B. Morrell, 'The University of Edinburgh: Its Scientific Eminence and Academic Structure', *Isis* 62 (1971): 158–71; Carson, *History of the Medical Department*, 65–66.
14. University of Pennsylvania Archives, memo no. 1173, 21 Apr. 1817, and memo no. 1166, 20 Nov. 1815.
15. Carson, *History of the Medical Department*, 86–98.
16. Ibid., 61, 65.
17. Sloan, 159–60.
18. Joseph Black, 'Lectures on Chemistry', Joseph Black Manuscripts, no. 1, 8 vols., Royal College of Physicians, Edinburgh; Benjamin Rush, 'Lectures on Chemistry', E.F. Smith Collection, Van Pelt Library, University of Pennsylvania; Wyndham Miles, 'Benjamin Rush, Chemist', *Chymia* 4 (1953): 37–77. Cf. Donald J. D'Elia, *Benjamin Rush: Philosopher of the American Revolution* (Philadelphia, 1974), 26–27.
19. Caspar Wistar, 'Notes on Chemistry', E.F. Smith Collection, Van Pelt Library, University of Pennsylvania; James Woodhouse, [Notes on Chemistry 1809], ibid., and 'Notes from the Lectures on Chemistry', CPP, 10c 53.
20. See the following items in the Alexander Monro *secundus* MSS, Royal College of Physicians, Edinburgh: 'Anatomical Lectures delivered by Dr. Monro, 1774/5', no. 10, 4 of 6 vols. extant, and 'Anatomy and Physiology of Dr. Monro', no. 6, 4 vols.; William Shippen, 'Anatomical Lectures taken from Dr. William Shippen . . . by William McWilliams, 1777', CPP, 10b 49; William Shippen, 'Anatomical Annotations . . . from Dr. William Shippen, 1783', University of Pennsylvania Library, MS Am. 67.
21. John Morgan, 'M.S. Lectures. Physiology of Dr. Morgan', CPP, 10a 92; Christopher J. Lawrence, 'Medicine as Culture: Edinburgh and

the Scottish Enlightenment' (Ph.D. diss., University College London, 1984), 135–39, 148–55.

22. Lawrence, 'Medicine as Culture', 259–75, 322–71; John Thomson, *An Account of the Life, Lectures and Writings of William Cullen, M.D.*, 2 vols. (Edinburgh, 1859), 1:258–428; Rosalie Stott, 'Health and Virtue, or How to Keep Out of Harm's Way: Lectures on Pathology and Therapeutics by William Cullen c. 1770', *Medical History* 31 (1987): 123–42.
23. *The Letters of Benjamin Rush*, ed. L.H. Butterfield, 2 vols. (Princeton, 1951), 1:49.
24. Adam Kuhn, 'Notes on the Lectures of the Practice of Physick . . . Taken by Mr. Stratton', CPP, 10a 77; Adam Kuhn, 'Lectures on the Institutes of Medicine', CPP, 10a 68; Benjamin Smith Barton, 'Notes from a Course of Lectures on the Institutes and Practice of Medicine', CPP, 10a 402.
25. Adam Kuhn, 'Notes from a Course of Lectures on the Materia Medica', CPP, 10a 72; Adam Kuhn, 'Lectures on the Materia Medica. Marcus Kuhl. 1790', CPP, 10a 74; Benjamin Smith Barton, 'Notes on the Materia Medica 1808–9', CPP, 10a 7.
26. *The Autobiography of Benjamin Rush*, ed. George W. Corner (Princeton, 1948), 363–66; Richard Shryock, *Medicine and Society in America, 1660–1860* (Ithaca, N.Y., 1984), 67–72; Thomson, *Life of Cullen*, 2:227–79.
27. Benjamin Rush, 'Notes from Dr. Rushes Lectures, vol. 2, 1797:1798 Elijah Griffiths', CPP, 10a 106, 30.
28. Benjamin Rush, *Syllabus of a Course of Lectures upon Physiology, Pathology, Hygiene, and the Practice of Medicine* in *Sixteen Introductory Lectures* (1811; rpt. Oceanside, N.Y., 1977); Nathaniel Chapman, 'Notes on the Lectures of Nathaniel Chapman, 1818–19–20', CPP, 10a 271; John Syng Dorsey, 'Notes on the Lectures of John Syng Dorsey, Professor of Materia Medica by John Clark 1816–1817', CPP, 10a 306; John Redman Coxe, 'Notes from the Lectures of John Redman Coxe by William S. Wallace, 1821–22', CPP, 10a 37.
29. Carson, *History of the Medical Department*, 142–44, 149–58, 172–73; EUL MS Da., 1791–95, 1801–3.
30. James Riley, *The Eighteenth-Century Campaign to Avoid Disease* (New York, 1987).
31. Nathaniel Chapman, *Elements of Therapeutics and Materia Medica*, 3rd ed., 2 vols. (Philadelphia, 1823), 1:41.
32. Adam Kuhn, 'Notes from a Course of Lectures on the Materia Medica', CPP, 10a 72, 7.
33. Benjamin Rush, 'Notes taken from Doctor Rush's Lectures upon the Institutes and Practice of Medicine . . . by William Darlington . . . 1802–3', CPP, 10a 105, n.p.
34. Susan Lawrence, 'Entrepreneurs and Private Enterprise: The Development of Medical Lecturing in London, 1775–1820', *Bulletin of the History of Medicine* 62 (1988): 171–92.
35. Carson, *History of the Medical Department*, 104.
36. Wright-St Clair, *Doctors Monro*, 82–87, 102–4. For a similar curricular reform in France, see Colin Jones, 'Montpellier Medical Students and the Medicalisation of Eighteenth-Century France', in *Problems and Methods in the History of Medicine*, ed. Roy Porter and Andrew Wear (London, 1987), 57–80.

37. Bell, *John Morgan*, 137–40.
38. Lisa Rosner, 'Students and Apprentices: Medical Education at Edinburgh University, 1760–1810' (Ph.D. diss., Johns Hopkins University, 1985).
39. Carson, *History of the Medical Department*, 60–61, 95–96, 117–19.
40. Ibid., 218–19; D.B. Horn, *A Short History of the University of Edinburgh, 1556–1889* (Edinburgh, 1967), 44–46.

15

ANNE MCCLENNY KRAUSS

James Bremner, Alexander Reinagle and the Influence of the Edinburgh Musical Society on Philadelphia

Although little has been written about the impact of Scotland's musical life on late eighteenth-century Philadelphia, it is clearly evident from a study of the careers of two Scottish musicians who settled there. The professional efforts of James Bremner, who arrived in Philadelphia in 1763, and Alexander Reinagle, who arrived in 1786, spanned the last forty years of the eighteenth century. This chapter focuses on the Scotland they knew in their early years and the ways in which they moulded Philadelphia's musical development in the image of their Scottish experiences.

Both men had the advantage of living in Edinburgh during the Scottish Enlightenment, a golden period in the musical history of the city. During those years there was a significant rise in concert activity, reflecting both the taste of the many professional people who earlier had gone abroad to study and the cultural needs of young men whose families had sent them on the grand tour of Europe.[1] There was also a great emphasis then on folk or national music, as part of Scotland's search for its identity after the Union of 1707 and the defeat of Bonnie Prince Charlie at Culloden in 1746.

Music played an important role in the lives of many people in Edinburgh during the Enlightenment. Edward Topham, a young English cavalry officer stationed there in 1775, wrote:

> Music in general in this country, exceeds belief. It is not only the principal entertainment, but the constant topic of every conversation; . . . how trifling does it appear to a stranger, to find so many philosophers, professors of science, and respectable characters, disputing on the merits of an Italian fiddle, and the preciseness of a demiquaver; while poetry, painting, architecture, and theatrical amusements, whose province it is to instruct as well as to amuse, here couch beneath the dominion of an air or a ballad, which at best were only invented to pass away a vacant hour, or ease the mind from more important duties![2]

Music was everywhere. Children and young adults were taking lessons, and an ever increasing number of dancing assemblies and concerts featured more and more professional musicians from Europe. Much of this activity was under the control of the Edinburgh Musical Society, the most important and powerful musical organisation in the country. The EMS counted among its members such prominent figures as George Drummond, William Cullen, Joseph Black, Henry Mackenzie and Lord Kames.[3] Because non-members ran the risk of being socially ostracised,[4] there was a constant waiting list for vacant places and a great demand for concert tickets.

The EMS was officially formed in March 1728, when a group of amateur gentlemen musicians who regularly played together drew up a set of rules to govern themselves and began keeping records of their meetings. At first there were approximately seventy members, performing either as singers or instrumentalists, as well as a few professionals employed to augment their efforts. They met on Friday evenings at six o'clock in St Mary's Chapel in Niddry's Wynd (pictured on p. 277 below) and paid annual dues of one guinea. It was always an aristocratic organisation, and the professional musicians were never members; rather, they were called 'masters'.[5]

Expenses mounted steadily but so, fortunately, did interest in the society. In its first five years dues were increased from one to two guineas, and thirty new members were admitted. The waiting list for vacant places was long enough for the directors to declare that anyone not paying dues would forfeit his place in the society (EMSSB, 1:36). Because membership needed to be increased to augment operating funds, it became necessary to admit people who simply wanted to listen. To encourage performing members, the treasurer was authorised to give them guest tickets for the Friday concerts whenever they played (EMSSB, 1:79).

Throughout the years leading up to the time of James Bremner's involvement with the EMS (1756–60), the sederunt books show an ever increasing budget requiring a larger membership and higher dues to meet the demands of adding more professional musicians. There were other needs as well. Music had to be added to the society's library and instruments bought. An inventory of 1747 lists twenty-one instruments belonging to the society (EMSSB, 2:preface). Among them were a harpsichord, an organ, a pair of French horns with crooks, two double basses, two tenore fiddles (violas) an old vn (violin), a German flute, two hautboys (oboes), two flagolets, two kettledrums and three bassoons. This list does not give a complete picture of the orchestra. Needless to say, there would also have been many violins, but the gentlemen playing them would have owned their instruments.

The mid-eighteenth century saw the society approaching its peak in membership and extravagances. There were 150 members, and the £616.2.8 paid out from June 1755 to June 1756 was the largest amount to that date (EMSSB, 2:78). But numbers do not tell the whole story. The society had contacts in places as far away as Russia. A letter dated 28 April 1749 states that 'the Musical Society of Edinburgh have agreed with Senor Passerini and Madame Passerini his wife for performing in the concerts here and are to give them six hundred Rubles yearly, and have sent a contract to Muscow' (EMSSB, 2:12). News of the high quality of the concerts had evidently also reached George Frederick Handel, for he gave the society access to any of his oratorios not in print, as a letter of 27 April 1754 from William Douglas, treasurer, to Christopher Smith in London confirms: 'Mr. Handel has been so good as to allow the Musical Society of Edin[h] the Favour of a Copy of such of his compositions which are not published as they shall call for, and has Directed them to apply to you for the same' (EMSSB, 2:62). Through these oratorios the EMS introduced Scotland to the art of choral singing.[6] The performances were so popular that a hall larger than St Mary's Chapel had to be rented for many of them (EMSSB, 2:76).

I

James Bremner's contact with the society began in January 1756 when he received an allowance of £5.5 (EMSSB, 2:77). He came from a musical family, for the previous year the society had paid £15 for music to Robert Bremner, presumably his father (EMSSB, 2:68), who had a music store 'opposite the head of Blackfriars Wynd in the High Street'.[7] The next Bremner reference is on 18 October 1756: 'The Directors considering that Mr. Gilson and the Messrs. Bremner were now of considerable use to the society by performing in the concerts and finding a vacant Sallary by the death of Mr. McGibbon agreed to divide his Sallary amongst the three Masters to Each £8.6.8 Sterling yearly comensing the 25th of Sept[r] last.'[8] The three were filling the place of an outstanding master who had served the society since its inception as both performer and composer, and had been one of its highest paid instrumentalists.

James's ability was recognised and appreciated. In 1759 his salary was raised to £10 yearly, while that of his brother Robert remained the same. One of the Bremners also had the society's backing as a teacher, without which very few musicians could build a class. William Douglas wrote to a contact in London who was trying to find a singer for the EMS: 'You can also tell him what a small part of their income our Sallarys make, only Serves as a feather in their Caps and to give them a Character in this place. I can assure you that the Taste for singing and playing the Guitar is very great at present and young Bremner has given up everything Else to teach that instrument and had not an hour to spare this twelve months' (EMSSB, 2:107). If 'young Bremner' was James, the teaching experience would stand him in good stead when he settled in Philadelphia a few years later.

James Bremner's annual salary of £10 continued until June 1760, but there is no evidence that he ever played in the Edinburgh concerts after that date. Later that same year he left for study in Naples. On 15 January 1761 he had a letter from William Douglas that shows the society's interest in his welfare:

> We have the pleasure by your brother often to hear of you. . . . We were all much pleased lately with a letter Mr. Walter Stewart had from a cousin of his in Naples who [spoke] of the success of your studys which gives us great hopes of offering first fiddle of our own soon. I put the Gentlemen in mind of their promises to which they cheerfully agreed and you have subjoined a Letter of Cred^{t}. for £50 Ster^{g}. which you may draw for as you please. There is one Thing I must beg your Endeavor to procure for us and that is a Right Singer. . . . You know very well what would answer here – a woman preferable to a man. Good looks you know bespeaks favour and if she has Common Sense it would be a great addition. (EMSSB, 2:120)

The EMS members had a high opinion of his worth as well as confidence in his judgement.

Although there are no extant plan books for EMS programmes when James Bremner played in the concerts, a description of them can be constructed by studying the society's accounts. They list money paid for the music of Corelli, Vivaldi, Geminiani and Handel, especially his oratorios, together with other composers whose works were in private collections bought by the society. Much of this music was heard for the first time in Scotland at the Friday concerts.[9] Also in the society's library was William Thomson's *Scots Songs*, showing interest in the national music that was gaining in popularity. The so-called 'Ladies Night' concerts were especially brilliant occasions. All concert programmes were divided into three parts, or acts, and were mixtures of vocal and instrumental music. The two intervals or intermissions were great times for socialising.

James Bremner was fortunate to have had weekly exposure to good music, and he had the great advantage of being employed by the society at a time when such notables as Lord Kames and the sixth earl of Kelly were members. Before he became Lord Kelly in 1756, at the age of twenty-four, Thomas Erskine, Lord Pittenweem had been sent by his family on the grand tour of Europe. When he got to Mannheim, he was so impressed by the music he heard there that he stayed for some time to study with Johann Stamitz. Stamitz was the founder of a new style of orchestral writing, called the Mannheim School,[10] characterised by homophonic music or melody with accompaniment, as opposed to the old contrapuntal style. By introducing the classical sonata form into orchestral compositions, Stamitz laid the foundation for the overtures and symphonies of Haydn and Mozart.

The earl of Kelly gave the people of Scotland and England their first taste of this important new style of writing for orchestra. When he got back to Edinburgh, he encouraged the EMS to put works of Stamitz, and later Haydn, on its programmes, in essence changing the course of its concert offerings. Gradually the programmes came to include music that was modern, or 'galant', often of Kelly's own composition,[11] alongside the contrapuntal, or 'antient', music the members loved and demanded.

Because James Bremner was in the society's orchestra when the earl of Kelly returned from Mannheim, he learned the new style of playing and the more modern repertoire before going to America. Just why he decided to emigrate after his study in Naples is not known, and the matter is especially puzzling because he would have been well received at home. Perhaps he had visions of a better life both financially and socially. In Edinburgh, even though good professional musicians were highly respected, there was a barrier between them and the people of higher rank. Members of the EMS were very much aware of their place in a tightly ordered class structure. For example, when conditions got crowded at the Friday concerts, they wanted to keep out people of 'Low Meen' (EMSSB, 1:66). When Mr Rochetti, a well-paid former master, was getting old, they decided to give him a maintenance fund, noting with condescension: 'Besides his Discretion and obliging manner and the merit of his being an old servant of the society he might still be of some use' (EMSSB, 2:47–48). These attitudes were probably hard for a talented and well-travelled young man to accept.

The exact date of Bremner's arrival in America is not known, but a newspaper announcement shows that he was in Philadelphia in 1763. The same announcement confirms that he was a well-rounded musician prepared to teach a variety of instruments. He gave notice that he was opening

> his Music School . . . at Mr. Glover Hunt's near the Coffee House in Market Street where young Ladies may be taught Harpsichord or Guitar, on Mondays, Wednesdays, and Fridays from 10 in the morning until 12. Likewise young Gentlemen may be taught Violin, German flute, or Guitar from 6 in the evening till 8 on Mondays, Wednesdays, and Fridays.[12]

Bremner was the musician who most deeply influenced the musical activity of Philadelphia in colonial days. Having known a rich concert life in Edinburgh, he was well qualified to direct Philadelphia's first subscription concerts. On 12 January 1764 the *Pennsylvania Packet* printed the following notice, the first of its kind in the city's musical history:

On Thursday, the 19th instant, at the Assembly Room in Lodge Alley, will be performed a CONCERT OF MUSIC, to be continued every Thursday, till the 24th of May, following.

No more than 70 subscribers will be admitted, and each, on paying Three Pounds for the season, to have one Lady's Ticket, to be disposed of every Concert night, as he thinks proper. Subscriptions to be taken in at Messrs. Rivington and Brown's Store, and by Mr. Bremner, at Mr. Glover Hunt's, in Market Street, near the Coffee House.

N.B. The concert to begin at precisely 6 o'clock.[13]

Because Bremner is the only musician mentioned, it is logical to think he directed the series. Unfortunately, none of the programmes have survived, although some idea of the concerts becomes apparent by piecing together certain clues. In the 1760s there were several people known to have been playing in the city. Lieutenant-Governor John Penn, John Schneider and Stephen Forage played violin along with Bremner, who probably played leading fiddle. Francis Hopkinson would have played the harpsichord, and John Schneider could also have played the French horn. Ernst Barnard and George D'Eisenburg would have played German flute. No doubt there would have been a number of gentlemen amateurs proficient enough as violinists to join the group.[14] Having played a concert for the benefit of the organ fund at St Peter's Church,[15] Bremner would probably have known a few singers from there who could have appeared, giving the evenings a balance of vocal and instrumental music similar to the programmes he knew in Edinburgh.

In addition to having a good knowledge of orchestral literature, Bremner had the advantage of close contact with his family's music businesses, which provided him with quick news of the latest music in print. For instance, Robert Bremner (presumably the senior) had published the earl of Kelly's *Six Overtures*, Op. 1, in Edinburgh in 1761 and in London a year later.[16] On 10 April 1765 Philadelphians had the opportunity to hear one of the overtures of the man James Bremner had known in Scotland. They are thought to have been the first Americans to hear this music. The programme, directed by Bremner, was given in College Hall for the benefit of the Boys and Girls Charity Schools that belonged to the College of Philadelphia. It was reminiscent of the EMS Friday concerts. Divided into three acts, it provided a mixture of ancient and modern styles so characteristic of the society's programmes after the earl of Kelly's return to Scotland. The former style was represented by the music of Geminiani and the latter by Stamitz and his pupil Kelly. An air in the first act and a chorus in the last made the affair a combination of vocal and instrumental music.[17]

In 1769 a wine merchant from Italy, Giovanni Gualdo, who came to

Philadelphia from London, had a benefit concert. It opened and closed with overtures by the earl of Kelly. Gualdo also directed a subscription series that year, and Kelly's name was among those whose works were to be played. Obviously, Philadelphia audiences liked the music of the adventurous Scotsman.[18] Apart from a Kelly overture performed in Boston in 1771,[19] Philadelphia was the only eighteenth-century American city where his music was heard in public performances.

Bremner's life in America was enriched by his friendship with Francis Hopkinson, the country's first native composer. Hopkinson was a distinguished statesman, a delegate to the Continental Congress and a signer of the Declaration of Independence.[20] The two would have been friends because of their common love of music, but Hopkinson also probably welcomed the opportunity to have discussions with a person who had known such prominent literati as Lord Kames. Certainly the two must have made music together often.

Hopkinson is thought to have studied with Bremner. In his handwritten book of *Lessons* are four pieces by the Scotsman and an overture by the earl of Kelly that Bremner arranged for keyboard for his friend.[21] Their association extended over many years. When Hopkinson went to London, he was received by the Robert Bremners.[22] After he returned to America, he took Bremner's place as organist at Christ Church when the Scottish musician went back to London to open a branch of the family business.[23] Hopkinson remarked on receiving a letter from his friend: 'I had two and a half lines from Bremner. . . . he is a good friend but a wretched Correspondent!'[24] Bremner eventually returned to Philadelphia, but his days of directing concerts were over. Except for random programmes, all concert activity had ceased because of the war. He died in 1780, before people could once again enjoy the luxury of public performances.

During his years in America, James Bremner had successfully launched the plan for subscription concerts in Philadelphia and had given audiences the benefit of his broad knowledge of music, gained largely when he played in the Friday concerts of the EMS. Above all, he had acquainted Philadelphians with the Mannheim style and specifically with the music of the earl of Kelly, giving the city the distinction of premiering his works in America.

II

Six years went by before another talented Scottish musician settled in Philadelphia. Alexander Reinagle arrived in 1786, already a sophisticated composer and performer. He and James Bremner came to America with remarkably similar backgrounds. Both had studied on the Continent, and both came from musical families connected with the EMS.

The first entry for a Reinagle in the society's sederunt books appears exactly one year after the last one for James Bremner. Accounts show that in January 1761 £9.10 was paid to Alexander's father, Joseph 'Reniagale' (the Scots always had trouble spelling the Hungarian name). The senior Reinagle's wife, Annie Laurie, was from nearby Prestonpans.[25] By 1762 Joseph Reinagle had moved his family from Portsmouth to Edinburgh. He was affiliated with the EMS and through its influence and the help of the earl of Kelly was appointed a trumpeter to the king.[26] A letter written on 22 November 1766 explains the society's connexion and is yet another example of its control over the musical affairs of Edinburgh: 'For several years past when any vacancy happened amongst the King's Trumpeters, the Lords of the Judiciary have allowed the gentlemen of the Musical Society to recommend proper persons whom their Lordships got appointed for the Vacancy by which means we got several good hands for the concert which otherwise our small Sallarys could not accomplish' (EMSSB, 2:178).

Joseph had already made it clear that his salary from the EMS was not enough 'to keep him in this place' (EMSSB, 2:131). It was fortunate that he could add the money he received as a trumpeter (£4.3.4 quarterly) to the small amount he received from the EMS, allowing him to live in Edinburgh. Financial records show that he got this quarterly payment from 21 May 1762 until 1785.[27] During those years he and several of his children were deeply involved with the EMS.

Joseph, Jr was receiving a master's salary in 1774, when he was just twelve years old (EMSSB, 3:92); and he continued on the payroll until 1785. His sister Mary married the famous cellist Johann Georg Christoff Schetky in 1774. For many years he was one of the highest paid masters in the EMS (EMSSB, 3:79). Their son George, a cellist like his father, followed his uncle Alexander Reinagle to America in 1792 and lived in Philadelphia.[28] By the early nineteenth century he had become one of the city's musical leaders and was a founding member of the Musical Fund Society, an organisation whose main purpose was to give financial help to the families of ailing or deceased musicians. Thus, another immigrant from Scotland enriched Philadelphia's musical life.

The years of Alexander Reinagle's contact with the EMS, both as a child of a master and as a professional himself, were flourishing ones for the society. It built a handsome concert hall, named after the patron saint of music, St Cecilia, and designed by the Scottish architect Robert Milne. Financed by members' subscriptions, it was completed in 1762.[29] Here the music of Haydn and Mozart was heard for the first time in Scotland, and audiences were thrilled by performances of Scots songs by well-known Italian singers employed by the society, Tenducci among them.[30] In this hall Alexander Reinagle heard the concerts that did much to mould his musical taste, and by 1771 the society's library contained several hundred books of music available for his perusal (EMSSB, 3:50).

Throughout his early life Reinagle lived in the midst of a musical culture unique to Scotland, one in which classical and folk music coexisted and intermingled in various ways.[31] Classical traditions were rooted in the musical soil of western Europe, while the native music of Scotland had qualities peculiarly its own. As one writer remarked, 'the old Scots songs, or melodies, have always been admired for that wild pathetic sweetness which distinguishes them from the music of every other country.'[32] The old folk tradition was deepened in 1723 with the publication of the first volume of Allan Ramsay's *Tea Table Miscellany*, the first important collection of national songs in print. Ramsay put no music to the songs, assuming readers would know the tunes. Shortly thereafter he saw the success William Thomson had achieved by offering music with the songs and employed Alexander Stewart to arrange a volume entitled *Musick for Allan Ramsay's Collection of Scots Songs*.[33] Scottish fiddlers used the familiar Scots tunes as a basis for complicated variations, combining elements of folk and classical music.[34] The folk tunes would be stated simply, but the variations that followed would contain figurations common to European art music. Performing musicians, especially fiddlers, knew both types, playing classical music in St Cecilia's Hall one night and filling an evening playing native tunes in a tavern the next. Moreover, because concert audiences in Edinburgh wanted to hear their native music as well as classical works, both would often be on the same programme.[35] In the dancing assemblies, too, both types were represented. Dignified allemandes and minuets were followed by more boisterous country dances and energetic strathspeys, with characteristic short-long rhythmic patterns known as the 'Scots snap'. Thus, any musician living in Edinburgh during the Enlightenment would have found it quite natural to embrace both folk and classical music with equal enthusiasm. This special musical culture found its way to Philadelphia through Alexander Reinagle, but not before he had established himself at home.

Reinagle's early professional career was a varied one, as was typical of the times; it provided the background he needed to succeed in America. He began his professional life in Glasgow in 1778, advertising that he intended to teach spinet in classes, then a progressive method of instruction in Britain.[36] He also got good experience managing concerts in Glasgow, the only eighteenth-century city in Scotland that could boast of public subscription concerts,[37] the kind Reinagle would manage later in Philadelphia. As a young composer in Glasgow he experimented with the Scottish way of combining folk and classical elements in the same piece. In a *Collection of the Most Favorite Scots Tunes with Variations for the Harpsichord*,[38] he used the formula popular with fiddlers: stating the tune simply and following with elaborate variations. Some of his other compositions show this duality in a different way. In 1783, for example, he published *Six Sonatas for the Piano-Forte or Harpsichord with an Accompaniment for a Violin* and put Scots tunes in the final movements of two of the six pieces: 'Up in the Morning Early' in the second sonata and 'Dainty Davie' in the fifth. In both instances the Scots tunes are used as rondo themes.

If Reinagle was in London in 1783, as some evidence suggests, he could have heard many fine programmes in the great concert rooms of the city. They presented some real differences, however, from those in St Cecilia's Hall. The mixing of folk and classical music on the same programme was not done. Furthermore, Londoners preferred evenings devoted mainly to contemporary music, whereas Edinburgh audiences demanded works from both the ancient and modern styles.[39] A less important difference was the way the programmes were arranged. In Edinburgh there were always three acts, but in London there were only two. In both cities, however, concerts mixed vocal and instrumental music, and both cities often shared the same performers.

Although never a master, Alexander Reinagle was highly regarded by the EMS. In the eight months he lived in the city in 1784 he was allowed three benefit concerts, a special privilege indeed, for even masters were seldom granted more than one a year. Reinagle also played for the Friday concert on 4 April and for Stephen Clark's benefit on 16 April. Programmes for three of the five performances survive, indicating that he played the pianoforte. The 4 April programme is the first in the plan books to specify that instrument, clearly suggesting that Reinagle was the first to play the pianoforte in the Friday concerts at St Cecilia's Hall. The programme for his benefit on 11 May was printed in the *Edinburgh Evening Courant* on 8 May 1784 and is distinctive in its pianoforte offerings.

Act I

Overture . . . . Haydn
Song
Concerto Piano Forte . . . . Schroeter

Act II

Organ Concerto . . . . Mr. Clark
Song
Concerto Violoncello . . . . Mr. Schetky

Act III

Piano Forte Fantasy, ex temporore
Sonata . . . . Mr. Reinagle
Rondeau . . . . of Carlo Bach
Violin Concerto . . . . Mr. Reinagle
Overture . . . . Haydn

Seldom had this much pianoforte music been put on a single programme, even in London. The EMS had given Alexander Reinagle a rare opportunity to test the audience appeal of such a programme and in so doing had prepared him to take a strong stand in its favour in America.

Two years later Reinagle was in Philadelphia, where on 21 September he appeared on the benefit programme of cellist Henri Capron at the City Tavern and on 12 October had his own benefit there. A comparison of the two programmes shows Reinagle's preference for the repertoire he knew in Edinburgh. His benefit was organised in the customary three acts, opening and closing with an overture by Haydn and including a concerto by Corelli in ancient style. That he named the composers is significant in marking him as the more experienced musician. In the eighteenth century, identification was vague at best. When only one name was listed it usually meant that the performer was playing his own music. Reinagle's use of the word 'of' before Haydn and Corelli is especially useful, for it implies that the others named were both performers and composers.[40]

Capron's Benefit		Reinagle's Benefit	
Part First		Act I	
Overture to the Deserter		Overture	of Haydn
Song		Song	Mr. Reinagle
Concerto Violoncello . .	Mr. Capron	Concerto Violoncello . .	Mr. Capron
Simphonia			
Concerto Violin	Mr. Juhan	Act II	
		Sonata Piano forte	Mr. Reinagle
		Concerto flute	Mr Brown
		Concerto	of Corelli
Part Second			
Overture to La Belle Arsiene		Act III	
Sonata Piano Forte	Mr. Reinagle	Sonata Piano Forte	Mr. Reinagle
Simphonia		Concerto Violin	Mr. Juhan
Concerto Flute	Mr. Brown	Overture	of Haydn
A Glee		Trio and Glee	

Exactly one week later, on 19 October 1786, the City Concert Series began under the management of Alexander Juhan, William Brown, Henri Capron and Alexander Reinagle – the same four musicians who had appeared on the benefit evenings. There had been subscription series in 1783–84 and 1784–85, managed by John Bentley, but no programmes have survived. As soon as Reinagle arrived he exerted his leadership capabilities, moving the concerts from the old Assembly Room to the newer City Tavern, the most elegant building of its kind in the city. More significant was the announcement made by the managers in the *Pennsyl-*

vania Packet on 16 October 1786: 'The Public may be assured that the greatest endeavors will be used to render every performance agreeable and satisfactory to the lovers of music. A new orchestra is erected, and the greatest care will be taken to make the room agreeable.'

In the passage just quoted the term 'orchestra' may refer either to a platform for the musicians or, as seems more likely, to the musicians themselves. If the latter, it is possible that what made the orchestra 'new' was the addition of instruments modelled on those used at EMS concerts.[41] Of the four directors Reinagle was the leading performer; all but two programmes carried his name. Nine out of twelve offered works by Haydn, and the series included pieces by Corelli and the earl of Kelly. When a comparison is made with EMS programmes, the similarities are obvious.

Edinburgh
Musical Society Plan[42]

Act I	
Overture, Op. 1	Abel
Song	
Overture to Esther	[Handel]
Act II	
Overture	Haydn
Song	
8 Concerto	Corelli
Act III	
Shaw's Concerto	Mr. Reinagle
Song	
Overture	Haydn, in D

Philadelphia
City Concert Plan[43]

Act I	
Overture	Vanhall
Duett, Violin and Violoncello	Breval
Concerto	Corelli
Act II	
Concerto, Violin	Pesch
Symphony	Stamitz
Sonata, Piano Forte and Violin	Reinagle
Act III	
Quartet	Kamel
Concerto, Flute	Mr. Brown
Symphony	Haydn

Both concerts are organised into three acts, offering works by Haydn as well as Corelli, thus giving a typical balance between ancient and modern music. The major difference is the absence of any songs in Philadelphia. The EMS had the funds to hire singers, but the managers of the City Concerts did not. In the next season, however, a song was put on the programme of each City Concert.

The City Concert Series of 1786–87, so clearly reflecting the influence of the EMS, did much to raise the level of Philadelphia's concert programmes. Indeed, that year's series is a landmark in the history of American music because all twelve programmes included a work for the pianoforte. This extensive use of the new keyboard instrument had not happened before in the United States. Reinagle had given Philadelphians a reason to be proud, and he owed a debt of gratitude to the EMS for encouraging his use of the pianoforte in 1784.

During the summer of 1787 Reinagle brought to the city's music lovers another side of his Scottish heritage. *The Pennsylvania Packet* printed this notice on 29 August 1787: 'NEW MUSIC, just composed, three dollars. A select *Collection of the Most Favorite Scots Tunes, with Variations for the Piano Forte or Harpsichord.* Composed by A. Reinagle, printed for the Author, and sold by T. Dobson and W. Young at their respective book-stores, Second Street.' What the notice did not explain was Reinagle's courage in having them 'printed for the Author'. That meant, of course, at his expense. The only other secular keyboard music known to have been published earlier in America was *Three Rondos* by Brown.[44] Reinagle had confidence in the appeal of the Scots tunes. His set of twenty-two with variations, composed in Glasgow, had seen two editions in 1782. The American edition was similar enough to raise expectations for equal success. In it Reinagle used two tunes not found in the earlier set, 'Laddie Lie Near Me' and 'Dainty Davie', and he wrote more intricate variations to 'Lee Rigg'. Eight of the tunes and variations are the same.[45]

These tunes exemplify many characteristics of Scottish folk music. 'Moss Plate' and 'Lee Rigg' feature scales that omit the fourth and seventh scale steps, known as 'gapping' scales. In 'Moss Plate' the lowered seventh is also used. 'East Nook of Fife' and 'Dainty Davie' modulate from the major mode to relative minor, and 'Steer Her Up and Had Her Gawn' illustrates possibly the most colorful characteristic of all, the use of the double tonic, where the tune starts in one key and soon introduces a melodic fragment in a key a whole step lower before shifting back to the original key, thus using two keys or tonics. These four musical characteristics are found often in Scottish folk music.

Apart from giving a feeling for the native music of Scotland, these tunes provided the keyboard player in America with the same kind of music enjoyed by Scottish fiddlers. They are examples of a trend prominent in the music of the Scottish Enlightenment – the combining of classical and folk traditions in the same piece. In the years between the British and American editions the piano was replacing the harpsichord in popularity, so Reinagle was wise to name it in the American title. He was also correct in thinking the music would sell easily in America. There was enough demand for a second edition, which changed only the title of one tune. 'Laddie Lie Near Me' became 'Over Hills and Dales'.[46]

Scottish influences brought over by Reinagle were undoubtedly strongest during the early years of his life in Philadelphia. After 1792 he, together with the actor Thomas Wignell, formed a stock company to build the New Theatre on Chestnut Street. It opened briefly on 2 February

1793 but after a week closed until 17 February 1794 while a yellow fever epidemic raged in the city. Reinagle continued to exert his leadership in musical affairs, but now by directing musical productions at his theatre. Of course, he sometimes put Scottish dances between the two plays of the evening or conducted a Scottish medley in the orchestra pit, but these touches of Scotland were slight.[47] Since nothing is known of any association he ever had with a theatre in Scotland, tracing Scottish influences in this connexion is impossible.

III

James Bremner and Alexander Reinagle brought much from Scotland to Philadelphia. Indeed, taken together the careers of these two Scottish immigrants reflect a very full picture of musical life and taste as they were carried across the Atlantic to America during the late eighteenth century. Both men had been involved with the EMS at times of change, not only in the society but also in the world of music generally. Bremner experienced the introduction of the Mannheim style of composition into Scotland by the earl of Kelly, who had studied with its leader. After the earl's return from Mannheim, the EMS concert repertoire was no longer dominated by works of Handel, Corelli and Vivaldi but included the music of Stamitz, Haydn and Kelly himself. Because of Bremner, Philadelphia was the first city in America to hear not only the works of Scotland's most noted composer, the earl of Kelly, but perhaps also Stamitz.

Reinagle reaped the benefit of the change Bremner had helped begin. The EMS concerts he heard in St Cecilia's Hall were planned with an emphasis on a balance between the old and new, and this balance he made a part of his own concert planning. For him the change was from use of the harpsichord exclusively to the gradual introduction of the pianoforte. Unlike Kelly, Reinagle did not stay in Scotland to enjoy the praise his performances and compositions would surely have earned. Instead, like Bremner, he emigrated to America and injected a new element into the musical life of Philadelphia, giving it the distinction of being the first American city to embrace the pianoforte.

NOTES

1. David Johnson, *Music and Society in Lowland Scotland in the Eighteenth Century* (London, 1972), 12–13.
2. Edward Topham, *Letters from Edinburgh, Written in the Years 1774 and 1775* (London, 1776), 378–79.
3. David Fraser Harris, *St. Cecilia's Hall in the Niddry Wynd*, 2nd ed. (Edinburgh, 1911), 290–99.

4. W. Forbes Gray, 'The Musical Society of Edinburgh', *Book of the Old Edinburgh Club* 19 (1933): 190.
5. EMSSB, 1:1–2. That the professionals were never members is clear from a list of members (3) and accounts showing that William McGibbon, Adam Craig and Alexander Stewart were paid £9.9 'for performing last winter session' (6). Not one of the three is on the member list, and this practice is consistent throughout the records.
6. Gray, 'Musical Society of Edinburgh', 199.
7. Harris, *St. Cecilia's Hall*, 122.
8. EMSSB, 2:79. It seems likely that 'Messrs. Bremner' were not father and son but rather two sons of Robert Bremner – Robert, Jr and James. Accounts for 1757 show a salary for both Robert and James (EMSSB, 2:82). When accounts twice mention 'Bremner's Boy' (EMSSB, 2:76), the identity is impossible to establish.
9. Gray, 'Musical Society of Edinburgh', 190.
10. Johnson, *Music and Society*, 68–84.
11. EMS Plan Books, 3 vols. (1768–71 and 1778–86), EUL, La.III.562–64. For example, Kelly's compositions were heard in twenty-two of the thirty-nine concerts presented in 1768.
12. Quoted in Oscar G. Sonneck, *Francis Hopkinson . . . and James Lyon . . .: Two Studies in Early American Music* (1905; rpt. New York, 1967), 27–28.
13. Ibid., 42.
14. Ibid., 45.
15. Oscar G. Sonneck, *Early Concert-Life in America (1731–1800)* (1907; rpt. New York, 1978), 66.
16. Johnson, *Music and Society*, 73.
17. Sonneck, *Early Concert-Life*, 67–68.
18. Ibid., 72–73.
19. Ibid., 262–63.
20. See the Preface to Hopkinson's *Seven Songs for the Forte Piano or Harpsichord*, ed. Maurice Hinson and Anne McClenny Krauss (Chapel Hill, N.C., 1987).
21. *Francis Hopkinson's Lessons*, facsimile ed. (Washington, D.C., 1979), 112, 114, 117, 119, 144.
22. Sonneck, *Francis Hopkinson*, 36.
23. Charles Humphries and William C. Smith, *Music Publishing in the British Isles* (Oxford, 1970), 83.
24. Quoted in Sonneck, *Francis Hopkinson*, 46.
25. Harris, *St. Cecilia's Hall*, 67, 79. That Alexander Reinagle's mother was Scottish can be demonstrated by his admission in 1794 to the St Andrew's Society of Philadelphia, which was restricted to native Scots and their descendants (the society's constitution and membership list are in the HSP). Also 'A Memoir of Baron Joseph von Reinagle and His Children', ed. I.M. Price (1889) – an unpublished and unpaginated manuscript in possession of the family – states that Joseph Reinagle's wife was the daughter of Hugh Laurie from 'Preston Pans'.
26. Harris, *St. Cecilia's Hall*, 76–77.
27. 'Treasury Books of North Britain', Scottish Record Office RH 2/4, vol. 466:238 – vol. 481:480.
28. Lawrence Oliphant Schetky, *The Schetky Family: A Compilation of*

Letters (Portland, Oreg., 1942), 48. For a more detailed review of the Reinagle family, see Anne McClenny Krauss, 'Alexander Reinagle: His Family Background and Early Professional Career', *American Music* 4 (1986): 425–29.

29. Hugo Arnot, *The History of Edinburgh* (Edinburgh, 1779), 379.
30. Harris, *St. Cecilia's Hall*, 122.
31. Johnson, *Music and Society*, 3.
32. Arnot, *History of Edinburgh*, 624.
33. Johnson, *Music and Society*, 140–41.
34. Ibid., 118.
35. For example, the third act of the EMS Friday concert in St Cecilia's Hall on 5 May 1784 included 'Concerto Solo, Mr. Schetky; Scots Song; Duetto; Overture of Lord Kelly with Tenore oblig^{o}' (EMS Plan Book, vol. 3).
36. *Glasgow Mercury*, 12 Nov. 1778.
37. Henry G. Farmer, 'Concerts in Eighteenth-Century Scotland', *Proceedings of the Royal Philosophical Society* 69 (1945): 111–12.
38. There were two London editions, ca. 1782: one printed for and sold by J. Aird in Glasgow (copy in the Farmer Collection, Glasgow University Library) and one 'printed for the Author' (copy in the NLS).
39. Arnot, *History of Edinburgh*, 380.
40. *Pennsylvania Packet*, 21 Sept. and 12 Oct. 1786
41. Arnot, *History of Edinburgh*, 380: 'The band consists of a *Maestro di capella*, an organist, two violins, two tenors [violas], six or eight *ripienos* [accompanying rather than solo instruments, usually strings], a double or *contra*-base, and harpsichord; and occasionally two French horns, besides kettle-drums, flutes, and clarinets.' 'The band' (the eighteenth-century term for orchestra) refers here to the instrumentalists who played in the EMS Friday concerts in St Cecilia's Hall.
42. EMS Plan Book, vol. 3, 30 Jan. 1784.
43. *Pennsylvania Packet*, 19 Oct. 1786.
44. Anne McClenny Krauss, 'The First Keyboard Pieces Published in America', *Piano Quarterly*, no. 130 (1985): 62.
45. Alexander Reinagle, *A Selection of the Most Favorite Scots Tunes, with Variations for the Piano Forte or Harpsichord* (Philadelphia, 1787).
46. A copy of the second edition, made from music belonging to Eleanor Parke Custis (Nelly), George Washington's adopted daughter, is in the Free Library of Philadelphia. Like the first edition, it was 'printed for the Author' in Philadelphia with no date.
47. Dunlap's Daily American Advertiser, 29 Mar. 1794.

16

CHARLES E. PETERSON

Robert Smith, Philadelphia Builder-Architect: From Dalkeith to Princeton

Robert Smith was the most important builder-architect in colonial America. He had appeared on the Philadelphia scene by early 1749 and quickly established himself as a member of the inner circle of the Carpenters' Company. From then until his death in 1777 Smith designed, and often built, a substantial number of major edifices from Virginia to Rhode Island. These included private homes, such as the mansion he built for Benjamin Franklin in the mid-1760s; churches, such as the Second and Third Presbyterian, St Peter's, St Paul's, Zion and the steeple at Christ Church he designed and/or built in Philadelphia between 1749 and 1777; public institutions, such as the east wing of the Pennsylvania Hospital he designed in 1755–56, the Williamsburg, Virginia, madhouse he planned in 1770 and the huge, fireproof Walnut Street Prison he designed and built in 1773–74; and even public fortifications, such as the system of Delaware River obstructions he laid out in 1775 in collaboration with Benjamin Franklin. The central buildings at three major colonial colleges – now Princeton, Brown and the University of Pennsylvania – all bore the marks of his skill and vision. Though building projects like these sometimes took him far from home, Philadelphia remained the centre of Smith's personal and professional life. It is therefore fitting that one of his great buildings, Carpenters' Hall (designed 1768; built 1770–74), stands today as a tribute to Smith and the master carpenters of early Philadelphia[1] and is the scene every January of a celebration in honour of his birthday.

Yet it was not always so. Though it is clear that Robert Smith was well known and respected in his own day, for the better part of the past two centuries his name faded into obscurity. No doubt this neglect was partly owing to the very thin paper-trail that remains. His drawings survived him but disappeared long ago,[2] and his correspondence is almost totally lost. Smith published nothing. There is no known portrait or description of his appearance. Until recently even his place of birth and family background were a mystery. It was sometimes said that Smith was a native of Glasgow, but nothing more was known of the matter, and commentators on Scottish-American affairs showed no interest. Smith was in danger of becoming a mere footnote to the colonial histories of American architecture and the city of Philadelphia.[3]

Several of his important buildings remained stubbornly in view, however, and from surviving institutional records and private papers it has been possible to reconstruct a long list of projects with which Smith was associated, as well as a few details about his life. Having been engaged in this process of reconstruction for more than forty years, I am painfully aware that the record is far from complete. But much ground has been gained.[4] In some cases it is now possible to determine not only which buildings Smith worked on but also how and when he did so. It is also possible to reconstruct some of the Scottish background that prepared him for a successful career as a builder-architect in colonial America. The present study marks a beginning along these lines. Part I presents the little that is known with certainty about Smith's background in Scotland and discusses the sort of training he could have received there. Part II concentrates on the first five major projects of Smith's career as a builder-architect in Philadelphia: the Second Presbyterian Church; Bush Hill mansion; the New College, Academy, and Charity School of Philadelphia; Christ Church Steeple; and Nassau Hall at the College of New Jersey in Princeton.

I

The Dalkeith parish registers reveal that Robert Smith was born on 14 January 1722 to John Smith, a baxter (baker) in the nearby hamlet of Lugton, and his wife Martha Lawrie.[5] Correspondence from Franklin's printing partner David Hall to the Edinburgh booksellers Hamilton and Balfour shows that by the 1760s Smith was sending money from America to his widowed mother, who still lived in Lugton.[6] These bits of information constitute the only firm facts now known about Smith's Scottish background. Yet from this meagre information it is possible to speculate constructively about Smith's early years. Geographically, he lived just eight miles from Edinburgh, Scotland's cultural and architectural capital. His particular region was dominated by the powerful dukes of Buccleuch, whose grand house, Dalkeith Palace, featured a fine Palladian front built by James Smith (ca. 1645–1731), a possible relation. Chronologically, Robert Smith was almost contemporary with John Witherspoon (1723–94) as well as with William Robertson (1721–93), Adam Smith (1723–90) and many other leading lights of the Scottish Enlightenment. Both Robertson and his cousin John Adam (1721–92), eldest of the distinguished Adam brothers, who followed their father William into the architectural pro-

Figure 1. St Mary's Chapel, Edinburgh. When the Incorporation of Masons and Wrights remodelled the front of its old headquarters on Niddry's Wynd, it featured an elegant 'Palladian' window designed by John Yates, wright. In 1737 he was paid three guineas 'for drawing the draught of the Chappel Gavel [Gable] but also in overseeing the workmen'.

Candidates for membership in that ancient craft guild were required to produce 'essays' – designs incorporating the architectural 'orders', as delineated in Palladio's books – to prove their professional competence. [Engraving from William Maitland, *The History of Edinburgh* (Edinburgh, 1753)] fession, attended Dalkeith Grammar School during the late 1720s and early 1730s, and it is quite possible that Smith was known to them. In the 1740s the Adam firm did some work for the duchess of Buccleuch around Dalkeith Palace. It is not known if Smith was ever taken into the Adam organisation, but that firm remains one possible source of his architectural training.

There are several other possibilities as to where he learned his craft. He might have been apprenticed in Dalkeith itself, where the carpenters or wrights formed part of the local incorporation of hammermen. He might have gone off to London to learn his trade, as did the architect Robert Mylne a decade later. Another possibility is that he served an apprenticeship in the Glasgow area and sailed to America from there: an alternative that could help to explain the nineteenth-century claim that Smith was a Glasgow native.[7] Or perhaps he joined the building trades as an apprentice in Edinburgh, though his name has been located neither on the list of organised wrights in the Canongate (embracing the lower part of the old city) nor among the records of the masons and wrights in the upper part of Edinburgh, who were incorporated jointly into a guild known as St Mary's Chapel (fig. 1).

Even though a connexion with St Mary's Chapel cannot be proved, that incorporation's remarkable manuscript minutes, now located in the Edinburgh City Archives, are of great value for understanding how a Scotsman just twenty-seven years old, trained and qualified in the old country, could have found ready acceptance as a designer in Philadelphia. There were, of course, no formal architectural schools in the eighteenth century. But the records of St Mary's Chapel, which are probably typical of builders' incorporations all over Scotland, reveal a qualifying procedure that ensured a high degree of preparation and competence. To attain the independent status of 'wright burgess' and the privilege of practicing his trade, an aspiring candidate had to prove his skill by undertaking 'essays' or examinations.[8] Besides samples of shop work, each candidate was required to make drawings incorporating the classical orders – Doric, Ionic or Corinthian, as the case might be – in the presence of 'essay-masters' appointed for the occasion. In every instance except one, the style of Palladio was specified.

Some examples from the incorporation's records illustrate these points. On 2 July 1709 the following minute was recorded regarding one William Ritchie, who had presented his petition to be qualified after serving an apprenticeship with a wright burgess: 'The house ordained him to make for his essay ane press [cupboard] of the Corinthian order Conform to paladoe [Palladio] pedestall way, with base & subase with four Lids of raist work of this Timber itself angled in the joynts from poynt to poynt and to draw the draught of his Essay befor the Deacons masters & essay masters And to put on the iron work himself.' In 1712 James Mack, mason, was assigned the drawing of two floor plans for a double house 36' x 60', no particular style specified, in the presence of the deacon and masters. The following examples from 1736, to be done in a style 'after Palladio', involved boys of approximately the same age as Smith:

1 January: James Scott, 'the Corinthian Order'
14 February: John Hume, 'the dorrich order'
14 February: Hugh Inglis, 'the Ionick order'
3 September: Thomas Short, 'the Ionick order'

This examination procedure, involving drawings made under close supervision, continued well into the second half of the eighteenth century. It reveals the unexpected extent to which the ideas of the Enlightenment permeated even the lower ranks of Scottish society, for in order to be a master carpenter in Edinburgh one had to have not only craft skill but some knowledge of classical design. If this system of training carpenters was indeed typical of organised wrights throughout Scotland,[9] it helps to explain how a young Scottish carpenter could have become competent to contribute to architectural advancement in America the moment he arrived there.

II

It is not known exactly how or when, let alone why, Robert Smith went to America. One likely possibility, however, is that Pennsylvania's lieutenant governor James Hamilton (1710–83) picked him up when Hamilton was in Britain during the 1740s to lobby for his appointment to Pennsylvania's proprietary government. The influential third duke of Argyll was cognizant of such appointments and could have introduced Smith to Hamilton. Argyll had a patron's eye for talent in a multitude of areas, including architecture, and he patronised a number of Smiths and Hamiltons in the Edinburgh vicinity. If not Argyll, perhaps another well-placed Scot brought Robert Smith to the attention of James Hamilton, who was well enough connected in Edinburgh to be granted membership in the 'old Revolution Club' by special diploma.[10] In any event, when Hamilton got his commission and returned to Philadelphia, arriving there on 23 November 1748,[11] Robert Smith turned up around the same time and was soon at work remodelling Hamilton's Bush Hill mansion. The fact that in his 1749 Bush Hill accounts Hamilton referred to Smith as 'my architect' certainly suggests a close association.

Yet Bush Hill was not Robert Smith's first American commission. That honour belongs to Philadelphia's Second Presbyterian Church on Arch Street. The congregation of that church had been born in controversy. In 1741, as a result of the general religious ferment of the 'Great Awakening', the 'New Side' or evangelical faction of the Presbyterian Church had been expelled from the main body, which continued to occupy the public meeting house on Market Street.[12] The Revd Gilbert Tennent was called to lead the dissident congregation. By the beginning of 1749 it was meeting temporarily in the so-called 'New Building' that had recently been erected for use by itinerant preachers of all denominations. But on 25 January an ad hoc committee was established to buy lots on which to erect a permanent church and a burial ground.

In just two weeks the purchase was reported of a site in the northern section of the city, described as a lot 98' 6'' on Arch Street and 80' on Third Street.[13] A committee of eighteen was then appointed as a body of trustees, charged with the responsibility to 'consult about, the General Form & Plan of the said Presbyterian Church, or Meeting House, now to be erected, upon the Lot of Ground aforsd.', decide 'who shall be the Head Workmen to build the Same', and appoint a smaller committee to oversee the project. Further, Thomas Bourne and William Shippen 'were desired to enquire about Materials, & Workmen for said House, by the next meeting of the Trustees'. Note that there is no mention here of the need for an 'architect'. That professional designation probably was not understood in Philadelphia at the time, except perhaps as translated by classical scholars. American communities relied on 'house carpenters' for building plans. Laymen seem to have taken building designs casually, so that the names of early American designers are rarely known today.

A key figure among the New Side Presbyterians of Philadelphia was Dr William Shippen, who kept an apothecary shop on Market Street.[14] He became an enthusiastic supporter of the famous itinerant preacher George Whitefield and, somewhat later, of the New Side College of New Jersey at Princeton. Shippen was busy at every stage of the church building committee's activities. He and Thomas Bourne carried out their assignment promptly, and the names of two young house carpenters were soon proposed: Gunning Bedford, a merchant's son originally from New Castle, Delaware, and Robert Smith. Bedford and Smith had evidently prepared plans in advance, making it possible for the committee to decide on detailed dimensions. Drawings were probably on the table at the meeting of 9 February, when

> it was agreed that the New Presbyterian Church aforesaid shall be built in the following Form, that is to say the Front upon Arch Street shall be eighty Feet Long & the Front or End upon Third Street, shall [be] Sixty Feet long, & shall be placed eight Feet back from the Arch Street, & six Feet back from Third Street, & that the Stone Work for the Foundat. shall be carried six Inches higher than the Regulation of the pavement at the North East Corner, & from thence levell'd towards Arch Street. That The Elevation of the Brick Work from the Top of the Foundation, to the Eves, shall be about Thirty

Figure 2. Second Presbyterian Church, Philadelphia. Robert Smith, in partnership with another house carpenter, Gunning Bedford, was awarded the construction of the New Side meeting house in February 1749. It is his first known commission in America. Here shown is the main block of the brick structure, as enlarged in 1809. A tall tower/steeple had been built and removed in the meantime. [Lithograph by W.L. Breton, 1830 (Courtesy HSP)]

> three, or thirty four Feet: That the South Front shall have two Doors made Pediment wise, & two arched Windows, equally disposed, between the Doors in the first Story; & four Windows in the Upper Story. That the East Front shall have an Arch'd door in the middle, & one Window on each Side the Door, & the North, or back Front have two Windows in each Story; & the same in the West End of the House. That the Roof of the said House shall be made with strait Rafters not Hipt. (fig. 2)

The arrangements for dealing with the carpenters were then spelled out with an unusual degree of detail:

> It is also agreed that the Managers hereafter named shall apply to Messrs. Smith & Bedford, to undertake the Carpenters Work of the said House, & agree with Them if they can, upon the following Terms, vizt. that when the Work is finished, it shall be valued by persons indifferently chosen on both Sides, & they shall be paid for it according to Valluation;[15] Unless the parties agree about the price of it among Themselves: & also that all such Carpenters as have

> subscribed to the House shall be employed by them in proportion to their Subscriptions & Merit.

It was also agreed that John Palmer, a leading Philadelphia builder, should be invited to do 'the Masons & Bricklayers Work upon the usual Terms'.

On 31 May 1750 the foundations were begun. In Philadelphia the building materials were ordinarily collected at the site in advance and the roofs framed and shingled before the first winter. In this case the floors, windows and doors and the interior finish were probably begun during the building season of 1751. On 5 December of that year the trustees met and agreed to a plan for selling the pews, and the following day Gilbert Tennent held a service in the new church. But the structure was not yet completely fitted out, for in June the congregation met and voted to build galleries.

At the appraised figure of £1500, the Second Presbyterian Church was a notable addition to colonial Philadelphia. A dozen years later Gunning Bedford 'surveyed' the church for fire insurance and described its features in carpenters' terms: '94 pews Below, A Galery and 40 pews therein – the frunt of Galery ornemented with the dorick intabliture Supported with 14 fluted Cullumns – a pulpitt and Circuler pew Rownd it – A Large publick pew and Canipy supported By 2 fluted Cullems – & a board Newel Stair – out Side of house, frunt of Galery, pulpitt, & Large publick pew painted – Roof 12 years old'.[16] A more detailed description of the interior arrangements was later provided by Samuel Hazard:

> In this building the pulpit was on the north side, with the pews facing it. The main door entered from Third Street, with an aisle across to the steeple-door at the west end. After some years the pews in the centre were built, filling up that portion of the east and west aisle. The pews were one hundred and four in number, of which thirty-nine were square pews, chiefly around the walls of the church. Opposite the pulpit, on the south side, was a large square pew with columns, designed for the use of the Governor and other public men who attended service. . . . It is not recollected whether stoves were in use at this early day in this church, but it is believed that two small ones were in use, which, not making the church very comfortable, the ladies were in the habit of having foot-stoves brought to church to keep their feet warm. These were small square boxes made of wood and tin, perforated with holes, in which was placed a small vessel containing hot coals.[17]

It seems that a steeple had been contemplated all along. The minutes of a meeting of the congregation for 9 April 1753 note that the committee chosen to regulate the pews was also directed to 'manage the Affair of the Steeple'. A public lottery was proposed to raise the £850 needed for that

Figure 3. Bush Hill. Before work began on the second Presbyterian Church Robert Smith was busy with the upgrading of Bush Hill Mansion, the newly inherited suburban house of Lieutenant Governor James Hamilton. Years later, stripped of its elegant landscape features (and probably of its rich furnishings), the house was drawn and engraved by James P. Malcolm for the *Universal Magazine* of December 1787.

purpose.[18] In the meantime the steeple on the Anglican Christ Church was under construction, and that may have stimulated the Arch Street Presbyterians. By the summer of 1754 two trustees were authorised to proceed with the 'Brick & stone Work of the Ste[eple]', though the following week it was necessary to borrow £700 on interest to 'carry on The Design of the Steeple'. The project dragged on for some years, during which Smith's name is not mentioned in the minutes. On 17 September 1761, however, another committee was appointed 'to wait on Robert Smith Carpenter for a plan for the Steeple & to know upon what Terms he will undertake & finish the Same'. This is the first time in the records that Smith was explicitly named as a designer.

We do not know precisely when the Arch Street steeple was completed. But even before it was built it graced the skyline of the panoramic view of Philadelphia, probably delineated from an architectural elevation now lost. The only view dating from after completion is a distant and somewhat dim rendering in the well-known engraved view down Arch Street by William Birch, dating from 1799. In the 1760s Thomas Nevell recorded expenditures for 'carved work on the clock' and other decorative touches on the steeple.[19] But Philadelphia carpenters lacked the expertise that made possible the New England church builders' ubiquitous, heaven-seeking steeples. Those on the Philadelphia State House and even Christ Church soon developed serious structural problems, and some time before 1809 the Arch Street steeple (like the State House one) was torn down, never to be replaced. The rest of the Second Presbyterian Church became redundant soon after and was finally removed in 1837–38.[20]

After plans had been approved for the Second Presbyterian Church, but before construction started, Robert Smith began work on the job of remodelling Bush Hill for Governor Hamilton. Bush Hill was still a new house, having been built in 1740 by Hamilton's famous father Andrew (d. 1741) on land he had acquired from the Penn family on the Springetsbury estate northwest of the city (fig. 3). Like his father, who had promoted and overseen the original building of the Pennsylvania State House (afterwards Independence Hall), James Hamilton was deeply interested in architecture and building. As mayor of Philadelphia in 1746, he presented the city treasurer with the handsome gift of £150 towards 'the erection of a city-hall and courthouse' instead of giving the customary large and expensive public dinner.[21] A collector of paintings and sculpture, Hamilton helped to subsidise the young Pennsylvania painter Benjamin West's travels abroad and contributed generously to building subscriptions at home. Thomas Lawrence described Hamilton as 'one of the most civilized young gentlemen bred in this part of the world'.[22] It would therefore have been quite in character for Hamilton to have recruited Robert Smith from Scotland for the purpose of introducing the latest British design fashions into his Philadelphia home.

Hamilton's cash book for 29 June 1749 contains a reference to a substantial payment of £30 to 'Robert Smith my Carpenter'.[23] The next month Hamilton wrote to London merchant David Barclay that 'I am about to alter my house at Bush Hill with an intent to reside there'. There followed a list of articles to be sent by the next available ship, including 250 squares of glass 12–1/4 by 8–1/2, 'two tables of Glass whole for two circular windows', 3 house bells, and many hinges and screws.[24] The renovation must have been impressive. Yankee preacher Ezra Stiles, later president of Yale University, visited the site with William Shippen on 30 September 1754 and recorded this account:

> We walkt to Govr. Hamilton's seat. Took a walk in his very elegant garden, in which are 7 statues in fine Italian marble curiously wrot; invited into his house; viewed the very splendid & grand apartments magnificently decorated & adorned with curious paintings, hangings, & statuary, & marble tablets, etc. After viewing these curious prospects we passed by the Centre House & returned into town.[25]

This is, unfortunately, the only known description of what must have been a local wonder. Clearly, Robert Smith was making a start near the top of the architectural ladder.

Figure 4. The College, Academy and Charitable School of Philadelphia. The large meeting house (left, originally built 1740–42) was divided and remodelled by Robert Smith in the 1750s. The multipurpose row to the right (newly constructed in the 1760s) and the Provost's House (further to the right, 1771, but not shown here) were built from Smith's plans. Later in the century the institution evolved into the University of Pennsylvania, which remained on the site for another century. [Undated pencil sketch by Pierre Eugéne du Simitière (Courtesy the Library Company of Philadelphia)]

He did not have long to wait for his next commission. A short distance west of the Second Presbyterian Church, on the south side of Arch Street between Fourth Street and the Christ Church burial ground, stood another product of the Great Awakening, the previously mentioned 'New Building'. A large 'tabernackle' built in 1740 to accommodate the great crowds of zealous worshippers, it was soon to be remodelled for educational functions and eventually evolved into the College of Philadelphia and, still later, the University of Pennsylvania. Robert Smith served as architect for both the remodelling and the new construction that followed.

On 1 February 1750 the trustees of the Academy of Philadelphia bought the property with a loan of £800.[26] They opened a school in a private house until the new structure could be properly fitted up. The existing New Building, at 70' by 100', was one of the largest structures in the colony; larger even than the main block of the State House and comparable in size to parliament's ancient Westminster Hall in London (fig. 4, left). On 6 February the remodelling was placed in the hands of Robert Smith.[27] Because Benjamin Franklin was chairman of the building committee, there began a long association between these two men that would include the construction of Franklin's own house and close collaboration on plans for the defence of Philadelphia in the period of the Revolution.

The huge interior of the New Building was then divided into two floors. Franklin described the upper story as 'A large Hall for occasional Preaching, publick Lectures, Orations, etc., it is 70 foot by 60, furnish'd with a handsome Pulpit, Seats, etc.'[28] In keeping with the arrangement agreed upon in the terms of purchase, the ground floor space was divided into four large classrooms for the Academy's teaching divisions – Latin, English, mathematics – and the Charity School. Improvements were made in the school yard to correct drainage problems, and the yard was expanded southwards by the purchase of more lots. A wooden fence was added along the west line to protect the Christ Church cemetery.[29] The eventual cost of the improvements was over £598, more than twice the original estimate.[30]

On 10 June 1755 a committee consisting of the president and others, including Governor Hamilton and Dr William Shippen, was 'desired to confer with Mr. Robert Smith, House-Carpenter, concerning the Alterations necessary to be made in the Hall, and to obtain a Plan and Estimate'. Three weeks later the committee produced 'a Memorandum of the several Things proposed to be done with an Estimate of the Charge thereof'. These included:

> A Gallery along three sides of the Hall finished like those of M^r. Tenent's Building, the Front painted, and under side of the Joice plaistered without any Pews made, but the Bottoms or Floors levelled.
>
> A Platform for accommodating the Trustees the Masters, Candidates for Degrees, and Strangers of Distinction, on publick Occasions according to plan annexed.
>
> Eight large circular Windows, and six Square Ditto, Cases, Sashes, Glass and Painting; and the sashes to be all hung.
>
> Plaistering the Partition Wall and Scaffolding for Ditto.
>
> Amounting in the whole, to Four hundred and forty three Pounds, all Materials and Workmanship of every kind included; And also three back Window-Shutters, and Bricking and stopping up the other windows, and painting the Pews on the Platform.[31]

Though the college had to be supported in part by public lotteries and though it was often rocked by personal and public rivalries, it continued to grow. On 26 November 1761 a special committee was appointed to make arrangements for constructing a new building. Two days later a general plan of Smith's was approved, and it was decided to put half of it under construction. This new unit, according to the trustees' minutes in the University of Pennsylvania archives, was '70 feet long by 30 feet wide and will have on the Ground Floor two Charity Schools, with a Kitchen and Dining Room, and in the upper Stories Sixteen Lodging Rooms, with cellar beneath the whole, which by an Estimate given to us may be executed for £1500'. It was largely built during the next year and was occupied on 8 February 1763 (fig. 4, right).[32] In September of that year Smith was asked to provide a fence for the new wood yard and to repair the enclosure along the street in front of the 'Academy Square'.

Apparently this work was soon completed, though payments for it dragged on – even to the year 1768, when the trustees thought 'the whole should be valued by two indifferent men, to be chosen by Him [Smith] and the Trustees'.

Robert Smith's last job on 'Academy Square' was a house for Provost William Smith at the corner of Fourth and Arch Streets. According to the trustees' minutes of 21 December 1773, the provost wanted to be 'at least nearly on an equal Footing with Gentlemen in the like Stations in the neighboring seminaries'. He spoke of the expense of providing for a growing family and of the need to live close to the school 'to have it immediately under my Eye'. On 22 February 1774 a committee was appointed to get a plan and estimate, and on 15 March these were presented. Robert Smith's detailed specifications have been preserved with the minutes, though the accompanying plan has been lost. By 19 March 1776 William Smith was in his house, which had two large rooms and a study on the ground floor, two upper floors with a finished garret above, an outdoor kitchen, a cellar, a yard and a fence. He did not stay there long, since his refusal to endorse the Revolution led to his imprisonment in 1777 and removal as provost in 1779. But the house Robert Smith designed for him survived, stripped of interiors, until the 1950s, when it was demolished by the Philadelphia Redevelopment Authority and replaced by the present Holiday Inn.

The earliest identified work of Robert Smith still standing is the steeple of Christ Church, which was, until the advent of modern skyscrapers, a dominant feature of the Philadelphia skyline (figs. 5 and 6). The main mass of Christ Church had been erected on North Second Street in the years 1727–44 from plans by an unknown designer.[33] From the outset a steeple had been contemplated, and as early as 1727 foundations were laid for such a structure at the west end.[34] When the body of the church was complete the vestry was reminded 'that it is the zealous inclination of very many inhabitants of this City to Contribute Handsome Sums of Money towards building a tower or Steeple for Holding a ring of Bells'.[35] Two years later a plan by a 'Mr. Harrison' was adopted (2 June 1746), but nothing is known to have come of it. As late as 28 October 1750 Richard Peters advised Proprietor Penn in England that the view of Philadelphia the latter had requested was hardly worth painting 'for want of steeples' on the skyline.[36]

In the race to put up Philadelphia's first steeple, Christ Church began its subscription list on 11 March 1750, three weeks before construction started on the steeple at the State House. But not until the following April were the managers of the building programme asked to proceed. From there on we are fortunate to have more or less connected and comprehensive building records, thanks in part to a little paperbound manuscript,

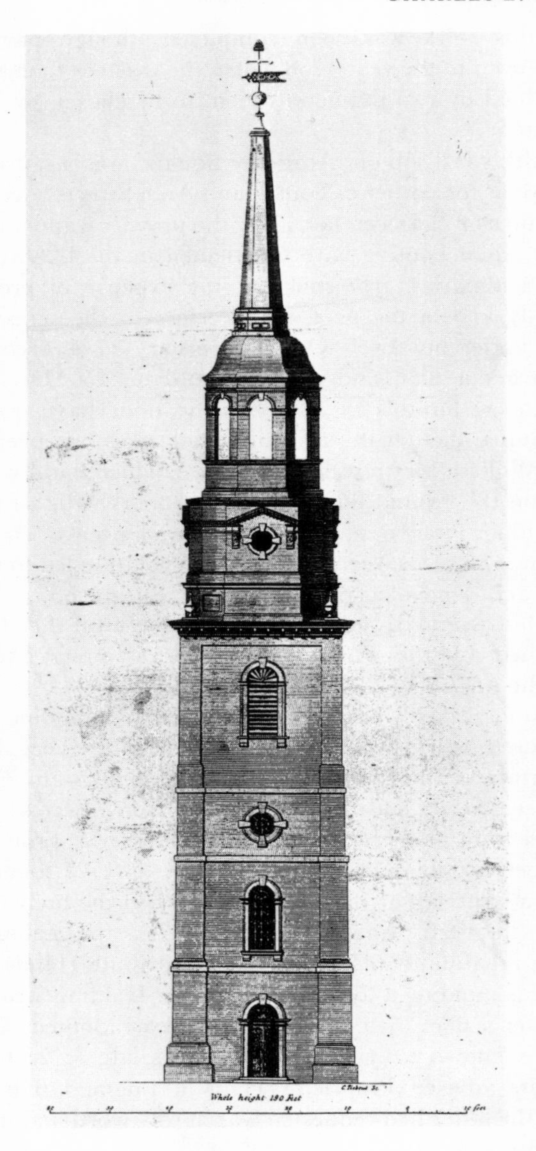

Figures 5 and 6. Christ Church Tower and Steeple. The original drawings from which the church was built have long been lost. The designer and date of construction of the tower (stone masonry veneered with brick) are not certain. Of the wooden steeple built by Robert Smith from his own designs in 1757 there is detailed record. It seems to have been derived from William Adam's design for George Gordon's Hospital in Aberdeen, never built but illustrated in William Adam's *Vitruvius Scoticus*.

Fig. 5. Plate 44 in *The Young Carpenter's Assistant* (Philadelphia, 1805) by Owen Biddle, 'Housecarpenter and Teacher of Architectural Drawing' and a member of the Carpenters' Company.

Fig. 6. Measured drawing by William Reimer, 1897, from *The Georgian Period*, ed. William Rotch Ware (New York, 1898), pt.2, plate 42. Robert Smith's steeple dominates the original block of the church begun a generation earlier.

neatly copied out in a professional hand and titled on the cover 'The Steeple Account'. It records the procurement of materials, including stone for the foundations of the tower,[37] lime and sand for mortar, poles for scaffolding and even rum for the riverboat crews that transported the stone. The bricklaying was handled by John Palmer, whose payments ran from July 1751 through May 1752. Vestry minutes tell of the usual financial problems: in October 1752 it was necessary to hold a lottery to raise funds for paying the tradesmen, with Benjamin Franklin, that reliable champion of civic progress, enlisted as a committeeman. The following February a 'Supplement' to the lottery was mounted to bring in additional funds for a set of bells from London.

A year later Robert Smith was at work on Christ Church steeple. He was possibly introduced there by the bricklayer John Palmer, with whom he had worked both at the Second Presbyterian Church and at Bush Hill. Actual work on the steeple began in the spring of 1753, when poles and spars were bought.[38] There followed a large order for cedar lumber and recapping of the brickwork on which the frame would be seated. Progress was fast. The basic frame, much of it undoubtedly prefabricated on the ground, was up by 11 July, when a cash distribution of 15 shillings was made to the carpenters. There were other payments in September and October, and by 30 October there was a celebration for 'raising the Spindle' of the weathervane. Smith received the last of eighteen payments on 19 December 1754, bringing his total to the very substantial sum of £396. On 7 January 1755 the *Pennsylvania Gazette* published a summary of the steeple's expenses, the magnitude of which must have astounded contemporaries. On 24 April the same paper reported, with obvious civic pride, on the church's great English bells, which had just been rung in honour of three provincial governors:

> The musical peal was cast by Lester and Pack, who are at present the most noted and ingenious artists of that kind in England. They were hung by Nicholas Nicholson, a native of Yorkshire, in a manner the most convenient and entirely new. And when a clock for the chimes is added, which he seems very desirous of, they will be the compleatest sett in America.

Christ Church steeple is today Robert Smith's greatest monument. It seems to have been generally admired by contemporaries also, certainly

Figure 7. Robert Smith's Own Vitruvius Britannicus. Smith's personal effects, inventoried after his death in 1777, included 'Sundry Books of Architecture' and drawing instruments valued at £23.16.6. Three volumes of Colen Campbell's popular work *Vitruvius Britannicus* are preserved in the Carpenters' Company library today. Volume 3 (1725) bears Smith's signature in ink on the title page; 1756 is presumably the date of purchase. [Courtesy the Carpenters' Company of the City and County of Philadelphia]

THE

THIRD VOLUME

OF

Vitruvius Britannicus:

OR, THE

BRITISH ARCHITECT.

CONTAINING

The *Geometrical* PLANS of the moſt Conſiderable *GARDENS* and *PLANTATIONS*; alſo the PLANS, ELEVATIONS, and SECTIONS of the moſt *Regular* BUILDINGS, not Publiſhed in the *Firſt and Second Volumes*. With *Large* VIEWS, in *Perſpective*, of the moſt Remarkable *Edifices* in *Great Britain*.

Engraven by the Beſt Hands *in* One Hundred *large Folio* PLATES.

By *COLEN CAMPBELL*, Eſquire,
Architect to His ROYAL HIGHNESS *the* PRINCE *of* WALES.

VITRUVIUS BRITANNICUS:

OU,

L'Architecte Britannique:

CONTENANT

Les *PLANS* des *JARDINS* les Plus Conſiderables, Auſſi les PLANS, ELEVATIONS, & SECTIONS des BATIMENS *Reguliers*, ne ſont pas encore publies dans les *Deux Premiers Tomes*. Avec quelques VEUES, en *Perſpective*, des *Maſons* les plus *Celebres* de la *Grande Bretagne*.

Compris en 100 *grandes* Planches *gravez en taille douce par les* plus habiles Maitres.

Par Le Sieur *CAMPBELL*,
Architecte de Son ALTESSE ROYALE *Le* PRINCE *de* GALLES.

TOME III.

CUM PRIVILEGIO REGIS.

LONDON,
Printed; And Sold by the AUTHOR, at his Houſe in *Middle Scotland-Yard*, *White-Hall*; And by JOSEPH SMITH, at the Sign of *Inigo Jones*'s Head, near *Exeter-Change*, in the *Strand*. M.DCC.XXV.

more than its rival on the State House. In 1805 Owen Biddle, a later member of the Carpenters' Company, published in his *Young Carpenters' Assistant: or, A System of Architecture Adapted to the Style of Building in the United States* a carefully engraved plate (fig. 5), along with a tribute to Robert Smith for his work on Christ Church steeple: 'For the justness of its proportions, simplicity and symmetry of its parts is allowed by good judges to be equal if not superior in beauty to any Steeple of the spire kind, either in Europe or America'. Biddle noted further:

> The superstructure of this steeple is composed of three distinct well-proportioned parts of Architecture, the first story, with its small Pediments and Attics, forming one; the octagonal part, with its ogee formed dome, being the second; and the spire and its pedestal, the third. These three parts are very dissimilar, no one having any thing in it that is common to the others; and yet they agree very well with each other, forming one complete and consistent whole.(56).

Biddle's plate notes that the total height is 190 feet.

The design of Christ Church steeple can be traced to William Adam's fine collection of engraved plates titled *Vitruvius Scoticus*, in the elevation for Robert Gordon's Hospital in St Andrew's Street, Aberdeen (unnumbered plate following no. 107). The hospital was actually built in 1730–32, but without its planned steeple. Even though the collection was not published in book form until 1812, the engraving of the plates (from Scottish designs mostly by Adam himself) had begun about 1727, with the printing of sheets in 1746 or shortly afterwards.[39] It seems likely that Robert Smith brought with him to America some of the plates long before they were bound in volumes. As noted earlier, a personal association between Smith and the Adam clan of architects may have existed in Scotland during the 1730s or 1740s. Moreover, Smith's use of William Adam's work demonstrates the extent of Scottish architectural influence in Philadelphia and colonial America generally.[40]

For all its handsome appearance, the proud new steeple was in deep trouble almost immediately. Concern for possible damage from weather in a vestry minute of 22 November 1756 had by 2 June 1762 turned into an order that the steeple 'be immediately repaired and painted'. Nothing was done, however, and by the spring of 1771 the situation was alarming. Robert Smith was called back on 7 May of that year. He found the wood sills on top of the brick tower decayed and the shingle walls leaking. He asked that some of the brickwork be removed for closer inspection. The vestry pressed him for his attendance at the site, and he reluctantly consented to undertake the repair work by 1 July. A week later members of the vestry who climbed the scaffold with the architect were appalled to see 'the Ends of the great Timbers so rotten as to be a mere Powder, and the other Parts likewise very much decayed'. As the repair work proceeded, Smith wrote that he 'shud. be pleased to see some of the Vestry now and then at the Steeple to see how we go on. I have a very difficult piece of Business. I think it is more so than any I Ever had before'. By 14 October it was all over but the painting, and when that was done Smith reported that the steeple was 'as strong as it Ever was'. In November 1772 the repair expenses of £644 caused a financial crisis in the church's affairs. If the problems that forced Christ Church to make such large, unanticipated expenditures were mostly attributable to Smith's inexperience in steeple design and construction, it says a great deal for his contemporary reputation that he was called back to make the necessary repairs, and a great deal for his skill that he succeeded in doing so.

Smith's reluctance to undertake the repair of Christ Church steeple may have been caused in part by his desire to get on with a new project: the building of what is now called Nassau Hall at the College of New Jersey in Princeton.[41] The college had been chartered in 1746 to educate New Side Presbyterian ministers, with some accommodation for lay students, too. After several years of uncertainty about its permanent location, it finally settled in at Princeton, then a village of some sixty houses halfway along the main highway between New York and Philadelphia. From the beginning the college owed much to Philadelphians and to the prominent Shippen family in particular. By 1753 Dr William Shippen, the apothecary whom we have already met at the Second Presbyterian Church, had worked out plans for the college with Robert Smith.[42] The preliminary financing took time to arrange, but by 22 July 1754 a building committee had been appointed and the architectural plan approved. The minutes state: 'That the Plan drawn by Doct^{r}. Shippen & Mr Robert Smith be in general the Plan of the College. That the College be . . . three Story high & without any Cellar'. It was further agreed that the structure should be of brick 'if good Brick can be made at Princeton & if Sand can be got reasonably cheap'.[43]

The project moved quickly at first: just a week after the plan was approved, Joseph Morrow 'set a man first to begin to Dig ye Colledge Cellar'.[44] The cornerstone was laid on 17 September 1754, with local notables in attendance.[45] Meanwhile, the Revd Samuel Davies of Virginia and the Revd Gilbert Tennent of Philadelphia were in Scotland raising money for the college. Perhaps because of uncertainty about funding or perhaps because his growing practice and repairs to Christ Church steeple kept him in Philadelphia, Robert Smith did not immediately settle in Princeton. As late as 28 October 1754 Aaron Burr, the president of the college, noted that stonemason William Worth was on the site but pleaded for 'a man to oversee the work *de die in diem*'.[46] The whole project probably lay dormant over the next winter. On the following 27 May, however, Robert Smith acknowledged by the hand of John Stockton the sum of

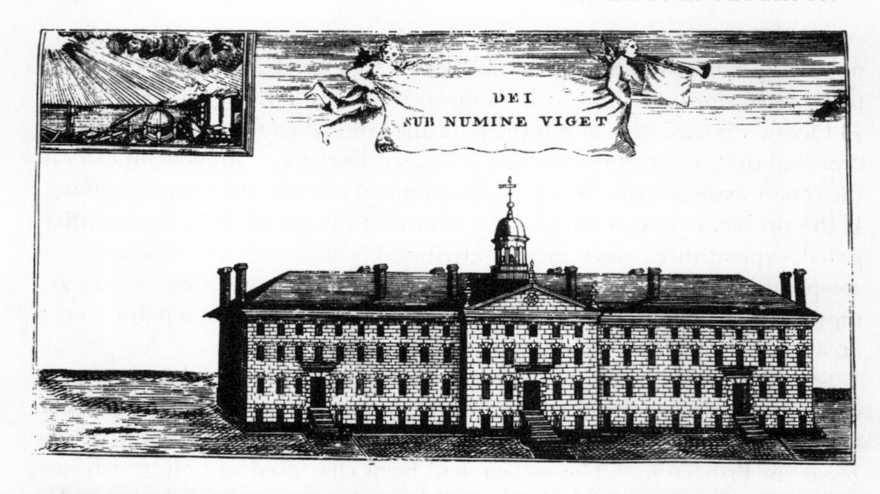

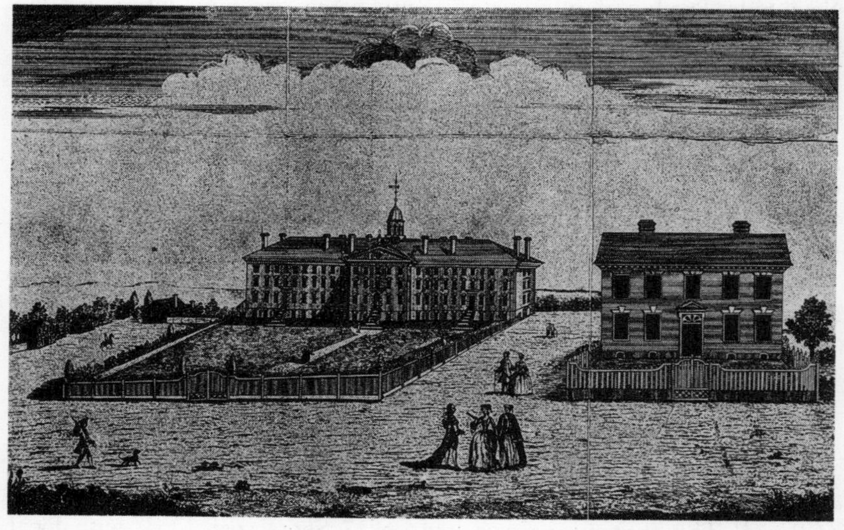

Figures 8 and 9. Nassau Hall, Princeton. Built for the College of New Jersey in the village of Princeton, Nassau Hall was widely advertised and served as a precedent for other American colleges.

Fig. 8. The most accurate image of Nassau Hall's architecture was the engraving in the *New American Magazine* for March 1760.

Fig. 9. The better known Tennent-Dawkins engraving of 1765 shows both Nassau Hall and the new President's House, also by Robert Smith. [Courtesy HSP]

£52.16 'on acc^{t}. of the bulding the College'.[47] By then the work of assembling the lumber and ironmongery was probably well under way and the setting of the floor joists begun. And by then the fundraising mission of Davies and Tennent had been successfully concluded.

For the construction season of 1755 we have five receipts signed by Smith totalling more than £1200. This phase of the work reached its climax in November, when FitzRandolph noted in his record book that 'the roof of s^{d}. College was Raised by M^{r}. Robert Smith the Carpenter that built the timberwork of ye College'. That undoubtedly meant that the roof framing and its covering of shingles had been completed. From then on flooring could be laid, doors and windows hung and finished trim and plaster applied. On 11 October Smith had written to Jonathan Sergeant, the trustees' treasurer, requesting him to pay Charles Read £37.3.9 for 8500 feet of pine scantling 'for Window Cases to the College'. Closed in, the new rooms could then be warmed, dried out and completed during the following winter. For 1756 we have another five receipts, totalling only £361.10.4. In the autumn of that year President Burr and seventy students moved up from their temporary location at Newark, and Burr preached the first sermon in the lecture hall of the new building. For that year we also have Smith's purchase of the third volume of *Vitruvius Britannicus*, by another Scot, Colen Campbell (fig. 7). Bills for work continued through the following year.[48] As late as March 1760 the building was still not entirely finished,[49] though Smith's role was presumably over by that time.

Of the four known eighteenth-century views of Nassau Hall, the copperplate in the *New American Magazine* for March 1760 (fig. 8) is the first and best. It is competently drawn and portrays a large, rather plain rectangular structure, twenty-six bays long. The lack of ornament was in keeping with President Burr's assurances, in a letter to Edinburgh during the fund-raising campaign of 1754, that 'we do everything in the plainest and cheapest manner, as far as is consistent with Decency & Convenience, having no superfluous Ornaments'.[50] The only decorative pretentions are the flat-topped, rusticated stone frontispieces at the three North entrance doors, a slightly projecting central bay surmounted by three urns and a bell turret or cupola typical of Robert Smith's later work. The turret design probably derived from William Adam, whose *Vitruvius Scoticus* displayed several like it. The new building was chiefly admired for its size. Esther Burr, wife of the president, boasted that it was 'the most commodious of any of the Colleges as well as much the largest of any upon the Continent. There is somthing very striking in it and a grandure and yet a simpliscity that cant well be expressed'.[51] Its contemporary influence was considerable, and it is believed to have provided the inspiration for similar buildings at American colleges such as Harvard, Brown, Dartmouth and Rutgers.[52]

The years were not kind to Nassau Hall. After it had endured the battle of Princeton (1777) and occupation by soldiers from both sides, 'the dilapidation and pollution of the college edifice' rendered the building 'utterly unfit' for student use.[53] The French diarist Moreau de St Méry wrote in 1794 that 'all in all, this building has an impressive appearance for America'. He described in some detail its exterior and interior, including 42 dormitory rooms housing up to 120 (but normally around 80) students, 'a chapel, a refectory, a library of about two thousand volumes, and the justly celebrated planetarium built by Dr David Rittenhouse' and 'a huge hall furnished with benches, as is any other classroom'. Yet he also found the front yard 'untidy' and the rear courtyard 'dirty and uncultivated, and everything in it is evidence of neglect'.[54] In 1802 and 1855 great fires completely destroyed Robert Smith's woodwork on the roof and the interiors, and later architects made further changes and additions. Today Nassau Hall continues to occupy an honoured place in the heart of Princeton University, but all that remains of the original building are the remnants of William Worth's sandstone walls.

Besides Nassau Hall, Smith's plans for the College of New Jersey included a residence for the president. The Tennent-Dawkins engraving of 1765 depicts the president's house as a double-pile structure that Smith almost certainly designed and built (fig. 9).[55] Thus, it appears that two of the greatest Scottish exports to the American Enlightenment – William Smith and John Witherspoon – as well as one of its greatest native products, Benjamin Franklin, lived parts of their lives in three distinct houses of Smith's design. In 1757 Smith worked on a Princeton farmhouse owned personally by President Burr, and his work there continued for more than a year after the president's death that September. In 1757 Smith also purchased land of his own in Princeton, suggesting a more than passing interest in that growing college town. But Philadelphia remained the focal point of his career, and for the next two decades he did more than anyone else to shape the physical appearance of that city. The significance of his achievements for the architecture of Philadelphia as well of Princeton and other colonial American sites suggests that Robert Smith, without ever publishing a word, made a contribution to the culture of the Scottish-American Enlightenment as profound in its way as that of any author or scholar.

NOTES

1. Charles E. Peterson, 'Carpenters' Hall', in *Historic Philadelphia: From the Founding Until the Early Nineteenth Century*, ed. Luther P. Eisenhart (Philadelphia, 1980), 96–128. This volume was originally published in the *Transactions of the American Philosophical Society*, 43, pt. 1 (1953).
2. Specimens of Smith's drawings were listed in the catalogue of a 1795 public exhibition by the Philadelphia Columbianum, the first gallery exhibition of architectural designs ever mounted in America.

3. The earliest published reference to Smith is Owen Biddle's high praise of Christ Church steeple in 1805, cited below. Brief, and somewhat inaccurate, accounts of Smith subsequently appeared in J. Thomas Scharf and Thompson Westcott, *History of Philadelphia, 1609–1884*, 3 vols. (Philadelphia, 1884), 1:290, and Joseph Jackson, *Early Philadelphia Architects and Engineers* (Philadelphia, 1924), 66–69. More substantial, but still relatively slight, biographical sketches appeared in the *Dictionary of American Biography* (by C.P. Stacey) and in Carl and Jessica Bridenbaugh, *Rebels and Gentlemen: Philadelphia in the Age of Franklin* (New York, 1942), 200–202.
4. This increase in knowledge was represented most dramatically by the 1982 Robert Smith Symposium in Newbattle, Edinburgh and Dalkeith, Scotland, which focused the attention of leading scholars.
5. Beatrice Garvan, 'Robert Smith, 1722–1777', in *Philadelphia: Three Centuries of American Art* (Philadelphia, 1976), 31–32.
6. Funds were transmitted several times by Hall through Hamilton's bookselling firm, Hamilton and Balfour. The discovery of this connexion was first made by Willman Spawn, reading Hall's letterbooks at the Library Company of Philadelphia.
7. C.A. Poulson, 'A Collection of Miscellaneous Scraps' (MS), Library Company of Philadelphia, 1:10–12.
8. Essays had been required since the beginning of the guild in 1475, but our knowledge of details dates from a later period. See Harry Carr, *The Minutes of the Lodge of Edinburgh St. Mary's Chapel, No. 1, 1598–1738* (London, 1962), 29. See also Charles E. Peterson, 'Philadelphia Carpentry according to Palladio', in *Building by the Book:3*, ed. Mario diValmarana (Charlottesville, Va., 1990).
9. Nothing comparable has been found among carpenter companies in English or Irish cities such as London, York and Dublin.
10. Diploma from Edinburgh, dated 13 Apr. 1750, HSP, James Hamilton Papers (brought to my attention by Beatrice Garvan).
11. Franklin, 3:283, n. 7.
12. Scharf and Westcott, *History of Philadelphia*, 1:1266.
13. Presbyterian Historical Society, Philadelphia, 'Minutes of the Presbyterian Congregation under the pastoral care of the Revd. Mr. Gilbert Tennent', 8 Feb. 1749. Unless otherwise noted, information about the building of this church has been drawn from this source.
14. Randolph Shipley Klein, *Portrait of an Early American Family: The Shippens of Pennsylvania across Five Generations* (Philadelphia, 1975). This William Shippen was the father of the medical professor of the same name who appears in Deborah Brunton's essay in chap. 14.
15. This archaic method of determining the price to be paid for a completed structure was much favoured in Philadelphia at the time. For a discussion of alternative methods, see *The Carpenters' Company of the City and County of Philadelphia 1786 Rule Book*, ed. Charles E. Peterson (Princeton, 1971), xiv.
16. Philadelphia Contributionship for the Insurance of Houses against Loss by Fire, surveys no. 801, 902, 903 (surveyed 7 June 1763).
17. Scharf and Westcott, *History of Philadelphia*, 1:1266.
18. Ibid.
19. Excerpts from Nevell's account book published by Charles E. Peterson in *The Robert Smith Newsletter*, no. 2 (1984). The original of

this recently rediscovered item is in the library of the University of Pennsylvania.

20. Scharf and Westcott, *History of Philadelphia*, 1:1279–80.
21. *A Historical Catalogue of the St. Andrew's Society of Philadelphia* (Philadelphia, 1907), 196.
22. Thomas Lawrence to George Charles, Philadelphia, 9 month 24, 1746, *PMHB* 7 (1883): 231.
23. HSP, James Hamilton Cash Book.
24. HSP, James Hamilton Letterbook, 1749–1783.
25. 'The Diary of Ezra Stiles', *PMHB* 16 (1892): 375.
26. J. Bennett Nolan, *Printer Strahan's Book Account* (Reading, Pa., 1939), 39.
27. William L. Turner, 'The Charity School, the Academy, and the College', in *Historic Philadelphia*, ed. Eisenhart, 180.
28. Franklin to Samuel Johnson of New York, 9 Aug. 1750, in Franklin, 4:39.
29. See the original 1750 description in HSP, Richard Peters Papers, 4:243–49.
30. Turner, 'Charity School', 180–81.
31. University of Pennsylvania Library, 'Minutes of the Trustees of the College, Academy and Charitable Schools', vol. 1, 10 Jan. 1755.
32. Thomas Montgomery, *A History of the University of Pennsylvania, 1740–1770* (Philadelphia, 1900), 355–59.
33. See Charles E. Peterson, 'The Building of Christ Church, Philadelphia', in the 1981 antiques show exhibition catalogue *Christ Church: Philadelphia, Arts, Architecture and Archives* (Philadelphia, 1981), 133–47. The designer was probably an Englishman, possibly Thomas Archer of London (ca. 1688–1743).
34. In eighteenth-century Philadelphia the distinction was often made between the tower of a building, which was generally of masonry, and the steeple or spire, a lighter wood frame construction topping it. In the case of Christ Church this distinction is important because the tower and steeple were designed by different parties at different times.
35. HSP, 'Christ Church Vestry Minutes', 3 Apr. 1744. Unless otherwise noted, these manuscript minutes are the source of the discussion that follows.
36. Nicholas B. Wainwright, 'Scull and Heap's East Prospect of Philadelphia', *PMHB* 73 (1949): 18.
37. It is not generally known that stone masonry, hidden under a veneer of brick, was used for this purpose both here and at the State House tower.
38. The purchases and payments recorded in this paragraph are drawn from various entries in 'The Steeple Account'.
39. The curious, complicated history of this work may be found in James Simpson's detailed essay in the 1980 Edinburgh reprint of *Vitruvius Scoticus*.
40. On this influence see Thomas T. Waterman, *The Mansions of Virginia, 1706–1776* (Chapel Hill, N.C., 1945), which includes many references and reproduces fine engravings.
41. The author acknowledges the encouragement of the late archivist

Henry L. Savage and the generous assistance of Constance M. Greiff, Princeton architectural historian. Savage's *Nassau Hall, 1756–1956* (Princeton, 1956) contains a comprehensive, well-documented essay by Paul Norton, 'Robert Smith's Nassau Hall and President's House', though much new information has become available since its publication. The story was carried further in Constance M. Greiff, Mary W. Gibbons and Elizabeth C. Menzies, *Princeton Architecture: A Pictorial History of Town and Campus* (Princeton, 1967).

42. Greiff et al., *Princeton Architecture*, 44; Klein, *Portrait*, 85.
43. Quoted in Greiff et al., *Princeton Architecture*, 44.
44. Nathaniel FitzRandolph, 'Book of Records', Princeton University Archives. FitzRandolph had donated four and a half acres for a building site.
45. Ibid. As in the case of the Second Presbyterian Church and most other building projects of the period, neither a formal agreement with the architect and builder nor an itemised account has survived. But a smattering of manuscripts allows us to follow progress.
46. Quoted in Norton, 'Robert Smith's Nassau Hall', 14.
47. Uncatalogued manuscript, Princeton University Archives. Other manuscripts, in various collections at the Princeton University Archives and Library, are the basis for much of the information that follows.
48. The last one extant, dated 2 Dec. 1758, includes an unspecified amount for the new task of 'Building the President's House'.
49. *New American Magazine* (March 1760): 104.
50. Quoted in Greiff et al., *Princeton Architecture*, 45.
51. *The Journal of Esther Edwards Burr, 1754–1757*, ed. Carol F. Karlson and Laurie Crumpacker (New Haven, Conn., 1984), 215 (3 Aug. 1756).
52. Greiff et al., *Princeton Architecture*, 45.
53. Ashbel Green's account in Joseph H. Jones, *The Life of Ashbel Green* (New York, 1849), 137.
54. *Moreau St. Méry's American Journey, 1793–1798*, trans. and ed. Kenneth Roberts and Anna M. Roberts (Garden City, N.Y., 1947), 103–5.
55. The present house is made of brick but retains many of the original features, including good interior trim of a kind common in eighteenth-century Philadelphia.

Index